BASIC
An Introduction to Computer Programming

Fourth Edition

■ Brooks/Cole Series in Computer Science

Program Design with Pseudocode, Third Edition
T. W. Bailey and Kris Lundgaard

BASIC: An Introduction to Computer Programming, Third Edition
Robert J. Bent and George C. Sethares

BASIC: An Introduction to Computer Programming with the Apple, Second Edition
Robert J. Bent and George C. Sethares

Business BASIC, Third Edition
Robert J. Bent and George C. Sethares

BASIC Programming with the IBM PC
Peter Mears

Absolutely BASIC Computing
Peter Mears

An Introduction to Personal Computing: BASIC Programming on the TRS-80
Robert R. Hare

Learning BASIC Programming: A Systematic Approach
Howard Dachslager, Masato Hayashi, Richard Zucker

Beginning Structured COBOL, Second Edition
Keith Carver

Structured COBOL Programming and Data Processing Methods
Thomas R. McCalla

Problem Solving and Structured Programming with Pascal
Ali Behforooz and Martin O. Holoien

Pascal Programming
Irvine Forkner

Pascal for the Eighties
Samuel Grier

FORTRAN 77 PDQ, 2nd Edition
Thomas A. Boyle

Problem Solving and Structured Programming with FORTRAN 77
Martin O. Holoien and Ali Behforooz

Introduction to ADA: A Top-Down Approach for Programmers
Phillip Caverly and Philip Goldstein

Introduction to DECSYSTEM-20 Assembly Programming
Stephen A. Longo

LOGO: Principles, Programming and Projects
George Lukas and Joan Lukas

BASIC
An Introduction to Computer Programming
Fourth Edition

Robert J. Bent
George C. Sethares
Bridgewater State College

Brooks/Cole Publishing Company
Pacific Grove, California

Brooks/Cole Publishing Company
A Division of Wadsworth, Inc.

Printed in the United States of America

10 9 8 7 6 5 4 3 2

Library of Congress Cataloging in Publication Data

Bent, Robert J. [date]
    BASIC : an introduction to computer programming.

    Includes index.
    1. BASIC (Computer program language) I. Sethares,
George C., [date] . II. Title.
QA76.73.B3B46 1989 005.13'3 89-15835
ISBN 0-534-12642-1

Sponsoring Editor: Michael Sugarman
Marketing Representative: John Moroney
Editorial Assistant: Sarah A. Wilson
Production Editor: Linda Loba
Manuscript Editor: Robert Burdette
Permissions Editor: Carline Haga
Interior and Cover Design: Roy R. Neuhaus
Art Coordinator: Lisa Torri
Typesetting: Interactive Composition Corporation
Printing and Binding: Malloy Lithographing

To Eleanor and Anita

Preface

This book is intended to serve as a general introduction to computer programming. The programming language used is BASIC, a general purpose and easy-to-use computer language that is available with essentially all computers. No prior experience with computers or programming languages is assumed. Included are descriptions of the computing equipment you will encounter and procedures for using this equipment. The programming language BASIC is described in detail and illustrated in numerous examples drawn from a wide range of application areas, including business, economics, mathematics, personal finance, and the natural and social sciences. Much of the material in this book is semitutorial and intended to be studied with a computer keyboard and display screen close at hand. For beginning programmers, hands-on experience with a real computer is the most effective way to learn about computers.

■ Organization and Coverage

We wrote this book with two principal goals in mind. First, we felt it important to present the elements of BASIC so that meaningful computer programs could be written at the earliest possible time. We adhere to the notion that one learns by doing. But the development of programming habits, both good and bad, will begin with the first programs written. For this reason, fundamental principles of program design are considered at the outset. Specifically, Chapter 2 describes the top-down approach to problem solving, illustrates the importance of input/output specification, modularization, and stepwise refinement, and points out some of the benefits to be gained by adhering to these problem solving principles.

Our second goal was to write a book that would serve as a general introduction to programming, not just to a programming language. Toward this end we have included examples that illustrate several major application areas of computer programming and that also describe important programming techniques that can be used effectively in many diverse programming situations. But a complete introduction to programming requires more than a description of application areas and programming techniques. Equally important is a consideration of the entire programming process that takes us from a problem statement to the finished product: a well-documented computer program that correctly carries out the task described in the problem statement. The approach we have taken toward achieving this objective is to use consistently the problem-solving methods introduced in Chapter 2, to introduce new programming principles as they can be appreciated in the context of the applications being considered, and to illustrate and reinforce these programming principles in the worked-out examples.

Throughout the book we have attempted to conform to the most common BASIC usage. In most cases, our presentation of BASIC conforms to the American National Standards Institute (ANSI) standard for BASIC. Phrases such as "Your system may allow you to . . ." indicate that the BASIC feature being introduced is not included in the BASIC standard. The material contained in this book, including the problem sets, has been carefully organized so that topics that are not a part of standard BASIC may be omitted with no loss in continuity.

A few remarks are appropriate concerning the order in which we have introduced the elements of BASIC. The INPUT statement (Chapter 5) is introduced early, before the READ and DATA statements, to emphasize the interactive nature of BASIC. In Chapter 6, the GOTO statement and a limited form of the IF statement are used to introduce the concept of a program loop. WHILE loops are also described in Chapter 6, since many versions of BASIC allow the WHILE statement as a convenient alternative to the IF and GOTO statements when coding loops. Chapter 7 expands upon the description of the PRINT statement given in Chapter 3 and introduces the PRINT USING statement. These output statements are introduced early so that well-formatted output can be illustrated in the examples and can be produced while carrying out all subsequent programming exercises. The general form of the IF statement and its use as a selection statement are described in Chapter 8. The BASIC statements described in Chapters 3–8 were selected because they allow meaningful structured programs to be written. Section 8.8 describes how structured algorithms can be coded as structured BASIC programs. Chapters 9–11 (FOR loops, READ/DATA statements, and subroutines) complete what is sometimes called Elementary BASIC. Selecting an order in which to present the remaining BASIC statements was not so easy. So that a person using this book will not be tied down to the order we have chosen, the introductory material for the remaining BASIC statements is presented in a way that allows these statements to be taken up in any order after Chapter 11.

■ Special Features

Several new features have been included in this revision. Following are brief descriptions of the more significant changes.

An Expanded Introductory Chapter on Problem Solving

Fundamental problem solving principles, including the top-down development of algorithms, are discussed in Chapter 2. Greater emphasis is placed on input/output specification, modularization, and stepwise refinement. The chapter also explains the sense in which computer programs and algorithms are equivalent and illustrates the steps leading to the discovery of algorithms.

Improved Examples and Programming Exercises

Work-out examples and programming exercises that illustrate application areas not covered in the previous edition have been added. Several examples and exercises, some of which were redundant, have been deleted. Also, many new programming exercises that are suitable for one- or two-week programming projects have been added to the problem sets.

A New Section on Menu-Driven Programs

The concept of a menu-driven program is described early (Chapter 7) and illustrated in several examples in the subsequent chapters. Writing BASIC code for menu-driven programs by using the ON GOTO statement is described in Section 7.8, and by using the ON GOSUB statement in Section 11.3. Programming exercises that call for menu-driven programs have been added to many of the problem sets beginning with Chapter 7.

An Expanded and Earlier Chapter on Subroutines

The topic of subroutines is taken up much earlier in this edition. Subroutines are described in Chapter 11, just after the READ and DATA statements, and their application is illustrated in many of the subsequent chapters.

A New Section on Table Processing

Section 14.3 illustrates the application of the array data structure to programming tasks that involve tables. The problem of deciding whether or not to use arrays to store tabular data is discussed and illustrated in the worked-out examples. New programming exercises that involve table processing have been included in the problem sets.

Increased Emphasis on the Application of String Variables

Many new string processing examples and programming exercises have been added. String arrays, which in the previous edition were introduced in a separate chapter after the numerical arrays, are now taken up with numerical arrays in a single chapter. The string conversion functions CHR$, ASC, STR$, and VAL are described earlier, with all other string and string-related functions, and their applications have been expanded to several new topics, including the conversion of lowercase letters to uppercase.

■ Acknowledgments

While preparing this revision, we were fortunate to have the comments of many users of the second edition. Their thoughtful criticisms and suggestions were carefully considered and, in many instances, incorporated as changes in the book. We are grateful for this assistance. So that we can continue to make improvements for future readers, we would welcome hearing of your experiences with this edition. A reader response form is provided at the end of the book for this purpose.

We wish to take this opportunity to acknowledge the helpful comments of our reviewers: Professor Nancy Boynton, State University of New York-Fredonia; Professor Marjorie Fitting, San Jose State University; and Professor Bushan Kapoor, California State University-Fullerton. We feel that their many thoughtful suggestions have led to a greatly improved book.

A very special thanks goes to Patricia Shea, our typist, proofreader, debugger, and general assistant. Her twelve years of cheerful cooperation are greatly appreciated. Finally, we are happy to acknowledge the fine cooperation of the staff at Brooks/Cole Publishing Company.

Robert J. Bent
George C. Sethares

Contents

1 Computer Systems

Any electronic device that can receive, store, process, and transmit data (information)—and can also receive and store the instructions to process these data—is called a **computer.** A **computer system** is any group of interrelated components that includes a computer as one of its principal elements. Figure 1.1 shows a complete table-top computer system that includes a computer with a disk storage unit, a detachable keyboard, a video display screen, and a printer for producing printed documents.

A computer has the ability to store large quantities of data, to process these data at very fast rates, and to present the results of this processing in ways that are meaningful to the task at hand. If the task is to prepare a payroll, for example, employee data will be transmitted to the computer, the computer will process these data to calculate relevant wage statistics, and the results will be presented in printed form, possibly including paychecks. This payroll example illustrates the three principal tasks involved in every com-

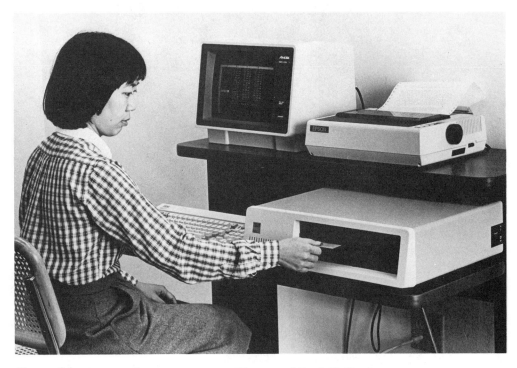

Figure 1.1 A personal computer system. (Courtesy of Frank Keillor.)

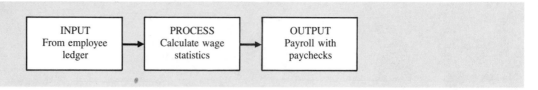

Figure 1.2 An INPUT–PROCESS–OUTPUT diagram.

puter application: data must be presented to the computer **(INPUT),** data must be processed **(PROCESS),** and results must be presented in a useful way **(OUTPUT).**

Applications involving these three steps are appropriately called **data processing applications,** an expression often used synonymously with *computer applications*. Data processing, however, is done by people as well as by computers. To plan an evening at the movies, you would want to know what movies are being shown and the cost and time of each showing (input). You, and possibly a companion, would consider the options in an attempt to match what is being shown with your individual likes (process), and having made a decision you would depart for the selected theater (output). As another illustration, consider the task of hiring new employees. Relevant input might be a resume, letters of reference, and an interview summary for each applicant. The company would carry out its selection process and notify each applicant of its decision (the output). As a final illustration, the INPUT–PROCESS–OUTPUT diagram in Figure 1.2 describes how you might prepare a payroll whether or not a computer is available.

Today, computer applications are so numerous and widespread that it is not always easy to distinguish between tasks we should assign to computers and tasks we should do ourselves. Certainly, tasks requiring large numbers of numerical calculations are best delegated to computers. Computers carry out thousands of calculations per second without error; we perform but a few per minute—even with a calculator in hand—and must exercise the greatest care and concentration to avoid errors. The very first computers were built precisely for such tasks (see Figure 1.3).

Figure 1.3 Presentation of the first UNIVAC I (first-generation UNIVersal Automatic Computer) to the Smithsonian Institution, where portions of it are now on display. Designed by John W. Mauchly and J. Presper Eckert, Jr., and built under their direction by Remington Rand Corporation, the UNIVAC I was the first commercially available electronic computer and the first computer to be used for business data processing. Unlike its predecessors, which were built for specific scientific applications, the UNIVAC I was a general-purpose computer. Early applications included the tabulation of U.S. census data—the first UNIVAC I was delivered to the U.S. Bureau of the Census in 1951—and the analysis of election returns during the 1952 presidential election. The early projection of Dwight D. Eisenhower as the winner over Adlai E. Stevenson was an impressive feat that greatly increased public awareness of computers. (Courtesy of Sperry Univac Corporation.)

Figure 1.4 Data terminals are rapidly replacing the typewriter as the standard office tool. With modern word processing systems, letters, memos, reports, and even entire books can be typed at terminal keyboards for transmission to a computer, which automatically stores the information on high-speed disk storage devices. The information can later be used in many ways. It can be displayed for reading on a video screen, modified by typing changes at the keyboard, formatted for output by typing special editing marks, and transmitted to an output device to obtain printed copy. If the word processing system is part of a communications system, the information can also be transmitted to other locations. (Courtesy of Texas Instruments.)

Applications of the computer, however, are no longer restricted to numerical tasks. Modern computers are useful tools in many application areas that have nothing to do with arithmetic. Word processing and communications systems, for example, allow for easy storage, retrieval, editing and transmission of most types of correspondence (see Figure 1.4).

In our rapidly changing technological society, an understanding of computers and how they are used is becoming more and more essential. But the purpose of this chapter is not to convince you that a computer can "do" many things nor even to indicate the computer applications you will be able to carry out after completing this book. Rather, the objectives of this chapter are to introduce you to the types of computing equipment you may encounter, to describe what a computer program is, and to introduce certain terminology that is helpful when talking about computers.

■ 1.1 Computer Hardware

Central to every computer system is an electronic computer whose principal function is to process data. The computer component that does this is called the **central processing unit (CPU).** The CPU contains an **arithmetic and logic unit (ALU),** consisting of circuitry that performs a variety of arithmetic and logical operations, and a **control unit** that directs the operation of the ALU and generally controls all electrical signals passing through the computer. In addition to the CPU, every computer has a **memory unit** that can store data and from which data can be retrieved for processing. In early computers these computer components were rather large, and a computer could occupy an entire room. This is no longer so. Figure 1.5 shows the main circuit board of a desktop computer. The ALU is labeled **microprocessor** because of its microminiaturized circuitry. It is an **integrated**

Figure 1.5   Main circuit board, keyboard, and power supply for an Apple Computer. (Courtesy of Apple Computer, Inc.)

circuit about the size of a fingernail and is housed in a special protective container.* In Figure 1.5, the memory unit is labeled **random access memory (RAM),** a term indicating that data can be obtained from or transmitted to any memory storage unit directly if its address is specified. [The term **read only memory (ROM)** refers to computer memory that can be accessed but not changed.]

Fortunately, you don't have to understand how a computer stores and processes data to make it work for you. The circuitry in a computer is not unlike that in an ordinary pocket calculator, and all who have used calculators know that no knowledge of their circuitry is needed to use them.

Data must be transmitted to the computer *(input),* and results of the processing must be returned *(output).* Devices that transfer data to and from a computer are called **input** and **output (I/O)** devices. The I/O devices you are most likely to encounter in your introduction to computer programming are as follows:

Keyboards. (Figure 1.6) A keyboard is the principal input device you will use while studying the material in this book. Keyboards are used with display screens or printers. To transmit information to the computer, you simply type it at the keyboard. The computer will automatically display what you are typing on the screen or with the printer.

Display screens and printers. (Figure 1.6) Display screens and printers are the principal output devices you will use in your study of computer programming. Most often, but not always, you will direct the computer to display the results of any processing on your screen or with a printer. Many computer systems contain several **data stations** (also called **data terminals**), each with a keyboard and display screen, that are connected to a single medium- or large-scale computer. On such systems a single high-speed printer is often used for all printed output. Figure 1.4 shows several data terminals that use one computer and share one high-speed printer. A computer system that provides for the simultaneous use of a computer by two or more data terminals is called a **time-sharing system.**

*An integrated circuit (IC) is an electronic circuit that has been etched into a small, thin wafer of a glasslike substance such as silicon. A single IC less than a square inch in area can contain several thousand distinct but interconnected electronic components such as transistors and diodes.

Figure 1.6   Top: a computer system with a display screen and detachable keyboard; bottom: DEC writer LA-36 terminal (keyboard and printer in a single unit). Photos (upper) courtesy of Frank Keillor, (lower) courtesy of Digital Equipment Corporation.

Most modern computer systems are equipped with data storage devices other than the computer's main memory unit. They are called **external** (or **secondary**) storage devices because, unlike the memory unit, they are not part of the computer. The following are the most common external storage devices.

Disk-storage units. Information is stored on rotating disks that resemble phonograph records. The disks have no grooves, however; the data are stored as sequences of magnetized spots appearing on concentric circles. A disk unit will contain one or more disks, each with one or more read/write heads. Disk units are called **random access devices.** As with RAM, the term *random access* indicates that the computer can directly access or change data stored on any part of a disk without having to read through the entire disk to find the data. Figure 1.7 shows a **floppy-disk unit.** The term *floppy* is used because the disk is flexible. The term **diskette** is used when referring to floppy disks. Figure 1.8 shows a disk pack containing several individual hard disks—that is, disks that are rigid, not flexible.

Figure 1.7 Diskette being inserted into an IBM PC floppy-disk unit.

Figure 1.8 IBM 5445 Removable Disk Pack and Drive. (Both courtesy of Judy Blamer.)

Magnetic-tape units. Information is stored on magnetic tapes as sequences of magnetized "spots." Although tape units can be rather "large" (Figure 1.9), some computer systems (especially personal computers) use ordinary cassette tape recorders. The computer "reads" data from a tape by reading through the tape sequentially until the desired data are found. For this reason, tape units are called **sequential access devices.**

Video display units, printers, tape units, disk units, and all other mechanical and electrical devices other than the computer itself are referred to as **computer peripherals.** The computer and all peripherals constitute the **hardware** of the computer system. Figure 1.10 illustrates the flow of information between a computer and its peripherals.

Figure 1.9   A computer system with magnetic-tape units.

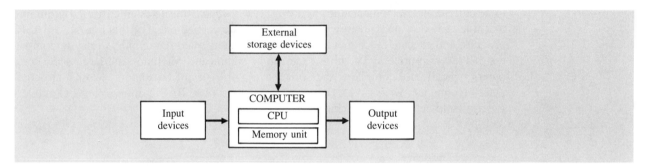

Figure 1.10   Flow of information through a computer and its peripherals. (Both courtesy of Frank Keillor.)

■ 1.2 Computer Software

The physical components, or hardware, of a computer system are inanimate objects. They cannot prepare a payroll or perform any other task, however simple, without human assistance. This assistance is given in the form of instructions to the computer. A sequence of such instructions is called a **computer program,** and a person who composes these instructions is called a **programmer.**

The precise form that instructions to a computer must take depends on the computer system being used. **BASIC** (Beginner's All-purpose Symbolic Instruction Code) is a carefully constructed English-like language used for writing computer programs.* Instructions in the BASIC language are designed to be understood by people as well as by the computer. Even the uninitiated will understand the meaning of this simple BASIC program:

```
1 LET A=3
2 LET B=A+5
3 PRINT B
4 END
```

A computer is an electronic device and understands an instruction such as
LET A = 3 in a very special way. An electronic device can distinguish between two distinct electrical or magnetic states. Consider, for instance, an ordinary on/off switch for a light fixture. When the switch is in the "on" position, current is allowed to flow and the bulb glows. If we denote the "on" position by the number 1 and the "off" position by the

*BASIC was developed at Dartmouth College under the direction of John G. Kemeny and Thomas E. Kurtz.

number 0, we can say that the instruction 1 causes the bulb to glow and the instruction 0 causes it not to glow. In like manner, we could envision a machine with two switches whose positions are denoted by the four codes 00, 01, 10, and 11 such that each of these four codes causes a different event to occur. It is this ability to distinguish between two distinct states that has led to the development of modern computers. Modern computers are still based on this principle. For example, each storage unit in a computer's main memory can store a sequence of 0s and 1s, and one or more such sequences can be used to represent either data (in coded form) or instructions to the central processing unit. All such primitive instructions that are meaningful to a particular computer are together called the **machine language** for that computer.

Although a computer understands only its machine language (it was built precisely for that purpose), you will not be required to write machine language programs. The computer you will use employs a **translator** that automatically translates your BASIC instructions into equivalent machine language instructions that are then executed by the computer. There are two different types of BASIC translators, called **interpreters** and **compilers.** An *interpreter* translates a BASIC instruction into machine code each time it is to be carried out. As indicated in Figure 1.11, a *compiler* translates an entire program into machine code only once, before any instructions are carried out. For this reason, a BASIC program will execute much more rapidly on computers that use compilers than on computers that use interpreters. The difference can be significant! Medium- and large-scale computers typically use compilers, but some have both types of translators. Most microcomputers (computers whose ALUs are microprocessors) use BASIC interpreters. Compilers are available but must be purchased separately.

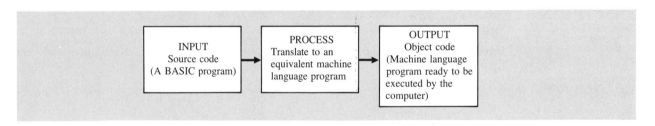

Figure 1.11   INPUT–PROCESS–OUTPUT diagram for a BASIC compiler.

BASIC interpreters and compilers are themselves computer programs. They are called **systems programs** because they are an integral part of the computer system itself. The BASIC programs in this book, as well as the programs you will write, are called **applications programs.** They are not an integral part of the computer system, so they are not called systems programs. All computer programs, both systems programs and applications programs, are called **computer software.**

In addition to a BASIC interpreter or compiler, your system will include other systems programs. These will be programs that produce listings of your programs, "save" your programs on secondary storage devices for later use, assist you in finding errors in the programs you write, and, most important of all, exercise general control over the entire system. This last program is called the **operating system.** It allows you to issue commands to the computer to "call up" and execute any of the other systems programs provided.

The emergence of computer science as a new discipline has been accompanied by a proliferation of new words and expressions. Although they are useful for talking about computers, they are for the most part absolutely unnecessary if your objective is to learn a computer language such as BASIC to help you solve problems. In our discussion of computer hardware and software, we have introduced only fundamental concepts and basic terminology. Even so, if this is your first exposure to computers, you may feel lost in this terminology. Don't be disheartened: much of the new vocabulary has already been introduced. You will become more familiar with it and recognize its usefulness as you study the subsequent chapters. You will also find it helpful to reread this chapter after you have written a few computer programs.

■ 1.3 Review True-or-False Quiz

1. Any electronic device that can process data is called a computer.   **T   F**
2. Input/output devices, external storage devices, and the central processing unit are called computer peripherals.   **T   F**
3. An automobile that uses a microprocessor to control the gas and air mixture is correctly referred to as a computer system.   **T   F**
4. A computer system must contain at least one printer.   **T   F**
5. Disk-storage units are called *random access devices* because information stored on a disk is accessed by randomly searching portions of the disk until the desired data are found.   **T   F**
6. Tape units are called *sequential access devices* because the computer reads information from a tape by reading through the tape until the desired data are found.   **T   F**
7. The term RAM refers to disk-storage units.   **T   F**
8. There is a significant difference between memory units called RAM and memory units called ROM.   **T   F**
9. The function of a BASIC compiler is to translate BASIC programs into machine language.   **T   F**
10. The terms *compiler* and *interpreter* are used synonymously.   **T   F**
11. To solve problems using the BASIC language, you must know and understand what a compiler is or what an interpreter is.   **T   F**
12. A computer program written to automate a payroll system is an example of a systems program.   **T   F**
13. An operating system is a computer system.   **T   F**

2 Problem Solving: Top-Down Approach

A computer program consists of a sequence of instructions to the computer. These instructions describe a step-by-step process for carrying out a specified task. Such a process is called an **algorithm.** Algorithms have been with us since antiquity: the familiar division algorithm was known and used in ancient Greece; the activities of bookkeepers have always been guided by algorithms (an algorithm to determine a tax assessment, an algorithm to calculate a depletion allowance, and so on); even the instructions for assembling a child's new toy are often given in algorithmic form.

Since a computer program describes an algorithm, the process of writing computer programs can be equated to the process of discovering algorithms. For this reason, an understanding of what is, and what is not, an algorithm is indispensable to a programmer.

In Section 2.1, we define the term *algorithm* and illustrate, with simple examples, the method of designing algorithms called the *top-down approach to problem solving.* In Section 2.2, we define the term *variable,* an essential concept in programming, and illustrate the use of variables in writing algorithms.

■ 2.1 Algorithms

An algorithm is a prescribed set of well-defined rules and processes for carrying out a specified task in a finite number of steps. Here is an algorithm giving instructions for completing a financial transaction at a drive-in teller port:

    a. Press the call button.
    b. Remove the carrier from the tray.
    c. Place your transaction inside the carrier.
    d. Replace the carrier.
    e. When the carrier returns, remove the transaction.
    f. Replace the carrier.

To see that these six steps describe an algorithm, we must verify that each step is well defined and that the process stops in a finite number of steps. For example, Step (a) requires that there be only one call button, Step (b) requires that there be but one tray containing a single carrier, and Step (e) requires that the carrier return automatically after being placed in the tray as specified in Step (d). Having verified that each step is well defined, and noting that the process stops after a transaction has been completed, we can be fairly confident that the six steps do indeed describe an algorithm for the specified task.

The drive-in teller example illustrates the following three properties of an algorithm:

1. Each step must be well defined—that is, unambiguous.
2. The process must halt in a finite number of steps.
3. The process must do what is claimed.

The examples in this section are intended to help you understand what an algorithm is and to allow you to gain some practice with the process of designing algorithms. In keeping with current terminology, we will refer to this process as the **problem-solving process.** In each example, we begin with a description of the task to be performed (the **problem statement**), illustrate the essential steps in the problem-solving process, and end with an algorithm for the specified task.

EXAMPLE 1   **Let's find an algorithm to produce a report showing the name, annual salary, and year-end bonus for each salaried employee in a firm. Employees are to receive 2% of their annual salary or $400, whichever is larger.**

To produce a bonus report, we will need to know the names and salaries of the employees. (These data are called the *input*.) To keep things as simple as possible, we'll assume that all names and annual salaries are contained in an employee ledger and are obtained simply by reading the ledger.

Since our algorithm is to produce a year-end bonus report (called the *output*), we must decide upon a format for this report. A quick reading of the problem statement suggests a report such as the following:

Year-end bonuses (1989)

Name	Salary	Bonus
Susan Andrade	27,000	540
Lester Barkley	16,500	400
.	.	.
.	.	.
.	.	.

To help us design a detailed algorithm to produce our bonus report, we'll begin with the following short algorithm that simply identifies what tasks must be performed:

a. Write the title and column headings for the bonus sheet.
b. Read the ledger to determine and fill in the name, salary, and bonus for each employee.

To carry out Step (a), a payroll clerk would simply copy the information from the output format already specified. To carry out Step (b), a clerk might proceed as follows:

b1. Open the employee ledger.
b2. Read the next employee's name and salary.
b3. Determine the employee's bonus.
b4. Write the employee's name, salary, and bonus on the bonus sheet.
b5. If all bonuses have not been determined, return to Step (b2).
b6. Close the ledger.

It is not difficult to see that Steps (b1) to (b6) constitute an algorithm for Step (b). Each step is well defined, and because a business can employ only a finite number of people, the algorithm will terminate in a finite number of steps. Moreover, if this algorithm is followed—without error—all employee bonuses will be determined as specified. Although the algorithm does what was asked, the process could be made more specific by including more detail in Step (b3). Recalling the method specified for calculating bonus amounts, we can substitute the following for Step (b3):

b3.1. Multiply the salary by 0.02 to obtain a tentative bonus.
b3.2. If the tentative bonus is less than $400, set the bonus to $400; otherwise make the bonus equal to the tentative bonus.

Making this change, or *refinement*, we obtain the following more detailed algorithm for Step (b):

b1. Open the employee ledger.
b2. Read the next employee's name and salary.
b3.1. Multiply the salary by 0.02 to obtain a tentative bonus.
b3.2. If the tentative bonus is less than $400, set the bonus to $400; otherwise make the bonus equal to the tentative bonus.
b4. Write the employee's name, salary, and bonus on the bonus sheet.
b5. If all bonuses have not been determined, return to Step (b2).
b6. Close the ledger.

Our final detailed algorithm consists of eight steps—Step (a) followed by this seven-step algorithm for carrying out Step (b).

In this example, we started with a problem statement describing the task to be carried out (produce a year-end bonus report) and ended with an algorithm describing how to accomplish this task. The steps you take while designing an algorithm are called a **problem analysis.** For simple problems, a description of the input and output may lead directly to a final algorithm. For more complicated problems, a thorough analysis of alternative approaches to a solution may be required. In any case, the term *problem analysis* refers to the process of designing a suitable algorithm.

The method used to design an algorithm for Example 1 illustrates three important principles of problem solving:

1. Begin by describing the input (information needed to carry out the specified task) and the output (the results that must be obtained). In the example, we described the input as salary information to be read from the employee ledger and the output as a table showing the names, salaries, and bonus amounts for the employees. An essential first step in the problem-solving process is to read and understand the problem statement. It is unlikely that a correct algorithm will be found if the task to be performed is not understood exactly. *Giving a clear and precise description of the input and output is an effective way to acquire an understanding of a problem statement*.

2. Identify individual subtasks that must be performed while carrying out the specified task. In Example 1 we identified the following two subtasks:

a. Write the title and column headings for the bonus sheet.
b. Read the ledger to determine and fill in the name, salary, and bonus for each employee.

If a complicated task can be broken down into simpler, more manageable subtasks, the job of writing an algorithm can often be simplified significantly: you simply describe the order in which the subtasks are to be carried out. This was especially easy to do in Example 1—simply carry out Subtask (a) followed by Subtask (b). The process of breaking down a task into simpler subtasks is called **problem segmentation** or **modularization**— the subtasks are sometimes called **modules.** As in Example 1, the details of how to carry out these modules can be worked out after an algorithm has been found.

3. If more details are needed in an algorithm, include the additional details separately for each step. In Example 1 we started with a two-step algorithm:

a. Write the title and column headings for the bonus sheet.
b. Read the ledger to determine and fill in the name, salary, and bonus for each employee.

Next, we included more detail in Step (b) by breaking it down into these six steps:

b1. Open the employee ledger.
b2. Read the next employee's name and salary.
b3. Determine the employee's bonus.
b4. Write the employee's name, salary, and bonus on the bonus sheet.
b5. If all bonuses have not been determined, return to Step (b2).
b6. Close the ledger.

Finally, we included more detail in the algorithm by rewriting Step (b3) as follows:

b3.1. Multiply the salary by 0.02 to obtain a tentative bonus.
b3.2. If the tentative bonus is less than $400, set the bonus to $400; otherwise make the bonus equal to the tentative bonus.

The important thing to notice is that we introduced details into the algorithm by refining the steps separately—that is, by breaking down the individual steps one at a time—and not by combining steps or otherwise changing the algorithm. This method of designing a detailed algorithm is called the **method of stepwise refinement.** You begin with a simple algorithm that contains few details but that you know is correct. If necessary, you refine one or more of the steps to obtain a more detailed algorithm. If even more detail is needed, you refine one or more of the steps in the derived algorithm. By repeating this process of stepwise refinement, you can obtain an algorithm with whatever detail is needed. Moreover, however complicated the final algorithm, you can be sure that it is correct simply by knowing that you started with a correct algorithm and that each step was refined correctly.

The approach to problem solving used in Example 1 is called the **top-down approach** to problem solving or the **top-down design** of algorithms. The expression *top-down* comes from using the methods of modularization and stepwise refinement. You start at the top (the problem statement), break that task down into simpler tasks, then break those tasks into even simpler ones, and continue the process, all the while knowing how the tasks at each level of refinement combine, until the tasks at the lowest (final) level contain whatever detail is desired. The advantages to be gained by adhering to the three problem-solving principles of the top-down approach will become more evident as you work through the examples and problems in this book. The following example should help you better understand these three principles and their application.

EXAMPLE 2   **A wholesale firm keeps a list of the items it sells in a card file. For each item, there is a single card containing a descriptive item name, the number of units in stock (this can be zero), the number of the warehouse in which the item is stored, and certain other information that will not concern us. Our task is to prepare a list of out-of-stock items for each warehouse.**

PROBLEM ANALYSIS

The problem statement says that a separate list of out-of-stock items is needed for each warehouse. Thus, we will need to know the warehouse numbers. Let's assume we are told there are three warehouses numbered 127, 227, and 327. With this information, we can include these numbers as input rather than reading through the entire card file to determine them. We can now specify the input and output for our algorithm:

Input: Warehouse numbers 127, 227, and 327.
Card file: one card for each item.

Output: Three reports formatted as follows:

WAREHOUSE 127
(Out-of-stock items)

Hammers—Model 2960
Hammers—Model 3375
Saws—Model 1233

.
.
.

WAREHOUSE 227
(Out-of-stock items)

.
.
.

WAREHOUSE 327
(Out-of-stock items)

.
.
.

Having given a precise description of the input and output, we should determine what subtask or subtasks must be performed. The problem statement specifies that three reports are to be produced, one for each warehouse. If we arrange things so that reports are produced one at a time (this is the common practice when using computers), we can use the same procedure for each report. Specifically, for each warehouse number W, we will carry out the following subtask (named R for report):

Subtask R. Prepare the report for warehouse W.

Of course, we will need to include details describing how to carry out this subtask. But even without these details, we can write a simple algorithm that obviously is correct:

    a. Assign 127 to W.
    b. Carry out Subtask R.
    c. Assign 227 to W.
    d. Carry out Subtask R.
    e. Assign 327 to W.
    f. Carry out Subtask R.

Notice that Subtask R specifies that a report is to be prepared. As in Example 1, we can break this subtask down into two subordinate subtasks R1 and R2 as follows:

    R1. Write the report header for warehouse W.
    R2. Read through the card file to complete the report.

At this point, we should recognize that Step R1 requires no additional details—the output specification shows how the report header should be formatted. We should, however, include more details in Step R2. In the following algorithm for Subtask R, Steps R2.1 to R2.4 show one way to carry out Step R2:

> **R1.** Write the report header for warehouse W.
> **R2.1.** Turn to the first card.
> **R2.2.** Read the warehouse number (call it N) and the units-on-hand figure (call it U).
> **R2.3.** If N = W and U = 0, read the item name and write it on the report.
> **R2.4.** If there is another card, turn to it and continue with Step R2.2.

Our final algorithm for the given problem statement consists of two parts: the original six-step algorithm [Steps (a)–(f)] that tells us when (but not how) to carry out Subtask R and the five-step algorithm (Steps R1, R2.1–R2.4) that shows us how Subtask R can be accomplished.

■ REMARK

Let's review the problem analysis carried out in this example:

Input/output specification. Our attempt to give a precise description of the input and output led us to include the warehouse numbers 127, 227, and 327 as input. As a consequence, the final algorithm is simpler than what would have been obtained had we begun by reading the entire card file just to determine the warehouse numbers.

Modularization. Our attempt to identify subtasks led us to conclude that there was but one major subtask, namely,

Subtask R. Prepare the report for warehouse W.

By using this subtask, it was easy to write an algorithm [Steps (a)–(f)] that lacked only the details needed to carry out Subtask R.

Stepwise refinement. Our next job was to show how to carry out Subtask R. We began by breaking it down into these two subordinate subtasks:

> **R1.** Write the report header for warehouse W.
> **R2.** Read through the card file to complete the report.

Notice that this two-step refinement of Subtask R represents an application of the principle of modularization applied to Subtask R. At this point we recognize that only Step R2 was lacking in details. We supplied these details by writing a short four-step algorithm (Steps R2.1–R2.4) for Step R2.

■ 2.2 Variables

Algorithms can often be stated clearly if symbols are used to denote certain values. Symbols are especially helpful when used to denote values that may change during the process of performing the steps in an algorithm. The symbols W, N, and U used in Example 2 illustrate this practice.

A value that can change during a process is called a **variable.** A symbol used to denote such a variable is the *name* of the variable. Thus W, N, and U in Example 2 are names of variables. It is common practice, however, to refer to the *symbol* as being the variable itself, rather than just its name. For instance, Step (a) of the algorithm for Example 2 says to assign 127 to W. Certainly this is less confusing than saying "assign 127 to the variable whose name is W."

The following two examples further illustrate the use of variables in algorithms.

EXAMPLE 3

Let's find an algorithm to determine the largest number in a list of numbers.

Input: A list of numbers.

Output: The largest number in the list.

One way to determine the largest number in a list of numbers is to read the numbers one at a time, remembering only the largest of those already read. To help us give a precise description of this process, let's use two symbols:

LGST to denote the largest of the numbers already read
NUM to denote the number currently being read

The following algorithm can now be written:

a. Read the first number and denote it by LGST.
b. Read the next number and denote it by NUM.
c. If NUM is larger than LGST, assign NUM to LGST.
d. If all numbers have not been read, go to Step (b).
e. Write the value of LGST and stop.

To verify this glorithm for the list of numbers

4, 5, 3, 6, 6, 2, 1, 8, 7, 3

we simply proceed step by step through the algorithm, always keeping track of the latest values of LGST and NUM. An orderly way to do this is to complete an assignment table, as follows:

Algorithm step	LGST	NUM	Output
a	4		
b		5	
c	5		
b		3	
b		6	
c	6		
b		6	
b		2	
b		1	
b		8	
c	8		
b		7	
b		3	
e			8

■ **REMARK 1**

If the numbers were written on a sheet of paper, you could look them over and select the largest. This process is heuristic, however, and does not constitute an algorithm.* To see

*A **heuristic process** is one involving exploratory methods. Solutions to problems are discovered by a continual evaluation of the progress made toward the final result. For instance, suppose you come upon an old map indicating that a treasure is buried in the Black Hills. You may be able to work out a plan that you know will lead to the location shown on the map. *That's an algorithm.* However, suppose you can find no such plan. Determined to find the location, or to verify that the map is a fake, you decide on a first step in your search, with no idea of what the next step will be. *That's exploratory.* Carrying out this first step may suggest a second step, or it may lead you nowhere, in which case you would try something else. Continuing in this manner, you may eventually find the location, or you may determine that the map is a fake. But it is also possible that the search will end only when you quit. Whatever the outcome, the process is heuristic. Someone else using this process will undoubtedly carry out entirely different steps and perhaps reach a different conclusion.

that this is so, imagine many hundreds of numbers written on a large sheet of paper. In that case, attempting to select the largest simply by looking over the numbers could easily result in an error. What we need is an orderly process that will ensure that the largest number is selected. Examining numbers one at a time, as in this algorithm, is such an orderly process.

■ **REMARK 2**   The task of finding the largest number in a list of numbers occurs as a subtask in many programming problems. When confronted with such a problem, you can use Steps (a)–(d) of the given algorithm to carry out the subtask. Should you need to find the smallest number, rather than the largest, simply change the word larger in Step (c) to smaller.

□

EXAMPLE 4   **Find an algorithm to prepare a depreciation schedule for a delivery van that costs $18,000, has a salvage value of $2,000, and has a useful life of 5 years. Use the straight-line method.**

[The straight-line method assumes that the value of the van will decrease by one-fifth of $16,000 (cost − salvage value) during each of the 5 years.]

PROBLEM ANALYSIS   For each year, let's agree to write one line showing the year, the depreciation allowance for that year, the cumulative depreciation (sum of yearly depreciations to that point), and the book value (cost − cumulative depreciation) at the end of the year. We can now describe the input and output.

Input: The purchased item (van), its cost ($18,000), salvage value ($2,000), and useful life (5 years).

Output: A report formatted as follows:

Depreciation schedule—van

Cost: $18,000 Life: 5 years		Salvage: $2,000 Method: Straight-line	
Year	**Depreciation allowance**	**Cumulative depreciation**	**Book value**
1990	$3,200	$3,200	$14,800
1991	3,200	6,400	11,600
.	.	.	.
.	.	.	.
.	.	.	.

It is not difficult to write an algorithm to produce this report if we leave out the details.

THE ALGORITHM   Look up the current year, item name, cost, salvage value, and useful life.
Write the report and column headers.
Determine and write the table values.

Steps (a) and (b) require no additional details—they are explained in the input/output description. To carry out Step (c) by hand, you might proceed as follows:

1. Determine the depreciation allowance for 1 year.
2. Subtract the depreciation allowance from the book value (initially the cost).
3. Add the depreciation amount to the cumulative depreciation (initially zero).
4. Write one line showing the year, the depreciation allowance for that year, the cumulative depreciation, and the book value at the end of the year.
5. Return to Step (2) until the schedule is complete.

To allow us to write a concise, detailed algorithm describing how to carry out Step (c), let's choose variable names to denote the various values of interest.

ITEM = name of purchased item
BV = book value (the initial book value is the cost)
SV = salvage value
Y = useful life in years
D = depreciation allowance for 1 year [D = (BV − SV)/Y]
C = cumulative depreciation (initially zero)
CY = current year

In the following detailed algorithm, Steps (c1) to (c7) tell how to accomplish Step (c). [Note that Step (a) has been changed only by the use of variable names in place of descriptive names.]

a. Look up (input) values for CY, ITEM, BV, SV, and Y.
b. Write the report and column headers.
c1. Start with C = 0.
c2. Calculate D = (BV − SV)/Y.
c3. Subtract D from BV.
c4. Add D to C.
c5. Write one line showing CY, D, C, and BV.
c6. Add 1 to CY.
c7. Return to Step (c3) until the schedule is complete.

For the input specified in the problem statement and with 1990 as the current year, this algorithm leads to the following depreciation schedule:

Depreciation schedule—van

Cost: $18,000 Life: 5 years		Salvage: $2,000 Method: Straight-line	
Year	Depreciation allowance	Cumulative depreciation	Book value
1990	$3,200	$ 3,200	$14,800
1991	3,200	6,400	11,600
1992	3,200	9,600	8,400
1993	3,200	12,800	5,200
1994	3,200	16,000	2,000

REMARK It is not often that a problem statement exactly describes the task to be carried out. Problem statements are written in a natural language, such as English, and thus are subject to the ambiguities inherent in natural languages. Moreover, they are written by people, which means that they are subject to human oversight and error. Since an algorithm describes a precise, unambiguous process for carrying out a task, the task to be performed must be clearly understood. If it appears ambiguous, the ambiguities must be resolved. If it appears that one thing is being asked but another is actually desired, the difference must be resolved. For instance, the problem statement in the present example asks for only a very limited algorithm (a book value of $18,000, a salvage value of $2,000, and a useful life of 5 years) when what is really desired is the more general algorithm that has a wider application.

■ 2.3 Problems

Problems 1–4 refer to the following algorithm for completing an invoice:

a. Let AMOUNT = 0.
b. Read QUANTITY and PRICE of an item.
c. Add the product QUANTITY × PRICE to AMOUNT.
d. If there is another item, go to Step (b); otherwise, continue with Step (e).
e. If AMOUNT is not greater than $500, go to Step (h); otherwise, continue with Step (f).
f. Evaluate the product 0.05 × AMOUNT.
g. Subtract this product from AMOUNT.
h. Record the value AMOUNT and stop.

1. What interpretation could be given to the product appearing in Step (f)?
2. What purpose would you say is served by Step (e)?
3. If the values (10, $3), (50, $8), and (25, $12) are read by Step (b), what value will be recorded by Step (h)?
4. If the values (100, $2) and (50, $1) are read by Step (b), what value will be recorded by Step (h)?

Problems 5–8 refer to the following algorithm, which is intended for use by a payroll clerk as a preliminary step in the preparation of a payroll:

a. Read the next time card.
b. Let H = number of hours worked.
c. If H is not greater than 32, assign 0 to G and B and go to Step (f); otherwise, continue with the next step.
d. Evaluate 6 × (H − 32) and assign this value to both G and B.
e. Let H = 32.
f. Evaluate 4 × H and add this value to G.
g. Write the values G and B on the time card.
h. If there is another time card, go to Step (a); otherwise, stop.

5. If the numbers of hours shown on the first four time cards are 20, 32, 40, and 45, respectively, what amounts will be written on these cards?
6. What is the base hourly rate for each employee?
7. What is the overtime rate?
8. Explain Step (c).

In Problems 9–12, what will be printed when each algorithm is carried out?

9. a. Let SUM = 0 and N = 1.
   b. Add N to SUM.
   c. Increase N by 1.
   d. If N ≤ 6, return to Step (b).
   e. Print the value SUM and stop.

10. a. Let PROD = 1 and N = 1.
   b. Print the values N and PROD on one line.
   c. Increase N by 1.
   d. Multiply PROD by N.
   e. If N ≤ 5, return to Step (b).
   f. Print the values of N and PROD on one line.
   g. Stop.

11. a. Let A = 1, B = 1, and F = 2.

   b. If F > 50, print the value F and stop.

   c. Assign the values of B and F to A and B, respectively.

   d. Evaluate A + B and assign this value to F.

   e. Return to Step (b).

12. a. Let NUM = 56, SUM = 1, and D = 2.

   b. If D is a factor of NUM, add D to SUM and print D.

   c. Increase D by 1.

   d. If D ≤ NUM/2, return to Step (b).

   e. Print the value SUM and stop.

Explain why the step-by-step processes given in Problems 13 and 14 do not describe algorithms.

13. a. Let N = 0.

   b. Increase N by 10.

   c. Divide N by 2.

   d. If N < 10, go to Step (b).

   e. Stop.

14. a. Let NUM = 25.

   b. Print the value of NUM.

   c. Add 2 or 3 to NUM.

   d. If NUM < 35, go to Step (b).

   e. Stop.

In Problems 15–21, write an algorithm to carry out each task specified.

15. A retail store's monthly sales report shows, for each item, the cost, the sale price, and the number sold. Prepare a three-column report with the column headings ITEM, GROSS SALES, and INCOME.

16. Each of several 3 × 5 cards contains an employee's name, Social Security number, job classification, and date hired. Prepare a report showing the names, job classifications, and complete years of service for employees who have been with the company for more than 10 years.

17. A summary sheet of an investor's stock portfolio shows, for each stock, the corporation name, the number of shares owned, the current price, and the earnings as reported for the most recent year. Prepare a six-column report with the column headings CORP. NAME, NO. OF SHARES, PRICE, EARNINGS, EQUITY, and PRICE/EARNINGS. Use this formula:

Equity = number of shares × price

18. Each of several cards contains a single number. Determine the sum and the average of all the numbers. (Use a variable N to count how many cards are read and a variable SUM to keep track of the sum of numbers already read.)

19. Each of several cards contains a single number. On each card, write the letter G if the number is greater than the average of all the numbers; otherwise, write the letter L. (You must read through the cards twice: once to find the average and again to determine whether to write the letter G or the letter L on the cards.)

20. A local supermarket has installed a check validation machine. To use this service, a customer must have an identification card containing a magnetic strip and a four-digit code. Instructions showing how to insert the identification card into a special magnetic-strip reader appear on the front panel. To validate a check, a customer must present the identification card to the machine, enter the four-digit code, enter the amount of the check, and place the check, blank side toward the customer, in a clearly labeled punch unit. To begin this process, the CLEAR key must be pressed, and, after each of the two entries has been made, the ENTER key must be pressed. Prepare an algorithm giving instructions for validating a check.

21. Write an algorithm describing the steps to be taken to cast a ballot in a national election. Assume that a person using this algorithm is a registered voter and has just entered the building in which voting is to take place. While in the voting booth, the voter should simply be instructed to vote. No instructions concerning the actual filling out of a ballot are to be given.

■ 2.4 Review True-or-False Quiz

1. The terms *algorithm* and *process* are synonymous.   **T F**
2. A computer program should describe an algorithm.   **T F**
3. Every algorithm can be translated into a computer program.   **T F**
4. The expression *heuristic process* refers to an algorithm.   **T F**
5. It is always easier to verify the correctness of an algorithm that describes a specific task than the correctness of a more general algorithm.   **T F**
6. The term *variable* refers to a value that can change during a process.   **T F**
7. The expressions *input/output specification*, *modularization*, and *stepwise refinement* refer to principles of problem solving.   **T F**
8. A *problem analysis* is the process of discovering a correct algorithm.   **T F**
9. The *method of stepwise refinement* is a method of problem solving in which successive steps in an algorithm are combined to produce an algorithm that is easier to read.   **T F**
10. *Top-down design* involves the process of *stepwise refinement*.   **T F**

3

A First Look at BASIC

We must communicate with a computer before it will perform any service for us. The medium for this communication is the computer program—for our purposes, a sequence of statements (instructions to the computer) in the English-like language BASIC. In this chapter we discuss some topics vital to understanding how a BASIC computer program must be written. These include the following: names of numerical and character string variables allowed in BASIC; how to write numerical expressions in a form suitable for computer evaluation; and how the REM, LET, PRINT, and END statements are used in BASIC programs. In the next chapter we explain how you get a completed program into the computer and cause it to be carried out, or executed.

Here is a BASIC program whose purpose is described in its first line:

```
100 REM PROGRAM TO AVERAGE THREE NUMBERS
110 REM   X, Y, AND Z DENOTE THE NUMBERS.
120 REM   AV DENOTES THE AVERAGE.
130 LET X=43
140 LET Y=27
150 LET Z=23
160 LET AV=(X+Y+Z)/3
170 PRINT "AVERAGE IS";AV
180 END
```

If a computer carries out the instructions in this program, it will produce the following output:

```
AVERAGE IS 31
```

The lines in this program are labeled with *line numbers* that determine the order in which the instructions are carried out by the computer. The program uses four words, called **keywords,** from the BASIC language: REM, to include remarks or comments as part of the program; LET, to associate certain numerical values with certain symbols (for example, line 130 associates 43 with the symbol X); PRINT, to display the results; and END, to indicate the last line of the program.

Unlike a natural language such as English, a programming language must not allow ambiguities. The computer must do precisely what it is instructed to do. For this reason, great care must be taken to write BASIC statements precisely according to the **BASIC syntax** (BASIC rules of grammar). The following sections describe how the keywords REM, LET, PRINT, and END can be used to form admissible BASIC programs. A complete treatment of these topics is not intended at this time; our immediate goal is to provide you with the minimal information you need to understand and write some BASIC programs.

■ 3.1 Numerical Constants and Variables

Three types of numerical constants are allowed in BASIC:

Type	Examples					
Integer	726	29234	−726	+423	−16023	0
Decimal	726.	−133.50	+10.001	−99234.	0.201	
Floating-point (exponential)	27.3E4	2.6E−3	1E3	−13.6E01	+2.345E−02	

Almost all of your numerical work in BASIC will deal with the first two types, *integer* and *decimal*. Integers are numbers with no decimal point, and decimals are numbers in which a decimal point appears. The use of commas and dollar signs in numbers is not allowed; using 29,234 to represent 29234 will result in an error.

The third type, the *exponential* constant, may be new to you. The E in 27.3E4 stands for exponent. Its meaning is *times 10 to the power*. Thus 27.3E4 means 27.3 times 10 to the power 4 or, in more mathematical symbols, 27.3×10^4. Hence,

$$27.3E4 = 27.3 \times 10^4 = 27.3 \times 10000 = 273000$$

Similarly,

$$2.6E-3 = 2.6 \times 10^{-3} = 2.6 \times .001 = .0026$$

Note that you could obtain the final result 273000 of 27.3E4 by moving the decimal point in 27.3 *four* places to the *right,* and the result .0026 of 2.6E − 3 by moving the decimal point in 2.6 *three* places the the *left*. The general form for a floating-point constant, together with its meaning, is

$$nEm = n \times 10^m$$

where *n* can be any integer or decimal, but *m* must be an integer (no decimal point). The values of the other floating-point numbers shown above are

$$1E3 = 1000$$

$$-13.6E01 = -136$$

$$2.345E-02 = .02345$$

Although in some programming languages you must be careful to represent numbers as integer, decimal, or floating-point constants, in BASIC you are free to use any form desired. For example, the following BASIC statements are equivalent; each assigns the value 230 to the variable A:

```
LET A=230
LET A=230.00
LET A=2.3E2
```

To form names for numerical variables, most BASIC systems allow sequences of alphanumeric characters (letters A–Z and digits 0–9) beginning with a letter. Thus, M, SUM1, SALARY, and DEPT32 are admissible numerical variable names on most systems. The careful selection of meaningful variable names can significantly improve a program's readability. You should be aware, however, that the following restrictions may apply on your system:

1. BASIC systems use certain words (such as LET, PRINT, and REM) for special purposes. These words are called **reserved words** and should not be used as variable names or, on some systems, as parts of variable names. Consult your BASIC manual for a complete list of reserved words.

2. Variable names may be restricted to a single letter or to a single letter followed by a single digit. On such systems, A and C2 are admissible but B13, AB3, and SUM are not.

3. In distinguishing one variable from another, BASIC recognizes only a fixed number of characters. For example, if the fixed number is 2, SUM1 and SUM2 are equivalent, since BASIC will recognize only the SU in each case. Experiment! You may find that the fixed number for your system is so large that such difficulties will not occur.

The variables just described are called **single precision real variables** or, more simply, **real variables.** They can be used to store numerical constants (real numbers) with approximately seven-digit accuracy. In addition to the *real variables,* your system may allow **integer variables** that can sometimes be helpful in applications involving only the integers from −32767 to 32767. Integer variable names differ from real variable names in one way only: their last character must be the percent symbol (%). Integer values for such variables are obtained by truncation, if necessary. Thus, the statement

```
LET A%=15.987
```

associates the integer 15 with A%. The fractional part (.987) is simply discarded.* Other than pointing out situations in which integer variables might be useful, we will restrict ourselves to real numerical variables. They are adequate for essentially all programming applications. In keeping with the most common BASIC terminology, we will use the expression *numerical variable* and *real variable* synonymously.

■ 3.2 String Constants and Variables

A **string constant** is a sequence, or **string,** of BASIC characters enclosed in quotation marks. The following are string constants:

```
"INCOME"          "NANCY JONES"
"X="              "567"
"19 APRIL 1775"   "*****"
"SUM "            " DISCOUNT"
```

The *value* of a string constant is the sequence of all BASIC characters, including blanks, appearing between the quotes. Thus the value of the string constant "NANCY JONES" is the 11-character string NANCY JONES and the value of "SUM " is the 4-character string consisting of SUM followed by a blank character. A string can contain at least as many characters as will fit on a line.

Variables whose values are strings are called **string variables.** Their names differ from numerical variable names in only one way: their last character must be a dollar sign ($). Thus, A$, CH$, TITLE$, and ITEM57$ are admissible names for string variables.

■ 3.3 Arithmetic Operations and Expressions

BASIC uses the following symbols to denote the usual arithmetic operations:

BASIC symbol	Meaning	Priority
∧ or ↑ or **	Exponentiation	1
*	Multiplication	2
/	Division	2
+	Addition	3
−	Subtraction	3

---

* Integer variables use half the memory space required for real variables, and on some BASIC systems operations involving integer variables are executed more quickly.

Any meaningful combination of BASIC constants, variable names, and operation symbols is called a **BASIC expression.** In a BASIC expression the order in which the operations are performed is determined first by the indicated priority and then, within any priority class, from left to right. This is in agreement with the usual order in which arithmetic operations are carried out.

EXAMPLE 1   **In the following expressions the circled numbers indicate the order in which the operations will be performed by the computer.**

$$
\begin{array}{c}
① \quad ② \\
\text{a. } 5 - 4 + 3 = \\
1 \quad + 3 = \\
4
\end{array}
$$

Since $+$ and $-$ have the same priority, they are performed from left to right. Note that performing the $+$ first gives the incorrect value -2.

$$
\begin{array}{c}
③ ① ② \\
\text{b. } 2 + 6/4 * 3 = \\
2 + 1.5 * 3 = \\
2 + \quad 4.5 = \\
6.5
\end{array}
$$

Since $/$ and $*$ have the same priority, they are performed from left to right. Note that performing the $*$ first gives the incorrect value 2.5.

$$
\begin{array}{c}
③ ① ④ ② \\
\text{c. } 5 * 2 \wedge 2 + 3 \wedge 2
\end{array}
$$

Performing the operations in (c) one at a time, we obtain

$$
\begin{array}{c}
5 * 2 \wedge 2 + 3 \wedge 2 = \\
5 * \quad 4 \quad + 3 \wedge 2 = \\
5 * \quad 4 \quad + \quad 9 \quad = \\
20 \quad \quad + \quad 9 \quad = \\
29
\end{array}
$$

Parentheses may be used in BASIC expressions just as in ordinary algebra. They are used to override the usual order in which operations are performed as shown in Example 2 and also to help clarify the meaning of numerical expressions. For example, $5/2 * 3$ and $(5/2) * 3$ have the same meaning in BASIC, but the second form is less likely to be misinterpreted. A third use of parentheses in BASIC is explained in Example 3.

EXAMPLE 2   **In this table, $P = 14$, $Q = -5$, and $R = 7$:**

BASIC expression	Value of expression
P+(Q−R)	2
P/(4*R)	0.5
(Q+P)/(R−4)	3
Q+P/R−4	−7
(Q+R)^2+P	18
3^(R+Q)	9

Expressions such as $+5$, -1.2, $+A$, and $-B$ are also allowed in BASIC. The expressions $+A$ and A have the same meaning, and the expression $-B$ denotes the negative of B. When $+$ and $-$ are used in this way, they are called **unary operations.** It is unlikely that you will ever have cause to use the unary operation $+$, but you may sometimes find it convenient to use the unary operation $-$. For example, if you need the negative of the sum of A and B, you can use the expression

    -(A+B)

Unfortunately, BASIC systems differ in how numerical expressions containing the unary operation $-$ are evaluated. On some systems, unary operations have the highest priority so that -5^2 would be evaluated as $(-5)^2$ to give 25. On other systems, they have the same priority as addition and subtraction so that -5^2 would be evaluated as $-(5^2)$ to give -25. Although you should determine how your computer handles unary operations, the best, and safest, practice is to use parentheses so that no confusion can arise.

EXAMPLE 3

In this table, $A = 3$, $B = -2$, and $C = 4$.

BASIC expression	Value of expression
$-A$	-3
$+B$	-2
$-B$	2
$-A+B$	-5
$-(A+B)$	-1
$1+3^C$	82
$4-3+2/4+A$	4.5
$A/B*C$	-6 (not $-.375$)
$(C-5)^(-2)$	1
-2^4	system dependent (-16 or 16)
$(-2)^4$	16

■ **REMARK**

The parentheses surrounding -2 in the expression $(C - 5)^{(-2)}$ are necessary so that two operation symbols do not appear adjacent to each other. Failure to observe this rule will result in an error on many BASIC systems.

Roots of numbers are indicated in BASIC by using the exponentiation operator $^$. Recall from algebra that

$$\sqrt{9} = 9^{1/2} = 3$$

In BASIC, we write this as

    9^(1/2)   or   9^0.5

EXAMPLE 4

In this table, $M = 4$ and $N = 5$.

Algebraic expression	Equivalent BASIC expression	Value
$\sqrt{M}$	$M^(1/2)$	2
$\sqrt{M + N}$	$(M + N)^0.5$	3
$\sqrt[3]{2M}$	$(2 * M)^(1/3)$	2

CAUTION

BASIC systems are not designed to take roots of negative numbers. For example, the cube root of -8 is -2, but the BASIC expression $(-8)^{(1/3)}$ will not give this value. BASIC expressions such as A^B will result in an error if A is negative and B is not an integer.

■ 3.4 Problems

1. Evaluate the following.
   a. 2+3*5   **b.** 5*7−2   **c.** −4+2
   d. −(4+2)   **e.** −3*5   **f.** −3^2
   g. 1+2^3*2   **h.** 6/2*3   **i.** 1/2/2
   j. −2*3/2*3   **k.** 2^2^3   **l.** (2+(3*4−5))^0.5

2. For A = 2, B = 3, and X = 2, evaluate each of the following.
   a. A+B/X   **b.** (A+B)/2*X   **c.** B/A/X
   d. B/(A*X)   **e.** A+X^3   **f.** (A+B)^X
   g. B^A/X   **h.** B+A/B−A   **i.** A^B+X
   j. B^(X/A)   **k.** −A^B   **l.** (−A)^B

3. Some of the following are not admissible BASIC expressions. Explain why.
   a. (Y+Z)X   **b.** X2*36   **c.** A*(2.1−7B)
   d. −(A+2B)   **e.** 2X+2   **f.** X2+2
   g. X−2^2   **h.** A+(+B)   **i.** A2−(−A2)
   j. 5E1.0   **k.** −9^0.5   **l.** −9^1/2

4. Write BASIC expressions for these arithmetic expressions.
   a. $0.06P$ **b.** $5x + 5y$ **c.** $a^2 + b^2$
   d. $\dfrac{6}{5a}$ **e.** $\dfrac{a}{b} + \dfrac{c}{d}$ **f.** $\dfrac{a + b}{c + d}$
   g. $ax^2 + bx + c$ **h.** $\sqrt{b^2 - 4ac}$ **i.** $(x^2 + 4xy)/(x + 2y)$

5. Write equivalent BASIC expressions without using parentheses.
   a. ((X+1)+Y)   **b.** (A+B)*(A−B)   **c.** A*(A*(A+B)+1)
   d. (A*B)/C   **e.** A/(B*C)   **f.** X*(X*(X*(X+D)+C)+B)+A
   g. P^(Q*R)   **h.** 1/(A*B*C*D)

■ 3.5 The LET Statement: Assigning Values to Variables

In Section 3.3 you saw how to write arithmetic expressions in a form acceptable to the computer. You will now learn how to instruct the computer to evaluate such expressions.

A BASIC **program statement,** also called a **programming line,** consists of an instruction to the computer preceded by an unsigned integer called the **line number.** The general form is

    line number   BASIC instruction

For example,

    100 LET A=2+5

is a BASIC statement with line number 100. This statement, called a LET statement, will cause the computer to evaluate the sum 2 + 5 and then assign this value to A.

A **BASIC program** is a collection of BASIC program statements. The instructions are executed by the computer in the order determined by increasing line numbers, unless some instruction overrides this order. In this book we'll often use the expression *BASIC statement* to refer to a BASIC program statement without its line number. This practice conforms to current programming terminology.

The general form of our first BASIC statement, the LET statement, is

    ln LET **v** = **e**

or, more simply,

    ln v = **e**   (LET is optional.)

where **ln** stands for line number, **v** denotes a variable name, and **e** denotes a BASIC expression that may simply be a constant. This statement directs the computer to evaluate the expression **e** and then assign this value to the variable **v**. Only numerical values may be assigned to numerical variables and only strings to string variables.

The next two examples contain BASIC programs ready to be typed at the keyboard and executed. (The next chapter will show you how to do this.) The columns to the right of each program show how the values of variables are changed during program execution.

EXAMPLE 5 **Assignment of numerical values.**

The program	After execution of each statement	
	Value of P	Value of Q
100 LET P=12	12	
110 LET Q=P/2+1	12	7
120 LET P=Q/2+1	4.5	7
130 LET Q=P/2+1	4.5	3.25
140 END		

■ REMARK 1 Note that no value is shown for Q after execution of line 100. Many, but not all, BASIC systems assign an initial value of zero to all numerical variables.

■ REMARK 2 The END statement causes program execution to terminate. BASIC systems differ in how the END statement can be used. Some require a single END statement as the final statement (highest line number) of each program. Others allow you to include more than one END statement in each program. In this book we'll include a single END statement at the end of each program.

■ REMARK 3 The practice of incrementing line numbers by something other than 1 is a good one. (Using increments of 10 is very popular.) This practice allows you to insert additional statements, which may have been forgotten or are needed to modify a program, in their proper places.

■ REMARK 4 Newly written programs seldom do what they were meant to do. The programmer must find and correct all errors. (The errors are called **bugs,** and making the corrections is referred to as **debugging** the program.) A useful debugging technique is to pretend that you are the computer and prepare a table of successive values of program variables, as was done in this example. Such a table is called a **trace of the program** or, more simply, a **trace.**

□

EXAMPLE 6 **Assignment of string values.**

The program	After execution of each statement		
	Value of A$	Value of B$	Value of C$
200 LET A$="AND"	AND		
210 LET B$="SO"	AND	SO	
220 LET C$=B$	AND	SO	SO
230 LET B$=A$	AND	AND	SO
240 LET A$=C$	SO	AND	SO
250 END			

■ REMARK 1 Strings appearing in LET statements *must* be within quotation marks. However, note that it is the *string* and not the *quoted string* that is assigned to the variable.

■ **REMARK 2**   Note that no values are shown for B$ and C$ before the assignment of values to these variables in lines 210 and 220. Many systems assign an initial empty string (written " ") to each string variable.

■ **REMARK 3**   The maximum length of a string that may be assigned to a string variable varies from system to system. Most BASIC systems, however, allow at least as many characters as will fit on a programming line.

The BASIC statement

```
40 LET N=N+1
```

does not mean that N is equal to N + 1 (since that is impossible). It means that the expression N + 1 is *evaluated* and this value is *assigned* to the variable N. For example, the effect of the two programming lines

```
30 LET N=5
40 LET N=N+1
```

is that the value 6 is assigned to N. Similarly, the statement

```
70 LET S=S+Y
```

evaluates S + Y and then assigns this new value to S. Thus, line 40 increases the value of N by 1 and line 70 increases the value of S by Y.

EXAMPLE 7   In this table, *S* = 3, *Y* = −2, *H* = −4, *Z* = 6, and *M* = 10.

BASIC statement	After execution
35 LET S=S+Y	S has the value 1.
90 LET H=H+2*Z	H has the value 8.
40 LET M=2*M−Z	M has the value 14.

■ 3.6 The PRINT Statement

Every computer language must be designed so that the results of its programs can be made available in a usable form. In BASIC, the PRINT statement meets this requirement. The simplest form of this statement is

ln PRINT **e**

where **ln** denotes a line number and **e** denotes any string or numerical expression. When executed, this statement displays (or prints) the value of the expression **e** and then causes a RETURN to be executed—that is, the screen cursor (or printer mechanism) is positioned at the left margin of the next line. Here are four admissible PRINT statements:

```
100 PRINT "THIS IS A MESSAGE."
110 PRINT 3-8*7
120 PRINT X
130 PRINT A$
```

If X has the value 723.45 and A$ has the string value END OF MESSAGE, these four lines will produce the output:

```
THIS IS A MESSAGE.
-53
 723.45
END OF MESSAGE
```

Most BASIC systems will display 723.45 with a leading blank as shown. This is the sign position, which is left blank when positive numbers are displayed.

As illustrated in the next example, BASIC allows you to display the values of more than one expression on a single line.

EXAMPLE 8   **Displaying labels for output values.**

```
100 REM AUTOMOBILE SALES TAX PROGRAM
110 REM
120 PRINT "TAXATION DEPARTMENT"
130 LET PRICE=7295
140 PRINT "PRICE:";PRICE
150 PRINT "SALES TAX:";.05*PRICE
160 END
```

When this program is executed, it will produce the following output:

```
TAXATION DEPARTMENT
PRICE: 7295
SALES TAX: 364.75
```

Both lines 140 and 150 display a numerical value preceded by a label identifying what this value represents. Separating two expressions in a PRINT statement by a *semicolon* as in lines 140 and 150 causes the two values to be displayed next to each other—the blank space preceding each number in the output is the sign position mentioned previously.*

■ REMARK   In this program, string constants are included in PRINT statements to display a heading (TAXATION DEPARTMENT) and two labels (PRICE: and SALES TAX:) identifying the numerical output values. You can also use string *variables* for this purpose. For instance, if you add the line

```
135 LET P$="PRICE:"
```

to the program and change line 140 to

```
140 PRINT P$;P
```

□   the program will produce exactly the same output as before.

■ 3.7 The REM Statement: Remarks as Part of a Program

In the program shown at the outset of this chapter, certain comments are included (lines 100–120) to indicate the purpose of the program and to identify what values the variables X, Y, Z, and AV represent. The BASIC statement that allows you to insert such comments is the REM (REMARK) statement. The general form is

ln REM comment

where **comment** denotes any comment or remark you may wish to include. REM statements cause nothing to happen when a program is executed by a computer. Their sole purpose is to allow you to include documentation as part of your programs. The following example further illustrates the use of REM statements.

---

*The forms of the PRINT statement described in this section are adequate for many programming tasks. Chapter 8 presents a more complete description of how BASIC allows you to format your output values.

EXAMPLE 9   **Typical uses of REM statements.**

```
100 REM PROGRAM TO DETERMINE THE RATE OF RETURN
110 REM GIVEN THE CURRENT PRICE AND EARNINGS
120 REM
130 REM    P DENOTES THE CURRENT PRICE OF A SECURITY.
140 REM    E DENOTES THE RECENT ANNUAL EARNINGS.
150 REM    R DENOTES THE RATE OF RETURN.
160 REM
170 LET P=80.00
180 LET E=6.00
190 REM
200 REM CALCULATE THE RATE OF RETURN AND
210 REM PRINT SUMMARY RESULTS.
220 LET R=100*E/P
230 PRINT "PRICE:";P
240 PRINT "EARNINGS:";E
250 PRINT "RATE OF RETURN:";R
260 END
```

If this program is executed, the output will be as follows:

```
PRICE: 80
EARNINGS: 6
RATE OF RETURN: 7.5
```

In the program, REM statements are used for four different purposes: to give a brief description of the program (lines 100 and 110); to separate one section of the program from another (lines 120, 160, and 190); to describe the values represented by the variables used (lines 130, 140, and 150); and to describe the action of certain groups of programming lines (lines 200 and 210). Using REM statements as illustrated in this example is an excellent programming practice. Your programs will be easier to read and understand, easier to modify at some later date (should that be required), and easier to debug.

The comments in REM statements and the quoted messages in PRINT statements are intended for two different audiences. REM statements give information to people who actually read the program, whereas the messages in PRINT statements give information to users of the program. The needs of these two audiences are very different. For instance, a reader of your program may want to understand how the program carries out its task, but the user would be interested only in the results. To illustrate, consider the following statement:

```
200 REM --- CALCULATE THE GROSS PAY G ---
```

This informs the reader that the gross pay is denoted by G and that the programming lines that follow this statement will calculate this value. A user of the program, however, has no need for this information. To assist the user, you would include a statement such as

```
500 PRINT "GROSS PAY $";G
```

so that the output value G is labeled in a meaningful way. You would not use

```
500 PRINT "G=$";G
```

since the user neither cares nor needs to know that G is used to denote the gross pay. Messages in PRINT statements should never presume that a user has read the program and is familiar with the variable names.

Good programming practice dictates that you include clarifying REM statements for someone reading your program and messages in PRINT statements that are useful to the user of the program. For example, the following two programs calculate and display exactly the same value (278.16), but Program A gives no information to the reader concerning the purpose of the program nor to the user as to what the output value 278.16 represents. Program B, on the other hand, gives useful information to both the reader and the user.

```
Program A                      Program B
10 LET X=38                    10 REM PROGRAM TO COMPUTE GROSS PAY
20 LET Y=7.32                  20 REM    H DENOTES HOURS WORKED.
30 LET Z=X*Y                   30 REM    R DENOTES HOURLY RATE.
40 PRINT Z                     40 LET H=38
50 END                         50 LET R=7.32
                               60 REM CALCULATE THE GROSS PAY G.
Output:  278.16               70 LET G=H*R
                               80 PRINT "GROSS PAY";G
                               90 END

                              Output:  GROSS PAY 278.16
```

Many BASIC systems allow you to end any programming line with a comment. In some versions of BASIC such comments must begin with an apostrophe and in others with an exclamation mark:

In BASIC instruction   'comment   (or **!comment**)

The careful use of such comments can significantly improve the readability of your programs. If your system uses the apostrophe to indicate comments, you might write Program B as follows:

```
10 REM PROGRAM TO COMPUTE GROSS PAY
20 REM
30 LET H=38                   ' Hours worked
40 LET R=7.32                 ' Hourly rate
50 LET G=H*R                  ' Gross pay
60 PRINT "GROSS PAY";G
70 END
```

In this book, we use the REM statement and the apostrophe symbol to document programs.

■ 3.8 Problems

1. Write LET statements to perform the indicated tasks.
   a. Assign the value 7 to M.
   b. Increase the value assigned to B by 7.
   c. Double the value assigned to H.
   d. Assign the value of the expression $(A - B)/2$ to C2.
   e. Assign the tenth power of $1 + R$ to A.
   f. Decrease the value assigned to X by twice the value assigned to Y.
   g. Assign the string COST to C$.
   h. Replace the value of A$ by the string DOE, JANE.
   i. Store the contents of P$ in Q$.
   j. Assign the string ***** to S$.

2. Which of these are admissible BASIC statements? Explain.

   a. `10 LET X=(A+B)C`   **b.** `15 LET M=A1-A2`
   c. `20 LET A3=A*A*A`   **d.** `25 LET A+B=S`
   e. `30 LET X=2.3E-05`   **f.** `35 LET Y=4E0.5`
   g. `40 LET A$=DISCOUNT`   **h.** `45 LET "DIVIDEND"=D$`
   i. `50 LET SUM=SUM+SALARY` **j.** `55 LET M="MONTHLY RENT"`
   k. `60 PRINT "RATE-OF-RETURN"` **l.** `65 PRINT PRICE=;P`
   m. `70 PRINT "5+13=";S`   **n.** `75 PRINT "5+13=";5+13`
   o. `80 PRINT ITEM #35`   **p.** `85 PRINT S$;A`

3. Show the output of each program.

   a.
```
100 LET A=5
110 LET B=A+2
120 LET C=A+B
130 PRINT "RESULT";C
140 END
```
   b.
```
10 LET P=100
20 LET R=8
30 LET I=R/100
40 LET A=P+I*P
50 PRINT "AMOUNT=";A
60 END
```

```
c. 500 LET X=0
   510 LET X=X-1
   520 LET Y=X^2+3*X
   530 PRINT "RESULT";Y
   540 END
```

```
d. 10 LET A=2
   20 LET B=6
   30 LET A=2*A
   40 LET B=B/2
   50 LET C=(A^2+B^2)^(1/2)
   60 PRINT "RESULT"; C
   70 END
```

```
e. 100 LET L=10        'Length
   110 LET W=5         'Width
   120 LET H=4         'Height
   130 LET V=L*W*H     'Volume
   140 PRINT "VOLUME";V
   150 LET L=W
   160 LET H=W
   170 PRINT "VOLUME";V
   180 END
```

```
f. 10 LET A=1
   20 LET B=3
   30 LET C=2
   40 LET D=B^2-4*A*C
   50 LET X=(-B+D^.5)/(2*A)
   60 PRINT "SOLUTION";X
   70 END
```

```
g. 10 PRINT "BOBBY LOVES"
   20 LET M$="MARY"
   30 LET B$="BARB"
   40 LET B$=M$
   50 LET M$=B$
   60 PRINT M$
   70 END
```

```
h. 10 LET L$="LIST PRICE"
   20 LET D$="DISCOUNT"
   30 LET S$="SELLING PRICE"
   40 LET L=45
   50 LET D=(10/100)*L
   60 LET S=L-D
   70 PRINT L$;L
   80 PRINT D$;D
   90 PRINT S$;S
   99 END
```

4. Complete each table as was done in Examples 6 and 7.

```
a. 100 LET A=1
   110 LET B=2
   120 LET C=1
   130 LET C=C+B
   140 LET A=B^2
   150 LET B=C-B+A
   160 LET C=C-1
   170 LET B=A*B
   180 LET A=A/C
   190 LET C=B/A+1
   200 END
```

A	B	C

```
b. 100 LET N=1
   110 PRINT N
   120 LET N=N*(N+1)
   130 PRINT N
   140 LET N=N*(N+1)
   150 PRINT N
   160 LET N=N*(N+1)
   170 PRINT N
   180 END
```

N	Output

	X	Y	Z	Output

```
c. 100 LET X=0
   110 LET Y=X+7
   120 LET Z=Y+X^2
   130 PRINT Z
   140 LET X=Z
   150 LET Y=X*Y*Z
   160 PRINT Y
   170 END
```

5. Prepare tables showing the successive values of all variables and the output.

```
a. 100 LET S=0
   110 LET A=25
   120 LET S=S+A
   130 PRINT S
   140 LET S=S+A
   150 PRINT S
   160 LET S=S/2
   170 PRINT S
   180 END
```

```
b. 100 LET X=1.5
   110 LET Y=3/(2*X+2)
   120 PRINT Y
   130 LET X=-X
   140 PRINT X
   150 PRINT Y
   160 END
```

```
c. 10 LET N=130      'COUNT
   20 LET C=3.00     'COST
   30 LET S=1.2*C    'PRICE
   40 LET G=N*S      'SALES
   50 PRINT "SALES";G
   60 LET P=G-N*C
   70 PRINT "PROFIT";P
   80 END
```

```
d. 100 PRINT "NTH POWERS OF 7"
   110 LET A=7
   120 LET P=7
   130 PRINT "FOR N=1:";P
   140 LET P=A*P
   150 PRINT "FOR N=2:";P
   160 LET P=A*P
   170 PRINT "FOR N=3:";P
   180 LET P=A*P
   190 PRINT "FOR N=4:";P
   200 REM "END OF TABLE"
   210 END
```

■ 3.9 Review True-or-False Quiz

1. Parentheses may be used only to override the usual order in which operations are performed by the computer. **T F**
2. A BASIC program is a collection of BASIC programming lines. **T F**
3. 2/3 is a numerical constant in BASIC. **T F**
4. $(A + B)^{.5}$ and $(A + B)^{1/2}$ have the same meaning. **T F**
5. 50 LET B$ = BALANCE is a valid BASIC statement. **T F**
6. If A = 3, the statement 43 LET 1 + A^2 = B1 assigns the value 10 to the variable B1. **T F**
7. 150 LET A3 = A3 * A3 is a valid BASIC statement. **T F**
8. 1.0E1 has the value 10. **T F**
9. 300 LET M = "1984" is a valid BASIC statement. **T F**
10. 40 PRINT DEPT#3 TOTAL; T is a valid BASIC statement. **T F**
11. REM statements are often used to explain the purpose of groups of programming lines. **T F**
12. REM statements can be used to display messages during program execution. **T F**
13. Comments appearing in REM statements must be enclosed in quotation marks. **T F**
14. The BASIC statement LET X = X + 1 is a valid BASIC statement but will result in an error because there is no value X for which X = X + 1. **T F**

4 First Session at the Keyboard

hapter 3 presented examples of BASIC programs ready to be transmitted to the computer. Two devices will serve as the principal means of communication between you and the computer: a *keyboard* at which you type information (such as programs) for transmission to the computer and either a *video display screen* or a *printer*, which the computer uses to transmit information back to you.

Your keyboard will resemble an ordinary typewriter keyboard. It will contain keys for the 26 letters of the English alphabet, the digits 0 through 9, and certain other familiar characters such as $ # , . ; : = ( ) − /. In addition, the keyboard has a space bar, a RE-TURN key, and several other keys whose functions will be explained as the need arises.

Before you begin typing a program, you must establish communication with the computer. When this has been accomplished you are *on line*. With small computer systems such as personal computers, going on line can be as simple as pushing a button. Larger time-sharing systems require a slightly more complicated *log-in procedure*. A typical log-in procedure is described in Appendix A. In what follows, we will assume that you are on line.

To get the most out of this chapter, you are urged to read through the material quickly to get a general idea of what is involved and then to read it again, this time being sure to try all the examples on your computer.

■ 4.1 Entering a Programming Line: The RETURN Key

Here is a program ready to be entered at the keyboard:

```
100 REM SUM AND DIFFERENCE PROGRAM
110 LET P=5
120 LET Q=8
130 LET SUM=P+Q
140 LET DIFF=Q-P
150 END
```

To enter this program, you first type

```
100 REM SUM AND DIFFERENCE PROGRAM ⏎
```

where ⏎ denotes the RETURN key on your keyboard. This key is also called the ENTER key. Pressing ⏎ causes two things to happen:

1. The line just typed is entered as part of the program.

2. The cursor (printer mechanism if you are using a printer) moves to the beginning of the next line.

You then continue typing:

```
110 LET P=5
120 LET Q=8
130 LET SUM=P+Q
140 LET DIFF=Q-P
150 END
```

Remember you must press ⏎ to enter each line. If you make a typing error, simply press ⏎ and retype the entire line, including the line number.

Since this program contains no PRINT statement, there will be no output if it is executed. To rectify this situation, you could add PRINT lines simply by typing the following:

```
135 PRINT "SUM IS";SUM
145 PRINT "DIFFERENCE IS";DIFF
```

BASIC allows you to enter these lines out of their natural numerical order; the program will still be carried out according to the sequence of line numbers from smallest to largest. Thus, if you omit a line in typing a program, you can insert it at any time before execution simply by typing it.

You have undoubtedly discovered that making an entry on the last line of the display screen causes the entire display to move up one line and the top line to scroll off the screen. Scrolling a line off the screen in no way affects what has already been stored in memory.

■ 4.2 Spacing

Spaces may be used to improve the appearance and readability of BASIC programs. During program execution, the only significant spaces are those that appear in strings and those that separate BASIC keywords from other items in a programming line. All other spaces are ignored; thus, the three programming lines

```
130 LET S=P+Q
130 LET     S = P + Q
130        LET S=P+Q
```

are equivalent BASIC statements.

Good programming practice dictates that you use this freedom of spacing to advantage: a program listing should be easy to read. Here are two rules you should follow (on many systems, these rules *must* be observed):

1. Insert at least one space before and after each BASIC keyword such as LET, PRINT, REM, and END. Thus, write 130 LET S = P + Q, but not 130LETS = P + Q.
2. Do not insert spaces within BASIC keywords, variables, line numbers, or constants. Thus, write 250 LET S = X1 + 24.75, but not 2 5 0 L E T S = X 1 + 24. 75.

■ 4.3 The System Commands LIST and RUN

A listing of all program statements already transmitted to the computer can be obtained by typing LIST. This is the first of several commands referred to as **system commands.** A system command has no line number and is not part of a BASIC program. It is an instruction to the computer to do a specific task at the time the command is issued. We illustrate for the program entered in Section 4.1:

```
LIST ↵                                    (You type this.)

100 REM SUM AND DIFFERENCE PROGRAM   (This is displayed by the computer.)
110 LET P=5
120 LET Q=8
130 LET SUM=P+Q
135 PRINT "SUM IS";SUM
140 LET DIFF=Q-P
145 PRINT "DIFFERENCE IS";DIFF
150 END
READY
```

Note that lines 135 and 145 have been inserted in their proper places even though they were actually typed after line 150. READY is the computer's signal that it is ready for you to make another entry (your system may use something other than READY).

When you are reasonably certain that the program has been typed correctly, you can cause it to be executed (run) with the system command RUN. This command will cause the program instructions to be carried out according to the sequence of their line numbers. We illustrate for the program just entered:

```
RUN ↵                    (You type this.)

SUM IS 13                (This is displayed by the computer.)
DIFFERENCE IS 3
READY
```

In subsequent examples we will show the BASIC prompt READY and the return symbol ↵ only if doing so helps to clarify what is being illustrated.

■ 4.4 Making Corrections

During a session at the keyboard you will most likely make occasional typing errors. As mentioned previously, you can change any line in a program simply by retyping the entire line, including its line number. To erase a line, type its line number and then press ↵.

EXAMPLE 1   **Changing and deleting program lines.**

```
30 LET Z=5        (You type this.)
40 PRINT X
50 LET Z-7=X
60 PRINT X
70 END
40                (Delete line 40.)
50 LET X=Z-7      (Correct line 50.)
LIST
30 LET Z=5        (This is displayed by the computer.)
50 LET X=Z-7
60 PRINT X
70 END
```

■ REMARK   Some systems will not allow a typing error such as

```
50 LET Z-7=X
```

to go undetected. If such a line is entered, the computer will immediately display a message indicating that this is not a BASIC statement.

BASIC also allows you to make corrections as you are typing a line—that is, before you press ↵. For example, while typing the line

```
55 LET S=35.2
```

you notice that you have typed

    55 LRT

At this point, press the BACKSPACE key two times to erase the characters T and R.* You then type the correct characters ET and continue typing to the end of the line. By using this method, you can erase as many characters as is required; simply press the BACKSPACE key once for each character to be erased. What the computer actually displays when you erase characters this way depends on the system you are using. (Experiment!)

■ 4.5 Error Messages

You may not always be fortunate enough to detect syntax errors (violations of BASIC rules of grammar) before attempting to "run" your program. Should you issue the RUN command for such an incorrect program, appropriate error messages will be displayed. These messages will indicate the type of error and, on many systems, the line number in which the error occurs. The exact forms of such messages depend on the BASIC system being used. The following example illustrates how such error messages can help you correct a program.

EXAMPLE 2   **Finding and correcting syntax errors.**

```
10 LET X=7              (You type this.)
20 LET X+9=Z
30 PRINT 'ANSWER IS';Z
40 END
RUN

ILLEGAL STATEMENT AT 20    (This is displayed by the computer.)

20 LET Z=X+9            (You type this.)
RUN

ILLEGAL STATEMENT AT 30    (This is displayed by the computer.)

30 PRINT "ANSWER IS";Z     (You type this.)
RUN

ANSWER IS 16               (This is displayed by the computer.)
READY
```

■ **REMARK 1**   When you issue the RUN command, your system may display the error messages one at a time, as in the example, or it may display all of the error messages together.

■ **REMARK 2**   When displaying the output of a program, we include a blank line immediately after the RUN command. If your system does not skip this line, you can insert

    5 PRINT

□ in the program. This statement will produce no output but will cause a RETURN to be executed.

As illustrated in the following example, error messages are sometimes displayed even though a program contains no syntax errors.

EXAMPLE 3   **Here is a syntactically correct program with an error.**

The following program is designed to compute the ratio

---

* The BACKSPACE key (labeled ← on some keyboards) is not standard; your system may instead require you to press the RUBOUT key, the DELETE key, or to type some combination of keys, such as SHIFT/O or CTRL/H.

$$\frac{\text{Cost } + \text{ Markup}}{\text{Cost } - \text{ Markup}}$$

```
10 REM C DENOTES THE COST.
20 LET C=100
30 REM M DENOTES THE MARKUP.
40 LET M=100
50 LET R=(C+M)/(C-M)
60 PRINT "RATIO=";R
70 END
RUN

DIVISION BY ZERO AT 50
READY
```

Each line in this program is an admissible BASIC program statement; hence the program is syntactically correct. When run, the computer assigns 100 to C (line 20), assigns 100 to M (line 40), and then attempts to evaluate the expression in line 50. The error message tells you that the computer does not "know" how to divide by zero. Programming errors that cause error messages during program execution are called **run-time errors.**

Unfortunately, error messages are not always displayed when incorrect programs are run. Here is a program with an error that the computer will not detect.

```
10 REM COMPUTE THE AVERAGE OF X AND Y.
20 REM THIS PROGRAM IS SYNTACTICALLY CORRECT
30 REM BUT PRODUCES INCORRECT RESULTS.
40 LET X=10
50 LET Y=5
60 LET AV=X+Y/2
70 PRINT "AVERAGE IS";AV
80 END
RUN

AVERAGE IS 12.5
```

The computer does precisely what you instruct it to do; it does not do what you meant it to do. The programming error in line 60 is an error in the *logic* of the program. It is not a syntax or run-time error. Such programming errors can be very difficult to find.

If a system command (rather than a programming line) is typed incorrectly, the system will respond with a message indicating that the command is unrecognizable. Thus, you needn't worry about harming the system with novice mistakes.

■ 4.6 Immediate Execution Mode

On many computer systems you can cause BASIC statements to be carried out as soon as they are entered simply by typing them without line numbers. This mode of operation is called **immediate execution mode.** (You will recall that statements with line numbers, even though they appear on the screen as you type them, are actually carried out only after you type a RUN command—this is called **deferred execution mode.**) If you type

```
LET A=32
```

without a line number, the statement will be executed as soon as you press the RETURN key, and the value 32 will be assigned to A. (If you obtain an error message, your computer does not allow immediate mode and the rest of this section is not applicable to that computer.) If you then type

```
PRINT 3*A
```

the computer will display the value 96 of the expression 3 *A.

Immediate execution mode can often be used to help you debug a program. After you run a program, the final values of all variables are retained by the computer. Thus if your program produces incorrect results, you can use immediate mode PRINT statements to examine these final values. This information may be just what you need to locate the error. We illustrate with a short program that contains a single error.

EXAMPLE 4   **Immediate mode and debugging.**

```
10 REM INCREASE SALARY BY 4.5 PERCENT.
20 REM    S=OLD SALARY
30 REM    R=RAISE
40 REM    N=NEW SALARY
50 LET S=24500
60 LET R=4.5*S
70 LET N=S+R
80 PRINT "OLD SALARY:";S
90 PRINT "NEW SALARY:";N
99 END
RUN

OLD SALARY: 24500
NEW SALARY: 134750
```

Clearly this program has a bug—the new salary amount is much too large. Let's examine the final values of the variables:

```
PRINT S
 24500
PRINT R
 110250
```

At this point we can see that S is correct (assigned in line 50), but R (assigned in line 60) cannot be what we want. Thus the error must be in line 60. You would now correct the programming error by typing

```
60 LET R=.045*S
```

and run the program again to get the correct results.

■ 4.7 Obtaining Hard Copy

If your system uses a display screen as the principal output device, every character typed by you at the keyboard, or generated as the result of some action by the computer, has appeared only on the display screen. Often, though, you will want a printed copy (hard copy) of your program or its output. Table 4.1 shows how to obtain hard copy for several widely used computer systems. In the table, the two entries

CTRL/P   and   CTRL/PrtSc

mean to press the indicated key (P or PrtSc) while holding down the key labeled CTRL.

■ 4.8 On Writing Your First Program

You are now ready to write your first program. Since a computer program is an algorithm (that is, a set of instructions to the computer to carry out a specified task), the principles of algorithm design described in Chapter 2 are also principles of program design. They will help you design algorithms that are both correct and easily translated into BASIC programs. Following is a brief summary of these principles:

Table 4.1 Hard copy output

Computer	Keyboard entries	
Apple	PR#1	Select printer plugged into slot #1
	LIST or RUN	Produce hard copy
	PR#0	Return to display screen
Commodore	OPEN 3,4	Assign channel 3 to printer
	CMD 3	Channel 3 will accept commands
	LIST or RUN	Produce hard copy
	PRINT #3	Clear the output buffer
	CLOSE 3	Return to screen output
CDC (Cyber)	ROUTE	The form of the ROUTE and other commands needed to produce hard copy differ significantly for different installations. If a terminal with a printer is not available, get help from your computer center.
DEC Rainbow	LLIST	Hard copy program listing
	CTRL/P	Select printer
	LIST or RUN	Produce hard copy
	CTRL/P	Return to display screen
DEC VAX-11	SAVE PROG.BAS	Save program as PROG.BAS
	EXIT	Leave BASIC subsystem
	PRINT PROG.BAS	Hard copy program listing
	BASIC PROG	Compile PROG.BAS
	LINK PROG	Prepare for execution
	ASSIGN PROGOUT AS SYS$OUTPUT	Select file PROGOUT for output
	RUN PROG	Output to file PROGOUT
	PRINT PROGOUT	Hard copy of program output
IBM PC and compatibles	LLIST	Hard copy program listing
	CTRL/PrtSc	Select printer
	LIST or RUN	Produce hard copy
	CTRL/PrtSc	Return to display screen
	LPRINT	Using LPRINT instead of PRINT will cause output to be transmitted to the printer instead of the screen.
TRS-80	LLIST	Hard copy program listing
	LPRINT	Using LPRINT instead of PRINT will cause output to be transmitted to the printer. (Other methods of obtaining hard copy output depend on the model being used.)

Your system: _____

_____

_____

_____

_____

_____

_____

_____

_____

_____

1. *Input/output specification.* Begin by describing the input (information needed to carry out the specified task) and the output (the results to be obtained and the form in which they should appear). Giving a clear and precise description of the input and output is an effective way to acquire an understanding of a problem statement. This principle of program design should be observed even for the relatively simple problems you will first encounter. The experience you gain while identifying and describing the input and output

for simple problems will help you when you are confronted with problems that are not so simple.

2. *Modularization.* Identify individual subtasks that must be performed while carrying out the specified task. As illustrated in Chapter 2, the job of writing an algorithm (or program) is often simplified if the given task is broken down into simpler more manageable subtasks. The importance of this principle of program design will become increasingly more evident as you learn more of the BASIC language and are confronted with more substantial programming problems.

3. *Stepwise refinement.* As illustrated in Chapter 2, you begin with a simple algorithm that contains few details but that you know is correct. (This initial algorithm can be a one-step algorithm describing the task to be carried out.) If necessary, you refine (break down) one or more of the steps to obtain a more detailed algorithm. If even more detail is needed, refine one or more steps in the derived algorithm. This process of stepwise refinement is repeated until you obtain an algorithm with whatever detail you need. The significance of this approach is that you can be sure that the final detailed algorithm is correct just by knowing that you started with a correct algorithm and that each step was refined correctly. As with modularization, the value of this principle of program design will become increasingly more evident as you progress in your study of programming.

The development of programming habits, both good and bad, begins with your first program. The following five-step approach to programming is presented to help you get started. It is not a complete description of the programming process but is adequate for many programming tasks, including those you will first encounter. Example 5 illustrates the application of this five-step process. At the end of this chapter you will be asked to write some programs. To learn good programming habits from the start, you should follow this five-step approach to programming.

1. *Be sure you thoroughly understand what is being asked in the problem statement.* A good way to do this is to identify the following items:

   Input: Data to be presented to the computer for processing.

   Output: The results called for in the problem statement. This may involve identifying what the output values are and in what form they are to be displayed.

2. *Identify what, if any, mathematical equations will be needed.* For example, to find the total cost C, including the 5% sales tax, of a television set listed at L dollars, you could use the equation

   $$C = L + 0.05 \times L$$

3. *Devise a step-by-step process (algorithm) that, if carried out, will result in a correct solution.* For simple programming tasks, this step usually is not difficult. For example, to find the total cost of the television set referred to above, you could use the following algorithm:

   a. Assign a value to L.
   b. Calculate $C = L + 0.05 \times L$.
   c. Print the result C and stop.

4. *Write the program statements to carry out the algorithm you have described.* This is called *coding the program.* Be sure to include adequate and meaningful REM statements.

5. *Debug the program.* This means running it to test for syntax errors and also to convince yourself that the program produces correct results.

EXAMPLE 5   **Write a program to calculate the simple interest and the amount due for a loan of *P* dollars, at an annual interest rate *R*, for a time of *T* years. Use the program to find the interest and amount due when *P* = $600, *R* = 0.1575, and *T* = 2.**

A quick reading of this problem statement shows that the input and output values are as follows:

Input: P, R, and T.

Output: Simple interest and the amount due.

We should all recognize the familiar formulas that govern this situation:

Simple interest: $I = P \times R \times T$

Amount due: $A = P + I$

Knowing these formulas, we can write the following algorithm:

a. Assign values to P, R, and T.
b. Calculate the interest I and the amount due A.
c. Display the results (I and A) and stop.

THE PROGRAM

```
100 REM SIMPLE INTEREST PROGRAM
110 REM   P DENOTES AMOUNT OF LOAN.
120 REM   R DENOTES ANNUAL INTEREST RATE.
130 REM   T DENOTES TERM OF LOAN IN YEARS.
140 REM
150 REM ASSIGN VALUES TO P, R, AND T.
160 LET P=600
170 LET R=.1575
180 LET T=2
190 REM
200 REM CALCULATE THE INTEREST I AND AMOUNT DUE A.
210 LET I=P*R*T
220 LET A=P+I
230 REM
240 REM PRINT THE RESULTS.
250 PRINT "INTEREST:";I
260 PRINT "AMOUNT DUE:";A
270 END
RUN

INTEREST: 189
AMOUNT DUE: 789
```

REMARK 1   To find the interest and amount due for other loans, simply change the given values at lines 160, 170, and 180. To test the program, try values for P, R, and T for which you know the results. For instance, P = 100, R = 0.06, and T = 1 should yield

```
INTEREST: 6
AMOUNT DUE: 106
```

Another good test would be P = 1, R = 0, and T = 1, which should yield

```
INTEREST: 0
AMOUNT DUE: 1
```

In Chapter 5 you will see how different values can be assigned to P, R, and T without having to retype programming lines.

REMARK 2   Notice that the REM statements in lines 150, 200, and 240 correspond to the three steps in the algorithm written for this example. Not only does this emphasize how the coding process follows from the algorithm, but it also suggests that each step in an algorithm should contain enough detail so that it can be coded easily. Writing your algorithms according to this principle and using the individual steps as REM statements are excellent programming practices.

■ 4.9 Problems

In Problems 1–4 show what will be displayed if the LIST command is entered; the RUN command.

```
1. 100 LET A=14
   110 LET B=20
   120 LET S=A+B
   130 PRINT "SUM IS S"
   140 END
   110 LET B=30
   130 PRINT "SUM IS";S
```

```
2. 100 LET X=5
   110 LET X=10
   120 LET Y=20
   130 PRINT "X+Y"=S
   110
   125 LET S=X+Y
   130 PRINT "X+Y=";S
   140 END
   150 RUN
   150
```

```
3. 100 PRINT "DISCOUNT CALCULATION"
   100 REM DISCOUNT PROGRAM
   100
   110 LET P=120
   120 LET D=0.1*P
   130 LET P=P-D
   140 PRINT "DISCOUNT";D
   150 PRINT "COST";C
   130 LET C=P-D
   160 END
```

```
4. 100 LET L$=AVERAGE
   110 LET A=5
   120 LET B=7
   130 LET M=A+B/2
   140 PRINT L$;M
   150 END
   110 LET A=9
   130 LET M=(A+B)/2
   100 LET L$="AVERAGE"
```

The programs in Problems 5–10 contain one or more bugs—either syntax errors (violations in the BASIC rules of grammar) or programming errors (errors in the logic of a program). Find each bug, tell which type of error it is, correct the programs, and show what will be displayed if the corrected programs are run.

```
5. 10 REM PROGRAM TO COMPUTE
   20 REM SIX PERCENT OF $23,000
   30 LET D=23,000
   40 LET R=6
   50 LET R*D=A
   60 PRINT "ANSWER IS";A
   70 END
```

```
6. 10 REM PROGRAM TO AVERAGE
   20 REM TWO NUMBERS
   30 LET N1=24
   40 LET N2=15
   50 LET A=N1+N2/2
   60 PRINT AVERAGE IS;A
   70 END
```

```
7. 10 REM SALES TAX PROGRAM
   20 REM    T=TAX RATE
   30 REM    P=PRICE
   40 LET 5=T
   50 LET P=120.00
   60 LET S=P+T*P
   70 PRINT "TOTAL COST"=S
   80 END
```

```
8. 10 REM PROGRAM TO FIND A SOLUTION X
   20 REM TO THE FOLLOWING EQUATION:
   30 REM    35X+220=0
   40 LET A=35
   50 LET B=220
   60 LET A*X+B=0
   70 PRINT "SOLUTION IS";X
   80 END
```

9.
```
100 REM PROGRAM TO SWAP THE
110 REM VALUES OF A$ AND B$
120 LET A$="STOCK"
130 LET B$="BOND"
140 PRINT "A$=";A$
150 PRINT "B$=";B$
160 REM INTERCHANGE A$ AND B$.
170 LET A$=B$
180 LET B$=A$
190 PRINT "A$=";A$
200 PRINT "B$=";B$
210 END
```

10.
```
100 REM "PROGRAM TO COMPUTE THE"
110 REM "EXCISE TAX T ON TWO CARS"
120 REM "VALUED AT V DOLLARS, IF THE"
130 REM "RATE IS 66 DOLLARS PER 1000."
140 LET V=4500
150 LET R=66/1000
160 LET T=V*R
170 PRINT TAX ON FIRST CAR IS T
180 LET V=5700
190 PRINT TAX ON SECOND CAR IS T
200 END
```

Listed below are several tasks to be performed. Write a BASIC program for each. Be sure to follow the guidelines suggested in Section 4.8. Use PRINT statements to label all output values, and be sure to include adequate REM statements. (If your system allows it, use meaningful variable names rather than single-letter names in these and all subsequent programming exercises.)

11. Compute the selling price S for an article whose list price is L if the rate of discount is D percent.

12. Compute the original price if an article is now selling at S dollars after a discount of D percent.

13. Compute the state gasoline tax in dollars paid by a driver who travels M miles per year if the car averages G miles per gallon and the tax is T cents per gallon.

14. Find the commission C on sales of S dollars if the rate of commission is R percent.

15. Find the principal P that, if invested at a rate of interest R for time T years, yields the simple interest I. (Recall that $I = P \times R \times T$.)

16. Compute the weekly salary, both gross G and net N, for a person who works H hours a week for D dollars an hour (no overtime). Deductions are S percent for state taxes and F percent for federal taxes.

17. Compute the batting average A of a baseball player who has S singles, D doubles, T triples, and H home runs in B times at bat. (A = number of hits/B.)

18. Compute the slugging percentage P of the baseball player who is described in Problem 17 (P = total bases/B.)

19. Find the total cost C of four tires if the list price of each is L dollars, the federal excise tax is E dollars per tire, and the sales tax is S percent.

20. Compute the total cost C of a table listed at L dollars selling at a discount of D percent if the sales tax is S percent.

21. Convert degrees Celsius to degrees Fahrenheit [F = (9/5)C + 32]. Run the program for several values of C, including C = 0 and C = 100.

22. Convert degrees Fahrenheit to degrees Celsius. Run the program for several values of F, including F = 0, F = 32, and F = 212.

23. Convert pounds L to grams G (1 oz = 28.3495 g).

24. Convert grams G to pounds L.

25. Convert yards Y to meters M. Run for several values of Y, including 1760 (1 in. = 2.54 cm).

26. Convert meters M to yards Y. Run for several values of M, including 1 and 1000.

27. Compute the area of a triangle of base B and height H.

28. Compute both the circumference and the area of a circle given the radius. Use $\pi = 3.14159$.

29. Solve the equation AX + B = 0. Run the program for several values of A and B, including the case A = 0.
30. Find the total taxes T on the McCormick property assessed at D dollars if the rate is R dollars per 1,000. If the community uses X percent of all taxes for schools, find how much of the McCormick tax is spent for schools.
31. The market value of a home is M dollars, the assessment rate is A percent of the market value, and the tax rate is R dollars per 1,000. Compute the property tax.
32. Compute the volume and surface area of a rectangular solid.
33. Compute the area of a triangle whose sides are *a*, *b*, and *c*. (Heron's formula for such a triangle is $A = \sqrt{s(s - a)(s - b)(s - c)}$, where $s = (a + b + c)/2$.)
34. A tin can is H inches high and the radius of its circular base is R inches. Calculate the volume and surface area. (Volume = area of base × height. Curved surface area = circumference of base × height.)
35. The equation

$$A = P \times \left(1 + \frac{R}{C}\right)^{N \times C}$$

is an alternative form of the compound interest formula that gives the amount A in an account after N years on an investment of P dollars at an annual rate R if the interest is compounded C times per year. Use this form in a program to help you determine the better investment: $1,000 for one year at 8% compounded semiannually or $1,000 for one year at 7.75% compounded daily. (Note that, for the rate 8%, R must be 8/100 or 0.08 and not 8.)

■ 4.10 Review True-or-False Quiz

1. System commands are carried out as soon as they are entered.   **T   F**
2. To correct an error made while typing a program, you must retype the entire line.   **T   F**
3. A line can be deleted from a program simply by typing its line number and then pressing the RETURN key.   **T   F**
4. The program statement 20 PRINT "13(2 + 3) = 500" contains a syntax error.   **T   F**
5. The statements

```
10 LET A=5000
20 LET R=12.5
30 PRINT R*A
```

will display 12.5% of 5000.   **T   F**
6. A program containing no syntax errors can cause error messages to be displayed.   **T   F**
7. Each step in an algorithm for a computer program should correspond to a single program statement.   **T   F**
8. A good programming practice is to choose REM statements to correspond to the individual steps of an algorithm.   **T   F**
9. Coding a BASIC program involves determining the programming lines to carry out a known algorithm.   **T   F**
10. The input values required in a program should be identified before an algorithm has been written, whereas it is best to identify the required output values after the algorithm has been described.   **T   F**

5 Interacting with the Computer

Most computer programs are written to process input data that will be different each time a program is run. The LET statement (Chapter 3) is not intended as a means for presenting such data to the computer. As we have mentioned, the use of LET statements to assign input values to variables requires that you retype these statements each time you run the program for different input data. If a program is to process 100 different input values, you would have to type 100 LET statements. Not only is this inconvenient, but it means that only those who know how to write correct LET statements can use the program. This violates an important rule of programming: the users of a program should not be required to have any knowledge of programming.

The BASIC language includes several statements intended specifically for data input. In this chapter we discuss the INPUT statement, which allows you to type values for variables during program execution. Thus, by using INPUT statements to obtain data from the keyboard, you will be able to run your programs for different input data without having to change programming lines in any way. In a sense, the INPUT statement allows you to *interact* with the computer while a program is running—the computer displays a message (PRINT statement) concerning the value or values to be typed, you type the input value or values, and then the computer processes the input data and displays the results. As you progress in your study of BASIC, you will learn other ways to effect meaningful "dialogues" between the user and the computer.

5.1 The INPUT Statement

The INPUT statement is best illustrated by example. (The general forms for the INPUT statement are shown at the end of this section.)

EXAMPLE 1 **Here is a program to display the square of any number typed at the keyboard.**

```
10 PRINT "TYPE A NUMBER."
20 INPUT T
30 LET A=T^2
40 PRINT "SQUARE IS";A
50 END
```

When line 20 is executed, a question mark (BASIC's *input prompt*) will be displayed. Nothing further will take place until you type a BASIC constant and enter it by pressing

■ **REMARK**

☐

⏎. The value of the constant will be assigned to T, and only then will the program execution continue. Let's run this program:

```
RUN                  (You type RUN ⏎.)

TYPE A NUMBER.       (Displayed by the computer.)
? 13                 (You type 13 ⏎.)
SQUARE IS 169        (Displayed by the computer.)
```

Some computers automatically leave a blank space after the input prompt **?**, as shown. If your computer doesn't do this but you want the blank space to appear in the display, simply press the space bar before typing the input value. In BASIC, the computer ignores blank spaces preceding input values.

More than one value may be assigned by an INPUT statement. The program statement

```
90 INPUT X,Y,Z
```

causes a question mark to be displayed, and three numerical constants, separated by commas, should be typed. If you type 5,3,24 after the question mark and then press ⏎, the value 5 will be assigned to X, 3 to Y, and 24 to Z. What happens if you do not type exactly three values is system dependent. Experiment!

EXAMPLE 2   **Here is a program to compute the cost *C* of renting a car for *D* days and driving it *M* miles. The rental rate is \$19 per day and 23¢ per mile.**

```
10 PRINT "ENTER NUMBER OF DAYS AND NUMBER"
20 PRINT "OF MILES, SEPARATED BY A COMMA."
30 INPUT D,M
40 LET C=19*D+0.23*M
50 PRINT
60 PRINT "TOTAL COST:";C
70 END
RUN

ENTER NUMBER OF DAYS AND NUMBER
OF MILES, SEPARATED BY A COMMA.
?
```

At this point simply follow the instructions and type two numbers separated by a comma. Let's complete this run as follows.

```
? 3,253     (Underlined characters are typed by the user.)

TOTAL COST: 115.19
```

■ **REMARK**

☐

Lines 10 and 20 display a message telling the user how to respond when the input prompt ? is encountered. Without this explanation, a user would have no way of knowing what to type. It is a cardinal rule of programming never to confront the person using the program with an unexplained input prompt.

Although lines 10 and 20 in the previous example instruct the user how to respond to the input prompt, there is the possibility that the inexperienced user will not follow instructions exactly. For example, the user might type

```
253,3
```

This will cause 253 to be assigned to D and 3 to M, and incorrect results will follow. You can prevent the user from making such errors by requiring only one response to each input prompt. Replacing lines 10, 20, and 30 by

```
10 PRINT "NUMBER OF DAYS"
15 INPUT D
20 PRINT "NUMBER OF MILES"
30 INPUT M
```

is one way to do this. Let's run this revised program:

```
RUN

NUMBER OF DAYS
? 3                   Underlined characters are typed by the user.)
NUMBER OF MILES
? 253                 Underlined characters are typed by the user.)
TOTAL COST: 115.19
```

EXAMPLE 3   **This example shows that the INPUT statement can be used to input string values for string variables.**

```
10  PRINT "ENTER A NAME."
20  INPUT N$
30  PRINT "ENTER THE DATE."
40  INPUT D$
50  PRINT
60  PRINT N$
70  PRINT "INITIATION DATE: ";D$
80  END
RUN

ENTER A NAME.
? STEVE MARTIN      (Underlined characters are typed by the user.)
ENTER THE DATE.
? MAY 1988

STEVE MARTIN
INITIATION DATE: MAY 1988
```

Note that the two input strings STEVE MARTIN and MAY 1988 were typed without quotation marks. Unlike strings in PRINT and LET statements (which must always be quoted), strings typed in response to INPUT statements usually are not quoted. Most BASIC systems require that you use quotes in only two situations:

1. *When significant blanks begin or end the input string.* If such a string is not enclosed in quotation marks, the leading and trailing blanks are ignored.
2. *When a comma is included in the input string.* BASIC uses the comma as a delimiter (separator) of input values. Thus, it would be correct to type

```
"STEVE MARTIN, JR"
```

in response to the statement INPUT N$. But it would not be correct to type

```
STEVE MARTIN, JR
```

It is always correct to enclose input strings in quotes, even if quotes are not required.

The readability of your output can often be improved by having an input value appear on the same line as the message identifying that value. This can be accomplished by placing a semicolon at the end of the PRINT statement that displays the message. If you end a PRINT statement with a semicolon, the RETURN normally occurring after execution of the PRINT statement is suppressed. Thus, if you type 345 in response to the programming lines

```
200  PRINT "NUMBER OF MILES";
210  INPUT M
```

the computer will display

```
NUMBER OF MILES? 345
```

Many versions of BASIC allow you to include a string input prompt as part of the INPUT statement. Simply place the quoted string after the keyword INPUT and separate it from any variables whose values are to be input with a semicolon. Thus, your system may allow you to replace lines 200 and 210 with the single line

```
200 INPUT "NUMBER OF MILES";M
```

Before you use this single line form, we suggest you experiment to see precisely what happens. Some systems will not display the question mark. If this happens you may want to include it in the string prompt:

```
200 INPUT "NUMBER OF MILES?";M
```

If your system does display the question mark, you may find that you can suppress it by using a comma instead of a semicolon.

EXAMPLE 4   Determine the yearly income and savings of a person whose weekly income and average monthly expenses are given.

Two values must be specified (weekly income and monthly expenses), and two values must be determined (yearly income and savings). Let's agree to use the following variable names:

Input: WI = weekly income
            ME = monthly expenses

Output: YI = yearly income (note that YI = 52 × WI)
            YS = yearly savings (note that YS = YI − 12 × ME)

An algorithm for solving this problem can now be written:

a. Assign values to WI and ME.
b. Determine yearly income and savings.
c. Display the results.

Before this algorithm can be coded, you must decide how to assign values to WI and ME. Available are the LET and INPUT statements. Since we may use this program for different weekly incomes and monthly expenses, the decision is easy: use an INPUT statement.

THE PROGRAM

```
100 REM PROGRAM TO FIND YEARLY INCOME AND SAVINGS
110 REM GIVEN THE WEEKLY INCOME AND MONTHLY EXPENSES
120 REM
130 PRINT "WEEKLY INCOME";
140 INPUT WI
150 PRINT "MONTHLY EXPENSES";
160 INPUT ME
170 REM COMPUTE YEARLY INCOME AND SAVINGS.
180 LET YI = 52*WI
190 LET YS = YI-12*ME
200 PRINT "YEARLY INCOME:";YI
210 PRINT "YEARLY SAVINGS:";YS
220 END
RUN

WEEKLY INCOME? 350        (Underlined characters are typed by the user.)
MONTHLY EXPENSES? 1300
YEARLY INCOME: 18200
YEARLY SAVINGS: 2600
```

The preceding examples illustrate the general forms of the INPUT statement:

ln INPUT **input list**
ln INPUT quoted string; **input list**

where **input list** denotes a list of variable names separated by commas. (Most often just one variable name will be included.) When executed, the first form displays the input prompt (**?**) and the second displays the string followed, on some systems, by a question mark. In either case, you must respond by typing a value for each variable in the input list. The values you type must be separated by commas, and their types (numerical or string) must agree with the types of the input variables.

■ 5.2 Problems

*Complete the following partial program so that it will perform the tasks specified in Problems
1–23. Be sure that messages displayed by the line numbers 100 and 130 are appropriate to the
problem being solved. Do not refer to the variable names X and A in these messages.*

```
100  PRINT "        "
110  INPUT X
120  LET A=
130  PRINT "        ";A
140  END
```

1. Determine how much $100 earning 6% interest compounded annually will be worth in X years
   [value after X years is $100(1 + 0.06)^x$].
2. Determine the commission earned by a salesperson who sells a $625 television set if the rate of
   commission is X percent.
3. Determine the total cost of an article whose selling price is X dollars if the sales tax is 4.5%.
4. Determine the weekly salary of a part-time employee working X hours at $4.47 per hour (no
   overtime).
5. Determine the cost per driving mile for a car that averages 19.2 miles per gallon if gasoline
   costs X cents per gallon.
6. Determine the average of the four grades for a student who has received grades of 73, 91, 62,
   and X on four exams.
7. Determine the equivalent hourly salary, assuming a 40-hour week, for a worker whose annual
   salary is X dollars.
8. Determine the amount of sales for a salesperson whose commission is X dollars if the rate of
   commission is 14%.
9. For a single taxpayer whose taxable income X is more than $17,850, the federal tax due is
   $2,677.50 plus 28% of the amount by which X exceeds $17,850. Determine the tax due for
   such a taxpayer.
10. Determine the amount that must be invested at X percent simple interest to yield $1,000 at the
    end of 1 year.
11. Convert dollars to yen (1 dollar = 133.84 yen).
12. Convert yen to dollars.
13. Convert dollars to deutsch marks (1 dollar = 1.8045 deutsch marks).
14. Convert deutsch marks to dollars.
15. Convert deutsch marks to yen.
16. Convert yen to deutsch marks.
17. Determine the area of a circle given its diameter.
18. Determine the diameter of a circle given its area.
19. Convert inches to centimeters (1 in. = 2.54 cm).
20. Convert centimeters to inches.
21. Convert degrees to radians (1 degree = $\pi/180$ radians; use π = 3.14159).
22. Convert radians to degrees.
23. Determine the distance A to the horizon as viewed over a smooth ocean from a vantage point
    X feet above sea level. (Consider the right triangle in the following diagram.)

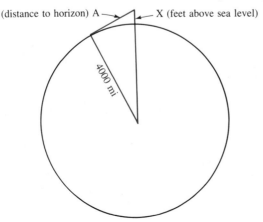

Write a program to perform each task specified in Problems 24–32. Be sure to label results and to instruct the user concerning what values are to be entered.

24. For any three numbers A, B, and C, determine the three sums A + B, A + C, and B + C, and find the average of these sums.

25. For any three numbers P, Q, and R, determine the mean M, the differences P − M, Q − M, and R − M, and the sum of these differences.

26. Semester grades are based on three 1-hour tests and a 2-hour final examination. The 1-hour tests are weighted equally, and the final counts as two 1-hour tests. (All exams are graded from 0 to 100.) Determine the semester average for a student whose grades are G1, G2, G3, and F (F for final).

27. Janet and Jim are bricklayers. In 1 hour Janet can lay J1 bricks and Jim can lay J2. Determine how long it will take both of them to complete a job if the number of bricks required is known.

28. A baseball player is to be paid P dollars the first year of a 3-year contract. Find the total dollar value of the contract over 3 years if the contract calls for an increase of I percent the second year and J percent the third year.

29. Determine the yearly gross pay, net pay, combined tax deductions, and retirement deductions for a person whose monthly salary is given. The combined tax rate is R percent, and 6% of the gross salary is withheld for retirement.

30. A manufacturer produces three items that sell for $550, $620, and $1,750. A profit of 10% is realized on items selling below $1,000, and 15% is realized on all other items. Determine the profit before and after taxes for a particular year, given the quantity of each item sold. The current tax rate on profits is R percent.

31. The monthly payment M on a loan of L dollars at the annual rate R for T years is given by

$$M = \frac{L \times R/12}{1 - (1 + R/12)^{-12 \times T}}$$

The Hendersons apply for a $65,000 mortgage for 25 years at an annual rate of 12.5%. Determine their monthly payment and the total amount repaid to the bank during the lifetime of their mortgage. (Note that in the given formula, R is a rate. Thus, for a 12.5 percent loan, R must be .125, not 12.5.)

32. Determine driving expense statistics for Charlene's parents, who are visiting her at college. They note that at the outset of the trip, the odometer reads M1 miles and the tank is full. Just before returning they fill the tank with G1 gallons of gasoline at a cost of C1 dollars. After they arrive home the tank is filled again, this time taking G2 gallons at a cost of C2 dollars. The odometer now reads M2 miles. The output should be as follows:

```
GALLONS OF GASOLINE _____
COST OF GASOLINE _____
NUMBER OF MILES DRIVEN _____
COST PER DRIVING MILE _____
MILES PER GALLON OF GASOLINE _____
```

Try your program, using 12,347 and 12,903 for odometer readings, and 13.4 gallons at $12.75 and 12.7 gallons at $11.20 as the two purchases. These values are to be typed during program execution.

■ 5.3 Review True-or-False Quiz

1. The PRINT and INPUT statements provide the means for two-way communication between a user and a running program.   **T F**
2. Using a PRINT statement immediately following an INPUT statement is an effective method of identifying what values should be typed at the keyboard.   **T F**
3. BASIC allows you to type 3/4 in response to the statement INPUT X.   **T F**
4. BASIC allows you to type 3/4 in response to the statement INPUT X$.   **T F**

5. It is never correct to type THORPE,JIM in response to an INPUT statement.   **T   F**
6. The statement 50 INPUT B,A$ is admissible.   **T   F**
7. The statement 60 INPUT A;B;C is admissible.   **T   F**
8. Quotation marks must always be used when a string is included in a LET statement or a PRINT statement or is typed in response to an INPUT statement.   **T   F**

6. A First Look at Loops

All programs presented up to this point have executed sequentially according to the order of the line numbers. In this chapter we show how you can override this normal sequential order. Specifically, we show how you can direct the computer to execute sections of a program repeatedly (this is called **looping**) and thus cause it to perform many hundreds of calculations with only a few programming lines. In addition we describe a form of the PRINT statement that is sometimes useful for generating reports in tabular form. (A complete description of the PRINT statement is given in Chapter 7.)

In Section 6.2 we describe the WHILE statement and show how it is used to code loops. Some BASIC systems, however, do not allow the WHILE statement. For this reason, we begin in Section 6.1 by introducing the IF and GOTO statements, which can be used to code loops in any version of BASIC. Although IF and GOTO statements provide a simple way to code loops, they are intended for other purposes, as explained in Chapter 8. The common practice is to code loops by using IF and GOTO statements only if the WHILE statement is not allowed. The principal reasons for this practice are explained in Section 6.2.

An alternative method of coding loops, which in certain situations is more convenient than the methods described in this chapter, uses the FOR statement. To keep this introductory chapter on loops as simple as possible, the FOR statement is considered in Chapter 9.*

The BASIC statements WHILE, IF, GOTO, and FOR are called control statements because they control the order in which the statements in a program are executed.

■ 6.1 Coding Loops with the IF and GOTO Statements

If you need to calculate 6% of several different amounts, you can use these programming lines:

```
100 PRINT "AMOUNT";
110 INPUT A
120 PRINT "6% OF AMOUNT IS";0.06*A
130 PRINT
140 GOTO 100
```

---

* The introductory material on the FOR statement in Chapter 9 is written so that it can be taken up at this time, should that be desired.

The statement GOTO 100 in line 140 (your system may require GO TO instead of GOTO) transfers program control back to line 100. Thus, these five BASIC statements will be executed repeatedly. We illustrate for the input values 43, 100, and 89:

```
RUN

AMOUNT? 43
6% OF AMOUNT IS 2.58

AMOUNT? 100
6% OF AMOUNT IS 6

AMOUNT? 89
6% OF AMOUNT IS 5.34

AMOUNT?
```

If you need 6% of other amounts, simply type them one at a time. Notice, however, that the five programming lines do not provide a means for stopping execution. You must stop it manually. How this is done depends on the system being used. Some require you to press a special key such as S, I, ESC, or BREAK; others require you to press a combination of keys such as CTRL C, CTRL S, or CTRL BREAK. In this book we will indicate that execution has been terminated manually by including the following in the output display:

```
*TERMINATED*
READY
```

The use of GOTO statements to execute BASIC statements repeatedly can transform the computer into a very fast and useful calculator. The following is another example of using the computer as a calculator. [The values N * (N + 1)/2 in this example are called IRS values because they are used in certain tax calculations.]

```
100 LET N=10
110 PRINT "NUMBER";N
120 PRINT "IRS VALUE";N*(N+1)/2
130 PRINT
140 LET N=N+1
150 GOTO 110
RUN

NUMBER 10
IRS VALUE 55

NUMBER 11
IRS VALUE 66

NUMBER 12
IRS VALUE 78

NUMBER 13
IRS VALUE 91

NUMBER 14
  *TERMINATED*        (Execution halted manually.)
READY
```

Unlike the loop in the previous example, this loop contains no INPUT statement to slow it down, so the results may be scrolled off the display screen before you can read them. To assist you in such situations, your system provides special keys or key combinations to stop program execution temporarily to give you time to read the results. (Consult your BASIC manual since systems differ greatly in how this is done.)

The key or key combinations that halt program execution are programmer's tools; they are not intended for people who use programs. Unless you are using the computer as a calculator, your programs should always halt automatically when the intended tasks have been carried out. This means that you should not code loops using only the GOTO statement. In the following examples, we describe a limited form of the IF statement that can be used to cause an exit from a loop when its task has been completed.

EXAMPLE 1   **Here is a program to display the IRS values *N* * (*N* + 1)/2 for *N* = 6, 12, 18, and 24.**

```
110 LET N=6
120    PRINT "NUMBER:";N
130    PRINT "IRS VALUE:";N*(N+1)/2
140    PRINT
150    LET N=N+6
160 IF N<=24 THEN 120
170 END
RUN

NUMBER: 6
IRS VALUE: 21

NUMBER: 12
IRS VALUE: 78

NUMBER: 18
IRS VALUE: 171

NUMBER: 24
IRS VALUE: 300

READY
```

The expression N <= 24 in line 160 is how you write N ≤ 24 in BASIC. This IF statement transfers control back to line 120 if the condition N <= 24 is true. If the condition is false, the sequential execution of the program statements is not interrupted and control passes to the line immediately following the IF statement—line 170 in this program. Thus, the action of the program is as follows:

Line 110 assigns the initial value 6 to N, lines 120–140 display this number and its IRS value followed by a blank line, and line 150 increases N by 6 to give 12. Since 12 is less than 24, the condition N <= 24 is true and the IF statement transfers control back to line 120. This looping continues until the condition N <= 24 is false. This happens when line 150 increases N from 24 to 30. Control then passes out of the loop to line 170, which in this program stops execution.

■ **REMARK 1**   This program provides for no interaction between the user and the computer. It simply displays the specified output and halts when it has finished. The user doesn't have to stop execution manually.

■ **REMARK 2**   The IF statement in this program sets up a loop in which statements in lines 120–150 are executed repeatedly. Indenting these statements as shown in the program listing improves the readability of the program. The practice of indenting program statements is not new to us. In several of the examples considered thus far, REM statements describing the meanings of variable names used in a program were indented. Other situations in which indentations should be used to improve the readability of your programs will be mentioned as they arise.

□

EXAMPLE 2   **Here is a program to determine the sum *S* of any number of input values.**

```
100 PRINT "TYPE NUMBERS TO BE ADDED, ONE PER LINE."
110 PRINT "TYPE 0 WHEN ALL NUMBERS HAVE BEEN TYPED."
120 LET S=0
```

```
130 INPUT X
140 IF X=0 THEN 180
150     LET S=S+X
160     INPUT X
170 GOTO 140
180 PRINT "THE SUM IS";S
190 END
RUN

TYPE NUMBERS TO BE ADDED, ONE PER LINE.
TYPE 0 WHEN ALL NUMBERS HAVE BEEN TYPED.
? 25
? 30
? -10
? 15.75
? 0
THE SUM IS 60.75
```

Lines 100 and 110 instruct the user, and line 120 starts with a sum S of 0. (It is a good programming practice to include line 120 even if your computer automatically assigns the initial value 0 to S. By including this statement, your program will be easier to read and will work on any computer—even those that do not initialize numerical variables to 0.)

Line 130 displays the first ? and we type 25 for X. Since the condition X = 0 in the IF statement is false, program execution continues with line 150, which adds 25, the value of X, to S. Line 160 displays another ? and we type the next number. The GOTO statement in line 170 then transfers control back to line 140 and the condition X = 0 is tested again. This looping continues until we type 0 for X. When this happens, the IF statement transfers control out of the loop to line 180 and the final sum is displayed.

■ **REMARK**   You may have noticed that we used two INPUT statements when one would have sufficed. For instance, we could replace lines 130–170 by

```
130     INPUT X
140     IF X=0 THEN 180
150     LET S=S+X
160 GOTO 130
```

Both forms are correct. The first, however, conforms to an important programming principle: *When coding a loop, the statement that causes an exit from the loop should start the loop or end it*. Experience has shown that programs written according to this principle will be easier to read and considerably easier to modify, should that be required.

In Example 2 we used the statement

```
140 IF X=0 THEN 180
```

to transfer control to line 180 if the condition X = 0 is true. This condition is called a **relational expression**—it is true if the equals symbol correctly describes the *relationship* between X and 0. In Example 1, we used the relational expression N <= 24 to test if the symbol <= correctly describes the relationship between N and 24. The symbols BASIC allows in relational expressions are as follows:

BASIC symbol	Arithmetic symbol	Meaning
=	=	Equal
<	<	Less than
>	>	Greater than
<>	≠	Not equal to
<=	≤	Less than or equal to
>=	≥	Greater than or equal to

Here are some correctly written IF statements:

BASIC statement	Meaning
`100 IF X>50 THEN 240`	Transfer control to line 240 if X is greater than 50.
`200 IF A<>B THEN 120`	Transfer control to line 120 if A and B are not equal.
`300 IF 2*N+1>=75 THEN 150`	Transfer control to line 150 if the value of $2 * N + 1$ is greater than or equal to 75.
`400 IF T$="YES" THEN 700`	Transfer control to line 700 if the string value of T$ is YES.

Notice that strings appearing in relational expressions must be enclosed in quotation marks. It would not be correct to write

```
400 IF T$=YES THEN 700
```

The condition in each IF statement used in this chapter is a single relational expression. In Chapter 8 we explain how you can use keywords such as AND and OR to write conditions that involve two or more comparisons. For instance, the statement

```
300 IF A$<>"Y" AND A$<>"N" THEN 200
```

transfers control to line 200 if the value of A$ is neither Y nor N.

A good use of string comparisons involves testing a user's response to input prompts. For instance, a program containing the lines

```
250 PRINT "ARE YOU DONE (Y OR N)";
260 INPUT A$
270 IF A$="N" THEN 100
280 END
```

will transfer control back to line 100 if the user types N in response to the prompt

```
ARE YOU DONE (Y OR N)?
```

If the user types anything other than N, control will pass to line 280, and execution will halt. To ensure that the user types either Y or N, you can include the line

```
265 IF A$<>"Y" AND A$<>"N" THEN 250
```

This will cause the prompt

```
ARE YOU DONE (Y OR N)?
```

to be repeated until the user types Y or N. String comparisons involving the relational symbols <, <=, >, and >= are discussed in Chapter 13.

Programming tasks often involve generating reports in tabular form. These reports usually consist of one or more columns of data, each with a descriptive column heading. In the next example, we use a loop containing a PRINT statement of the form

```
PRINT expression1, expression2, expression3
```

to display the values in a three-column salary report. It is the commas in this PRINT statement that cause the values of the expressions to line up in columns. We also use PRINT statements of the same form to display the column headings. A more detailed description of the use of commas in PRINT statements is given in Chapter 7.

EXAMPLE 3 **Prepare a report showing the weekly and annual salaries for persons working 40 hours a week if their hourly rates are $4.50, $4.60, $4.70, . . . , $5.50.**

PROBLEM ANALYSIS

The weekly pay W for a person who is working H hours a week at R dollars an hour is W = H × R dollars; the annual salary A for this person is A = 52 × W dollars. The hourly rates R = 4.50, 4.60, 4.70, and so on, should not be input. Since successive R values differ by the same amount (0.10), you can start with R = 4.50 and simply keep adding 0.10 to R (LET R = R + 0.10) to get the other values.

THE ALGORITHM

a. Display column headings.
b. Let H = 40 and R = 4.50.
c. Evaluate W = H × R and then A = 52 × W.
d. Display R, W, and A on one line.
e. Add 0.10 to R and go to Step (c) if R ≤ 5.50.
f. Stop.

THE PROGRAM

```
100 REM SALARY REPORT PROGRAM
110 REM    H DENOTES HOURS WORKED.
120 REM    R DENOTES HOURLY RATE.
130 REM    W DENOTES EQUIVALENT WEEKLY SALARY.
140 REM    A DENOTES EQUIVALENT ANNUAL SALARY.
150 PRINT "HOURLY RATE","WEEKLY SALARY","ANNUAL SALARY"
160 PRINT "-----------","--------------","--------------"
170 LET H=40
180 LET R=4.50
190     LET W=H*R
200     LET A=52*W
210     PRINT R,W,A
220     LET R=R+0.10
230 IF R<5.51 THEN 190
240 END
RUN
```

HOURLY RATE	WEEKLY SALARY	ANNUAL SALARY
4.5	180.	9360.
4.6	184.	9568.
4.7	188.	9776.
4.8	192.	9984.
4.9	196.	10192.
5.	200.	10400.
5.1	204.	10608.
5.2	208.	10816.
5.3	212.	11024.
5.4	216.	11232.
5.5	220.	11440.

■ **REMARK 1**

Lines 190–230 constitute the loop used to display the table values. Since the column headings must be displayed first, and only once, the statements that do this (lines 150 and 160) must be executed before the loop is entered.

■ **REMARK 2**

Note that in line 230 we use the IF condition R < 5.51 rather than R <= 5.50. Your computer will store integers exactly but in most cases will store only close approximations of numbers with fractional parts—just as you might use 0.66666 or 0.66667 for 2/3. The number 0.10 is one of the numbers your computer does not store exactly. Thus, if you start with R = 4.50 and repeatedly add 0.10 to R, you may get an approximation such as 5.500001 or 5.499998 instead of 5.50. By using the condition R < 5.51 we ensure that the last output line will be displayed. To see for yourself that R will not attain the exact value 5.50, type and run these lines (you'll need to halt execution manually):

```
10 LET R=4.50
20 PRINT R
30 LET R=R+0.10
40 IF R<>5.50 THEN 20
```

In light of Remark 2, we state an important rule of programming:

Never test numbers for equality unless they are known to be integers.

We conclude this section with an example illustrating the following programming practices that we have been stressing:

1. To discover a correct algorithm for a given problem statement, carry out a complete problem analysis and record it in writing. The first step should be to determine precisely what is being asked. Determining the input and output values is a good way to begin.
2. Use PRINT statements (or INPUT statements containing string prompts) to tell the user what values are to be input during program execution. Also use PRINT statements to label all output values. The precise form of these statements is often determined during the coding process.
3. Use comments to make your program more readable and to clarify what is being done at every point.

EXAMPLE 4

A man lives in a large house with many rooms. He wants to paint the walls and ceiling of each room, but before buying paint he naturally needs to know how much paint is necessary. On the average, each window and door covers 20 square feet. According to the label, each quart of paint covers 110 square feet. Write a program that will allow the man to enter the dimensions of each room and the number of doors and windows in each room and then determine how many quarts of wall paint and how many quarts of ceiling paint he needs for that room.

PROBLEM ANALYSIS

Although this problem statement is somewhat lengthy, it should not be difficult to identify the input and output:

Input: Name of each room.
 Length, width, and height of each room.
 Number of doors and windows in each room.

Output: Quarts of wall paint and quarts of ceiling paint needed for each room.

To determine how many quarts of wall paint are needed for a particular room, we must determine the wall area (in square feet) to be covered and divide this value by 110 since 1 quart of paint covers 110 square feet. Similarly, the amount of ceiling paint is obtained by dividing the ceiling area by 110.

Before attempting to write an algorithm for carrying out this task, let's choose variable names for the values of interest. This will allow us to write a concise algorithm by using variable names rather than verbal descriptions for these values.

ROOM$ = name of the room in question
L, W, H = length, width, and height of ROOM$ (in feet)
 DW = total number of doors and windows in ROOM$
 AW = area of all walls in ROOM$ including door and window space
 $(AW = 2 \times (L + W) \times H)$
 ADW = area of the DW doors and windows $(ADW = 20 \times DW)$
 AC = area of a ceiling $(AC = L \times W)$
 QWP = quarts of wall paint needed $(QWP = (AW - ADW)/110)$
 QCP = quarts of ceiling paint needed $(QCP = AC/110)$

Using these variable names, we can write the following five-step process (note that the order in which the steps are to be taken is just how you might carry out this task with tape measure, pencil, and paper):

  a. Enter values for ROOM$, L, W, H, and DW.
  b. Determine the areas AW, ADW, AC.

c. Determine the number of quarts of paint needed (QWP and QCP).
d. Display the values of QWP and QCP.
e. Go to Step (a) and repeat the process for the next room.

There is a difficulty with this five-step process. It does not describe how the process will end—thus, we don't have an algorithm. Noting that the first item to be input for any room is the room name ROOM$, we will instruct the user to type END for the room name after all results have been obtained. The following algorithm incorporates this change. Note that only Step (a) of our five-step process was changed.

THE ALGORITHM

a1. Enter a value for ROOM$.
a2. If ROOM$ is END, stop.
a3. Enter values for L, W, H, and DW.
b. Determine the areas AW, ADW, AC.
c. Determine the number of quarts of paint needed (QWP and QCP).
d. Print the values of QWP and QCP.
e. Go to Step (a1) and repeat the process for the next room.

THE PROGRAM

```
100 PRINT "PAINT CALCULATION PROGRAM"
110 PRINT
120 PRINT "WHEN DONE, TYPE END FOR ROOM NAME."
130 PRINT
140 PRINT "ROOM NAME";
150 INPUT ROOM$
160 IF ROOM$="END" THEN 460
170     PRINT "LENGTH";
180     INPUT L
190     PRINT "WIDTH";
200     INPUT W
210     PRINT "HEIGHT";
220     INPUT H
230     PRINT "TOTAL NUMBER OF WINDOWS AND DOORS";
240     INPUT DW
250     REM
260     REM ------ CALCULATE AREAS ------
270     REM
280     LET AW=2*(L+W)*H          'AREA OF WALLS
290     LET ADW=20*DW             'AREA OF DOORS AND WINDOWS
300     LET AC=L*W                'AREA OF CEILING
310     REM
320     REM ------ QUARTS OF WALL AND CEILING PAINT ------
330     REM
340     LET QWP=(AW-ADW)/110      'QUARTS OF WALL PAINT
350     LET QCP=AC/110            'QUARTS OF CEILING PAINT
360     REM
370     REM ------ DISPLAY RESULTS FOR ROOM ROOM$ ------
380     REM
390     PRINT "QUARTS OF WALL PAINT";QWP
400     PRINT "QUARTS OF CEILING PAINT";QCP
410     PRINT
420     REM ------ GET NEXT ROOM NAME OR END ------
430     PRINT "ROOM NAME";
440     INPUT ROOM$
450 GOTO 160
460 END
RUN

PAINT CALCULATION PROGRAM

WHEN DONE, TYPE END FOR ROOM NAME.

ROOM NAME? KITCHEN
LENGTH? 13
WIDTH? 13
HEIGHT? 9
```

```
TOTAL NUMBER OF WINDOWS AND DOORS? 5
QUARTS OF WALL PAINT: 3.34545
QUARTS OF CEILING PAINT: 1.53636

ROOM NAME? FRONT BEDROOM
LENGTH? 12
WIDTH? 9
HEIGHT? 9
TOTAL NUMBER OF WINDOWS AND DOORS? 4
QUARTS OF WALL PAINT: 2.70909
QUARTS OF CEILING PAINT: .981818

ROOM NAME? END
READY
```

■ 6.2 WHILE Loops

The WHILE statement is used only for writing loops. If your version of BASIC allows this statement, you can code loops as follows:

WHILE *condition*

_____ (Statements to be repeated)

_____

_____

_____

NEXT   (Some systems use WEND for NEXT)

The statements between the WHILE and NEXT (or WEND) statements are executed repeatedly as long as the *condition* is true—that is, *while* the condition is true. Loops coded with WHILE statements are called WHILE loops.

EXAMPLE 5   **Here is a WHILE loop to display the numbers 1, 3, 5, 7, and 9.**

```
100 LET N=1
110 WHILE N<=9
120     PRINT N
130 LET N=N+2
140 NEXT (or WEND)
150 END
RUN

1
3
5
7
9
READY
```

The WHILE loop (lines 110–140) instructs the computer to execute lines 120 and 130 repeatedly while the condition $N <= 9$ is true. Thus the action of this program is as follows:

Line 100 assigns the initial value 1 to N, and line 110 tests the condition $N <= 9$. Since $1 <= 9$ is true, execution continues with line 120, which displays the value 1 of N. Line 130 then increases N to 3, and the NEXT (or WEND) statement instructs the computer to test the WHILE condition again. This looping continues until line 130 increases N from 9 to 11. When this happens, the WHILE condition $N <= 9$ is false so that program control passes to the line immediately following the NEXT (or WEND) statement, which in this program halts program execution.

We could have coded the loop in Example 5 in the following equivalent way:

```
100 LET N=1
110 IF N>9 THEN 150
120    PRINT N
130       LET N=N+2
140 GOTO 110
150 END
```

The only differences are that we used an IF statement instead of the WHILE statement and a GOTO instead of a NEXT or WEND. There are two good reasons for writing WHILE loops; both concern program readability:

1. The WHILE statement is used only to code loops, whereas the IF statement has many uses, as explained in Chapter 8. Thus, when you see a WHILE statement you know that it starts a loop. When you see an IF statement, it may start a loop, it may end a loop, or it may have nothing to do with looping.
2. The condition in a WHILE statement is *always* the condition needed to *continue* looping. In Example 5 this condition is N <= 9. This is not so with the IF statement. For instance, the IF/GOTO form of the loop uses the IF condition N > 9—that is, the condition needed to *stop* looping. The following form of the loop, however, uses the condition N <= 9.

```
100 LET N=1
110    PRINT N
120    LET N=N+2
130 IF N<=9 THEN 110
```

EXAMPLE 6   **In this example, we show how the loops in Examples 1–4 of Section 6.1 can be coded as WHILE loops.**

a. Changes for the program in Example 1:

```
115 WHILE N<=24
160 NEXT (or WEND)
```

b. Changes for the program in Example 2:

```
140 WHILE X<>0
170 NEXT (or WEND)
```

c. Changes for the program in Example 3:

```
185 WHILE R<5.51
230 NEXT (or WEND)
```

d. Changes for the program in Example 4:

```
160 WHILE ROOM$<>"END"
450 NEXT (or WEND)
```

We conclude this section with two examples further illustrating the application of WHILE loops. Example 7 involves compound interest calculations. Example 8 shows that WHILE loops can be **nested**—that is, the statements being repeated in one WHILE loop can contain another WHILE loop.

EXAMPLE 7   **A local bank pays interest at the annual rate of R percent compounded monthly. Let's write a program to show how a single deposit of A dollars grows until it doubles in value.**

PROBLEM ANALYSIS

Input: R = annual percentage rate
A = amount of the single deposit

Output: A table showing the account balance, month by month, until the balance is at least twice the initial deposit. (A two-column table with the column headings MONTH and BALANCE is appropriate.)

It is not difficult to write an algorithm for the specified task if we leave out the details:

    a. Input values for A and R.
    b. Display the column headings MONTH and BALANCE.
    c. Calculate and display the table values.

Steps (a) and (b) are not new to us. To carry out Step (c), we must decide how to carry out the required compound interest calculations. First, notice that the problem statement specifies that the annual rate R is a percentage. This means that we must use R/100 instead of R in any calculations. Since interest is compounded monthly, the interest rate for one month is (R/100)/12 or R/1200. Thus, if the balance at the beginning of a month is A, the balance at the end of the month will be A + (R/1200) * A or A * (1 + R/1200).

    Having determined how the balance will increase for a single month, it is not difficult to code Step (c). In the following program segment for Step (c) we use two additional variables:

TARGET = double the amount of the initial deposit
    M = month number (initially 0)

```
LET TARGET=2*A
LET M=0
WHILE A<=TARGET
    LET M=M+1              'Move on one month.
    LET A=A*(1+R/1200)     'Balance at end of month.
    PRINT M,A              'Display one line of table.
NEXT  (or WEND)
```

Writing code to complete the program is routine and is left as an exercise.

■ **REMARK 1**   Notice that by using WHILE instead of IF to code the loop, we were able to write down the BASIC code without referencing line numbers. Writing program segments without line numbers is an excellent programming practice—the line numbers would be included while typing the program at the keyboard. The result will almost always be a program whose action is reasonably easy to follow.

■ **REMARK 2**   Notice that the expression 1 + R/1200 is evaluated on each pass through the WHILE loop. It isn't necessary to do this. Simply include the statement

```
LET FACTOR = 1+R/1200
```

before the WHILE statement and change 1 + R/1200 in the WHILE loop to FACTOR.

    It is permissible, and often desirable, to have one WHILE loop contained in another. When nesting loops in this way, there is one rule that must be observed:

    If the statements to be repeated in a WHILE loop contain any part of a second WHILE loop, they must contain the *entire* second WHILE loop. The following schematic illustrates correctly nested WHILE loops and shows how you might include comments to indicate matching WHILE and NEXT(WEND) statements.

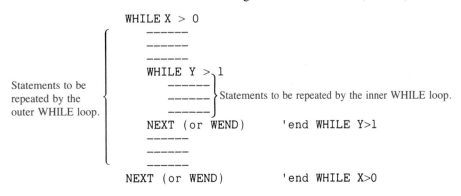

EXAMPLE 8   **Nested WHILE loops. This program allows the user to obtain many sums during a single program run.**

```
100 PRINT "THIS PROGRAM IS USED TO ADD LISTS OF NUMBERS."
110 PRINT
120 PRINT "DO YOU HAVE A LIST TO ADD (Y OR N)";
130 INPUT C$
140 WHILE C$="Y"
150    PRINT "ENTER NUMBERS ONE PER LINE."
160    PRINT "TYPE 0 WHEN LIST IS IN."
170    LET SUM=0                          'Start with zero sum.
180    INPUT X                            'First number in list.
190    WHILE X<>0                         'Test for end of list.
200       LET SUM=SUM+X
210       INPUT X                         'Next number in list.
220    NEXT (or WEND)                     'end WHILE X<>0
230    PRINT "LIST TOTAL: ";SUM
240    PRINT
250    PRINT "IS THERE ANOTHER LIST (Y OR N)";
260    INPUT C$
270 NEXT (or WEND)                        'end WHILE C$="Y"
280 END
RUN

THIS PROGRAM IS USED TO ADD LISTS OF NUMBERS.

DO YOU HAVE A LIST TO ADD (Y OR N)? Y
ENTER NUMBERS ONE PER LINE.
TYPE 0 WHEN LIST IS IN.
? 23
? 39
? 0
LIST TOTAL: 62

IS THERE ANOTHER LIST (Y OR N)? Y
ENTER NUMBERS ONE PER LINE.
TYPE 0 WHEN LIST IS IN.
? -15
? 25
? -30
? 0
LIST TOTAL:-20

IS THERE ANOTHER LIST (Y OR N)? N
```

The inside WHILE loop consists of lines 190-220. This loop is used to determine the sum of all input values up to the input value zero. The outside WHILE loop consists of lines 140-270. This outer WHILE loop is included to allow the user to determine many sums during a single program run. By typing Y in response to the INPUT statement at line 130 or 260, the user instructs the computer to repeat this outer WHILE loop.

□

■ 6.3 Problems

1. Show the output produced by each IF loop.

a.
```
10 LET S=0
20 LET N=1
30 IF  N>=25 THEN 80
40      LET S=S+N
50      PRINT N,S
60      LET N=2*N
70 GOTO 30
80 END
```

b.
```
10 LET P=1
20 LET X=1
30     LET P=P*X
40     PRINT X,P
50     LET X=X+1
60 IF P<1000 THEN 30
70 END
```

c.
```
100 LET A=1
110     PRINT A;
120     LET A=A+1
130 IF A<3 THEN 110
140 PRINT
150     LET A=A+1
160     PRINT A;
170 IF A<6 THEN 150
180 END
```

d.
```
100 LET R=3
110     LET S=1
120       PRINT R;
130       LET S=S+1
140     IF S<=R THEN 120
150     PRINT
160     LET R=R-1
170 IF R>0 THEN 110
180 END
```

2. Show the output produced by each WHILE loop.

a.
```
10 LET N=9
20 WHILE N>1
30     PRINT N,N^2
40     LET N=N-2
50 NEXT  (or WEND)
60 END
```

b.
```
10 LET S=0
20 LET K=1
30 WHILE K<8
40     LET S=S+K^2
50     PRINT K,S
60     LET K=K+1
70 NEXT   (or WEND)
80 END
```

c.
```
10 LET A=1
20 LET B=0
30 LET FIB=A+B
40 WHILE FIB<10
50     PRINT FIB
60     LET A=B
70     LET B=FIB
80     LET FIB=A+B
90 NEXT  (or WEND)
99 END
```

d.
```
10 LET X=10
20 WHILE X>0
30     PRINT X
40     WHILE X>4
50        LET X=X-1
60     NEXT  (or WEND)
70     LET X=X-2
80 NEXT   (or WEND)
90 PRINT X
99 END
```

e.
```
100 LET A$="A"
110 LET B$="B"
120 LET C$="C"
130 LET T$=""
140 WHILE T$<>"A"
150     PRINT A$,B$,C$
160     LET T$=A$
170     LET A$=B$
180     LET B$=T$
190     PRINT A$,B$,C$
200     LET T$=C$
210     LET C$=A$
220     LET A$=T$
230 NEXT  (or WEND)
240 END
```

3. Code each loop in Problem 1 as a WHILE loop.

4. If your version of BASIC does not allow WHILE, code each loop in Problem 2 by using IF and GOTO statements.

5. If A = 1, B = 2, and C = 3, which of the following relational expressions are true?

   a. A+B<=C   **b.** A+B=C

   c. 3<>C   **d.** A*B*C>=6

   e. A/C=.333   **f.** 3-(C/B)=3-C/B

6. Explain what is wrong with each statement. The problem may be a syntax error, or the statement may serve no useful purpose.

   a. 10 IF A<B THEN 10   **b.** 20 IF X<X-B THEN 21

   c. 30 IF A$=OK THEN 150   **d.** 40 IF A^2<0 THEN 100

   e. 50 IF M-N<27, THEN 80   **f.** 60 IF "DONE" THEN 150

   g. 70 WHILE A$=OK   **h.** 80 WHILE "NOT DONE"

   i. 90 WHILE M<5 THEN 200

7. Correct each IF loop in the following programs:

   a.
```
10 REM PROGRAM TO DISPLAY THE ODD
20 REM WHOLE NUMBERS THROUGH 15
30 LET N=1
40 PRINT N
50 LET N=N+2
60 IF N<15 THEN 30
70 END
```

   b.
```
100 REM PROGRAM TO DO SUBTRACTION
110 PRINT "FOLLOWING EACH ? TYPE TWO NUMBERS."
120 PRINT "MAKE THEM EQUAL TO STOP."
130 INPUT A,B
140 IF A<>B THEN 190
150     LET D=A-B
160     PRINT "SECOND-FIRST =";D
170     INPUT A,B
180 GOTO 150
190 END
```

   c.
```
10 REM PROGRAM TO DISPLAY AN
20 REM 8 PERCENT TAX TABLE
30 LET X=100
40 LET T=8*X
50 PRINT "PRICE","TAX"
60 PRINT X,T
70 LET X=X+1
80 IF X<=110 THEN 40
90 END
```

   d.
```
10 REM PROGRAM TO DISPLAY A TABLE OF
20 REM SQUARE ROOTS FOR N=2,3,4,...,10
30 PRINT "NUMBER","SQUARE ROOT"
40 LET N=2
50 LET R=N^1/2
60 PRINT N,R
70 LET N=N+1
80 IF N<=10 THEN 60
90 END
```

8. Correct each WHILE loop in the following programs:

   a.
```
10 REM PROGRAM TO DISPLAY THE ODD
20 REM WHOLE NUMBERS THROUGH 15
30 WHILE N<=15
40     LET N=1
50     PRINT N
60     LET N=N+2
70 NEXT (or WEND)
80 END
```

   b.
```
100 REM PROGRAM TO DO MULTIPLICATION
110 PRINT "FOLLOWING EACH ? TYPE TWO NUMBERS."
120 PRINT "MAKE THEM EQUAL TO STOP."
130 INPUT A,B
140 WHILE A=B
```

```
150    LET P=A*B
160    PRINT "PRODUCT IS";P
170 NEXT (or WEND)
180 END
```
c.
```
10 REM PROGRAM TO DISPLAY 8 PERCENT
20 REM OF THE AMOUNTS 100,101,102,...,110
30 LET A=100
40 WHILE A<=110
50    PRINT "AMOUNT","8% OF AMOUNT"
60    LET A=A+1
70    PRINT A,.08*A
80 NEXT (or WEND)
90 END
```

Write a program to display each table described in Problems 9–24. Begin each program with a PRINT statement describing the table. If a table has more than one column, display column headings.

9. The first column contains the number of dollars (1, 2, 3, . . . , 10), and the second column gives the corresponding number of yen (1 dollar = 146.55 yen).

10. The first column contains the temperature in degrees Celsius from −10 to 30 in increments of 2, and the second column gives the corresponding temperature in degrees Fahrenheit [$F = (9/5)C + 32$].

11. The first column gives the amount of sales ($500, $1,000, $1,500, . . . , $5,000), and the second gives the commission at a rate of R percent.

12. The first column contains the principal (50, 100, 150, . . . , 500), and the second column gives the corresponding simple interest for 6 months at an annual interest rate of R percent.

13. The first column contains the annual interest rate (7.0%, 7.25%, 7.5%, . . . , 9.0%), and the second column gives the simple interest on a principal of $1,000 for 9 months.

14. The first column gives the list price of an article ($25, $50, $75, . . . , $300), the second gives the amount of discount at 25%, and the third gives the corresponding selling price.

15. Ucall Taxi charges 45 cents for a ride plus 13 cents for each tenth of a mile. The first column gives the number of miles (0.1, 0.2, 0.3, . . . , 2.0), and the second gives the total charges.

16. The first column contains the number of years (n = 1, 2, 3, . . . , 15); the second shows the amount to which an initial deposit of A dollars has grown after n years. The interest rate is R percent compounded annually. [The value of A dollars after 1 year is $(1 + R/100) \times A$.]

17. Produce a two-column table showing how a single deposit of A dollars grows until it doubles in value. The annual interest rate is R percent compounded monthly. (See text Example 7.)

18. Interest is earned at the annual rate R percent, compounded quarterly. Produce a table showing how a single deposit of A dollars will grow, quarter by quarter, until it doubles in value. R and A are to be input.

19. A one-column table (list) containing the terms of the arithmetic progression a, $a + d$, $a + 2d$, $a + 3d$, . . . , $a + 10d$. Values for a and d are to be assigned by the user.

20. A one-column table (list) of the terms of the geometric progression a, ar, ar^2, ar^3, . . . , ar^{10}. Values for a and r are to be assigned by the user.

21. The first column contains the radius of a circle in inches (1, 2, 3, . . . , 15), and the second and third columns give the circumference and area of the circle.

22. The first column shows the radius in inches (1.0, 1.1, 1.2, . . . , 2.5) of the circular bottom of a tin can; the second gives the volume of the can if its height is H inches. (H must be input.)

23. The first column contains the number of miles (1, 2, 3, . . . , 15); the second column gives the corresponding number of kilometers (1 mi = 1.6093 km).

24. You require an accurate sketch of the graph of

$$y = \sqrt{1.09}x^3 - \sqrt[3]{8.51}x^2 + (1.314/1.426)x - 0.8$$

on the interval $1 \le x \le 3$. To make this task easier, produce a table of x and y values where the x's are in increments of 0.1.

In Problems 25–31, write a program for each task specified.

25. A young man agrees to begin working for a company at the very modest salary of a penny per

week, with the stipulation that his salary will double each week. What is his weekly salary at the end of 6 months and how much has he earned?

26. Find the total amount credited to an account after 4 years if $25 is deposited each month at an annual interest rate of 5.5% compounded monthly.

27. Mary deposits $25 in a bank at the annual interest rate of 6% compounded monthly. After how many months will her account first exceed $27.50?

28. A list of numbers is to be typed at the keyboard. After each number is typed, the program should cause two values to be displayed: a count of how many numbers have been typed and the average of all numbers entered to that time. The program should halt when the user types 0.

29. A person wishes to determine the dollar amount of any collection of U.S. coins simply by specifying how many of each type of coin are included. Your program should assist the user in this task and should halt only when the user so specifies.

30. Two numbers X and Y are to be typed. If the sum of X and Y is greater than 42, the computer should display the message SUM IS GREATER THAN 42. If the sum is not greater than 42, increase X by 10, decrease Y by 3, display these new X and Y values, and again check to see if the sum is greater than 42. This process should be repeated until the message SUM IS GREATER THAN 42 is displayed. When this happens, the user should be able to type two new values for X and Y or end the program.

31. Division of one positive integer A by another positive integer B is often presented in elementary school as repeated subtraction. Write a program to input two positive integers A and B, and determine the quotient Q and the remainder R by this method.

■ 6.4 Review True-or-False Quiz

1. If the condition in an IF statement is false, the normal sequential execution of the program is interrupted.   **T F**

2. String constants appearing in relational expressions must be quoted.   **T F**

3. If the statements

```
149 PRINT "FIRST","SECOND","THIRD"
150 PRINT A,B,C
```

appear in a loop, all A, B, and C values will be displayed in columns with the headings FIRST, SECOND, and THIRD.   **T F**

4. If the statement

```
50 PRINT X,Y
```

appears in a loop, the column of X values and the column of Y values will be aligned according to decimal points.   **T F**

5. The WHILE statement is used only to code loops.   **T F**

6. The condition in a WHILE statement is always the condition that must be true for looping to continue.   **T F**

7. If an IF statement that controls execution of a loop is the last statement of the loop, the IF condition is precisely the condition that must be true for looping to continue.   **T F**

8. The statement

```
50 IF X$<>NO THEN 90
```

will transfer control to line 90 if X$ has the value YES.   **T F**

9. The statement

```
WHILE LOOP$=YES
```

will cause looping to continue if LOOP$ has the value YES.   **T F**

10. A computer can store every number between 0 and 1 exactly, but it must use approximations for some numbers larger than 1.   **T F**

11. The following program will display the integers 1 through 10 and no other numbers:

```
10 LET N=0
20 WHILE N<>1          (IF N=1 THEN 60)
30   LET N=N+0.1
40   PRINT 10*N
50 NEXT (or WEND)      (GOTO 20)
60 END
```

T   F

7

More on the
PRINT Statement

Up to now we have been working with very limited forms of the PRINT statement. As a consequence, we have had little control over the format of the output generated by a program. In this chapter we'll show how you can display many string and numerical values on a line (Sections 7.1 and 7.2) and how the spacing function TAB can be used to specify precise positions along a line for these values (Section 7.4). In Section 7.6, we describe the PRINT USING statement, an extended form of the PRINT statement that provides a convenient way to specify an exact format for all output values. In Sections 7.8 and 7.9 we introduce the topic of menu-driven programs and show how the formatting methods illustrated in this chapter can be used to produce neat and uncluttered screen displays for menu-driven programs.

■ 7.1 Displaying More Values on a Line

The number of characters that can be printed or displayed on a single line depends on both the output device and the version of BASIC being used. If you are using a display screen, this number may be as small as 24, but 80 characters per line is common. Printers usually print 80 or more characters per line. For the sake of discussion, we will assume an output device that allows 80 characters per line. In BASIC, these are numbered 1 through 80 (0 through 79 on some early BASIC systems).

When programming in BASIC, we consider a line to be divided into units called **print zones.** The number of characters per zone is system dependent—for instance, 14 for Vax BASIC and Microsoft BASIC, 15 for BASIC on Cyber computers, and 16 for Applesoft BASIC. If a print zone consists of 15 character positions, we would visualize an 80-character display line as follows:

zone 1	zone 2	zone 3	zone 4	zone 5	partial zone
1–15	16–30	31–45	46–60	61–75	76–80

The statement PRINT A,B,C,D,E will display the values of the five variables, one per zone. BASIC interprets *commas* in PRINT statements as instructions to *move to the beginning of the next print zone*. Thus, the two commas in the statement

```
PRINT , , A
```

instruct the computer to skip *two* print zones and display the value of A in zone 3.

You can include as many expressions separated by commas in a single PRINT statement as will fit on a programming line. The output values will be displayed, one per zone, by using as many display lines as needed. When using commas in PRINT statements, the usual practice is to include no more output expressions than will fit on a single line of output. Thus, for an 80-character display line divided into 15-character print zones we would use the statement PRINT A,B,C,D,E but not the statement PRINT A,B,C,D,E,F.

EXAMPLE 1   **Displaying numerical values.**

```
100 LET A=20
110 LET B=-3
120 LET C=3.123
130 PRINT A,B,C,A,B
140 END
RUN
```

zone 1	zone 2	zone 3	zone 4	zone 5
20	-3	3.123	20	-3

■ **REMARK**   On most BASIC systems, when a numerical value is displayed, the first position in its zone is reserved for the sign of the number. However, if the number is positive or zero, the sign is omitted and the first position is left blank.

In the same way as displaying numerical values, up to five *strings* can be displayed on one line, provided that each string fits in its zone. Strings are displayed beginning in the first position of a zone.

EXAMPLE 2   **Displaying string values.**

```
100 PRINT "FIRST COLUMN","THE SECOND COLUMN","THIRD COLUMN"
110 END
RUN
```

zone 1	zone 2	zone 3	zone 4	zone 5
FIRST COLUMN	THE SECOND COLUMN		THIRD COLUMN	

The second string uses all 15 positions in zone 2 and 2 positions from zone 3. This means that the third string must start in zone 4.

■ **REMARK**   If the string variables A\$, B\$, and C\$ have the values FIRST COLUMN, THE SECOND COLUMN, and THIRD COLUMN, respectively, the statement

```
100 PRINT A$,B$,C$
```

produces the same output.

Many values can be displayed on a single line if *semicolons* instead of commas are used to delimit the expressions in a PRINT statement. If this is done, zones will be ignored and the output values will be packed more closely. On most systems one space will separate numbers, with a possible second space if a number is not negative (the sign position). As many numbers will be displayed on a line as will fit. If line 130 of Example 1 is changed to

```
130 PRINT A;B;C;A;B
```

the output will be*

```
20 -3  3.123  20 -3
```

If *string constants* or *string variables* are separated by semicolons in a PRINT state-ment, the output will be merged. For example, if A$ = "TO", B$ = "GET", and C$ = "HER!!!" the two statements

```
100 PRINT A$;B$;C$
```

and

```
100 PRINT "TO";"GET";"HER!!!"
```

will both produce the same output

```
TOGETHER!!!
```

If spaces are desired, they must be included as part of a string. Or you can write

```
100 PRINT A$;" ";B$;" ";C$
```

A PRINT statement, whether it uses semicolons or commas as delimiters, may con-tain any combination of constants, variables, and expressions. In the next example, we use a single PRINT statement to display the values of two string expressions ("PERCENT OF" and "IS") and three numerical expressions (R, A, and A*R/100).

EXAMPLE 3   **Here is a program further illustrating the use of semicolons in PRINT state-ments.**

```
10 PRINT "ENTER A NUMBER";
20 INPUT A
30 LET R=5
40 WHILE R<=8              (IF R>8 THEN 80)
50    PRINT R;"PERCENT OF";A;"IS";A*R/100
60    LET R=R+1
70 NEXT (or WEND)          (GOTO 40)
80 END
RUN

ENTER A NUMBER? 500
 5 PERCENT OF 500 IS 25.
 6 PERCENT OF 500 IS 30.
 7 PERCENT OF 500 IS 35.
 8 PERCENT OF 500 IS 40.
```

■ 7.2 Suppressing the Carriage Return

It often happens that a program contains a loop in which a new value to be displayed is determined each time the loop is executed. If the PRINT statement is of the form

```
PRINT T
```

successive values of T will be displayed on separate lines. However, if you terminate this PRINT statement with a comma or a semicolon, more than one value will be displayed on each line: as many as there are zones if a comma is used and as many as will fit on the line if a semicolon is used.

---

*Some BASIC systems implemented on personal computers leave no spaces between numbers when semicolons are used. On these systems the output would be 20−33.12320−3. If your system works this way, you must in-sert spaces between numerical values being displayed as explained in what follows. In this book, we assume that numerical values are always separated in the output.

EXAMPLE 4   **Displaying many values per line.**

```
100 LET N=1
110 WHILE N<=14            (IF N>14 THEN 160)
120     LET T=2*N-1
130     PRINT T;
140     LET N=N+1
150 NEXT (or WEND)          (GOTO 110)
160 PRINT
170 PRINT "THAT'S ALL FOLKS!"
180 END
RUN

  1  3  5  7  9  11  13  15  17  19  21  23  25  27
THAT'S ALL FOLKS!
```

■ REMARK

☐

When the last number (27) is displayed by line 130, the semicolon prevents the cursor from being positioned at the beginning of the next line. The PRINT statement in line 150 causes a RETURN so that the subsequent output will appear on a new line.

EXAMPLE 5   **Here is a program to display a row of N dashes.**

```
10 PRINT "HOW MANY DASHES";
20 INPUT N
30 LET DASHES=0
40 WHILE DASHES<N     (IF DASHES>=N THEN 80)
50     PRINT "-";
60     LET DASHES=DASHES+1
70 NEXT (or WEND)     (GOTO 40)
80 END
RUN

HOW MANY DASHES? 19
-------------------
```

☐

Note that the number of dashes already displayed (DASHES) is compared with the number desired (N) as soon as the loop is entered (line 40). This ensures that no dash will be displayed if 0 is input for N.

■ 7.3 Problems

1. Show the exact output (line by line and space by space) of each program.

a.
```
100 PRINT "BASEBALL'S HALL OF FAME"
110 PRINT "COOPERSTOWN, NY ";
120 PRINT "13326"
130 END
```

b.
```
10 PRINT "PASCA";
20 PRINT "GOULA RIVER"
30 PRINT "BAYOU";
40 PRINT " COUNTRY, U.S.A."
50 END
```

c.
```
10 LET X=5
20 LET Y=X+3
30 PRINT X;"TIMES";Y;"=";X*Y
40 END
```

d.
```
10 PRINT "HAPPY"
20 PRINT,"HAPPY"
30 PRINT,,"HOLIDAY"
```

e.
```
10 LET N=0
20 WHILE N<38
30     PRINT N,
40     LET N=N+5
50 NEXT (or WEND)
60 PRINT "FINI"
70 END
```

```
f. 10 LET X=5
   20 WHILE X<=15
   30    PRINT "IF A=";
   40    PRINT X;
   50    PRINT "A+2=";
   60    PRINT X+2
   70    PRINT
   80    LET X=X+5
   90 NEXT (or WEND)
   99 END
```

2. Assuming that X = 1 and Y = 2, write PRINT statements to display the following. No numbers are to appear in the PRINT statements.

    a. 1 / 2 = .5   **b.** X + Y = 3   **c.** X − 2 = −1

    d. SCORE: 2 TO 1   **e.** DEPT. NO. 5   **f.** BLDG 4.25

3. The following programs fail to do what is claimed. Correct them.

```
a. 100 REM A PROGRAM TO PRINT
   101 REM      TEA FOR TWO
   110 PRINT "TEA";"FOR";"TWO"
   120 END
```

```
b. 10 REM A PROGRAM TO DISPLAY
   20 REM    SLEEPING BEAR DUNES
   30 PRINT "SLEEPING",
   40 PRINT "BEAR",
   50 PRINT "DUNES"
   60 END
```

```
c. 100 REM A PROGRAM TO PRINT
   101 REM      7A7A7A
   110 LET X=1
   120 WHILE X<=3
   130    PRINT 7;"A"
   140    LET X=X+1
   150 NEXT  (or WEND)
   160 END
```

```
d. 100 REM A PROGRAM TO PRINT
   101 REM      1  2  3
   102 REM      4  5  6
   110 LET X=1
   120 WHILE X<=3
   130    PRINT X;
   140    LET X=X+1
   150 NEXT (or WEND)
   160 WHILE X<=6
   170    LET X=X+1
   180    PRINT X
   190 NEXT (or WEND)
   200 END
```

Write a program to perform each task specified in Problems 4–13.

4. Fifteen years ago the population of Easton was 3571; it is currently 7827. Find the average increase in population per year. The output should be

```
FIFTEEN YEAR POPULATION INCREASE IS _____ .
THIS REPRESENTS AN AVERAGE INCREASE OF _____ PER YEAR.
```

5. An item has a list price of L dollars but is on sale at a discount of D percent. Find the selling price. The output should be.

```
LIST PRICE $ _____
DISCOUNT OF _____ PERCENT IS $ _____
SELLING PRICE $ _____
```

6. The wholesale price of a car is W dollars and the markup is P percent. Determine the retail price. The output should be

```
WHOLESALE PRICE IS _____ DOLLARS.
MARKUP IS _____ PERCENT.
RETAIL PRICE IS _____ DOLLARS.
```

7. A manufacturer produces an item at a cost of C dollars per unit and sells each unit for S dollars. In addition to the cost of C dollars per unit, a fixed yearly cost of F dollars must be absorbed in the manufacture of the item. The number of units that must be sold in 1 year to break even (breakeven volume) is given by the formula.

$$\text{Breakeven volume} = \frac{F}{S - C} \text{ units}$$

Your program is to process several sets of input values C, S, and F and end when the user types 0 as the cost per unit amount. The output for each set of input values should be

```
COST PER UNIT? _____
FIXED COST PER YEAR? _____
PRICE PER UNIT? _____
_____ UNITS MUST BE SOLD TO BREAK EVEN.
THIS REPRESENTS _____ DOLLARS IN SALES.
```

8. Display a row containing M dashes followed by the string THE END. M is to be input.
9. Display THE END beginning in column position N. N is to be input. (Use the statement PRINT " "; to display a space.)
10. Display a square array of asterisks with M rows and M columns. M is to be input.
11. Display a square array of # symbols with N rows and N columns. The display is to begin in column position P. N and P are to be input.
12. Display a square array of asterisks with 12 rows and 12 columns. The design is to be centered.
13. Display a rectangular array of + signs with R rows and C columns. The design is to be centered. R and C are to be input.

■ 7.4 The TAB Function

By using the semicolon in PRINT statements, you can specify exact positions for your output values. However, as you probably found while writing the programs for the preceding problem set, this process can be cumbersome. To alleviate this difficulty, BASIC provides the spacing function TAB, which is included in PRINT statements to specify positions for output values. TAB(n) specifies that the next output value is to begin in column position n. The following three examples illustrate the use of the TAB function.

EXAMPLE 6

```
10 PRINT "12345678901234567890"
20 PRINT TAB(7);"WET"
30 PRINT TAB(6);"PAINT"
40 PRINT
50 PRINT "BEWARE!";TAB(10);"ATTACK DOG"
60 END
RUN

12345678901234567890
      WET
     PAINT

BEWARE!  ATTACK DOG
```

■ **REMARK 1**   Note the use of semicolons in the PRINT statements. Remember that a comma specifies that subsequent output is to commence at the beginning of the next print zone.

■ **REMARK 2**   It would be correct to replace line 50 by

```
50 PRINT TAB(1);"BEWARE!";TAB(10);"ATTACK DOG"
```

but not by

```
50 PRINT TAB(10);"ATTACK DOG";TAB(1);"BEWARE!"
```

☐   The TAB function is used only to specify positions to the right of the current cursor position. Violating this rule will have different effects on different systems.

EXAMPLE 7

```
10 PRINT "12345678901234567890"
20 PRINT "--------------------"
30 LET K=1
40 WHILE K<=5                    (IF K>5 THEN 80)
50    PRINT TAB(K);3*K
60    LET K=K+1
70 NEXT (or WEND)                (GOTO 40)
80 END
RUN

12345678901234567890
--------------------
  3
   6
    9
     12
      15
```

Each time line 50 is executed, TAB(K) causes the value of 3 * K to be displayed beginning in column position K as shown. (The apparent discrepancy is due to the suppressed plus sign, which, if displayed, would occupy column position K.)

EXAMPLE 8

```
10 PRINT "12345678901234567890"
20 PRINT "--------------------"
30 LET C=5
40 LET K=1
50 WHILE K<=6                    (IF K>6 THEN 90)
60    PRINT TAB(C);"N";TAB(C+K);"N";TAB(C+7);"N"
70    LET K=K+1
80 NEXT (or WEND)                (GOTO 50)
90 END

RUN
12345678901234567890
--------------------
    NN      N
    N N     N
    N  N    N
    N   N   N
    N    N N N
    N       NN
```

Each time line 60 is executed, the letter N is displayed in column positions C, C + K, and C + 7. To display the design beginning in a column position C other than C = 5, simply change line 30.

We conclude this section by giving the general form of the PRINT statement that includes the TAB function.

ln PRINT TAB(**a**);**e**;TAB(**b**);**f**; . . .

where

> **a,b, . . .** are numerical expressions whose values are rounded to integers (truncated on some systems) to determine positions for the values to be displayed.
> **e,f, . . .** are BASIC expressions (arithmetic or string) whose values are to be displayed.

A semicolon or comma may terminate such a PRINT statement, in which case the RETURN will be suppressed.

■ 7.5 Problems

1. Show the exact output of each program.

   a.
   ```
   10 PRINT TAB(5);"SALES";TAB(15);"COMMISSION"
   20 PRINT TAB(5);"-----";TAB(15);"----------"
   30 LET SALES=2000
   40 WHILE SALES<=5000
   50    LET COMM=0.10*SALES
   60    PRINT TAB(5);SALES;TAB(17);COMM
   70    LET SALES=SALES+500
   80 NEXT (or WEND)
   90 END
   ```

   b.
   ```
   10 LET B$="BASIC"
   20 LET N=1
   30 WHILE N<=15
   40    PRINT TAB(N);B$;
   50    LET N=N+6
   60 NEXT (or WEND)
   70 END
   ```

   c.
   ```
   10 PRINT "1234567890"
   20 LET T=0
   30 WHILE T<=4
   40    PRINT TAB(2*T+1);-T
   50    LET T=T+1
   60 NEXT (or WEND)
   70 PRINT "THAT'S ENOUGH"
   80 END
   ```

   d.
   ```
   10 PRINT " 7777777"
   20 LET N=1
   30 LET S=6
   40 WHILE S>=1
   50    PRINT TAB(S);S+N
   60    LET N=N+1
   70    LET S=S-1
   80 NEXT (or WEND)
   90 END
   ```

   e.
   ```
   10 PRINT "1234567890"
   20 LET X=1
   30 WHILE X<=5
   40    PRINT TAB(2*X);"*";
   50    LET X=X+1
   60 NEXT (or WEND)
   70 END
   ```

   f.
   ```
   10 LET X=0
   20 PRINT TAB(5);"X";TAB(15);"X^2"
   30 WHILE X<4
   40    PRINT
   50    LET X=X+1
   60    PRINT TAB(4);X;TAB(14);X^2;
   70 NEXT (or WEND)
   80 END
   ```

2. Write PRINT statements to do the following. (Use the TAB function.)

   a. Display the letter B in position 6 and the digit 3 in position 10.

   b. Display the values of X, .04X, .06X, and .08X on one line about equally spaced.

   c. Display six zeros on one line equally spaced along the entire line.

   d. Display your name centered on a line.

Write a program to perform each task specified in Problems 3–9. Use the TAB function.

3. Display your name on one line, street and number on the next line, and city or town and state on the third line. Your name should be centered, and successive lines should be indented.

4. Display a row of 15 A's beginning in position 21 and a row of 13 B's centered under the A's.

5. Display a rectangular array of asterisks with five rows and eight columns. The display is to be centered.

6. Display a square array of # symbols with M rows and M columns. M is to be input. The display is to be centered.
7. Display the numbers 1, 10, 100, 1000, 10000, 100000, and 1000000 in a column that lines up on the right.
8. Display the numbers .33333, 3.3333, 33.333, 333.33 and 3333.3 in a column so that the decimal points line up.
9. Display the following designs:

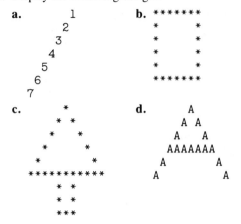

■ 7.6 The PRINT USING Statement

Consider the following simple program and its output:

```
100 REM PRINT COLUMN HEADINGS.
110 PRINT TAB(5);"N";TAB(14);"1/N^2"
120 PRINT
130 REM PRINT TABLE VALUES.
140 LET N=1
150 WHILE N<=10                    (IF N>10 THEN 190)
160    PRINT TAB(4);N;TAB(13);1/N^2
170    LET N=N+1
180 NEXT (or WEND)                 (GOTO 150)
190 END
RUN

     N         1/N^2

     1         1
     2         .25
     3         .111111
     4         .0625
     5         .04
     6         2.77778E-2
     7         2.04082E-2
     8         .015625
     9         1.23457E-2
    10         .01
```

Even though the TAB function is used to control the output format, the second column appears rather cluttered. The PRINT USING statement provides a simple way to rectify this situation. BASIC systems differ in how this statement must be written. We present the most common forms to show how this extended version of the PRINT statement can be used to help you produce improved output displays.

A PRINT USING statement not only includes the variables and expressions whose values are to be displayed, but also specifies the format to be used in displaying these values. The following example illustrates the three most common forms of the PRINT USING statement.

EXAMPLE 9   **Each of parts (a), (b), and (c) contains a program segment to produce the output ASSETS INCREASED BY 23.5 PERCENT.**

a. 100 LET F$="ASSETS INCREASED BY ##.# PERCENT."
110 LET A=23.487
120 PRINT USING F$,A

(Your system may require PRINT USING F$;A)

The PRINT USING statement displays the value of A in the form specified by the contents of a string variable (F$ in this example). The specification ##.# included in F$ says to display the value of A by using two positions to the left and one to the right of the decimal point. The value 23.487 of A is rounded to fit the specification ##.#.

b. 110 LET A=23.487
120 PRINT USING "ASSETS INCREASED BY ##.# PERCENT.",A

This equivalent form of the PRINT USING statement shown in part (a) does not require a separate statement to assign the form of the output to a string variable. The output format is simply enclosed in quotation marks and placed immediately after the keywords PRINT USING, as shown.

c. 110 LET A=23.487
120 PRINT USING 130,A
130 :ASSETS INCREASED BY ##.# PERCENT.

The PRINT USING statement displays the value of A in the form specified in line 130. The statement at line 130, whose keyword is the colon (:), is called an IMAGE statement since it contains an image of the output to be produced.

The three forms of the PRINT USING statement shown in Example 9 are included in the following general form.

PRINT USING **s,a,b,c, . . .**

or

PRINT USING **s;a,b,c, . . .**

a,b,c, . . . denote numerical or string expressions whose values are to be output. The commas serve only as delimiters; they do not affect the output format as do commas in regular PRINT statements.

s denotes a string variable [as in Example 9(a)], a string constant [as in Example 9(b)], or the line number of an IMAGE statement that contains a string [as in Example 9(c)].

The string referenced by **s** is called the **format string.** It consists of two types of *format specifications:* strings that specify how the output values are to be displayed—such as ##.# in Example 9, which specifies the form for the numerical value of A; and strings that are to be included in the output—such as the strings ASSETS INCREASED BY and PERCENT in Example 9. Such strings are displayed exactly as they appear, including any blanks.

The next two examples further illustrate the use of strings and pound symbols (#) as format specifications. In these and all subsequent examples, we will use the form of the PRINT USING statement in which **s** denotes a string variable. If your system requires one of the other forms, it is a simple matter to make the necessary changes as illustrated in Example 9.

EXAMPLE 10   **If X = 453, the program segment**

```
100 LET A$="12345678901234567890"
110 LET M$="ITEM NUMBER #####"
120 PRINT A$
130 PRINT USING M$,X
```

will cause the display

```
12345678901234567890
ITEM NUMBER    453
```

Lines 100 and 120 are included for reference only. The format specification ##### in the string M$ is used to specify how 453 is to appear in the output. Since 453 uses only three of the possible five positions, it is displayed *right justified;* that is, it appears in the rightmost three positions reserved by the specification. (Notice that only one space precedes ##### in the format string M$, whereas three spaces precede 453 in the output.)

EXAMPLE 11   **If A = 42.237 and B = 25, the program segment**

```
200 LET A$="12345678901234567890"
210 LET H$="####.## ####.##"
220 PRINT A$
230 PRINT USING H$,A,B
```

will cause the display

```
12345678901234567890
  42.24   25.00
```

This example illustrates two points: numbers are rounded (not truncated) to fit a format specification (42.237 is rounded to 42.24), and all positions specified to the right of the decimal point will be displayed (25, the value of B, is displayed as 25.00).

The numerical format specifications illustrated in the preceding examples (pound symbols and the period) are allowed in all versions of BASIC that include the PRINT USING statement. BASIC systems provide characters other than the pound symbol and period that can be used to specify a format for numerical output values. Here are two formatting characters that you may find useful if they are allowed in your version of BASIC.

1. Place $$ just to the left of a numerical format specification. The numerical output value will be displayed with a signal $ just before the leftmost digit. If A = 495.37, the program segment

```
200 LET F$="EQUITY IS $$###.##"
210 PRINT USING F$,A
```

will cause the display

```
EQUITY IS $495.37
```

If A = 7.45, the display will be

```
EQUITY IS   $7.45
```

2. Place a single comma anywhere to the left of the decimal point in a numerical format specification. The output value will be displayed with a comma to the left of every third digit as required—for instance, 2,253,000.1234 instead of 2253000.1234. If A = 2756.13825, the two lines

```
300 LET F$="EQUITY IS $$#,###.##"
310 PRINT USING F$,A
```

will cause the display

```
EQUITY IS $2,756.14
```

If F$ = "EQUITY IS $$####,.##", the output will be exactly the same.

BASIC allows you to specify exact forms for *string* as well as numerical output values. BASIC systems, however, differ significantly in the formatting characters used for this purpose. The next two examples illustrate the most common methods of writing string format specifications.

EXAMPLE 12

Parts (a) and (b) of this example illustrate the use of the pound symbol to specify a position for either a digit in a numerical output value or a character in a string output value. (Versions of BASIC implemented on Cyber computers use this method of writing format specifications for string output values.)

a. If N = 16, and B$="BLDG.", the program segment

```
50 LET A$="12345678901234567890"
60 LET Z$="######## ##"
70 PRINT A$
80 PRINT USING Z$,B$,N
```

will cause the display

```
12345678901234567890
BLDG.    16
```

Since BLDG., the value of B$, uses only five of the eight positions reserved by the specification ########, it is displayed *left justified;* that is, it appears in the leftmost five positions reserved by the format specification. Thus, integer values are displayed right justified (see Example 10), and strings are displayed left justified.

b. If N$ = "CARLTON", the two lines

```
120 LET F$="NAME: ####"
130 PRINT USING F$,N$
```

will cause the display

```
NAME: CARL
```

If a format specification does not provide enough positions to display an output string, the output string is truncated on the right to fit the specification. In the example, only four positions are specified for the output variable N$; hence only the first four characters in N$ are displayed.

EXAMPLE 13

Parts (a) through (d) illustrate the following string formatting characters.

!   Specifies that only the *first* character of the output string is to be displayed. (This formatting character is allowed in Vax BASIC, BASIC-PLUS, Microsoft BASIC, and BASIC on the TRS-80.)

&   Specifies that the *entire* output string is to be displayed. (Allowed in Microsoft BASIC)

'E   Specifies that the *entire* output string is to be displayed. (Allowed with recent versions of BASIC on DEC computers.)

\n spaces\   Specifies n + 2 character positions for the output string. Thus, to display two characters, include no spaces between the two backslashes; to display three characters, include one space; and so on. If you specify more positions than needed, the output string is displayed *left justified* with trailing blanks. If you specify too few positions, the output string is truncated on the right. Note that the format specification itself occupies n + 2 character positions. (Allowed in Vax BASIC, BASIC-PLUS, and Microsoft BASIC. BASIC on the TRS-80 uses *%n spaces%* instead of *\n spaces\.*)

a. If N = 16, and B$="BLDG.", the program segment

```
50 LET A$="12345678901234567890"
60 LET Z$="\         \ ##"
70 PRINT A$
80 PRINT USING Z$,B$,N
```

will cause the display

```
12345678901234567890
BLDG.    16
```

The format string Z$ specifies eight positions for the output variable B$ (two back-slashes separated by six spaces). Since BLDG., the value of B$, requires only five of these eight spaces, it is displayed left justified with three trailing blanks.

b. IF N$="CARLTON", the two lines

```
120 LET F$="NAME: \  \"
130 PRINT USING F$,N$
```

will cause the display

```
NAME: CARL
```

The format string F$ specifies four positions for the output variable N$ (two back-slashes separated by two spaces). Since CARLTON, the value of N$, contains more than four characters it is truncated to CARL to fit the specification.

c. If A$ = "ABC", B$ = "DEF", and C$ = "GHI", the two lines

```
150 LET F$="! !!"
160 PRINT USING F$,A$,B$,C$
```

will cause the display

```
A DG
```

d. With A$, B$, and C$ as in part (c), the two lines

```
250 LET F$="& &&"
260 PRINT USING F$,A$,B$,C$
```

will cause the display

```
ABC DEFGHI
```

With recent versions of Vax BASIC or BASIC-PLUS, you would use

```
250 LET F$="'E 'E'E"
```

The PRINT USING statement is especially useful when you have to produce reports in which the columns must line up on the decimal points. The next two examples illustrate this use of the PRINT USING statement.

EXAMPLE 14   **Here is an improved version of the program shown at the beginning of this section.**

```
100 REM DISPLAY HEADINGS AND ASSIGN OUTPUT FORMATS.
110 PRINT "    N          1/N^2"
120 LET F$="    ##         #.####"
130 PRINT
140 REM PRINT TABLE VALUES
150 LET N=1
160 WHILE N<=10              (IF N>10 THEN 200)
170   PRINT USING F$,N,1/N^2
180   LET N=N+1
190 NEXT (OR WEND)           (GOTO 160)
200 END
RUN

      N          1/N^2

      1          1.0000
      2          0.2500
      3          0.1111
      4          0.0625
      5          0.0400
      6          0.0278
      7          0.0204
      8          0.0156
      9          0.0123
     10          0.0100
```

Notice that the second column in the output now lines up on the decimal points and the exponential forms of numbers are not displayed. The format specification #.#### in the format string F$ controls this.

EXAMPLE 15

```
100 REM ***************** PROPERTY TAX PROGRAM ********************
110 REM
120 REM THIS PROGRAM PRODUCES PROPERTY TAX TABLES
130 REM BASED ON THE FOLLOWING INPUT VALUES:
140 REM
150 REM      P    PROPERTY IS ASSESSED AT P PERCENT OF MARKET VALUE.
160 REM    L,H   LOWEST AND HIGHEST MARKET VALUES FOR TAX TABLE.
170 REM          (SHOWN FROM LOWEST TO HIGHEST IN INCREMENTS OF $100.)
180 REM      R    TAX RATE IN DOLLARS PER THOUSAND.
190 REM
200 REM **************** DATA ENTRY SECTION ********************
210 REM
220 PRINT "ASSESSMENT PERCENT ";
230 INPUT P
240 PRINT "LOWEST AND HIGHEST MARKET VALUES ";
250 INPUT L,H
260 PRINT "TAX RATE PER THOUSAND ";
270 INPUT R
280 REM
290 REM ***** DISPLAY COLUMN HEADINGS AND ASSIGN FORMAT STRING F$ *****
300 PRINT
310 PRINT "   MARKET      ASSESSED     TOTAL    SEMIANNUAL     MONTHLY"
320 PRINT "   VALUE        VALUE        TAX        BILL         BILL"
330 LET F$=" ######.##    ######.##   ####.##    ####.##      ###.##"
340 PRINT
350 REM ************ CALCULATE AND DISPLAY TABLE VALUES **************
360 REM
370 LET MV=L                                    'Lowest market value.
380 WHILE MV<=H              (IF MV>H THEN 440)
390    LET ASV=(P/100)*MV                        'Assessed value.
400    LET TAX=ASV*R/1000                        'Tax for one year.
410    PRINT USING F$;MV,ASV,TAX,TAX/2,TAX/12    'Display one line.
420    LET MV=MV+100                             'Next market value.
430 NEXT (or WEND)           (GOTO 380)
440 END
RUN

ASSESSMENT PERCENT ? 87
LOWEST AND HIGHEST MARKET VALUES ? 12500,13400
TAX RATE PER THOUSAND ? 56.45

    MARKET      ASSESSED     TOTAL    SEMIANNUAL     MONTHLY
    VALUE        VALUE        TAX        BILL         BILL

    12500.00    10875.00    613.89     306.95        51.16
    12600.00    10962.00    618.80     309.40        51.57
    12700.00    11049.00    623.72     311.86        51.98
    12800.00    11136.00    628.63     314.31        52.39
    12900.00    11223.00    633.54     316.77        52.79
    13000.00    11310.00    638.45     319.22        53.20
    13100.00    11397.00    643.36     321.68        53.61
    13200.00    11484.00    648.27     324.14        54.02
    13300.00    11571.00    653.18     326.59        54.43
    13400.00    11658.00    658.09     329.05        54.84
```

Here are two points concerning the use of PRINT USING statements that have not been mentioned, but that you may find helpful:

1. Placing a semicolon or comma at the end of a PRINT USING statement has the same effect as placing a *semicolon* at the end of a PRINT statement. Thus, the loop

```
200 LET N=1
210 WHILE N<=3                    (IF N>3 THEN 250)
220   PRINT USING "COLUMN#    ",N;
230   LET N=N+1
240 NEXT (or WEND)                (GOTO 210)
250 PRINT
```

will produce the output

```
COLUMN1    COLUMN2    COLUMN3
```

If the final semicolon in line 220 is changed to a comma, the output will remain as shown. (In PRINT USING statements, commas do *not* specify that subsequent output is to begin in the next print zone.)

2. If an output format contains *fewer* format specifications than output values, the *output format* is repeated. Thus,

```
PRINT USING "#",1,2,3,4,5
```

will produce the output

```
12345
```

If separating spaces are desired, you can use " #" or "# " instead of "#".

Here is a simple way to code the loop shown in item (1):

```
PRINT USING "COLUMN#   ",1,2,3
```

This single statement is equivalent to lines 200–250.

■ 7.7 Problems

1. Show the exact output of each program.

   a.
   ```
   10 LET A=23.60
   20 LET W$="123456789"
   30 LET X$="  ##.##"
   40 PRINT W$
   50 PRINT USING X$,A
   60 PRINT TAB(3);A
   70 END
   ```

   b.
   ```
   10 LET N=9
   20 LET F$="##.##"
   30 WHILE N>1
   40   PRINT USING F$,N
   50   LET N=N/2
   60 NEXT (or WEND)
   70 END
   ```

   c.
   ```
   10 LET J=1
   20 LET Y$="TIME## A= #.##"
   30 WHILE J<=3
   40   LET A=0.004*J
   50   PRINT USING Y$,J,A
   60   LET J=J+1
   70 NEXT (or WEND)
   80 END
   ```

   d.
   ```
   10 REM STOCK FRACTION VALUES
   20 LET F$="  #/#=.###"
   30 LET D=8
   40 LET N=1
   50 WHILE N<=7
   60   PRINT USING F$,N,D,N/D
   70   LET N=N+2
   80 NEXT (or WEND)
   90 END
   ```

2. Show the exact output of each program (for systems that use pound symbols to specify positions for characters in output strings).

a.
```
10 LET A$="EYELIDS"
20 LET B$="POPULAR"
30 LET C$="###"
40 PRINT USING C$,B$;
50 PRINT USING C$,A$
60 END
```

b.
```
10 LET A$="RIVER#####"
20 LET B$="          ####SWAIN"
30 PRINT USING A$,"BOAT"
40 PRINT USING B$,"BOAT"
50 END
```

c.
```
10 LET A$="BOBBY"
20 LET B$="JUDITH"
30 LET C$="######LOVES #######"
40 LET D$="#### LOVES ###"
50 PRINT USING C$,A$,B$
60 PRINT USING D$,B$,A$
70 END
```

d.
```
10 LET F$="###-#### ##    "
20 LET T$="TAXATION"
30 LET R$="RATE"
40 LET R=15
50 WHILE N=35
60   PRINT USING F$,T$,R$,R;
70   LET N=N+10
80 NEXT (or WEND)
90 END
```

3. Show the exact output of each program (for systems that use the form \ *spaces* \ to specify a format for string output values).

a.
```
10 LET A$="EYELIDS"
20 LET B$="POPULAR"
30 LET C$="\ \"
40 PRINT USING C$,B$;
50 PRINT USING C$,A$
60 END
```

b.
```
10 LET B$="BOAT"
20 PRINT USING "RIVER\  \",B$
30 PRINT USING "          \  \SWAIN",B$
40 END
```

c.
```
10 LET A$="BOBBY"
20 LET B$="JUDITH"
30 LET C$="\   \ LOVES \      \"
40 LET D$="\  \ LOVES \  \"
50 PRINT USING C$,A$,B$
60 PRINT USING D$,B$,A$
70 END
```

d.
```
10 LET F$="\ \-\  \ ##    "
20 LET T$="TAXATION"
30 LET R$="RATE"
40 LET R=15
50 WHILE R<=35
60   PRINT USING F$,T$,R$,R;
70   LET R=R+10
80 NEXT (or WEND)
90 END
```

Write a program to perform each task specified in Problems 4–9.

4. Display the numbers 1, 10, 100, 1000, 10000, 100000, and 1000000 in a column that lines up on the right.

5. Display the numbers .33333, 3.3333, 33.333, 333.33, and 3333.3 in a column so that the decimal points line up.

6. An employer is considering giving all employees a flat across-the-board raise R in addition to a percentage increase P. P and R are to be input. A three-column report with the column headings PRESENT SALARY, AMOUNT OF RAISE, and NEW SALARY is to be displayed. The first column is to list the possible salaries from $10,000 to $15,000 in increments of $500. Columns must line up on the decimal points.

7. Produce a six-column tax table showing 5%, 6%, 7%, 8%, 9%, and 10% for the amounts $100 to $300 in increments of $25. The table should have a centered title, and each column should be labeled appropriately. Columns must line up on the decimal points.

8. Produce a table showing 1%, 2%, 3%, . . . , 8% of the values from 10¢ to $2 in increments of 10¢. Your table should have nine columns, each with a column heading, and all columns are to line up on the decimal points.

9. Agaze Motors offers a new car buyer a 4-year loan at an annual rate of R percent after a 25% down payment. Write a program to determine the monthly payment if the cost of the car is input. Part of the monthly payment is for interest and part is used to reduce the principal. Interest is charged only on the unpaid principal. The program should produce a table with four columns showing the month number, the interest for the month, the amount by which the principal is reduced, and the loan balance after the payment is made. Columns must line up on the decimal points. Conclude the table with one line indicating the total amount of interest paid during the four years. (See Problem 23 of Section 5.2 for the monthly payment formula.)

■ 7.8 Menu-Driven Programs

Many programming applications require a program that can carry out several tasks but that will perform only those specified by the user. In such situations, it is natural to write a **menu-driven program.** This means that the program displays a list of the options available to the user (this is the **menu**) and permits the user to select options from the list.

It is customary to include two special options in each menu-driven program: an option to end the program and one to display instructions to the user. The following algorithm can be used for many menu-driven programs:

Algorithm for menu-driven programs

a. Display instructions to the user. (This step may be omitted if one of the options in the menu is to display instructions.)
b. Repeat the following until the end option:
   b1. Display the menu.
   b2. Specify an option at the keyboard.
   b3. Carry out the specified task.

The following programming lines show how you might write a BASIC program for this menu:*

```
1  Carry out Task A.
2  Carry out Task B.
3  End the program.


200 REM ———————— DISPLAY THE MENU ————————
210 PRINT
220 PRINT "MENU:"
230 PRINT
240 PRINT "    1   Carry out Task A."
250 PRINT "    2   Carry out Task B."
260 PRINT "    3   End the program."
```

* When coding menu-driven programs, the usual practice is to code the individual tasks as subroutines, as described in Chapter 11. If you are already familiar with the topic of subroutines, you should check that only these changes need to be made:

Insert GOSUB after THEN in lines 300–320.
Change GOTO 340 in lines 1900, 2900, and 3900 to RETURN.

```
270 PRINT
280 PRINT "OPTION NUMBER";
290 INPUT OP
300 IF OP=1 THEN 1000
310 IF OP=2 THEN 2000
320 IF OP=3 THEN 3000
330 IF OP<>3 THEN 200        'Check for End option.
340 GOTO 9999               'End of program.
350 REM
1000 REM ----- CODE FOR TASK A ------
   .
   .
   .
1900 GOTO 330
2000 REM ----- CODE FOR TASK B -----
   .
   .
   .
2900 GOTO 330
3000 REM -- ANY CODE THAT MUST BE EXECUTED --
3010 REM --     BEFORE THE PROGRAM STOPS    --
   .
   .
   .
3900 GOTO 330
9999 END
```

Notice that the program segment for each option ends with the statement GOTO 330. If OP is not 3, line 330 returns control to line 200 so that the menu is displayed again and the user can select another option. If OP is 3, the condition OP<>3 in line 330 is false and control passes to line 340, which ends the program.

The program segment (lines 3000–3900) that is executed when the End option is specified might simply display a concluding message to the user. As you learn more about the BASIC language, you will find situations in which other, more significant tasks must be carried out just prior to halting a program. In any case, it is excellent programming practice to include such a program segment in every menu-driven program. By doing so, each option, including the End option, is handled in exactly the same way. This makes the action of the program easier to follow and also makes the program easier to modify at a later date, should that be required.

With the given programming lines as a model, you can write a menu-driven program to carry out any tasks, provided only that you know how to write BASIC code for each task. We illustrate in Example 16 with a short menu-driven program designed to assist the user in carrying out simple and compound interest calculations.

EXAMPLE 16   **Here is a menu-driven program to perform interest calculations.**

```
100 REM      A MENU-DRIVEN PROGRAM
110 REM
120 REM *******************
130 REM * DISPLAY THE MENU *
140 REM *******************
150 REM
160 PRINT
170 PRINT
180 PRINT TAB(10); "TYPE AN OPTION AS FOLLOWS:"
190 PRINT
200 PRINT TAB(12); "1  FOR INSTRUCTIONS"
210 PRINT TAB(12); "2  FOR SIMPLE INTEREST"
220 PRINT TAB(12); "3  FOR COMPOUND INTEREST"
230 PRINT TAB(12); "4  TO END PROGRAM"
240 REM
250 REM *****************
260 REM * SELECT OPTIONS *
270 REM *****************
280 REM
```

```
290     PRINT
300     PRINT
310     PRINT "ENTER OPTION NUMBER";
320     INPUT OP
330     IF OP=1 THEN 500
340     IF OP=2 THEN 600
350     IF OP=3 THEN 700
360     IF OP=4 THEN 900
370 IF OP<>4 THEN 160          'Check for End option.
380 GOTO 999                   'End of program.
390 REM
400 REM ********************************************
410 REM * PROGRAM SEGMENTS TO PERFORM THE OPTIONS *
420 REM ********************************************
430 REM
500 REM -------- CHOICE 1 : DISPLAY INSTRUCTIONS --------
510 PRINT
520 PRINT "THIS PROGRAM COMPUTES EITHER THE SIMPLE OR THE"
530 PRINT "COMPOUND INTEREST ON A ONE-YEAR INVESTMENT. YOU"
540 PRINT "MUST CHOOSE THE METHOD OF CALCULATION AND ENTER"
550 PRINT "THE NECESSARY INFORMATION. MAKE YOUR CHOICE FROM"
560 PRINT "THE LIST OF OPTIONS."
570 GOTO 370
600 REM -------- CHOICE 2 : SIMPLE INTEREST --------------
610 PRINT
620 PRINT "AMOUNT OF INVESTMENT";
630 INPUT P
640 PRINT "RATE OF INTEREST AS PERCENT";
650 INPUT R
660 PRINT USING "SIMPLE INTEREST: $$########.##";P*R/100
670 GOTO 370
700 REM -------- CHOICE 3 : COMPOUND INTEREST -----------
710 PRINT
720 PRINT "AMOUNT OF INVESTMENT";
730 INPUT P
740 PRINT "RATE OF INTEREST AS PERCENT";
750 INPUT R
760 PRINT "NUMBER OF TIMES COMPOUNDED PER YEAR";
770 INPUT T
780 LET AMT=P*(1+R/100/T)^T
790 PRINT USING "COMPOUND INTEREST: $$########.##";AMT-P
800 GOTO 370
900 REM -------- CHOICE 4 : END THE PROGRAM -------------
910 PRINT
920 PRINT "PROGRAM TERMINATED"
930 GOTO 370
999 END
```

This program consists of three parts, as described by the REM statements at lines 130, 260, and 410. The first displays the menu, the second allows the user to choose from four options by typing option numbers, and the third contains the four program segments that carry out the tasks corresponding to the option numbers.

The action of the program should not be difficult to follow. It begins (lines 160–230) by displaying the menu. The PRINT statement in line 310 prompts the user for an option number, and the IF statements in lines 330–360 transfer control to the program segment that carries out the specified task. Option 1 (lines 500–570) displays instructions to the user; Option 2 (lines 600–670) prompts the user for input data and displays the result of a simple interest calculation; Option 3 (lines 700–800) does the same for compound interest; and Option 4 (lines 900–930) displays the message PROGRAM TERMINATED. Each of these four program segments returns control to line 370, which causes the program to continue, but only if the End option (OP = 4) was not selected.

In the event of a bad choice (a number other than 1, 2, 3, or 4) the IF statement at line 370 returns control to line 160 to display the menu and prompt the user for another option number.

BASIC contains the ON GOTO statement, which you may find helpful in coding menu-driven programs.* This statement is used to transfer control to a selected line number depending on the value of a certain expression. For example,

```
ON X GOTO 300,700,300
```

will transfer control to

line 300 if X = 1
line 700 if X = 2
line 300 if X = 3

Thus, you can see that lines 330–360 of the program in Example 16

```
330 IF OP=1 THEN 500
340 IF OP=2 THEN 600
350 IF OP=3 THEN 700
360 IF OP=4 THEN 900
```

can be replaced by the single line

```
330 ON OP GOTO 500,600,700,900
```

This ON GOTO statement is not exactly equivalent to the IF statements in lines 330–360. The four IF statements will transfer control to one of the lines 500, 600, 700, or 900 only if OP is exactly 1, 2, 3, or 4. For any other value of OP, no transfer is made, and control passes to the line that follows line 360. The ON GOTO statement, however, is handled differently as we now explain.

The general form of the ON GOTO statement is

ln ON **e** GOTO **ln₁**, **ln₂**, . . . , **lnₖ**

where **e** denotes a numerical expression and ln_1, ln_2, . . . , ln_k denote line numbers (they don't have to be different). On execution, **e** is evaluated and rounded (truncated on some systems) to an integer. If this integer is 1, control transfers to line ln_1; if it is 2, control transfers to line ln_2; and so on. Care must be taken that this integer is a number from **1** to **k**. What happens if it is not is system dependent.

Thus, when the statement

```
330 ON OP GOTO 500,600,700,900
```

is encountered, the computer rounds (or truncates) OP if necessary to obtain an integer. If this integer is 1, 2, 3, or 4, control passes to line 500, 600, 700, or 900, respectively. To ensure that the integer is 1, 2, 3, or 4, you can include the statement

```
325 IF OP<1 OR OP>4 THEN 370
```

to skip over the ON GOTO statement should the user inadvertently enter an incorrect value for OP. Including such an IF statement just before each ON GOTO statement is a common programming practice.

■ 7.9 Screen Displays

Modern BASIC systems provide statements that give you greater control of the display screen than we have shown to this point. Significant are statements that cause the following actions:

1. *Clear the screen.* We'll use the pseudocode

clearscreen

---

* BASIC also contains the ON GOSUB statement, which is often used in menu-driven programs.   statement is described in Chapter 11 after BASIC subroutines are introduced. The effect of the ON GO⌣ , statement is similar but not identical to that of the ON GOTO statement described in this section.

to indicate any BASIC statement that clears the screen. Your system will require a different name—for instance, Microsoft BASIC uses CLS and Apple computers use HOME.

   2. Move the cursor to a specified screen position without affecting the current screen display. (This is called a **pure cursor move.**) We'll use the pseudocode

> **cursor l,p**

to indicate that the cursor will be moved to position **p** of line **l**. Your system may have a single statement to do this (for instance, Microsoft BASIC uses LOCATE **l,p**), or it may require two statements (for instance, Apple computers use VTAB **l** to specify screen line **l** and HTAB **p** to specify position **p** of this line).

   In the next example we illustrate the use of statements that clear the screen and reposition the cursor. Before proceeding, you may wish to determine the precise form of the BASIC statements your system provides for carrying out the **clearscreen** and **cursor l,p** pseudocode operations.

EXAMPLE 17 **Here are four program segments to illustrate the pseudocode operations clearscreen and cursor l,p.**

a. ```
10 clearscreen
20 cursor 12,38
30 PRINT "BASIC"
```

Line 10 clears the screen, line 20 moves the cursor to position 38 of screen line 12, and line 30 displays BASIC in positions 38–42 of screen line 12. If your screen has 24 lines with 80 positions on each line (a common situation), this program segment will display BASIC at the approximate center of an otherwise clear screen.

**b.**  ```
10 clearscreen
20 cursor 1,20
30 PRINT "FIRST LINE"
40 cursor 10,20
50 PRINT "TENTH LINE"
```

Lines 20 and 30 display FIRST LINE beginning at position 20 of line 1 on an otherwise clear screen. Then lines 40 and 50 display TENTH LINE beginning at position 20 of line 10 without affecting the rest of the display.

c. ```
10 cursor 15,5
20 PRINT "PINEAPPLE"
30 cursor 15,5
40 PRINT "BANANA"
```

Cursor moving statements will position the cursor at a location on the screen whether or not a character is already displayed at that location. Thus, lines 10 and 20 display PINEAPPLE beginning at the fifth position of display line 15, and then lines 30 and 40 display BANANA beginning at this same location. The effect is to display the characters BANANAPLE. If the intent is to replace PINEAPPLE by BANANA, you can include the statements

```
22 cursor 15,5
24 PRINT "                    "
```

to "erase" PINEAPPLE, by displaying enough blank characters over it, before displaying BANANA.

d. ```
150 clearscreen
160 cursor 3,1
170 PRINT TAB(10); "TYPE AN OPTION AS FOLLOWS:"
180 PRINT
190 PRINT TAB(12); "1 FOR INSTRUCTIONS"
200 PRINT TAB(12); "2 FOR SIMPLE INTEREST"
210 PRINT TAB(12); "3 FOR COMPOUND INTEREST"
220 PRINT TAB(12); "4 TO END PROGRAM"
```

This program segment displays the menu

```
TYPE AN OPTION AS FOLLOWS:

     1   FOR INSTRUCTIONS
     2   FOR SIMPLE INTEREST
     3   FOR COMPOUND INTEREST
     4   TO END PROGRAM
```

on screen lines 3–8 of an otherwise clear screen.

BASIC statements that clear the screen and move the cursor can be used effectively in menu-driven programs. They allow you to control the screen placement of the menu, of any user prompts, and of any output generated when the options are carried out. By using screen control statements in this way, you can improve your programs significantly by giving the user neat and uncluttered screen displays. Consider, for example, the menu-driven program shown in Example 16. If you change lines 150 and 160 to

```
150  clearscreen
160  cursor 3,1
```

the menu will always be displayed on screen lines 8–13 as shown in Example 17(d). Also, if you change the PRINT statement in line 510 to

```
510  clearscreen
515  cursor 20,1
```

and the PRINT statement in line 610 to

```
610  clearscreen
615  cursor 20,1
```

the displays associated with the options to calculate simple and compound interest will always be displayed near the bottom (beginning at screen line 20) of an otherwise clear screen.

■ 7.10 Problems

1. While studying the current day's receipts, a bookkeeper must perform numerous calculations to answer certain questions. Write a menu-driven program to assist the bookkeeper in obtaining answers to these questions.
   a. What is the selling price of an item whose list price and discount percent are known?
   b. What is the discount percent for an item whose list and selling prices are known?
   c. What is the list price of an item whose selling price and discount percent are known?
2. An investor must carry out several calculations while assessing the performance of the family's current stock portfolio. These include finding the equity (paper value) given the number of shares and the current price, and finding the profit (or loss) for a holding given the total price paid for all shares, the number of shares owned, and the current selling price. Write a menu-driven program to assist the investor in carrying out these calculations.
3. First write a menu-driven program as described in Problem 2. Then modify it by including a new option: allow the investor to find the sum of any column of numbers typed at the keyboard.

Write a program to produce each screen display described in Problems 4–11.

4. Display BASIC at the four corners and center of an otherwise clear screen.
5. Display a square block containing 36 X's at the center of an otherwise clear screen.
6. Successively display the digits 0 through 9 in the 36-character block described in Problem 4. Be sure to clear the screen after each 36-character block is displayed.

7. Produce the display

```
NUMBER  1   2   3    4    5
CUBE    1   8   27   64   125
```

in about the center of an otherwise clear screen.

8. Display the following table centered on screen lines 5–12:

```
  _____

  ITEM  PERCENT
   1.      0
   2.      0
   3.      0
   4.      0
   5.      0

  _____
```

9. Display the table described in Problem 8. Then allow the user to enter percent figures for items 1–5. Use the bottom portion of the screen to prompt the user for the next percent figures.

10. Display the following table centered on screen lines 5–10:

```
RANGE    COUNT    WEIGHT
_____    _____    _____
10-20      0        1
20-30      0        1
30-40      0        1
40-50      0        1
_____    _____    _____
```

11. Display the table shown in Problem 10. Then allow the user to make selective changes in the count and weight columns. Whatever dialogue you set up between the user and the computer, be sure to cause an orderly exit from the program when the user indicates that all desired changes have been made.

■ 7.11 Review True-or-False Quiz

1. A semicolon in a PRINT statement always causes a separation of at least one space between the items being displayed.   **T   F**

2. If you want to suppress the RETURN following execution of a PRINT statement, you must end the PRINT statement with a semicolon.   **T   F**

3. If commas are used to separate numerical output expressions in PRINT statements, columns will not necessarily be aligned according to decimal points.   **T   F**

4. To display a string centered on an output line, you must use the TAB function.   **T   F**

5. The two program statements

```
50 PRINT
51 PRINT "1";TAB(5);"5"
```

will cause the digits 1 and 5 to be displayed in column positions 1 and 5, respectively.   **T   F**

6. The statement

```
60 PRINT "GOOD";TAB(6);"GRIEF"
```

will always cause the same output as the statement

```
60 PRINT "GOOD GRIEF"
```
   T   F

7. The PRINT USING statement allows you to include an "image" of how you wish an output line to be formatted.   **T   F**

8. The program segment

```
10 LET X=123
20 LET F$="VALUE:####.###"
30 PRINT USING F$,X
```

will cause the display

```
VALUE:0123.000
```

(Assume F$;X in line 30 if your system requires it.)   **T   F**

9. If F$="A#", the statement

```
50 PRINT USING F$,1,2,3
```

will cause the display

```
A1A2A3
```

(Assume F$;1,2,3 in line 50 if your system requires it.)   **T   F**

10. If F$="!!!" and A$="ABC", the statement

```
60 PRINT USING F$,A$,A$,A$
```

will cause the display

```
AAA
```

(Assume F$;A$,A$,A$ in line 60 if your system requires it.)   **T   F**

11. Any program that performs several tasks is a menu-driven program.   **T   F**

12. A PRINT statement causes a pure cursor move.   **T   F**

8 The Computer as a Decision Maker

All of the programs shown in the preceding chapters share a common characteristic. In each program, the computations performed on data do not depend on the particular data values but are the same whatever these values are. For instance, to calculate the weekly gross salary W of a person who works H hours at an hourly rate of R dollars, we used the statement

```
LET W=H*R
```

(See Example 3 of Section 6.1.) In practice, however, you would take overtime into consideration and use a different formula should the overtime rate apply. If time and a half is paid for hours over 32, an appropriate LET statement for hours over 32 would be

```
LET W=32*R+(H-32)*(1.5*R)
```

It is in this sense that a computer makes *decisions*. You code the program so that the computer tests a condition (in this case, H <= 32) and selects one of two alternative actions depending on whether the condition is true or false.

In BASIC, the principal decision-making tool is the IF statement. Sections 8.1 and 8.2 describe the various forms of the IF statement allowed in BASIC and illustrate how they are used to transform the computer into a decision maker. Section 8.4 shows how a flowchart (pictorial representation of an algorithm) can clarify the logic of a program and how flowcharting can help you design algorithms.

Section 8.6 reviews the loop structure and its application to the repetitive process of summing. In Section 8.8 we consider the general structure of algorithms, discuss what is meant by a structured program, and discuss some of the benefits derived from writing structured programs.

■ 8.1 IF as a Selection Statement

In Chapter 6 we used the form

> IF *condition* THEN **ln**

to code loops. We now show how this and other forms of the IF statement are used to execute BASIC statements or groups of BASIC statements selectively.

EXAMPLE 1   **Here is a program to display 6% of any input value, but only if the input value is positive.**

```
100 PRINT "AMOUNT";
110 INPUT A
120 IF A>0 THEN PRINT "TAX:";0.06*A
130 END
RUN

AMOUNT? 43
TAX IS 2.58
```

After a value for A is input, the condition $A > 0$ in line 120 is tested. If it is true, the PRINT statement following the keyword THEN is executed. If it is false, the PRINT statement is not executed. In either case, control passes to the next line, which in this example is an END statement.

■ **REMARK**   Using only the form of the IF statement described in Chapter 6, we could code line 120 in the following equivalent way:

```
120 IF A<=0 THEN 130
125 PRINT "TAX:";0.06
```

The single-line form is more desirable because it is more readable. It reads, "If A is greater than zero, print the tax." The two-line form reads, "If A is less than or equal to zero, skip the line that prints the tax."

Line 120 of Example 1 illustrates the following form of the IF statement:

IF *condition* THEN *statement*

If the statement that follows the keyword THEN is a GOTO statement, you can omit the keyword GOTO. Thus, the following are equivalent:

IF *condition* THEN GOTO **ln**
IF *conditon* THEN **ln**

The next example shows that the statement that follows the keyword THEN does not have to be a PRINT or GOTO statement. It can, in fact, be any BASIC statement.

EXAMPLE 2   **Here is a program to count how many of three input values are greater than the average of all three.**

```
100 REM****A SIMPLE COUNTING PROGRAM****
110 REM    X, Y, AND Z DENOTE THE INPUT VALUES.
120 REM    A DENOTES THEIR AVERAGE.
130 REM    C COUNTS INPUT VALUES THAT EXCEED A.
140 PRINT "ENTER THREE NUMBERS."
150 INPUT X,Y,Z
160 LET A=(X+Y+Z)/3
170 REM***BEGIN COUNTING***
180 LET C=0
190 IF X>A THEN LET C=C+1
200 IF Y>A THEN LET C=C+1
210 IF Z>A THEN LET C=C+1
220 PRINT "AVERAGE:";A
230 PRINT "COUNT OF INPUT VALUES THAT EXCEED AVERAGE:";C
240 END
RUN

ENTER THREE NUMBERS.
? 79,70,85
AVERAGE: 78
COUNT OF INPUT VALUES THAT EXCEED AVERAGE: 2
```

Lines 140–160 accept input values for X, Y, and Z and assign their average to A. For the input values shown, $(79 + 70 + 85)/3 = 78$ is assigned to A. Line 180 sets the counter C to zero. The condition $X > A$ in the first IF statement is true, so the statement LET $C = C + 1$ is executed, and C becomes 1. The condition $Y > A$ is false, so the statement LET $C = C + 1$ in line 200 is skipped. The condition $Z > A$ is true, so the statement LET $C = C + 1$ in the third IF statement is executed to give $C = 2$. Finally, the PRINT statements cause the output shown.

■ **REMARK 1**   The first time the statement LET $C = C + 1$ is executed, it increases the value of C from 0 to 1; the second time from 1 to 2. Thus, the statement LET $C = C + 1$ actually does the counting. The use of such "counting" statements is widespread in computer programming.

■ **REMARK 2**   Since the keyword LET is optional, we could have written lines 190–210 as follows:

```
190 IF X>A THEN C=C+1
200 IF Y>A THEN C=C+1
210 IF Z>A THEN C=C+1
```

Thus far we have used two forms of the IF statement:

> IF *condition* THEN **ln**
> IF *condition* THEN *statement*

Many versions of BASIC allow more general forms of the IF statement. In the next example we illustrate the following useful and widely implemented form:

> IF *condition* THEN *statement1* ELSE *statement2*

This is called an IF–THEN–ELSE statement. In this form, *statement1* is executed if the condition is true, and *statement2* is executed if the condition is false. Thus, exactly one of the two statements will be executed. Control then passes to the next line unless the statement executed (*statement1* or *statement2*) causes a jump to another line. If either of the two statements is a GOTO statement, you can omit the keyword GOTO.

EXAMPLE 3   **Here is an illustration of the IF-THEN-ELSE statement.**

```
10 PRINT "ENTER A NON-ZERO NUMBER."
20 INPUT X
30 IF X=0 THEN 10
40 IF X>0 THEN PRINT "POSITIVE" ELSE PRINT "NEGATIVE"
50 END
```

If the input value X is 0, line 30 transfers control back to line 10, and you must type another value for X. Thus, this program "ignores" any zeros that are input.

If X is not 0, control passes to the IF–THEN–ELSE statement in line 40. If the condition $X > 0$ is true, the statement following the keyword THEN is executed, causing POSITIVE to be displayed. If the condition $X > 0$ is false, the statement following the keyword ELSE is executed, causing the word NEGATIVE to be displayed.

■ **REMARK 1**   If your system does not allow the IF-THEN-ELSE statement, you can code line 40 by using two lines as follows:

```
40 IF X>0 THEN PRINT "POSITIVE"
45 IF X<0 THEN PRINT "NEGATIVE"
```

■ **REMARK 2**   The input prompt ENTER A NON-ZERO NUMBER. does not prevent the user from typing 0 as a value for X. But if the user does, line 30 rejects 0 as an input value. If line 30 is omitted and the user types 0 for X, the condition $X > 0$ in line 40 will be false, and the word NEGATIVE will be displayed. But 0 is not a negative number. With line 30 included, this won't happen. You should always make an effort to design your programs to prevent incorrect input data from influencing results.

■ REMARK 3   The loop in lines 10–30 can be coded as a WHILE loop, as follows:

```
10 LET X=1          'Force a pass through the loop.
15 WHILE X<>0
20    PRINT "ENTER A NON-ZERO NUMBER."
25    INPUT X
30 NEXT  (or WEND)
```

The IF-THEN-ELSE statement in line 40 of Example 3 requires the execution of a single statement (PRINT "POSITIVE") if the condition is true and a single statement (PRINT "NEGATIVE") if the condition is false. Very often, however, programming problems require the selective execution of not one of two single program statements but one of two program segments. Suppose, for example, that you must carry out Task 1 if a condition is true and Task 2 if the condition is false. However simple or complicated the tasks might be, you can always code the selection as follows (the line numbers are for illustration only):

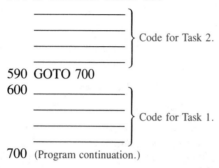

500 IF *condition* THEN 600

⎫
⎬ Code for Task 2.
⎭

590 GOTO 700

600 ⎫
    ⎬ Code for Task 1.
    ⎭

700 (Program continuation.)

This method is used in the next example.

■ EXAMPLE 4   **Let's write a program to count how many input values are positive and how many are negative and also to find the sum of the positive numbers and the sum of the negative numbers. The input value 0 will mean that all numbers have been typed.**

PROBLEM ANALYSIS

The input and output for this problem are as follows:

Input: A list of numbers terminated by 0.

Output: Two counts and two sums as specified in the problem statement.

Counting and summing problems are not new to us. The following algorithm describes one way to carry out the specified task. To keep the algorithm as short as possible, let's use variable names for the quantities of interest.

X = the value being input
CP = the number of positive values
SP = the sum of the positive values
CN = the number of negative values
SN = the sum of the negative values

THE ALGORITHM

a. Set CP, SP, CN, and SN to zero.
b. Input X.
c. While $X \neq 0$ do the following:
   c1. If $X > 0$, add X to SP and 1 to CP. Otherwise, add X to SN and 1 to CN.
   c2. Input X.
d. Display the results and stop.

■ REMARK

In the program we code Step (c1) as follows:

```
180 IF X < 0 THEN 230
190    REM---HANDLE POSITIVE VALUE---
200    LET SP=SP+X
210    LET CP=CP+1
220 GOTO 260
230    REM---HANDLE NEGATIVE VALUE---
240    LET SN=SN+X
250    LET CN=CN+1
```

Your version of BASIC may allow you to code Step (c1) more concisely. The extended forms of the IF statement that make this possible are described following this example.

THE
PROGRAM

```
100 REM *******A COUNTING AND SUMMING PROGRAM*******
110 LET CP=0      'Count of positive values
120 LET CN=0      'Count of negative values
130 LET SP=0      'Sum of positive values
140 LET SN=0      'Sum of negative values
150 PRINT "ENTER NUMBERS, ONE PER LINE - TYPE 0 WHEN DONE."
160 INPUT X
170 WHILE X<>0
180    IF X<0 THEN 230
190       REM---HANDLE POSITIVE VALUE---
200       LET SP=SP+X
210       LET CP=CP+1
220    GOTO 260
230       REM---HANDLE NEGATIVE VALUE---
240       LET SN=SN+X
250       LET CN=CN+1
260    INPUT X
270 NEXT     (or WEND)
280 PRINT "POSITIVE COUNT:";CP
290 PRINT "POSITIVE SUM:   ";SP
300 PRINT "NEGATIVE COUNT:";CN
310 PRINT "NEGATIVE SUM:   ";SN
320 END
RUN

ENTER NUMBERS, ONE PER LINE - TYPE 0 WHEN DONE.
? 23
? -15
? -29
? 10
? 7
? 0
POSITIVE COUNT: 3
POSITIVE SUM:    40
NEGATIVE COUNT: 2
NEGATIVE SUM:   -44
```

Some versions of BASIC allow you to write IF statements with more than one statement following the keywords THEN and ELSE. The most general form of the IF statement is

IF *condition* THEN *clause* [ELSE *clause*]

where *clause* denotes one or more statements separated by colons(:) or on some systems by backslash characters (\). The part in brackets is optional. If the *condition* is true, the statements immediately following the keyword THEN (the THEN *clause*) are executed. If the *condition* is false, the ELSE *clause*, if present, is executed.

Since the number of characters a screen or printer can display on a single line is limited, you will have to use more than one line when typing long programming lines. How this is done depends on the system being used. Here are two commonly used methods.

1. (Many personal computers use this method.) You simply keep typing when you reach the end of a display line—the computer will automatically continue the display to the next line. When the entire statement has been typed, you enter it by pressing the RETURN key. Typically, you can press up to 255 keys while entering a long programming line. Thus, if your BASIC system allows the general form of the IF–THEN–ELSE statement, you can replace lines 180–250 of the preceding program with the single programming line

```
180 IF X>0 THEN SP=SP+X : CP=CP+1
        ELSE SN=SN+X : CN=CN+1
```

After typing CP = CP + 1, simply press the space bar until the cursor moves to the desired position on the next line. If your system does not allow ELSE, you can use two IF statements:

```
180 IF X>0 THEN SP=SP+X : CP=CP+1
190 IF X<0 THEN SN=SN+X : CN=CN+1
```

2. (This method is used with Vax BASIC and BASIC–PLUS.) You include an ampersand (&) as the last character of a display line to indicate that the next display line is a continuation of the programming line being typed. These two versions of BASIC allow you to include a comment at the end of each display line but before any &. Vax BASIC allows the most general form of the IF–THEN–ELSE statement, so you can replace lines 180–250 of the program in Example 4 with

```
180 IF X>0 THEN                                         &
        LET SP=SP+X   !X IS POSITIVE                    &
        \LET CP=CP+1   !INCREASE POSITIVE COUNT         &
     ELSE                                               &
        LET SN=SN+X   !X IS NEGATIVE                     &
        \LET CN=CN+1   !INCREASE NEGATIVE COUNT
```

The last line does not end with & since the IF–THEN–ELSE statement does not continue on the next line. BASIC–PLUS does not allow the most general form of the IF–THEN–ELSE statement. It does, however, allow these limited forms:

IF *condition* THEN *clause*
IF *condition* THEN *statement* ELSE *clause*

Thus, in BASIC–PLUS you could use the following:

```
180 IF X>0 THEN                                         &
        LET SP=SP+X   !ADD TO POSITIVE SUM              &
        \LET CP=CP+1   !INCREASE POSITIVE COUNT
190 IF X<0 THEN                                         &
        LET SN=SN+X   !ADD TO NEGATIVE SUM              &
        \LET CN=CN+1   !INCREASE NEGATIVE COUNT
```

■ 8.2 Logical Expressions

A **logical expression** is an expression that is either *true* or *false*. The relational expressions encountered in the preceding sections are either true or false; hence they are logical expressions. BASIC allows you to write *compound* logical expressions by using the logical operators AND, OR, and NOT. These are best illustrated by example.

EXAMPLE 5   **Here are illustrations of the logical operators AND, OR, and NOT.**

a. The logical expression

```
C$="YES" OR C$="NO"
```

is true if either of the relational expressions C$ = "YES" and C$ = "NO" is true. Thus, the given logical expression is true if C$ has the string value YES or the string value NO; otherwise it is false.

b. The logical expression

```
A<B AND B<C
```

is true if *both* of the relational expressions A < B and B < C are true; otherwise, it is false. Thus, if X has the value 3, the expression 2 < X AND X < 5 is true; if X has the value 6, the expression 2 < X AND X < 5 is false.

c. The logical expression

```
A<B OR A<C
```

is true if *either* or *both* of the relational expressions are true. Thus, the given expression is true if A is less than B, if A is less than C, or if A is less than both B and C. You should verify that this expression is true only if the expression

```
A>=B AND A>=C
```

is false.

d. The logical expression

```
NOT (A<B)
```

is true if the relational expression A < B is *not* true: otherwise it is false. Note that the given expression NOT (A < B) is equivalent to the relational expression A >= B. By equivalent, we mean that for any values of A and B, the expressions are both true or both false.

■ **REMARK** In many versions of BASIC, the logical operator NOT has a higher priority than any of the relational operators =, <, >, <>, <= , and >=. The parentheses in Part (d) are included to ensure that the computer first determines the truth value of the expression A < B and then applies the logical operator NOT to this truth value. The logical operators AND and OR, however, have a lower priority than the relational operators. Hence, parentheses are not needed in Parts (a)–(c).

CAUTION In many versions of BASIC seemingly meaningless expressions such as (NOT A) < B, (A < B) < C, and A OR B have meaning—they do not contain syntax errors. The meaning and application of such expressions are beyond the scope of this introductory book. We mention the topic only to caution you. For example, if you write NOT A < B when you should have written NOT (A < B), your program may seem to run correctly, but it will probably produce incorrect results.

In Tables 8.1–8.3 we give precise definitions of the logical operators AND, OR, and NOT. In each table **le₁** and **le₂** denote logical expressions.

Table 8.1 The AND operator

le₁	le₂	(le₁)AND(le₂)
true	true	true
true	false	false
false	true	false
false	false	false

Table 8.2 The OR operator

le₁	le₂	(le₁)OR(le₂)
true	true	true
true	false	true
false	true	true
false	false	false

Table 8.3 The NOT operator

le₁	NOT(le₁)
true	false
false	true

EXAMPLE 6

The following illustrate typical uses of logical expressions containing the AND and OR operators.

a. The statement

```
IF A>0 AND B>0 THEN 200
```

will transfer control to line 200 if both A and B are positive. Otherwise, control passes to the line following the IF statement.

b. The statement

```
IF G>=80 AND G<=89 THEN PRINT "B"
```

will cause the letter B to be displayed only if the value of G is between 80 and 89, inclusive.

c. The statement

```
IF G<80 OR G>89 THEN 300
```

will cause a transfer to line 300 only if G is not between 80 and 89, inclusive.

d. If your system allows lowercase letters, the statement

```
IF C$="Y" OR C$="y" THEN 500
```

will transfer control to line 500 if C$ is either Y or y.

A logical expression may contain more than one of the operators NOT, AND, and OR. For example, an expression such as

```
M=0 OR A<B AND A<C
```

is admissible. The order in which the OR and AND operators are carried out, however, matters. For instance, if M has the value 0, the expression

```
M=0 OR (M<5 AND M>1)
```

is true, whereas the expression

```
(M=0 OR M<5) AND M>1
```

is false. If parentheses are not included, BASIC uses the following priorities:

Logical operator	Priority
NOT	highest
AND	intermediate
OR	lowest

In any logical expression, the order in which the logical operators are performed is determined first by the indicated priority and then, in any priority class, from left to right. As with arithmetic expressions, parentheses may be used to override this order or simply to clarify what order is intended. Thus, the logical expression

```
M=0 OR A<B AND A<C
```

is equivalent to the expression

```
M=0 OR (A<B AND A<C)
```

If you want the OR to be performed first, you must use parentheses and write

```
(M=0 OR A<B) AND A<C
```

EXAMPLE 7 **Here is a program to input four numbers and display IN ORDER if they are in increasing order, and NOT IN ORDER if they are not.**

```
10 INPUT A,B,C,D
20 IF A<B AND B<C AND C<D THEN PRINT "IN ORDER"
   ELSE PRINT "NOT IN ORDER"
30 END
```

If your system does not allow ELSE, you can write

```
10 INPUT A,B,C,D
20 IF NOT (A<B AND B<C AND C<D) THEN PRINT "NOT";
30 PRINT " IN ORDER"
40 END
```

This short example illustrates the importance of being able to make more than one comparison in an IF statement. The program was easy to code and is quite easy to read. As an exercise, we suggest that you write a program for the specified task, but making only single comparisons in IF statements. However you do this, your program will be more complicated than the one shown, and probably much more difficult to read.

■ 8.3 Problems

1. If A = 1, B = 2, and C = 3, which of the following logical expressions are true?
   a. A<B OR A>C
   b. A<C AND A+B=C
   c. (A>B OR B>C) AND C=3
   d. A=B OR 2*B-1=C
   e. NOT (A>B OR C>A)
   f. NOT (A>B) OR NOT (C>A)
   g. NOT (A>B) AND NOT (C>A)

2. Correct the following programs:
   a.
   ```
   10 REM TELL WHETHER AN INPUT VALUE
   20 REM IS POSITIVE OR NEGATIVE.
   30 INPUT N
   40 IF N>0 THEN PRINT "POSITIVE"
   50 GOTO 70
   60 IF N<0 THEN PRINT "NEGATIVE"
   70 END
   ```
   b.
   ```
   10 REM DISPLAY OK IF THE INPUT
   20 REM VALUE IS EITHER 7 OR 11.
   30 INPUT R
   40 IF R=7 OR 11 THEN PRINT OK
   50 END
   ```
   c.
   ```
   10 REM DISPLAY BETWEEN IF THE INPUT VALUE
   20 REM IS BETWEEN 2 AND 8, EXCLUSIVE.
   30 INPUT Y
   40 IF 2<Y<8 THEN PRINT "BETWEEN"
   50 END
   ```
   d.
   ```
   10 REM DISPLAY OK IF THE INPUT VALUE
   20 REM IS FROM 0 TO 100, BUT NOT 50.
   30 INPUT X
   40 IF X>=0 AND X<=100 OR X<>50 THEN PRINT "OK"
   50 END
   ```

3. Show the output of each of the following programs:
   a.
   ```
   10 LET A=3
   20 LET B=A
   30 LET C=(A+B)/B
   40 LET D=B/A-C
   50 IF D>=0 THEN D=13
   60 PRINT D
   70 END
   ```
   b.
   ```
   10 LET A=5
   20 LET B=-A
   30 IF A+B<>0 THEN 60
   40 LET A=-B
   50 PRINT A
   60 PRINT B
   70 END
   ```

```
c. 10 LET A$="JONES"
   20 LET B$="SMITH"
   30 LET C$=B$
   40 LET B$=A$
   50 LET A$=C$
   60 PRINT "THAT'S ALL"
   70 IF B$=C$ THEN PRINT B$
   80 IF C$=A$ THEN PRINT C$
   90 END
d. 10 LET S=5
   20 LET J=3
   30 IF S<7 AND J>10 THEN PRINT J
   40 LET J=S+J
   50 IF S+J<15 THEN PRINT S ELSE PRINT J
   60 PRINT "THAT'S ALL"
   70 END
e. 10 LET L=22
   20 WHILE L<40 OR L>60
   30    IF L<40 THEN LET L=L+50
   40    IF L>60 THEN LET L=L-10
   50 NEXT (or WEND)
   60 PRINT L
   70 END
```

In Problems 4–20, write a program to perform each task specified. Be sure to write each program so that the user can try any number of input values during a single program run.

4. Two numbers A and B are to be typed. If the first is larger, display LARGER; otherwise, display NOT LARGER.

5. Two numbers M and N are to be typed. If the sum equals 5, display 5; otherwise display NOT 5.

6. Two numbers X and Y are to be typed. If the product is less than or equal to the quotient, display PRODUCT; otherwise display QUOTIENT.

7. Three numbers are to be typed. If the second is less than the sum of the first and third, display LESS; otherwise display NOT LESS.

8. A person earns R dollars an hour with time and a half for all hours over 32. Determine the gross pay for a T-hour week.

9. The cost of sending a telegram is $1.35 for the first 10 words and 9¢ for each additional word. Find the cost if the number of words is input.

10. If the wholesale cost of an item is under $100, the markup is 20%. Otherwise the markup is 30%. Determine the retail price for an item whose wholesale cost is given.

11. A finance charge is added each month to the outstanding balance on all credit card accounts at Knox Department Store. If the outstanding balance is not greater than $33 the finance charge is 50¢; otherwise, it is 1.5% of the outstanding balance. Find the finance charge if the outstanding balance is input.

12. A number is to be typed. If it is between 7 and 35 inclusive, display BETWEEN. If it is less than 7, increase it by 5; if it is greater than 35, decrease it by 5. In either case, display the value obtained and check to see if this new value is between 7 and 35. Repeat the process until BETWEEN is displayed. Don't forget to allow the user to try several input values during a single program run.

13. For any two numbers M and N, display POSITIVE if both are positive and NEGATIVE if both are negative. Otherwise, display NEITHER.

14. For any three numbers input, display ALL NEGATIVE if all are negative, ALL POSITIVE if all are positive, and NEITHER in all other cases.

15. Using the information in the following table, find the tax due for a single taxpayer whose taxable income I is less than $89,560.

Taxable Income I	Tax due
$0 < I \le 17{,}850$	15% of I
$17{,}850 < I \le 43{,}150$	2677.50 + 28% of (I − 17,850)
$43{,}150 < I \le 89{,}560$	9761.50 + 33% of (I − 43,150)

16. Display the largest of the four input values N1, N2, N3, and N4.

17. Change Fahrenheit temperatures to Celsius and Celsius temperatures to Fahrenheit. Enter a letter (F or C to indicate the given scale) and a temperature, and then change this temperature to the other scale [F = (9/5)C + 32].

18. Determine the final checkbook balance given the beginning balance and a list of transactions, either deposits to the account or checks drawn on the account. Each transaction is to be entered by typing a letter and a number. The letter D indicates a deposit, C a check, and X that the final transaction has been entered; the number entered is the amount of the transaction. If the account becomes overdrawn, display an appropriate message and continue program execution. Typing X should be the only means of stopping program execution.

19. A menu-driven program is desired that will allow students to practice addition, multiplication, or taking powers. If addition is chosen, have the computer prompt the student for two numbers and then ask for their sum. If the correct answer is typed, have the computer say so. If the answer is not correct, display the correct answer. In either case, allow the student to try another addition or to return to the menu. Handle multiplication (of two numbers) the same way. If the student chooses to practice powers, have the computer ask for a number whose powers are to be found. If the student types 3, have the computer display, in order,

```
WHAT IS 3 TO THE POWER 2?
WHAT IS 3 TO THE POWER 3?
WHAT IS 3 TO THE POWER 4?
        .
        .
        .
WHAT IS 3 TO THE POWER 10?
```

Ask each question only if the previous answer is correct. If an answer is incorrect, display the correct answer. Congratulate a student successful to high powers, perhaps in a way reflective of how high the power. In any case, allow the student to try powers of another number or to return to the menu.

20. First write a menu-driven program as described in Problem 19. Then add an option to allow the student to practice summing any three numbers.

■ 8.4 Flowcharts and Flowcharting

The following diagram is a pictorial representation of a simple algorithm to recognize whether or not an input value is 5.

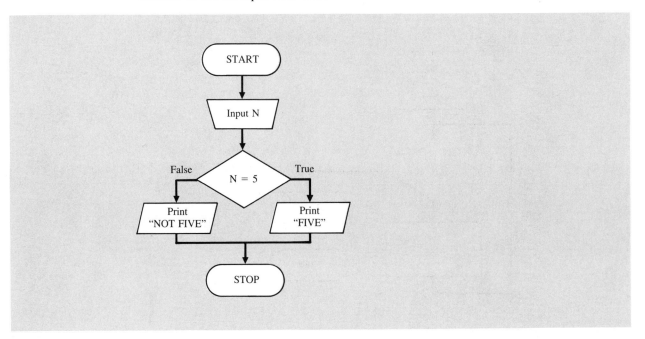

Such a pictorial representation of the sequence of steps in an algorithm or a program is called a **programming flowchart,** or simply a **flowchart.** Flowcharts are useful for program documentation. In addition, it is often easier to prepare a pictorial description of a process to be followed than to attempt a detailed description in words. The flowchart is an excellent way to do this. Some of the components used to construct flowcharts can be seen in the following examples.

EXAMPLE 8   **Here are two equivalent flowcharts for a program to display the numbers 100, 110, 120, . . . , 200.**

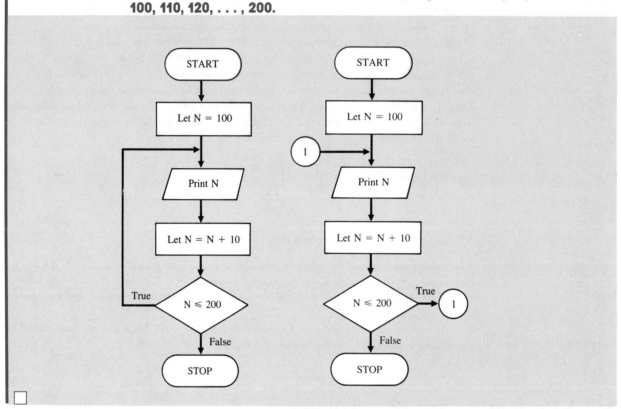

EXAMPLE 9   **Here is a flowchart displaying the process of adding the integers from 1 to 10.**

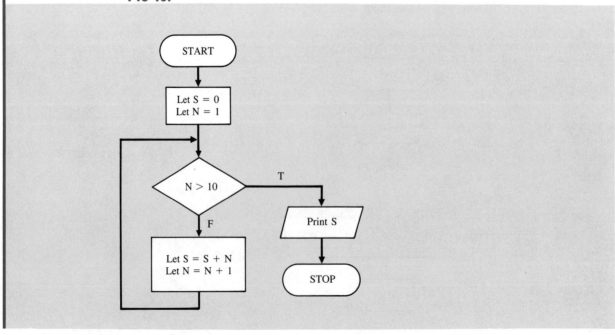

■ REMARK 1   When two or more statements are included in a single box they are carried out from top to bottom.

■ REMARK 2   Note that we have labeled the flow lines from the diamond-shaped decision symbol with the letters T and F for true and false, respectively.

In these examples, arrows connecting six different types of symbols are used to describe the sequence of steps in an algorithm. When possible, the flow should be directed from top to bottom or from left to right, as was done in the examples. Although there are many flowchart symbols in use,* the six shown here are adequate for displaying the flow of instructions for many BASIC programs. A brief description of how these symbols are used is given in Table 8.4.

We conclude this section with two examples illustrating the process of flowcharting—that is, of designing flowcharts. Once a flowchart is prepared, the task of writing the program is reasonably routine; it consists only of coding the steps indicated in the flowchart.

Table 8.4 Flowchart symbols

The symbol	Its use
⬭	To designate the start and end of a program
⬟	To describe data to be entered at the keyboard
▱	To describe the output
▭	To describe any processing of data
◇	To designate a decision that is to be made
○	A connector—used so that flow from one segment of a flowchart to another can be displayed and also to avoid drawing long lines

EXAMPLE 10   **Construct a flowchart to find the largest number in a list of input values. The special value 9999 is to be typed to indicate that all numbers in the list have been entered.**

One way to determine the largest number in a list is to read the numbers one at a time, remembering only the largest of those already read. (This method was illustrated and discussed in Chapter 2, Example 2.) To help us give a precise description of this process, let's use the following variable names:

L = largest of those numbers already read
N = the number currently being read

---

*Flowchart symbols as proposed by the American National Standards Institute (ANSI) are described in "Flowcharting with the ANSI Standard: A Tutorial," by Ned Chapin, *Computer Surveys,* Vol. 2, No. 2, June 1970.

It is not difficult to construct a flowchart describing an algorithm for this task. First, we must input the first number and assign it to L. Thus, we can begin with the following flowchart segment:

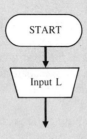

The next step is to input another value and compare it with 9999 to determine if the end of the input list has been reached. To display this step, we can add the following to our partial flowchart:

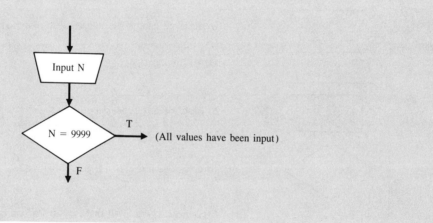

If N = 9999 (the *True* branch), we simply display L, the largest number, and stop. Thus, we can complete the T (*True*) branch by adding the following to our partial flowchart:

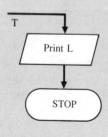

Note that while constructing the flowchart (that is, while discovering an algorithm), we always have a partial flowchart in front of us to help us decide what the next step should be.

As we continue this process of flowchart construction, a flowchart such as the following will emerge:

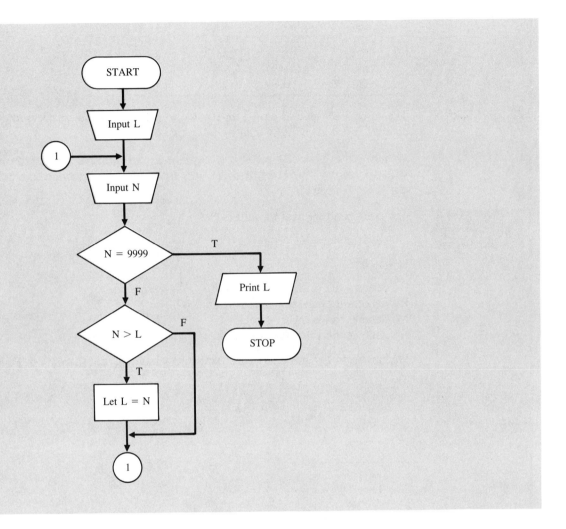

Here is one way to code this flowchart:

```
100 PRINT "AFTER EACH ? ENTER A NUMBER."
110 PRINT "WHEN FINISHED TYPE 9999."
120 INPUT L
130 INPUT N
140 WHILE N<>9999
150     IF N>L THEN L=N
160     INPUT N
170 NEXT (or WEND)
180 PRINT "LARGEST NUMBER ENTERED:";L
190 END
```

The following table summarizes the values of the variables when this program is run with the input list

8,3,9,2,9999

Line Number	N	L	Output
120	—	8	
130	3	8	
160	9	8	
150	9	9	
160	2	9	
160	9999	9	
180	9999	9	9

■
□ **REMARK**

The value 9999 used as a final input value to indicate that all numbers in the list have been entered is called an **EOD** (end of data) **tag.**

EXAMPLE 11

Construct a flowchart for a program to determine the number of years required for an investment of $1,000 earning 7.5% compounded annually to double in value.

PROBLEM ANALYSIS

The compound interest formula is

$$A = P(1 + R)^N$$

in which

P   denotes the principal (P = 1000)
R   denotes the rate per period (R = 0.075)
N   denotes the number of periods
A   denotes the value for N periods

We can begin our flowchart construction by assigning initial values to P, R, and N:

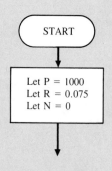

Next, we must compare the value of A after 1 year wth 2P. Since N denotes the number of years that have passed, we can add the following to our partial flowchart:

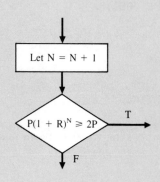

If the condition is true, we simply display N and stop. If it is false, we increase N by 1 and repeat the comparison. Adding these two steps to the partial flowchart we obtain the following complete algorithm.

THE FLOWCHART

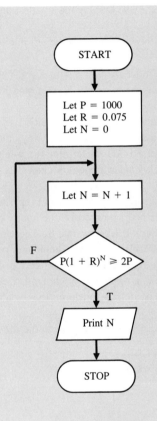

THE PROGRAM

```
100 LET P=1000
110 LET R=0.075
120 LET N=0
130    LET N=N+1
140 IF P*(1+R)^N<2*P THEN 130
150 PRINT "NUMBER OF YEARS TO DOUBLE:";N
160 END
RUN

NUMBER OF YEARS TO DOUBLE: 10
```

To code the loop in lines 130–140 as a WHILE loop, you can make these changes:

```
120 LET N=1
125 WHILE P*(1+R)^N<2*P
130    LET N=N+1
140 NEXT  (or WEND)
```

■ 8.5 Problems

In Problems 1–11, prepare a flowchart and then a program to accomplish each task specified. Try to avoid GOTO statements in your programs.

1. Input one number. If it is between 3 and 21, display BETWEEN. Otherwise, display NOT BETWEEN.

2. Input two numbers. If either one is positive, display EITHER. Otherwise, display NEITHER.
3. Input three distinct numbers. If the first is the largest, display LARGEST. Otherwise, display NOT LARGEST.
4. Input three distinct numbers. If the second is the largest, display LARGEST. If it is the smallest, display SMALLEST. Otherwise, display NEITHER.
5. Input two values A and B. Display the value 1 if A and B are both 0 or both 1. Display the value 0 in all other cases.
6. Input a list of numbers whose last value is 9999. Display the smallest and largest values in the list excluding the 9999.
7. Input a list of numbers whose last value is 9999. Display the largest number and a count of how many numbers are included in the list.
8. Several pairs (X, Y) of numbers are to be input. Any pair with X = Y serves as the EOD tag. Determine and display counts of how many pairs satisfy X < Y and how many pairs satisfy X > Y.
9. Each salesperson earns a base weekly salary of $185. In addition, if a salesperson's total weekly sales exceed $1,000, a commission of 5.3% is earned on any amount up to $5,000 and 7.8% is earned on any amount in excess of $5,000. Determine the weekly pay, before deductions, for any salesperson whose total weekly sales amount is input. Use an EOD tag to terminate the program.
10. A company payroll clerk needs a computer program to assist in preparing the weekly payroll. For each employee the clerk is to enter the hours worked H, the hourly pay rate R, the federal tax rate F, the state tax rate S, and the Social Security rate T. The clerk needs to know the gross pay, the net pay, and the amount of each deduction. Employees receive time and a half for each hour worked over 40 hours. (The algorithm should not be too detailed. For example, after H, R, F, S, and T have been called for, a single line might read "Determine the gross pay, the three deductions, and the net pay." The details for doing this would then be worked out during the flowchart construction.)
11. A salesperson's monthly commission is determined according to the following schedule:

Net Sales	Commission rate
Up to $10,000	6%
Next $4,000	7%
Next $6,000	8%
Additional amounts	10%

Determine the monthly commission given the total monthly sales.

■ 8.6 Summing as a Repetitive Process

As a programmer you will often encounter problems whose solutions require you to find the sum of many numbers. Since summing is a repetitive process, it is most conveniently done in a loop that terminates only after the required sum has been obtained. The examples in this section illustrate two ways to exit from a loop:

1. Before the loop is initiated, specify the exact number of terms to be added (Example 12).
2. Cause an exit from the loop when some prescribed condition has been satisfied (Example 13).

EXAMPLE 12

Construct a flowchart and write a program to evaluate the sum

$$S = 1^2 + 2^2 + 3^3 + \cdots + N^2$$

where N is to be specified by the user. If the input value N is less than 1, display the sum S = 0.

PROBLEM ANALYSIS

A simple algorithm for this task is as follows.

 a. Input N.
 b. Calculate the sum $S = 1^2 + 2^2 + \cdots + N^2$.
 c. Display S and stop.

To carry out Step (b), you can start with a sum S of 0 and add the squares of the numbers 1, 2, 3, . . . , N to S, one at a time. The following flowchart describes this process:

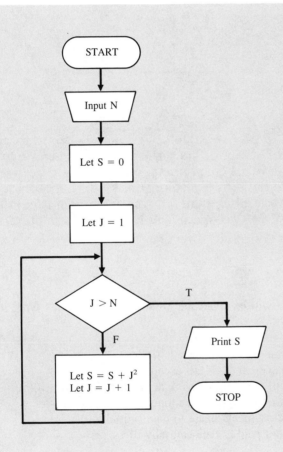

THE PROGRAM

```
100 PRINT "HOW MANY SQUARES SHOULD BE ADDED";
110 INPUT N
120 LET S=0
130 LET J=1
140 WHILE J<=N
150   LET S=S+J^2
160   LET J=J+1
170 NEXT  (or WEND)
180 PRINT "SUM:";S
190 END
RUN

HOW MANY SQUARES SHOULD BE ADDED? 5
SUM: 55
```

The following table traces the values of N, S, and J as the program is executed with the input value of N = 5:

110	5	—	—	
120	5	0	—	
130	5	0	1	
150	5	1	1	
160	5	1	2	
150	5	5	2	
160	5	5	3	
150	5	14	3	
160	5	14	4	
150	5	30	4	
160	5	30	5	
150	5	55	5	
160	5	55	6	
180	5	55	6	SUM:55

EXAMPLE 13   **A person wishes to borrow $1,000 but can only afford to pay back $40 per month. A loan officer at the bank states that such a loan is possible at an interest rate of 1.2% per month on the unpaid balance. Write a program to compute the total number of payments, the amount of the final payment, and the total amount the borrower must pay to the bank. (Assume that the first $40 payment is to be made 1 month after the date of the loan.)**

PROBLEM ANALYSIS

So that the program will be applicable to any problem of this type, let's assign the variables as follows:

R = the monthly rate of interest (R = .012).
P = the monthly payment (P = 40 except for last payment).
B = the balance still owed to the bank at any time (initially 1000).
I = the interest due for the previous month (I = B * R).
N = the number of payments made to date (initially 0).
T = the total amount paid to date (initially 0).

At the end of each month, the bank calculates the new balance as follows. The interest I = B * R for the month is added to the old balance (LET B = B + I). If this balance B is at least as great as P, the monthly payment is the regular monthly payment P ($40). If B is less than P, however, the monthly payment—the final one—is B dollars. We'll use the statement

```
IF B<P THEN P=B
```

so that the current payment is always denoted by P. In either case, the payment P is subtracted from B to give the new balance, 1 is added to N since 1 month has passed, and the current payment P is added to the total T of all payments. This process is repeated as long as the new balance B is greater than 0.

THE FLOWCHART

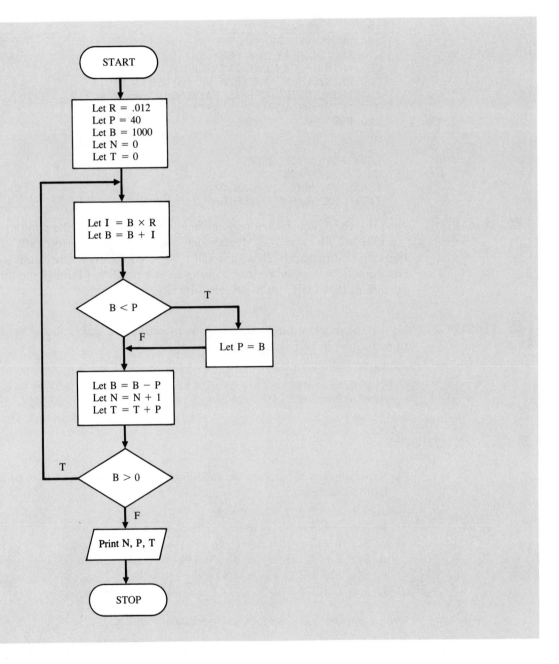

THE PROGRAM

```
100 REM INITIALIZE VARIABLES.
110 LET R=0.012
120 LET P=40
130 LET B=1000
140 LET T=0
150 LET N=0
160 WHILE B>.001
170     REM ADD INTEREST TO OLD BALANCE.
180     LET I=B*R
190     LET B=B+I
```

```
200     REM DETERMINE CURRENT PAYMENT P.
210     IF B<P THEN P=B
220     REM MAKE A PAYMENT OF P DOLLARS.
230     LET B=B-P
240     LET N=N+1
250     LET T=T+P
260 NEXT  (or WEND)
270 REM DISPLAY THE RESULTS.
280 PRINT "LOAN PAYMENT SUMMARY:"
290 PRINT USING "NUMBER OF PAYMENTS ##";N
300 PRINT USING "FINAL PAYMENT:    ####.##";P
310 PRINT USING "TOTAL REPAYMENT #####.##";T
320 END
RUN

LOAN PAYMENT SUMMARY:
NUMBER OF PAYMENTS 30
FINAL PAYMENT      36.07
TOTAL REPAYMENT  1196.06
```

REMARK 1   Note that the flowchart continues looping if $B > 0$, whereas the program continues looping if $B > .001$ (line 160). Remember, the computer may store only close approximations for real numbers. Thus, if a value $B = .000023$ is reached instead of $B = 0$, the condition $B > 0$ would be true, causing an unwanted pass through the loop. By using the conditions $B > .001$, we avoid this difficulty.

REMARK 2   So that the program can be used for other loans, R, P, and B should be input and not assigned values in LET statements.

■ 8.7 Problems

1. Write programs to compute the following sums S. If present, N is to be assigned with an INPUT statement.

   a. $S = 5 + 7 + 9 + \cdots + 91$
   b. $S = 3 + 8 + 13 + 18 + \cdots + 93$
   c. $S = 1 + 2 + 3 + \cdots + N$
   d. $S = 1 + 1/2 + 1/3 + \cdots + 1/99 + 1/100$
   e. $S = 1 + 1/2 + 1/3 + 1/4 + \cdots + 1/N$
   f. $S = 1 - 1/2 + 1/3 - 1/4 + \cdots + 1/99 - 1/100$

Write a program to perform each task specified in Problems 2–11.

2. Input a list of numbers whose last value is 999. Calculate the sum and average of all input values excluding 999.
3. Many numbers are to be input. The number 0 is used as the EOD tag. Determine the sum of all positive numbers and the sum of all negative numbers. Display both sums.
4. A list of numbers is to be input as in Problem 3. Determine and display the average of all positive numbers and the average of all negative numbers.
5. A young man agrees to begin working for a company at the very modest salary of a penny per week, with the stipulation that his salary will double each week. At the end of 6 months what is his weekly salary and how much has he earned?

6. Find the total amount credited to an account after 4 years if $25 is deposited each month at an annual interest rate of 5.5% compounded monthly.

7. Mary deposits $25 in a bank at the annual interest rate of 6% compounded monthly. After how many months will her account first exceed $27.50?

8. On the first of each month other than January, a person deposits $100 into an account earning 6% interest compounded monthly. The account is opened on February 1. How much will the account be worth in 5 years just before the February deposit?

9. Andrew's parents deposit $500 in a savings account on the day of his birth. The bank pays 6.5% compounded annually. Construct a table showing how this deposit grows in value from the date of deposit to his 21st birthday.

10. Sally receives a graduation present of $1,000 and invests it in a long-term certificate that pays 8% compounded annually. Construct a table showing how this investment grows to a value of $1,500.

11. Find the averages of several sets of numbers typed at the keyboard. The value 999, when typed, means that all entries for the set being typed have been made. The input value -999 means that all input sets have been processed.

■ 8.8 Structured Programming

The importance of preparing an algorithm before beginning the coding process cannot be overemphasized. However, just as unreadable programs are often written by people who begin a programming task while seated at a computer keyboard, so too unreadable algorithms can be written if certain guidelines are not followed. The algorithms we have presented in this book take one of two forms:

1. An English-like step-by-step process describing how to carry out a specific task. This mixture of the English language and programming statements is called **pseudocode.**
2. A flowchart displaying the steps to be followed.

In the pseudocode form, the individual steps often correspond to program segments rather than to single program statements. For instance, the following algorithm was written for the task given in Example 12:

a. Input N.
b. Calculate the sum $S = 1^2 + 2^2 + \cdots + N^2$.
c. Display S and stop.

If you can see how to code Step(b), there is no need to include more detail in this algorithm. However, if it is not obvious to you how to code Step(b), you can try to rewrite the step in more detail. Here is one way to do this:

b1. Let $S = 0$.
b2. For $J = 1, 2, 3, \ldots, N$, add J^2 to S.

This process of refining the steps in an algorithm is called the *method of stepwise refinement* and has been illustrated in several of the worked-out examples, beginning with those in Chapter 2.

With flowcharts, the same process of refinement can be used. For the example cited, you could have begun by writing the flowchart on the left:

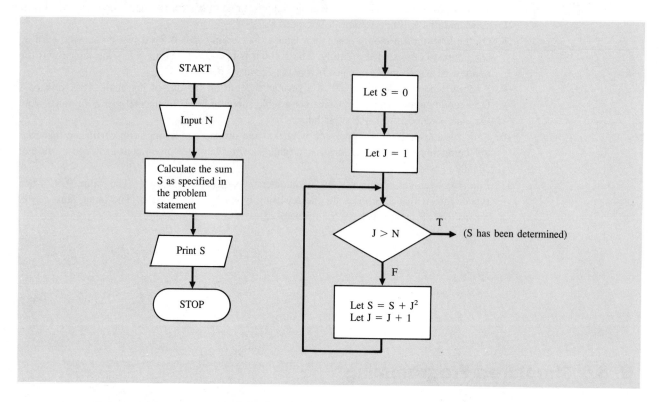

As before, if coding this flowchart is easy for you, there is no need to include more detail. However, if it is not clear how to code the box that calculates S, you should try to rewrite this step by including more detail. In Example 12 we displayed this detail by using the flowchart segment on the right.

When writing an algorithm, whether in pseudocode or as a flowchart, or in BASIC, you will encounter the following situations:

1. Two or more tasks are to be carried out in sequence (Figure 8.1).
2. One of two tasks is to be selected depending on a specified condition. It may be that one of the two tasks is to do nothing (Figure 8.2).
3. A task is to be carried out repeatedly (Figure 8.3).

These three control structures are referred to as **structured programming constructs.** It has been shown that any algorithm can be written using only these constructs.* The following diagram shows how two of these constructs (*sequence* and *repetition*) are used in the algorithm, shown in Example 12, to calculate the sum

$$S = 1^2 + 2^2 + 3^2 + \cdots + N^2$$

Note that Task 4 is an instance of the construct *repetition*, whereas the entire program is simply the *sequence* of Tasks 1 through 5 in that order. Note also that the task being repeated within Task 4 is the *sequence* of two LET statements.

---

* "Flow Diagrams, Turing Machines and Languages with Only Two Formation Rules," by Corrado Bohm and Giuseppe Jacopini, *Comm. A.C.M.*, 9 (May 1966), pp. 366–371.

Figure 8.1 Sequence.

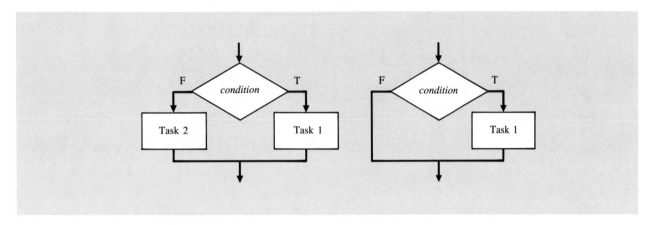

Figure 8.2 Selection.

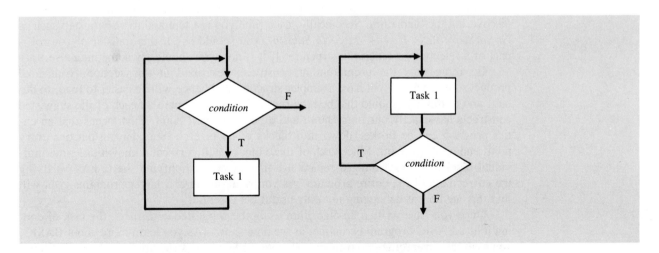

Figure 8.3 Repetition.

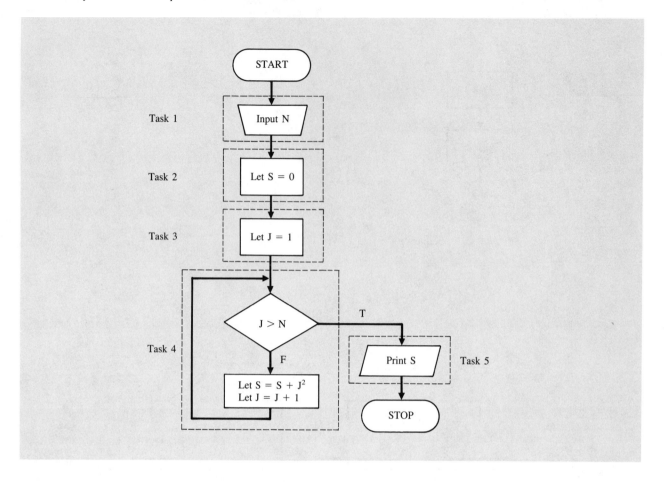

Algorithms written using only the constructs *sequence, selection,* and *repetition* are called **structured algorithms.** The process of writing such algorithms is called **structured programming,** and the resulting programs are called **structured programs.**

Because the BASIC language allows you to use GOTO and IF statements to transfer control to any line in a program, it is easy to write BASIC programs that are very difficult to understand. The time to avoid writing an unreadable program is during the process of discovering the algorithm. Specifically, each time you are tempted to write a step such as *Go to Step (b),* or *If N < 5, go to Step (b),* you should ask if this transfer of control is part of a selection or repetition structure. If it is not, you should try something else.

By using only the programming constructs described in this section, your final product, the program, will have a simpler structure and hence will be easier to read, to debug, and to modify, should that be required. For instance, note that each of the suggested constructs has exactly one entry point and exactly one exit point. This means that an entire program can be broken down into blocks of code, each block having but one entry point and one exit point. Since each of these blocks will perform a known task, the individual blocks can be debugged separately, thus greatly simplifying the task of verifying the correctness of the entire program. As you write larger and larger programs, you will find this method of debugging not only useful but essential.

Once you have written an algorithm using the suggested constructs, the task of coding it as a BASIC program is routine, as we now show. (As you learn more about BASIC, you will discover other convenient ways to code these structured programming constructs.)

EXAMPLE 14 **To code the selection construct**

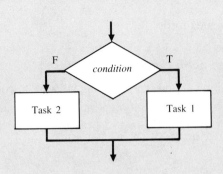

you can write (the line numbers are for illustration only):

500 IF *condition* THEN 600

$$\left.\begin{array}{l} \rule{3cm}{0.4pt} \\ \rule{3cm}{0.4pt} \\ \rule{3cm}{0.4pt} \end{array}\right\} \text{Code for Task 2.}$$

590 GOTO 700
600

$$\left.\begin{array}{l} \rule{3cm}{0.4pt} \\ \rule{3cm}{0.4pt} \\ \rule{3cm}{0.4pt} \end{array}\right\} \text{Code for Task 1.}$$

700 (Program continuation.)

If Task 1 and Task 2 denote single BASIC statements s_1 and s_2, respectively, you can write

IF *condition* THEN s_1 ELSE s_2

□

EXAMPLE 15 **To code the selection construct**

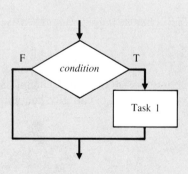

you can write

500 IF NOT *(condition)* THEN 600

$$\left.\begin{array}{l} \rule{3cm}{0.4pt} \\ \rule{3cm}{0.4pt} \\ \rule{3cm}{0.4pt} \end{array}\right\} \text{Code for Task 1.}$$

600 (Program continuation.)

If Task 1 denotes a single BASIC statement **s**, you would write

IF *condition* THEN **s**

If your system allows the extended forms

IF *condition* THEN *clause*
IF *condition* THEN *clause* ELSE *clause*

as described in Section 8.1, you will find more convenient ways to code the selection constructs in Examples 14 and 15.

EXAMPLE 16   To code the repetition construct

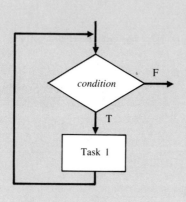

you can write

500 **WHILE** *condition*

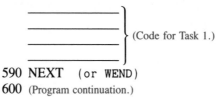

(Code for Task 1.)

590 **NEXT**   (or **WEND**)
600 (Program continuation.)

If your system does not allow WHILE, change lines 500 and 590 as follows:

```
500 IF NOT (condition) THEN 600
590 GOTO 500
```

■ REMARK   Note that the code for Task 1 must contain a statement that changes some variable appearing in the *condition*. Indeed, the *condition* must eventually become *false;* otherwise you have an infinite loop.

EXAMPLE 17   To code the repetition construct

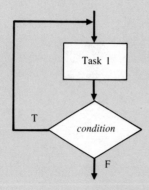

you can write

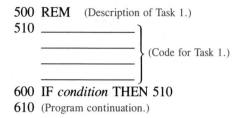

500 REM   (Description of Task 1.)
510 _____
     _____
     _____ (Code for Task 1.)
     _____
600 IF *condition* THEN 510
610 (Program continuation.)

If your system allows the WHILE statement you may wish to code this loop as a WHILE loop. If you do, you must make sure that *condition* is true before entering the loop. Having done this, you can make these two changes:

505 WHILE *condition*
600 NEXT (or WEND)

■ 8.9 Problems

Construct a flowchart for each algorithm shown in Problems 1–6. In each case use only the sequence, selection, and repetition constructs presented in Section 8.8.

1. **a.** Input values for N, R, and T.
   b. If N ≤ 40, let S = N × R. Otherwise, let S = 40 × R + (N − 40) × (1.5) × R.
   c. Reduce S by the amount S × T.
   d. Print S and stop.

2. **a.** Input a value for N.
   b. If N = 0, print the message GOODBYE and stop.
   c. If N > 0, print the integers from 1 up to N. Otherwise, print the integers from 0 down to N.
   d. Input another value for N and repeat Step (b).

3. **a.** Input values for A and B.
   b. If A and B have the same sign (the condition for this is A × B > 0), print POSITIVE or NEGATIVE according to whether A and B are positive or negative.
   c. If either A or B is 0, print FINI and stop. Otherwise, repeat Step (a).

4. **a.** Input an integer N.
   b. If N = 0, stop.
   c. Print BETWEEN if N is between 70 and 80, exclusive; otherwise print NOT BETWEEN.
   d. Go to Step (a).

5. **a.** Input values for X, Y, and Z.
   b. If X < Y, print Y − X and go to Step (d).
   c. Print Z − X only if X < Z.
   d. Print X, Y, and Z.
   e. Stop.

6. **a.** Input a value for N.
   b. If N is less than or equal to 0, go to Step (a).
   c. If N > 100, print VALUE IS TOO LARGE and go to Step (g).
   d. If N > 50, calculate SUM = 50 + 51 + 52 + · · · + N and go to Step (f).
   e. Calculate SUM = 1 + 2 + 3 + · · · + N.
   f. Print the value of SUM.
   g. Print the message GOODBYE and stop.

Reconstruct the flowcharts shown in Problems 7–10 by using only the sequence, selection, and repetition constructs shown in Figures 8.1, 8.2, and 8.3. In the given flowcharts, C1, C2, and C3 denote logical expressions, and S1, S2, and S3 denote single statements or groups of statements. To illustrate, the unstructured flowchart

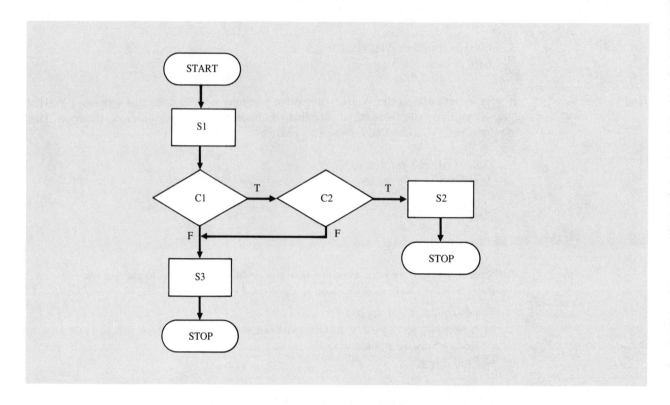

can be written in the equivalent structured form

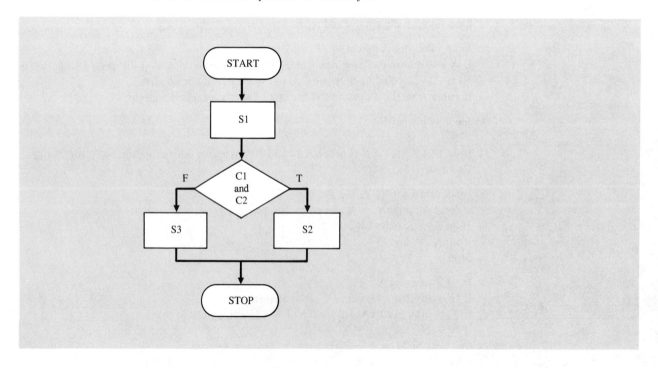

In this illustration, we had to combine two symbols. For the problems, you may also have to write a symbol more than once.

7.

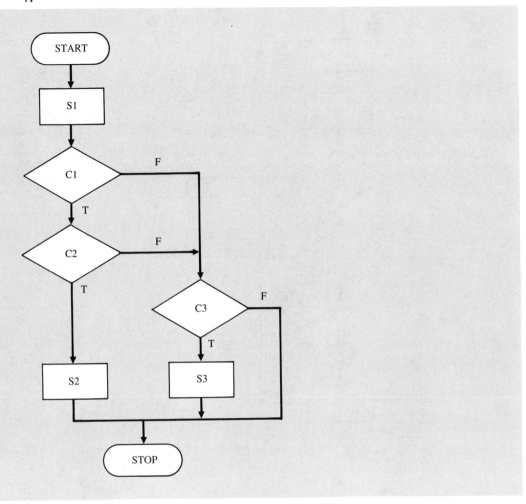

8.

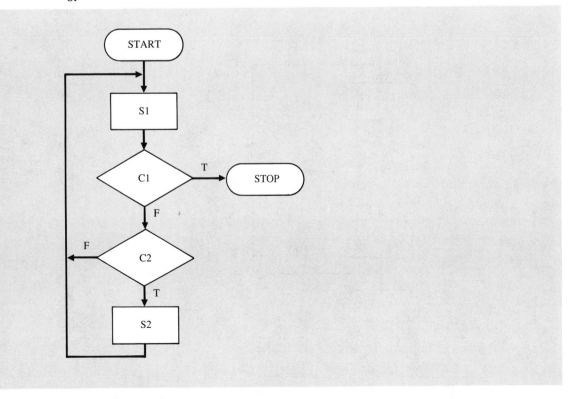

9.

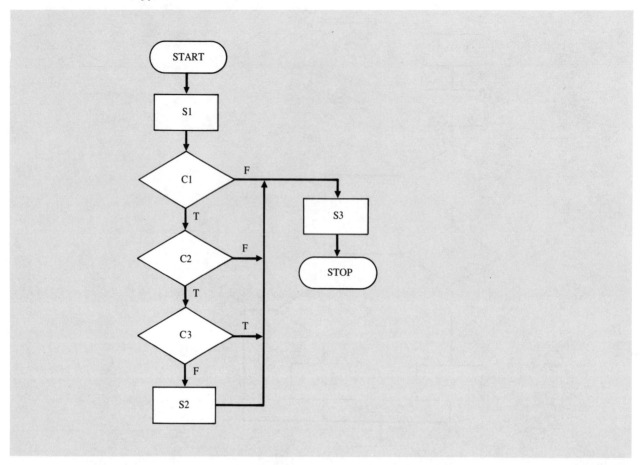

10.

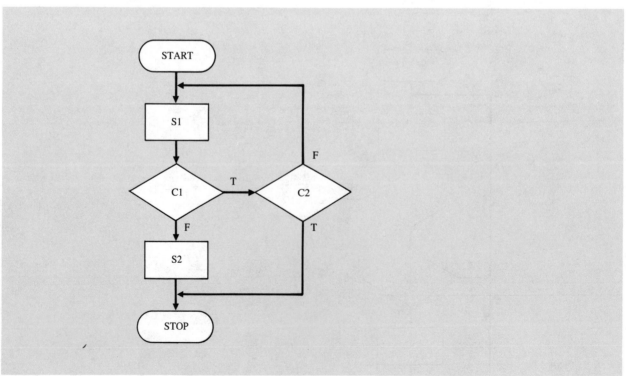

■ 8.10 Review True-or-False Quiz

1. In BASIC the IF statement is used for two fundamentally different purposes.   **T F**
2. A flowchart is a pictorial representation of an algorithm.   **T F**
3. A written algorithm will usually contain more detail than the corresponding flowchart.   **T F**
4. A flowchart is an excellent way to display the logic of a program, but flowcharting is of little value while writing the program.   **T F**
5. A BASIC program containing only LET, PRINT, and INPUT statements, together with a proper END statement, is necessarily *structured*.   **T F**
6. A similar program that also contains IF statements of the form IF *condition* THEN *statement*, where *statement* denotes a LET, PRINT, or INPUT statement, may or may not be structured.   **T F**
7. The statement

       50 IF X>0 THEN PRINT "GOOD" ELSE PRINT "BAD"

   is equivalent to the two statements

       50 IF X>0 THEN PRINT "GOOD"
       51 IF X<=0 THEN PRINT "BAD"   **T F**

8. If A = 1 and B = 2, this IF statement will print 3.

       IF B=1 AND A>B OR B<3 THEN PRINT A+B   **T F**

9. The statement

       IF A>5 THEN IF A<10 THEN PRINT A

   is equivalent to the statement

       IF A>5 AND A<10 THEN PRINT A   **T F**

10. These two logical expressions are equivalent:

        NOT (A=1 AND B=2)
        A<>1 OR B<>2   **T F**

9 Loops Made Easier

S o far we have coded each loop by using either an IF or a WHILE statement to specify a looping condition. BASIC also contains the FOR statement, which in many situations can be used to simplify writing loops and also to produce more readable programs. The FOR statement, like the WHILE statement, is used only to code loops. Loops constructed with the FOR statement are called FOR loops. In this chapter we describe how FOR loops are written and give guidelines to help you decide when loops should be coded as FOR loops and when they should not.

■ 9.1 FOR Loops

Here are two ways to display the integers from 1 to 5:

Program 1
```
100 LET N=1
110     PRINT N;
120     LET N=N+1
130 IF N<=5 THEN 110
140 END
RUN

  1  2  3  4  5
```

Program 2
```
100 LET N=1
110 WHILE N<=5
120     PRINT N;
130     LET N=N+1
140 NEXT (or WEND)
150 END
RUN

  1  2  3  4  5
```

The same thing can be accomplished by the following program:

Program 3
```
100 FOR N=1 TO 5
110     PRINT N;
120 NEXT N
130 END
RUN

  1  2  3  4  5
```

Program 3 simply instructs the computer to execute 110 five times, once for each integer N from 1 to 5. Just how the computer will accomplish this depends on the particular implementation of BASIC on your system. Our assumption in this text is that Program 3 is equivalent to Program 2. This assumption conforms to the BASIC standard. Thus, the action of Program 3 can be described as follows:

a. Line 100 (the FOR statement) assigns an initial value of 1 to N.
b. N is compared with the terminal value 5. If N > 5, control passes to the line follow-

ing the NEXT statement (line 130). The loop has been satisfied. If N ≤ 5, control passes to the line following the FOR statement (line 110).

c. Line 110 displays the current value of N.

d. When the NEXT statement, line 120, is encountered, N is incremented by 1, and the comparison in Step (b) is repeated.

The following three short examples further illustrate the use of the FOR and NEXT statements to construct loops. To clarify the meaning of the FOR loops, we have written each program in two ways—with and without the FOR and NEXT statements. The general form of a FOR loop is given after Example 3.

EXAMPLE 1   **Here is a program to calculate and display the price of one, two, three, four, five, and six items selling at seven for $1.**

```
100 REM U DENOTES THE        100 REM U DENOTES THE
105 REM UNIT PRICE.          105 REM UNIT PRICE.
110 LET U=1.00/7             110 LET U=1.00/7
120 FOR K=1 to 6             120 LET K=1
130    LET P=U*K             130 WHILE K<=6
140    PRINT K,P             140    LET P=U*K
150 NEXT K                   150    PRINT K,P
160 END                      160    LET K=K+1
                             170 NEXT (or WEND)
                             180 END
```

The FOR loop instructs the computer to execute the statements

```
LET P=U*K
PRINT K,P
```

six times, once for each integer K from 1 to 6. These two statements are called the **body** or **range** of the loop. It is an excellent programming practice to indent the body of each FOR loop to improve program readability.

EXAMPLE 2   **Here is a loop to display the numbers −4, −2, 0, 2, 4, 6.**

```
100 FOR J=-4 TO 6 STEP 2     100 LET J=-4
110    PRINT J;              110 WHILE J<=6
120 NEXT J                   120    PRINT J;
130 END                      130    LET J=J+2
RUN                          140 NEXT (or WEND)
                             150 END
-4 -2  0  2  4  6            RUN

                              -4 -2  0  2  4  6
```

The starting value for J is −4. Including STEP 2 in the statement

```
100 FOR J=-4 TO 6 STEP 2
```

specifies that J is to be increased by 2 each time NEXT J is encountered. Thus, the FOR loop instructs the computer to execute the statement

```
110 PRINT J;
```

for the successive J values −4, −2, 0, 2, 4, and 6.

EXAMPLE 3   **Here is a loop to display 5, 4, 3, 2, 1.**

```
100 FOR N=5 TO 1 STEP -1     100 LET N=5
110    PRINT N;              110 WHILE N>=1
120 NEXT N                   120    PRINT N;
130 END                      130    LET N=N-1
RUN                          140 NEXT (or WEND)
                             150 END
   5  4  3  2  1             RUN

                                5  4  3  2  1
```

This example illustrates that negative increments are allowed. The initial value of N is 5, and, after each pass through the loop, N is *decreased* by 1 (STEP–1). As soon as N attains a value *less* than 1 (as specified in the FOR statement), control passes out of the loop to the statement following the NEXT statement.

The general form of a FOR loop is

FOR **v** = **a** TO **b** STEP **c**

.

. (Body of the loop)

.

NEXT **v**

where **v** denotes a simple numerical variable name* and **a**, **b**, and **c** denote arithmetic expressions. (IF STEP **c** is omitted, **c** is assumed to have the value 1.) **v** is called the **control variable,** and the values of **a**, **b**, and **c** are called the **initial, terminal,** and **step** values, respectively. The action of a FOR loop is described by the following flow diagrams.

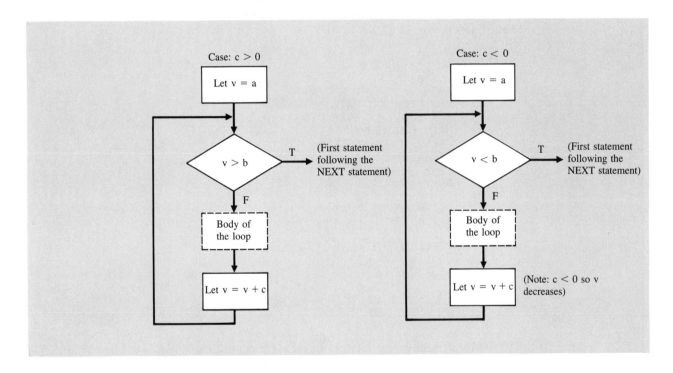

In each FOR loop shown in Examples 1–3, the control variable appears in a statement in the body of the loop. The next example shows that you are not required to do this. Indeed, in many cases, as in this one, the control variable serves only as a counter.

EXAMPLE 4   **Here is a loop to display a row of N dashes.**

```
200 FOR I=1 TO N
210     PRINT "-";
220 NEXT I
```

Of course, N must be assigned a value before line 200 is executed. If N is 15, a row of 15 dashes will be displayed.

If the terminal value N in Example 4 is 0, then the entire loop will be skipped, since the initial value, I = 1, will be greater than the terminal value, N = 0. However, as

---

*The numerical variables considered to this point are called *simple* to distinguish them from the *subscripted* variables considered in Chapter 14.

noted previously, the precise action caused by a FOR loop may differ on your system. Some BASIC systems are designed so that execution of a FOR statement results in at least one pass through the loop (the comparison is made at the end of the loop rather than at the beginning). If BASIC on your computer works this way, an unwanted dash will be displayed when N is 0. To rectify this, you could include a statement such as

```
195 IF N=0 THEN 230
```

to skip the loop entirely when N is 0. We restate this difference in BASIC systems as a caution.

CAUTION

On some BASIC systems, when the FOR statement beginning a FOR loop is executed, at least one pass is made through the loop.

In the next example, we use a FOR loop to produce a table of values. This is a common application of FOR loops. The example also illustrates that the initial, terminal, and step values of a FOR loop do not have to be integers.

EXAMPLE 5

Here is a program to produce a table showing the 5.5%, 6%, 6.5%, . . . , 8% discount on any amount A typed at the keyboard. The maximum discount, however, is $50.

```
100 REM *** DISCOUNT CALCULATIONS ***
110 PRINT "AMOUNT";
120 INPUT A
130 PRINT
140 PRINT "PERCENT RATE","DISCOUNT"
150 FOR R=5.5 TO 8 STEP 0.5
160    LET D=R/100*A
170    IF D>50 THEN LET D=50
180    PRINT R,D
190 NEXT R
200 END
RUN

AMOUNT? 700

PERCENT RATE    DISCOUNT
   5.5             38.5
   6               42
   6.5             45.5
   7               49
   7.5             50
   8               50
```

The FOR statement in line 150 specifies that the control variable R is to range from 5.5 to 8, with 0.5 as the increment. For R = 5.5, 6, 6.5, and 7, the discount values D determined by line 160 do not exceed 50; hence the statement LET D = 50 in line 170 is not executed. When R = 7.5 and 8, the D values determined by line 160 do exceed 50, so the statement LET D = 50 in line 170 is executed.

■ REMARK

Special care must be taken when writing FOR loops with initial, terminal, or step values that are not integers. As we have mentioned previously, the computer stores only close approximations for most numbers that are not integers. The loop in this example causes no difficulty because 0.5 is one of the fractional numbers computers store exactly. If we had used STEP 0.1 instead of STEP 0.5, however, the control variable R would take on only close approximations to the values 5.6, 5.7 , 5.8, . . . , 8. If your computer reaches R = 8.00010 instead of R = 8, the loop will not be executed for the final value R = 8. To avoid such awkward situations, many programmers use only integers for the initial, terminal, and step values in FOR loops. To write the program in this example so that the control variable R takes on only integer values, you can make these two changes:

```
150 FOR R=55 TO 80 STEP 5
160    LET D=R/1000*A
```

If increments of 0.1 instead of 0.5 are required, you can simply use STEP 1 rather than STEP 5.

In this section we have described and illustrated the syntax that must be used in writing FOR loops. Although the examples also illustrate certain situations in which loops are best coded as FOR loops, more needs to be said on this topic.

You may have noticed that all FOR loops share a common characteristic: the number of times the body of the loop must be executed to satisfy the loop (this is called the **iteration count** of the loop) can be determined before the loop is entered. For example, the statement

```
FOR N=1 TO 500
```

initiates a loop with iteration count 500, the statement

```
FOR N=1 TO 20 STEP 4
```

initiates a loop with iteration count 5 (the five N values are 1, 5, 9, 13, and 17), and if M has been assigned a positive integer value,

```
FOR K=1 TO M
```

initiates a loop with iteration count M.

There is a simple formula for determining the iteration count for any FOR loop. If **i**, **t**, and **s** denote the initial, terminal, and step values, respectively, the iteration count is the larger of the two values

$$\left[\frac{t - i + s}{s} \right] \text{ and } 0$$

where the expression in brackets is truncated, if necessary, to obtain an integer.

FOR statement	i, t, s	(t − i + s)/s	Iteration count
FOR N=1 TO 20 STEP 3	1, 20, 3	(20 − 1 + 3)/3 = 7 1/3	7
FOR K=1 TO 1000	1, 1000, 1	(1000 − 1 + 1)/1 = 1000	1000
FOR L=2 TO 100 STEP 50	2, 100, 50	(100 − 2 + 50)/50 = 2.96	2
FOR M=20 TO 1 STEP −3	20, 1, −3	(1 − 20 + (−3))/(−3) = 7 1/3	7
FOR P=10 TO 1	10, 1, 1	(1 − 10 + 1)/1 = −8	0
FOR R=5.5 TO 8 STEP .5	5.5, 8, .5	(8 − 5.5 + .5)/.5 = 6	6

A common method used by computers to process FOR statements is first to calculate the iteration count, and then to use a counter to control looping. An exit from the loop occurs when the predetermined number of passes has been made.* Loops that are controlled by such counters are called **counter-controlled loops.** Thus, every FOR loop that does not contain an IF or GOTO statement to terminate the loop prematurely is a counter-controlled loop.

The worked-out examples in this section and the preceding discussion of counter-controlled loops suggest this guideline concerning the use of FOR loops:

Use a FOR loop only if both of the following conditions are met:

1. *The number of times the loop will be repeated can be determined before the loop is entered.* It isn't necessary that you determine this count, but it is necessary that you know it can be determined. For instance, to produce a report showing the equivalent annual salaries for people working at the hourly rates 4.00, 4.25, 4.50, . . . , 9.00, we could use a FOR loop beginning

```
FOR H=4 TO 9 STEP 0.25
```

---

*The flow diagrams shown after Example 3 explain the effect of a FOR loop, but they are not intended to describe exactly how the computer causes this effect. For instance, our description of the action caused by the statement FOR R = 5.5 to 8 STEP 0.5 suggests that the computer first assigns 5.5 to R and then compares R with the terminal value 8. Although this helps us understand the effect of the FOR statement, it does not necessarily correspond to what actually happens.

We would not determine the iteration count, but it is obvious that it can be determined simply by counting the H values. As an example of a loop that should not be coded as a FOR loop, suppose we must find the smallest of these hourly rates that gives an equivalent annual salary of at least $11,500. In this case, an iteration count cannot be determined without actually performing some calculations—that is, without entering the loop. Thus, we would code the loop by including the condition SALARY < 11500 in a WHILE statement.

2. *A meaningful control variable can be found for the loop.* If you determine the iteration count C for a loop, you can use a counter, say N, as the control variable and use a FOR loop beginning

```
FOR N=1 TO C
```

Such a counter, however, is not always meaningful. For instance, in Example 5 we used a FOR loop beginning

```
FOR R=5.5 TO 8 STEP 0.5
```

to display R percent discounts. The iteration count for the loop is

$$\frac{8 - 5.5 + 0.5}{0.5} = \frac{3}{0.5} = 6$$

But it would not be particularly meaningful to code the loop by using

```
FOR N=1 TO 6
```

The control variable R, however, is meaningful—it denotes the discount rate.

Following are some points concerning the use of FOR loops that were not raised explicitly in this section:

1. The initial, terminal, and step values are determined once, when the FOR statement is executed, and cannot be altered within the body of the loop.
2. Entry into a FOR loop should be made only by executing the FOR statement.
3. Although the control variable can be modified inside the FOR loop, don't do it. The resulting program may be very difficult to understand.
4. Although it is allowed, never use IF or GOTO statements to transfer control out of a FOR loop to perform some task and then back into the body so that looping can continue. Programs written in this way can be very difficult to understand.
5. Never use an IF or GOTO statement to terminate a FOR loop. Doing so will give you a loop with two exit points and your program will not be structured (see Section 8.8). Moreover, on some BASIC systems this use of an IF or GOTO statement can cause unexpected and incorrect results.
6. When a FOR loop has been satisfied (that is, when an exit is made via the NEXT statement), the value of the control variable is the first value not used. On systems not conforming to the BASIC standard, however, this may not be the case.

■ 9.2 Problems

1. Show the output of each program.
   a.
   ```
   10 FOR J=2 TO 4
   20    PRINT J+2
   30 NEXT J
   40 END
   ```
   b.
   ```
   10 FOR N=5 TO -3 STEP -4
   20    PRINT N
   30 NEXT N
   40 END
   ```

```
c. 10 LET C=0
   20 LET X=1
   30 FOR Q=1 TO 4.9 STEP 2
   40     LET C=C+1
   50     LET X=X*Q
   60 NEXT Q
   70 PRINT "TIMES THROUGH LOOP=";C
   80 PRINT X
   90 END
```

```
d. 10 FOR I=1 TO 3
   20     PRINT "+";
   30 NEXT I
   40 FOR J=5 TO 7
   50     PRINT "/";
   60 NEXT J
   70 END
```

```
e. 10 FOR J=2 TO 2
   20     PRINT "LOOP"
   30 NEXT J
   40 END
```

```
f. 10 FOR J=5 TO 1
   20     PRINT "LOOP"
   30 NEXT J
   40 END
```

```
g. 10 PRINT "123456789"
   20 FOR V=1 TO 4
   30     PRINT TAB(V);"V";TAB(10-V);"V"
   40 NEXT V
   50 PRINT TAB(5);"V"
   60 END
```

```
h. 10 FOR N=1 TO 4
   20     PRINT USING "ITEM# ",N;
   30 NEXT N
   40 PRINT
   50 FOR N=1 TO 4
   60     PRINT USING "###    ",N;
   70 NEXT N
   80 END
```

2. Each of the following programs contains an error—either a syntax error that will cause an error message or a programming error that the computer will not recognize but that will cause incorrect results. In each case find the error and tell which of the two types it is.

```
a. 10 REM 6 PERCENT PROGRAM
   20 FOR N=1 TO 6
   30     INPUT X
   40     PRINT X,.06*X
   50 NEXT X
   60 END
```

```
b. 10 REM COUNT THE POSITIVE
   20 REM NUMBERS TYPED.
   30 FOR I=1 TO 10
   40     LET C=0
   50     INPUT N
   60     IF N>0 THEN C=C+1
   70 NEXT I
   80 PRINT C;"ARE POSITIVE."
   90 END
```

```
c. 10 REM SUMMING PROGRAM
   20 LET S=0
   30 FOR X=1 TO 4
   40     INPUT X
   50     LET S=S+X
   60 NEXT X
   70 PRINT "SUM IS";S
   80 END
```

```
d. 10 REM DISPLAY THE NUMBERS
   20 REM 1 3 6 10 15
   30 LET S=1
   40 FOR N=1 TO 15 STEP S
   50     PRINT N
   60     LET S=S+1
   70 NEXT N
   80 END
```

In Problems 3–13, write a program for each task specified.

3. A positive integer N is to be entered, followed by N numbers. Determine the sum and average of the N numbers.

4. A positive integer N is to be entered, followed by N numbers. Determine how many of the N numbers are negative, how many are positive, and how many are 0.

5. Display the integers from 1 to 72, eight to the line. *Hint:* Use a separate variable to count how many numbers have been displayed on a line.

6. Display the integers from 1 to 72, eight to the line, equally spaced.

7. A program is needed to assist grade school students with their multiplication tables. After an initial greeting, the computer should ask the student to type a number from 2 to 12 so that products involving this number can be practiced. (Call this number N, but don't confuse the student with this information.) Next, the student should be asked to answer the questions $2 \times N = ?, 3 \times N = ?, \ldots, 12 \times N = ?$ Of course, the *value* of N should be displayed, not the letter N. If a question is answered correctly, the next question should be asked; if not, the question should be repeated. If the same question is answered incorrectly twice, the correct answer should be displayed and then the next question should be asked. After all questions pertaining to N have been answered, display the student's score and give the student the choice of trying another multiplication table or stopping.

8. Produce a two-column table with column headings showing P percent of the amounts $1, $2, $3, . . . , $20. P is to be input.

9. Prepare a report showing the effect of a flat across-the-board raise of F dollars in addition to a percentage increase of P percent on the salaries $20,000, $20,500, $21,000, . . . , $30,000. F and P are to be input. Include three columns labeled PRESENT SALARY, RAISE, and NEW SALARY.

10. Produce each of the following designs. Use the TAB function.

```
a. ZZZZZZZ    b. V           V    c. N      N    d.         A
        Z          V       V         NN     N             A  A
        Z           V     V          N N    N           A      A
        Z            V   V           N  N   N          A        A
        Z             V V            N   N  N          AAAAAAAAA
        Z              V             N    NN        A              A
   ZZZZZZZ             V             N      N       A              A
```

11. Evaluate the following sums. If a value for N is required, it is to be input.
   a. $1 + 2 + 3 + \cdots + N$
   b. $1 + 3 + 5 + 7 + \cdots + 51$
   c. $1 + 3 + 5 + 7 + \cdots + (2N - 1)$
   d. $2 + 5 + 8 + 11 + \cdots + K$, where $N - 3 < K <= N$
   e. $(.06) + (.06)^2 + (.06)^3 + \cdots + (.06)^N$
   f. $1 + 1/2 + 1/3 + 1/4 + \cdots + 1/N$
   g. $1 + 1/4 + 1/9 + 1/16 + \cdots + 1/N^2$
   h. $1 + 1/2 + 1/4 + 1/8 + \cdots + 1/2^N$
   i. $1 - 1/2 + 1/3 - 1/4 + \cdots - 1/100$
   j. $4[1 - 1/3 + 1/5 - 1/7 + \cdots + (-1)^{N+1}/(2N - 1)]$

12. Produce a two-column table with the headings N and $1 + 2 + 3 + \cdots + N$. The first column is to show the N values 1, 2, 3, . . . , 20, and the second is to show the indicated sums. [*Hint:* The second column value for row N $(N > 1)$ is simply N plus the previous sum.]

13. For any positive integer N, the product $1 \times 2 \times 3 \times \cdots \times N$ is denoted by the symbol N! and is called N factorial. Also, zero factorial (0!) is defined to be 1. (Thus, $0! = 1! = 1$.) Produce a two-column table with column headings showing the values of N and N! for N = 0, 1, 2, . . . , 10. [*Hint:* For $N > 0$, $N! = (N - 1)! \times N$.]

■ 9.3 Nested Loops

It is permissible, and often desirable, to have one FOR loop contained in another. When nesting loops in this way, there is one rule that must be observed:

If the body of one FOR loop contains either the FOR or the NEXT statement of another loop, it must contain both of them. This is illustrated in Figure 9.1.

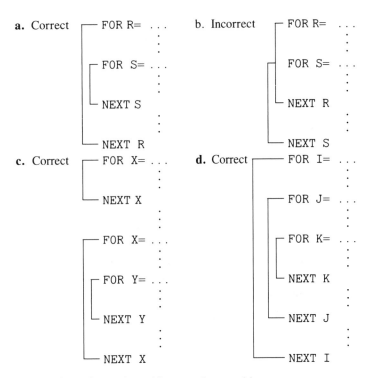

Figure 9.1 Correctly and incorrectly nested loops.

EXAMPLE 6   **Here is an illustration of nested FOR loops.**

```
10 FOR I=1 TO 3
20    FOR J=1 TO 5
30       PRINT I;
40    NEXT J
50    PRINT
60 NEXT I
70 END
RUN

 1  1  1  1  1
 2  2  2  2  2
 3  3  3  3  3
```

The FOR and NEXT statements in lines 10 and 60 cause the four program lines between them to be executed three times. The first three of these lines (20, 30, 40) display the value of I five times on one line, leaving the cursor positioned at the end of that line. Line 50 causes a RETURN to be executed so that subsequent output will appear on a new line. Since lines 20 to 50 are executed for the successive I values 1, 2, and 3, the program produces three lines of output as shown.

As shown in Section 9.1, the value of the control variable of a FOR loop can be used in the body of the loop in any way you wish. In the preceding example, the control variable I was used to supply output values; in the next example, we use the control variable of an outer loop to supply the terminal value for an inner loop.

EXAMPLE 7   **Here is a program to display five lines containing the word BASIC—once in the first row, twice in the second, and so on.**

```
10 FOR ROW=1 TO 5          'ROW counts the rows.
20    FOR COL=1 TO ROW     'COL counts times per row.
30       PRINT "BASIC ";
40    NEXT COL
50    PRINT
60 NEXT ROW
70 END
RUN

BASIC
BASIC BASIC
BASIC BASIC BASIC
BASIC BASIC BASIC BASIC
BASIC BASIC BASIC BASIC BASIC
```

To display the output nearer the center of the screen, you can use the TAB function. To cause the output of each row to begin in column position 20, for example, simply include the statement

```
15 PRINT TAB(20);
```

This statement causes the cursor to move to position 20 so that the loop in lines 20 to 40 will display BASIC ROW times beginning in position 20.

Nested FOR loops are especially useful when tables must be prepared in which the rows and columns each correspond to equally spaced data values. We conclude this chapter with an example illustrating one such application of nested loops.

EXAMPLE 8   **Prepare a table showing the possible raises for salaried employees whose salaries are $20,000, $21,000, $22,000, ... , $27,000. A raise is to consist of a flat across-the-board increase and a percentage increase of either 2, 3, or 4%.**

PROBLEM ANALYSIS

Let's agree on the following variable names.

     SALARY = present salary ($20,000, $21,000, . . . , $27,000)
       FLAT = flat across-the-board increase (to be input)
    PERCENT = percentage increase (2, 3, 4%)
      RAISE = amount of raise for a given SALARY, FLAT, and PERCENT

The formula governing this situation is

     RAISE = (PERCENT/100) * SALARY + FLAT

For each salary SALARY, we must display three possible raises RAISE—one for each of the indicated percentages PERCENT. Thus a four-column table is appropriate, the first showing the present salary SALARY and the others showing the three possible raises. The following program segment can be used to display these values.

```
FOR SALARY=20000 TO 27000 STEP 1000
    PRINT SALARY,
    FOR PERCENT=2 TO 4
        LET RAISE=(PERCENT/100)*SALARY+FLAT
        PRINT RAISE,
    NEXT PERCENT
    PRINT
NEXT SALARY
```

All that remains is to include an INPUT statement, so that a value can be typed for FLAT, and to add the PRINT statements needed to display a title for the table and appropriate column headings. We will use PRINT USING rather than PRINT statements to align the columns by decimal point.

**PROBLEM
ANALYSIS**

```
100 PRINT  "            SALARY INCREASE SCHEDULE"
110 PRINT
120 PRINT "ACROSS THE BOARD INCREASE ";
130 INPUT FLAT
140 PRINT
150 PRINT  "         **** ADDITIONAL PERCENTAGE INCREASE ****
160 PRINT
170 PRINT  " SALARY      2 PERCENT    3 PERCENT    4 PERCENT"
180 LET D$=" #####.##"
190 LET E$="       ####.##"
200 FOR SALARY=20000 TO 27000 STEP 1000
210    PRINT USING D$,SALARY;
220    FOR PERCENT=2 TO 4
230       LET RAISE=(PERCENT/100)*SALARY+FLAT
240       PRINT USING E$,RAISE;
250    NEXT PERCENT
260    PRINT
270 NEXT SALARY
280 END
RUN

          SALARY INCREASE SCHEDULE

ACROSS THE BOARD INCREASE ? 700

          **** ADDITIONAL PERCENTAGE INCREASE ****

    SALARY      2 PERCENT    3 PERCENT    4 PERCENT
    20000.00      1100.00      1300.00      1500.00
    21000.00      1120.00      1330.00      1540.00
    22000.00      1140.00      1360.00      1580.00
    23000.00      1160.00      1390.00      1620.00
    24000.00      1180.00      1420.00      1660.00
    25000.00      1200.00      1450.00      1700.00
    26000.00      1220.00      1480.00      1740.00
    27000.00      1240.00      1510.00      1780.00
```

■ 9.4 Problems

1. Show the output of each program.

a.
```
10 FOR I=1 TO 3
20    FOR J=2 TO 3
30       PRINT J;
40    NEXT J
50 NEXT I
60 END
```

b.
```
10 FOR J=9 TO 7 STEP -2
20    FOR K=4 TO 9 STEP 3
30       PRINT J+K;
40    NEXT K
50 NEXT J
60 END
```

c.
```
10 FOR X=1 TO 4
20    FOR Y=X+1 TO 5
30       PRINT Y;
40    NEXT Y
50    PRINT
60 NEXT X
70 END
```

d.
```
10 LET X=0
20 FOR P=1 TO 6
30    FOR Q=2 TO 7
40       FOR R=2 TO 4
50          LET X=X+1
60       NEXT R
70    NEXT Q
80 NEXT P
90 PRINT X
99 END
```

```
e. 10 LET F$="## "
   20 FOR R=7 TO 13 STEP 2
   30    FOR C=1 TO 3
   40       PRINT USING F$,R;
   50    NEXT C
   60    PRINT
   70 NEXT R
   80 END
```

2. Each of the following programs contains an error—either a syntax error that will cause an error message to be displayed or a programming error that the computer will not recognize but that will cause incorrect results. In each case, find the error and tell which of the two types it is.

```
a. 10 REM DISPLAY PRODUCTS.
   20 FOR I=1 TO 3
   30 FOR J=2 TO 4
   40 PRINT I;"TIMES";J;"=";I*J
   50 NEXT I
   60 NEXT J
   70 END
```

```
b. 10 REM DISPLAY SUMS.
   20 FOR A=3 TO 1
   30 FOR B=4 TO 1
   40 PRINT A;"PLUS";B;"=";A+B
   50 NEXT B
   60 NEXT A
   70 END
```

c. A program to display

```
1   2
1   3
1   4
2   3
2   4
3   4
```

```
10 FOR I=1 TO 4
20 FOR J=2 TO 4
30 IF I<>J THEN PRINT I;J
40 NEXT J
50 NEXT I
60 END
```

d. A program to display

```
XXXXX
 XXXX
  XXX
   XX
    X
```

```
10 FOR R=1 TO 5
20 FOR C=1 TO 5
30 IF R>=C THEN PRINT "X";
40 IF R<C THEN PRINT " ";
50 NEXT C
60 NEXT R
70 END
```

3. Produce the following designs. Each time a PRINT statement is executed, no more than one character should be displayed. (Do not use the TAB function.)

```
a. 1                         b. 5   5   5   5   5
   2  2                         4   4   4   4
   3  3  3                        3   3   3
   4  4  4  4                       2   2
   5  5  5  5  5                      1
c. 1                         d. 1
   1  2                         2  1
   1  2  3                      3  2  1
   1  2  3  4                   4  3  2  1
   1  2  3  4  5               5  4  3  2  1
```

In Problems 4–15, write a program to perform each task specified.

4. Produce a tax rate schedule showing the 4, 5, 6, and 7% tax on the dollar amounts $1, $2, $3, ... , $20.

5. Prepare a table showing the interest earned on a $100 deposit for the rates 0.05 to 0.08 in increments of 0.01 and for times 1, 2, ... , 8 years. Interest is compounded annually $(I = P(1 + R)^N - P)$.

6. Prepare the table for Problem 5 except that rates are to be in increments of 0.005 instead of 0.01.

7. Present the information required in Problem 6 by producing seven short tables, one for each interest rate specified. Label each of these tables and also the information contained in the tables.

8. For each of the tax rates 5, $5\frac{1}{8}$, $5\frac{1}{4}$, $5\frac{3}{8}$, and $5\frac{1}{2}$%, produce a table showing the tax on the dollar amounts, \$1, \$2, \$3, . . . , \$20. Each of the five tables is to have an appropriate title and is to contain two labeled columns—the first showing the dollar amounts \$1, \$2, \$3, . . . , \$20 and the second showing the corresponding tax amounts.

9. Produce a listing of all three-digit numbers whose digits are 1, 2, or 3. Spaces are not to appear between the digits of the numbers. (*Hint:* Use triple-nested loops with control variables I, J, and K ranging from 1 to 3. If I, J, and K are the digits, the number is $100 \times I + 10 \times J + K$.)

10. Produce a listing of all three-digit numbers as described in Problem 9. If no digit is repeated in a number, however, it is to be preceded by an asterisk. Thus a portion of your display should be as follows:

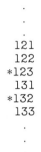

```
        .
        .
        .
      121
      122
     *123
      131
     *132
      133
        .
        .
        .
```

11. Let's define an operation whose symbol is & on the set A = {0, 1, 2, 3, 4, 5} as follows. The "product" of two integers **i** and **j** is given by

$$i \mathbin{\&} j = \text{the remainder when } i \times j \text{ is divided by } 6$$

Write a program to display a table showing all possible "products" of numbers in the set A. The table values should be labeled as follows:

```
&   0   1   2   3   4   5
   --- --- --- --- --- ---
0
1
2
3
4
5
```

12. Determine the largest value the expression $XY^2 - X^2Y + X - Y$ can assume if X and Y can be any integers from 1 to 5, inclusive.

13. Find the maximum and minimum values of the expression $3X^2 - 2XY + Y^2$ if X and Y are subject to the following constraints.

$$X = -4, -3.5, -3, \ldots, 4$$

$$Y = -3, -2.5, -2, \ldots, 5$$

14. The expression $X^3 - 4XY + X^2 + 10X$ is to be examined for all integers X and Y between 1 and 5 to determine those pairs (X, Y) for which the expression is negative. All such pairs are to be displayed, together with the corresponding negative value of the expression.

15. Find all pairs of integers (X, Y) that satisfy the following system of inequalities.

$$2X - Y < 3$$

$$X + 3Y \geq 1$$

$$-6 \leq X \leq 6$$

$$-10 \leq Y \leq 10$$

The solutions are to be displayed as individual ordered pairs (X, Y). (*Hint:* The last two conditions give the initial and terminal values of FOR loops.)

■ 9.5 Review True-or-False Quiz

1. If a group of statements is to be executed several times in a program, it is always a good practice to use a FOR loop.   **T F**
2. If a loop begins with the statement FOR K = 1 TO 35, the variable K must occur in some statement before the NEXT K statement is encountered.   **T F**
3. The statement FOR J = X TO 10 STEP 3 is valid even though X may have a value that is not an integer.   **T F**
4. In the statement FOR N = 15 TO 200 STEP C, C must be a positive integer.   **T F**
5. The initial, terminal, and step values in a FOR loop cannot be changed in the body of the loop.   **T F**
6. The control variable in a FOR loop can be changed in the body of the loop; moreover, doing so represents a good programming practice.   **T F**
7. The control variable of a loop containing a loop may be used as the initial, terminal, or step value of the inner loop.   **T F**
8. Some loops must be coded by using the FOR and NEXT statements.   **T F**
9. The statement FOR X = Y TO Z STEP W contains a syntax error.   **T F**
10. The statement FOR X$ = "A" TO "Z" contains a syntax error.   **T F**
11. All counter-controlled loops are best coded as FOR loops.   **T F**

10 Data as Part of a Program

To this point, values have been assigned to variables by using only LET and INPUT statements. BASIC provides alternative ways of presenting data to the computer. In this chapter, we describe three statements: the DATA statement, which allows you to include data as part of your programs; the READ statement, which is used to assign these data to variables; and the RESTORE statement, which allows you to "read" these data more than once during a single program run.

As you work through the examples in this chapter, you will see that these statements often provide a convenient, and sometimes necessary, alternative to the LET and INPUT statements.

■ 10.1 The READ and DATA Statements

These two statements are best illustrated by example. The general forms that must be used for READ and DATA statements, together with rules governing their use, are given following Example 5.

EXAMPLE 1   **Here is a program to "read" two numbers and display their sum.**

```
100 READ A
110 READ B
120 PRINT "VALUES:";A;B
130 PRINT "SUM:";A+B
140 DATA 17,8
150 END
RUN

VALUES: 17  8
SUM: 25
```

Line 140 contains the numbers to be added. Line 100 assigns the first of these (17) to A, and line 110 assigns the second number (8) to B. When line 140, the DATA line, is encountered, it is ignored, and control passes to the next line, which in this program terminates the run.

■ **REMARK**   Lines 100 and 110 can be replaced by the single READ statement

```
100 READ A,B
```

This statement obtains the first datum (17) for the first variable (A) and the second datum (8) for the second variable (B).

EXAMPLE 2   **Here is a program to "read" and display a list of numbers.**

```
100 PRINT "DATA VALUES:"
110 READ X
120 PRINT X
130 GOTO 110
140 DATA 7,-123,40
150 END
RUN

DATA VALUES:
 7
-123
 40
OUT OF DATA AT 110
```

Line 140 contains the list of numbers. When line 110 is first executed, the first datum (7) is assigned to X, and control passes to line 120, which displays the value of X. The GOTO statement transfers control back to line 110, which then assigns the next value (-123) to X. This process is repeated until the data list is exhausted. This will happen when the READ statement is executed a fourth time. Since only three values are supplied in the DATA line, the attempt to read a fourth value causes the error condition identified by the OUT OF DATA message, and the program terminates.

■
□   **REMARK**   OUT OF DATA errors should be avoided. The examples in this chapter illustrate the most common ways to do this.

EXAMPLE 3   **Here is a program to "read" and display three strings.**

```
100 READ A$,B$,P$
110 PRINT B$;" ";A$;P$
120 DATA FLIES,TIME,.
130 END
RUN

TIME FLIES.
```

The READ statement assigns the first datum (FLIES) to A$, the second (TIME) to B$, and the third (a period) to P$. The PRINT statement then produces the output shown.

■   **REMARK**   On BASIC systems that allow both upper- and lowercase letters, line 120 could be written

```
120 DATA flies,Time,.
```

to produce the output

□
```
Time flies.
```

Note that the strings in the DATA line of Example 3 are not in quotation marks. The same rules that apply to strings typed in response to INPUT statements apply to strings in DATA lines. We'll repeat these rules:

1. Strings included in DATA lines usually are not quoted. Most BASIC systems require that you use quotes in only two situations:
   a. When a comma appears in the string. The comma is used to delimit BASIC constants.
   b. When significant blanks begin or end the string. (If such a string is not enclosed in quotation marks, the leading and trailing blanks are ignored.)
2. It is always correct to enclose strings in quotation marks.

EXAMPLE 4   **Here is a program to illustrate quoted and unquoted strings in DATA lines.**

```
10 READ Z$
20 WHILE Z$<>"END-OF-DATA"
30    PRINT Z$
40    READ Z$
50 NEXT (or WEND)
```

```
60 DATA 12345678,VI,"  AL",TO GO,"CLARK,JACK"
70 DATA END-OF-DATA
80 END
RUN

12345678
VI
  AL
TO GO
CLARK,JACK
```

Quotes are needed for " AL" because of the leading blanks and for "CLARK,JACK" because of the comma. Quotes are not needed for the string TO GO because the blank is not a leading blank.

■ **REMARK 1**   Note that the string END-OF-DATA in line 70 is not displayed in the output. It serves only as an *end-of-data* (EOD) *tag*. The use of end-of-data tags in DATA statements represents a common method of avoiding OUT OF DATA errors.

■ **REMARK 2**   Note also that the string 12345678 is displayed without a leading blank. When the READ statement obtains the value 12345678 for the *string* variable Z$, the computer stores it as eight distinct characters. This would not be so if 12345678 were assigned to a *numerical* variable. The statement

```
LET Z=12345678
```

stores the numbers 12345678 in a special binary form the computer uses to store numerical values.

As illustrated in the next example, both string and numerical data can be included in a single DATA statement, and a single READ statement can be used to read values for both string and numerical variables.

EXAMPLE 5   **Here is a program to produce a table summarizing the information contained in DATA statements.**

```
100 REM ********* DISPLAY COLUMN HEADINGS *********
110 PRINT "NAME","SCORE1","SCORE2","AVERAGE"
120 PRINT
130 REM ******* READ THE NUMBER OF STUDENTS *******
140 READ N
150 REM **** READ THE DATA AND DISPLAY TABLE VALUES ****
160 LET COUNT=1
170 WHILE COUNT<=N
180     READ N$,S1,S2
190     LET A=(S1+S2)/2
200     PRINT N$,S1,S2,A
210     LET COUNT=COUNT+1
220 NEXT (or WEND)
230 REM
300 REM *** FIRST DATA ITEM IS THE NUMBER OF STUDENTS ***
310 DATA 4
320 DATA CARL,71,79
330 DATA MARLENE,82,88
340 DATA SUZANNE,89,62
350 DATA WILLIAM,58,96
999 END
RUN
```

NAME	SCORE1	SCORE2	AVERAGE
CARL	71	79	75
MARLENE	82	88	85
SUZANNE	89	62	75.5
WILLIAM	58	96	77

The first READ statement (line 140) assigns the first datum (4) to the variable N. This N is then used to ensure that exactly four names with their corresponding scores are read and processed. This procedure illustrates another common method of avoiding OUT OF DATA errors. Include a count as the first datum, and then use this count to cause an exit from the loop when the prescribed number of data values has been read.

■ **REMARK**

Note that the variable COUNT serves as a counter for the loop described by lines 160–220. Thus, the loop is a counter-controlled loop as described in Section 9.1 and is more conveniently coded as a FOR loop. To do this, delete line 210 and make these changes:

```
160 FOR COUNT=1 TO N
220 NEXT COUNT
```

The general forms of the READ and DATA statements are as follows:

ln READ   (list of variables separated by commas)
ln DATA   (list of BASIC constants separated by commas)

The following rules govern the use of these two statements:

1. As many DATA lines as desired may be included in a program, and as many values as will fit may appear on each line. The values must be constants.
2. All values appearing in the DATA lines constitute a single list called the **data list.** The order in which data appear in this list is precisely the order in which they appear in the program—that is, from lowest to highest line numbers and, within a DATA line, from left to right.
3. When a READ statement is executed, the variables appearing are assigned successive values from the data list. You must write your READ and DATA statements so that only numerical values are assigned to numerical variables and only string values to string variables. The data appearing in DATA lines constitute a *single* data list; no special treatment is given to string constants. The execution of a READ statement will attempt to assign the next value in this list to the variable being assigned. If this next value is not of the same data type as the variable, either an error message will be displayed or your program will simply produce incorrect results.
4. It is not necessary that all data values be read. However, an attempt to read more data than appear in DATA lines will result in an error condition that causes an OUT OF DATA message and program execution to stop. Errors that stop program execution are called **fatal errors.**
5. If a DATA statement is encountered during program execution, the statement is ignored and control passes to the next line. Thus, DATA lines may appear anywhere in the program, although you should position them to make your programs more readable. Placing them near the end of a program is a common practice, especially if different data will be processed each time the program is run. If DATA lines will never be changed, it is sometimes better to place them just after the READ statements that read the data.

In flowcharting, the symbol

is used to designate any input or output that is carried out automatically with no user interaction. The PRINT and READ statements designate such actions; hence this symbol is used for both of these statements. You will recall that we have used the flowchart symbol for all INPUT statements. In flowcharting, this symbol is used to designate any process that requires user interaction, thus causing a temporary halt in execution. The INPUT statement does precisely this—the program waits until you enter data at the keyboard.

There is no flowchart symbol for DATA statements. DATA statements simply provide a means of presenting data to the computer for processing. When encountered during program execution, they cause nothing to happen. Thus they have no place in a flowchart, whose purpose is to describe the flow of activity in a program.

We conclude this section with another example illustrating the use of an EOD tag. Using an EOD tag as the last datum, rather than a count as the first, relieves us of the burden of counting the values in a data list.

EXAMPLE 6

In this example, we are given the results of a golf tournament and must produce a two-column table showing the names and total scores of all golfers. We must also tell how many golfers are tied for the lead (lowest total score). If there is a single winner, however, the winner's name and total score are to be displayed instead of the count. The results of the tournament are given to us in DATA lines as follows:

```
DATA BROUHA,70,72,68,69
DATA HERMAN,66,68,73,76
DATA MITCHELL,66,75,72,74
DATA NICKLAUS,73,70,70,65
DATA SANDERS,73,73,71,72
DATA SMYTHE,68,72,77,68
DATA XXX
```

**PROBLEM
ANALYSIS**

Producing a two-column table as specified in the problem statement is not new to us. After displaying a title and column headings, we can process the DATA lines one at a time to produce the table values.

In addition to producing the table, the problem statement says that we must find the lowest total score and count how many golfers have achieved this lowest score. Moreover, if there is a winner, we'll need that winner's name. This short analysis suggests that we use variable names for the following values:

$$
\begin{aligned}
\text{N\$} &= \text{player's name.} \\
\text{S1,S2,S3,S4} &= \text{scores for player N\$.} \\
\text{TTL} &= \text{total score for N\$.} \\
\text{LOW} &= \text{lowest total score.} \\
\text{WIN\$} &= \text{winner's name.} \\
\text{CNT} &= \text{count of players with lowest score.}
\end{aligned}
$$

Each time we read N$ and the four scores S1, S2, S3, and S4, we will calculate TTL = S1 + S2 + S3 + S4 and display N$ and TTL. Then if TTL = LOW, we have another player with the best score LOW so we'll add 1 to CNT. If TTL < LOW we have a new lowest score, so we'll assign TTL to LOW, assign N$ to WIN$, and set CNT to 1. Since the first player's total TTL will be the lowest score to that point, we'll start with LOW = a large number to ensure that TTL < LOW will be true for the first player.

**THE
ALGORITHM**

a. Display a title and column headings.
b. Initialize: LOW = 9999.
c. Read N$ (first player's name).

   d. Repeat the following as long as N$ <> "XXX":

      d1. Read S1, S2, S3, S4.

      d2. Calculate their sum TTL.

      d3. Display N$ and TTL.

      d4. If TTL = LOW, add 1 to CNT.

      d5. If TTL < LOW, assign TTL to LOW, N$ to WIN$, and set CNT to 1.

      d6. READ N$ (next player's name).

   e. Display the lowest score LOW.

   f. If CNT = 1, display winner's name WIN$; otherwise display CNT.

   g. Stop.

THE PROGRAM

```
100 REM GOLF TOURNAMENT PROGRAM
110 REM
120 REM        N$        PLAYER'S NAME
130 REM        S1-S4     SCORES FOR N$
140 REM        TTL       TOTAL SCORE FOR N$
150 REM        LOW       LOWEST SCORE
160 REM        WIN$      WINNER'S NAME
170 REM        CNT       NUMBER OF PLAYERS WITH LOW SCORE
180 REM
190 REM **********************************
200 REM DISPLAY TITLE AND COLUMN HEADINGS.
210 REM
220 PRINT "   GOLF TOURNAMENT"
230 PRINT "     (ROUNDS 1-4)"
240 PRINT
250 PRINT "PLAYER","TOTAL"
260 PRINT
270 REM **********************************
280 REM READ DATA TO PRODUCE TABLE VALUES
290 REM AND TO FIND LOW, CNT, AND WIN$.
300 REM
310 LET LOW=9999
320 READ N$
330 WHILE N$<>"XXX"
340     READ S1,S2,S3,S4
350     LET TTL=S1+S2+S3+S4
360     PRINT N$,TTL
370     IF TTL=LOW THEN CNT=CNT+1
380     IF TTL>=LOW THEN 420
390     LET LOW=TTL
400     LET WIN$=N$
410     LET CNT=1
420     READ N$
430 NEXT (or WEND)
440 REM
450 REM *********************
460 REM DISPLAY FINAL RESULTS.
470 PRINT
480 PRINT "BEST FOUR-ROUND TOTAL:";LOW
490 IF CNT=1 THEN PRINT "TOURNAMENT WINNER: ";WIN$
500 IF CNT<>1 THEN PRINT CNT;"PLAYERS ARE TIED FOR THE LEAD."
510 REM
800 REM ****************
810 REM TOURNAMENT RESULTS
820 REM
830 DATA BROUHA,70,72,68,69
840 DATA HERMAN,66,68,73,76
850 DATA MITCHELL,66,75,72,74
860 DATA NICKLAUS,73,70,70,65
870 DATA SANDERS,73,73,71,72
880 DATA SMYTHE,68,72,77,68
890 DATA XXX
900 END
```

```
RUN

    GOLF TOURNAMENT
      (ROUNDS 1-4)

PLAYER          TOTAL

BROUHA          279
HERMAN          283
MITCHELL        287
NICKLAUS        278
SANDERS         289
SMYTHE          285


BEST FOUR-ROUND TOTAL: 278
TOURNAMENT WINNER: NICKLAUS
```

■ 10.2 Problems

1. Show the output of each program.

   a.
   ```
   10 READ X
   20 WHILE X>=0
   30    LET Y=X-5
   40    PRINT X;Y
   50    READ X
   60 NEXT (or WEND)
   70 DATA 2,5,0,-1
   80 END
   ```

   b.
   ```
   10 READ A,B$,M$
   20 LET M$=B$
   30 PRINT M$;
   40 READ A,B$,M$
   50 LET M$=B$
   60 LET B$=M$
   70 PRINT B$
   80 DATA 6,CAT,MOUSE
   90 DATA 8,"WOMAN","MAN"
   99 END
   ```

   c.
   ```
   10 LET N=0
   20 READ X
   30 WHILE X<>9999
   40    LET N=N+1
   50    PRINT X
   60    READ X
   70 NEXT (or WEND)
   80 PRINT N
   90 DATA 7,3,18,-5,9999
   99 END
   ```

   d.
   ```
   100 LET B=0
   110 READ V
   120 WHILE V<>0
   130    IF V>24 AND V<76 THEN 160
   140    PRINT "BAD VALUE:";V
   150    LET B=B+1
   160    READ V
   170 NEXT (or WEND)
   180 IF B=0 THEN PRINT "DATA ARE OK."
   190 DATA 36,42,71,22,63,68,84,51,0
   200 END
   ```

2. Find and correct the errors in these programs.

   a.
   ```
   10 READ X,X$
   20 PRINT X$;X
   30 DATA "1";A
   40 END
   ```

   b.
   ```
   10 READ Y;Z$
   20 PRINT Z$;" OF ";Y
   30 DATA 42,SUMMER
   40 END
   ```

   c.
   ```
   10 READ B$
   20 IF B$=HELLO THEN 10
   30 PRINT B$
   40 DATA HELLO,GOODBYE
   50 END
   ```

   d.
   ```
   10 READ N$
   20 READ A,B,C
   30 PRINT "NAME: ";N$
   40 PRINT "AVERAGE:";(A+B+C)/3
   50 DATA TOM DOOLEY,JR
   60 DATA 85,81,76
   70 END
   ```

3. The following programs do not do what they claim. Find and correct all errors.

a.
```
100 REM DISPLAY THE SQUARES OF:
110 REM     12,37,21,96
120 READ A
130 LET A=A*A
140 WHILE A<>999
150    PRINT A
160    READ A
170    LET A=A*A
180 NEXT   (or WEND)
190 DATA 12,37,21,96,999
200 END
```

b.
```
100 REM AVERAGE DATA VALUES.
110 REM (1E-30 IS EOD-TAG.)
120 LET SUM=0
130 LET C=1
140 READ X
150 WHILE X<>1E-30
160    LET SUM=SUM+X
170    LET C=C+1
180 NEXT   (or WEND)
190 PRINT "AVERAGE IS";SUM/C
200 DATA 18,23,17,22
210 DATA 1E-30
220 END
```

c.
```
100 REM COUNT DATA VALUES,
110 REM BUT NOT 999.
120 LET C=0
130 WHILE V<999
140    READ V
150    LET C=C+1
160 NEXT   (or WEND)
170 PRINT "DATA COUNT: ";C
180 DATA 275,863,1262,1344
190 DATA 2765,999
200 END
```

In Problems 4–11, write a program to perform each task specified.

4. Read values from DATA lines two at a time. Display each pair of values, their sum, and their average on one line. Run your program using the following DATA lines. The last two values $(-1,-1)$ are to be used to detect the end of the data.

```
800 DATA 70,80,90,65,75,85
810 DATA 50,40,65,80,78,76
820 DATA 62,60,65,50,60,85
830 DATA 35,45,60,90,96,92
890 DATA -1,-1
```

5. Read values three at a time from DATA lines and display them only if the third is greater than the average of the first two. Run your program using the data in Problem 4. (Change only line 890.)

6. Read values three at a time from DATA lines and display them only if they are in ascending order. Use the data in Problem 4. (Change only line 890.)

7. Find how many of the numbers appearing in DATA lines lie between 40 and 60, inclusive, and determine the average of these numbers. Use the data in Problem 4.

8. A list of scores in the range 0 to 100 is to be examined to determine the following counts:

$C1$ = number of scores less than 40

$C2$ = number of scores between 40 and 60, inclusive

$C3$ = number of scores greater than 60

Determine these counts for any list appearing in DATA lines. Use the data in Problem 4.

9. A list of scores in the range 0 to 100 is to be examined to determine the following counts:

   C1 = number of scores less than 20
   C2 = number of scores less than 40 but at least 20
   C3 = number of scores less than 60 but at least 40
   C4 = number of scores less than 80 but at least 60
   C5 = number of scores not less than 80

   Determine these counts for any list appearing in DATA lines. Use the data in Problem 4.

10. A candidate for political office conducted a preelection poll. Each voter polled was assigned a number from 1 to 3 as follows:

    1 = will vote for candidate
    2 = leans toward candidate but still undecided
    3 = all other cases

    Tally the results of this poll. Use DATA lines to present the data to the computer.

11. Modify Problem 10 by assigning two values to each voter. The first is as stated; the second is to designate whether the voter is female (F) or male (M). There are now six counts to be determined. (Use READ A,S$ to read the two values assigned to a voter.)

For Problems 12–16, write programs to produce reports as specified. Make sure each report has a title and each column has an appropriate heading. All data are to be presented in DATA lines.

12. The following DATA lines show the salaries for all salaried employees in a small firm. [The first value (10) denotes how many salaries are listed.]

    ```
    800 DATA 10
    810 DATA 19923,20240,20275,21390,22560
    820 DATA 22997,23423,24620,29240,32730
    ```

    Prepare a report showing the effect of a flat across-the-board raise of R dollars in addition to a percentage increase of P percent. R and P are to be input. Include three columns labeled PRESENT SALARY, RAISE, and NEW SALARY.

13. The following DATA lines show the annual salaries for all salaried employees in a firm. Each salary amount is followed by a count of the number of employees earning that amount. This firm has a salary step schedule. (The values 0, 0 are end-of-data tags.)

    ```
    800 DATA 19020,4,20250,8,22330,16,22940,30
    810 DATA 23570,21,24840,86,25920,28,26520,7
    820 DATA 0,0
    ```

    Prepare a three-column report as in Problem 12. In addition, conclude the report by displaying the total cost to the owners of the old salary package, the total cost of the new salary package, the total dollar amount of all raises (the difference of the previous two figures), and the overall percent increase this amount represents.

14. Given the following information, produce a three-column report showing the employee number, monthly sales, and commission for each employee if the commission rate for each person is 6%.

Employee number	Monthly sales
018266234	$4,050
026196551	6,500
034257321	3,750
016187718	3,640
023298049	7,150

15. Given the following information, produce a four-column report showing the employee name, the monthly sales, the commission rate, and the total commission for each employee.

Employee name	Monthly sales	Commission rate
Hart	$28,400	2%
Wilson	34,550	2.5%
Brown	19,600	3%
Ruiz	14,500	2%
Jensen	22,300	3.25%
Grogan	31,350	1.5%

16. (Electric Bill Problem) Given the following information, produce a report showing the customer number, total number of kilowatt hours (KWH) used, and the total monthly bill. The charges are computed according to the following schedule: $1.41 for the first 14 KWH, the next 85 KWH at $0.0389/KWH, the next 200 at $0.0214/KWH, the next 300 at $0.0134/KWH, and the excess at $0.0099/KWH. In addition, there is a fuel-adjustment charge of $0.0322/KWH for all kilowatt hours used.

Customer number	Previous month's reading	Current reading
0516	25,346	25,973
2634	47,947	48,851
2917	21,342	21,652
2853	893,462	894,258
3576	347,643	348,748
3943	41,241	41,783
3465	887,531	888,165

■ 10.3 The RESTORE Statement

We have described a *data list* as the list of all data values appearing in all DATA lines in a program. Associated with a data list is a conceptual *pointer* indicating the value to be read by the next READ statement. The pointer is initially set to the first value in the list; then each time a value is read, the pointer moves to the next value. The BASIC statement

ln RESTORE

positions the pointer back to the beginning of the data list so the values can be read again.

EXAMPLE 7   **This example illustrates the action caused by the RESTORE statement.**

The program segment

```
10 READ A,B
20 RESTORE
30 READ C
40 RESTORE
50 READ D,E,F
60 DATA 1,2,3,4,5,6
```

assigns values to A,B,C,D,E, and F as follows:

Line 10 assigns the first two data values (1 and 2) to A and B, respectively.
Line 20 positions the pointer back to the first datum.
Line 30 assigns the first datum (1) to C.
Line 40 once again restores the pointer to the first datum.
Line 50 assigns the values 1, 2, and 3 to D, E, and F, respectively.

Following are two examples that illustrate typical ways in which the RESTORE statement is used.

EXAMPLE 8   **Here is a program to display two lists obtained from a single data list.**

```
100 PRINT "SCORES 70 OR MORE:";
110 LET COUNT=0              'Data counter
120 READ X
130 WHILE X<>999
140    LET COUNT=COUNT+1
150    IF X>=70 THEN PRINT X;
160    READ X
170 NEXT   (or WEND)
180 PRINT
190 RESTORE
200 PRINT "SCORES LESS THAN 70:";
210 FOR K=1 TO COUNT
220    READ X
230    IF X<70 THEN PRINT X;
240 NEXT K
250 DATA 78,84,65,32,93,58,88,76,83
260 DATA 999
270 END
RUN

SCORES 70 OR MORE: 78  84  93  88  76  83
SCORES LESS THAN 70: 65  32  58  68
```

The PRINT statements in lines 100 and 200 describe what this program does. Since all numbers 70 or greater must be displayed before any number less than 70 is displayed, the data must be examined twice. The RESTORE statement in line 190 allows this to happen.

■ REMARK 1   Without the RESTORE statement, 10 variables would be needed for the 10 numbers appearing in the DATA lines. With the RESTORE statement, only one (X) is needed.

■ REMARK 2   Notice that the data are first read in a WHILE loop (lines 130–170) that counts the number of values other than the end-of-data tag 999. With this count, we were able to read
□   the data a second time by using a FOR loop.

EXAMPLE 9   **Here is program to search a list for any value typed at the keyboard.**

```
100 REM ***************** ON MIXING COLORS ******************
110 REM
120 REM    X$ = A COLOR INCLUDED IN DATA LINES
130 REM    Y$ = INFORMATION ABOUT COLOR X$
140 REM    C$ = A STRING INPUT VALUE
150 REM
160 PRINT "THIS PROGRAM GIVES INFORMATION ABOUT COLORS."
170 PRINT "ALL ENTRIES YOU MAKE MUST BE IN UPPER CASE."
180 PRINT
190 PRINT "COLOR (TYPE END TO STOP)";
200 INPUT C$
210 WHILE C$<>"END"
220    REM ---------- SEARCH DATA LIST FOR COLOR C$ ----------
230    READ X$,Y$
240    WHILE X$<>C$ AND X$<>"XXX"
250      READ X$,Y$
260    NEXT   (or WEND)
270    REM ----------------- DISPLAY OUTPUT -----------------
280    IF X$="XXX" THEN PRINT C$;" IS NOT IN MY LIST OF COLORS."
290    IF X$<>"XXX" THEN PRINT Y$
300    REM ---------- PREPARE FOR NEXT INPUT VALUE ----------
310    RESTORE
320    PRINT
330    PRINT "COLOR (TYPE END TO STOP)";
340    INPUT C$
350 NEXT   (or WEND)
500 DATA WHITE, USED FOR TINTING
510 DATA BLACK, USED FOR SHADING
```

```
520 DATA YELLOW, A PRIMARY COLOR
530 DATA RED, A PRIMARY COLOR
540 DATA BLUE, A PRIMARY COLOR
550 DATA ORANGE, MIX YELLOW AND RED.
560 DATA GREEN, MIX YELLOW AND BLUE.
570 DATA PURPLE, MIX RED AND BLUE.
580 DATA PINK, MIX RED AND WHITE.
590 DATA GRAY, MIX BLACK AND WHITE.
600 DATA MAGENTA, MIX RED WITH A SPECK OF BLACK.
610 DATA XXX,YYY
999 END
RUN

THIS PROGRAM GIVES INFORMATION ABOUT COLORS.
ALL ENTRIES YOU MAKE MUST BE IN UPPER CASE.

COLOR (TYPE END TO STOP)? BLUE
A PRIMARY COLOR

COLOR (TYPE END TO STOP)? MAGENTA
MIX RED WITH A SPECK OF BLACK.

COLOR (TYPE END TO STOP)? AQUA
AQUA IS NOT IN MY LIST OF COLORS.

COLOR (TYPE END TO STOP)? END
```

The list of colors being searched in lines 230–260 consists of every other datum—we use READ X$, Y$ to read the data and compare the input value C$ with X$, a color, and not with Y$ that contains information about the color.

When the value read for X$ by line 250 is the input value C$ or the end-of-data tag XXX, the WHILE condition in line 240 is false and an exit is made from the search loop to line 280. If X$ = "XXX", the input value C$ is not one of the colors included in the DATA lines and line 280 displays a message that this is so. If X$ ≠ "XXX", then X$ = C$ is one of the included colors and line 290 displays Y$, which contains information about this color.

After the output for the input value C$ is displayed, lines 310–350 restore the data pointer to the first datum, request another input value C$, and transfer control back to line 210. This process is repeated until the user types END.

■ **REMARK**   Note that the information in DATA lines does not represent input data in the usual sense. Rather, it represents more or less permanent data that the program uses while processing other information (values typed at the keyboard). This represents a common usage of DATA statements.

☐

Many applications require that the values given in DATA lines be used more than once. In Example 8, data included in DATA lines had to be examined twice to produce two lists, and in Example 9, a table of colors and color-mixing instructions had to be examined from its beginning to search for each input value typed at the keyboard. We conclude this chapter with a detailed analysis of another programming task that requires examining input data more than once.

EXAMPLE 10   **A clothing manufacturer has retail outlets in Miami, Orlando, Chicago, Austin, Seattle, and Montreal. Each month, the company compiles a report showing three amounts for each location: the month's sales, payroll, and building maintenance costs. Our task is to write a program that uses this information to help answer questions that management might ask concerning the company's financial operations. Following is a portion of last month's report:**

Location	Sales	Payroll	Maintenance
Miami	$45,620	$15,600	$3,400
Orlando	27,000	16,000	2,540
Chicago	64,000	14,280	5,250
.	.	.	.
.	.	.	.
.	.	.	.

PROBLEM ANALYSIS

The problem statement is incomplete—in practice, many are. We need to know what questions the program should answer. Even without this knowledge, however, there is something that we can do. Whatever tasks the program will carry out, it should begin by displaying a list of these tasks. It should also tell the user how to specify which tasks are to be performed. We'll assign the option numbers 1, 2, 3, and so on, to these tasks and require the user to select a task by typing its option number. Thus, we will write a menu-driven program.

This brief discussion allows us to write the following simple but complete algorithm. As in all menu-driven programs, one of the options will be to end program execution.

THE ALGORITHM

    a. Display a menu showing the available options.
    b. Repeat until the end option is selected:
        b1. Input an option number OP.
        b2. Carry out the task specified by OP.

In addition to the end option, let's include an option to display the menu and another to allow the user to see the current monthly report. Thus, we can begin by writing a program with only these three options:

1. Display this menu.
2. End the program.
3. Display this month's report.

We will use an ON GOTO statement of the form

    ON OP GOTO **ln₁, ln₂, ln₃**

to transfer control to the program segment that carries out the specified option OP. The program, however, must be organized so that it's a simple matter to include new options as they are determined. Toward this end, we will designate line 1000 for the menu option (OP = 1), 2000 for the End option (OP = 2), 3000 for the option to display the monthly report (OP = 3), and we will use line numbers less than 1000 for the rest of the program—that is, for all but the program segments that carry out the options. For the options mentioned, this program segment will contain the statement

```
ON OP GOTO 1000,2000,3000
```

for option selection. Each of the program segments at lines 1000, 2000, and 3000 will end by transferring control back to the statement that follows the ON GOTO statement.

Even though we have not yet written a single line of code (other than the ON GOTO statement), it isn't difficult to see how we will be able to include new options. For example, suppose we are told that management might ask for a report showing the sales/payroll ratio for each outlet. We could write the code for this new task at line 4000, being sure to end by transferring control back to the statement that follows the ON GOTO statement. The only other changes needed would be to add the option

4. Display the sales/payroll ratios.

to the menu and change the ON GOTO statement to

```
ON OP GOTO 1000,2000,3000,4000
```

Let's write a program to allow the four options already mentioned:

1. Display this menu.
2. End the program.
3. Display this month's report.
4. Display the sales/payroll ratios.

Writing BASIC code to carry out these options is rather routine and requires no new programming technique. Thus, we can proceed directly to the coding stage. Since both Options 3 and 4—and any new options to be added later—will require examining the current month's sales, payroll, and maintenance report, we will include these data in DATA statements and use RESTORE to allow the data to be read as many times as is necessary. Also, since the DATA lines must be changed each month, we'll place them in a prominent position near the beginning of the program.

THE PROGRAM

```
100 PRINT "PROGRAM TO EXAMINE MONTHLY REPORT OF:"
110 PRINT
120 PRINT "            SALES"
130 PRINT "            PAYROLL"
140 PRINT "            MAINTENANCE"
160 REM ***********************
170 REM *         DATA         *
180 REM ***********************
190 REM
200 REM LOCATIONS FOLLOWED BY:
210 REM SALES,PAYROLL,MAINTENANCE
220 REM
230 DATA MIAMI,45620,15600,3400
240 DATA ORLANDO,27000,16000,2540
250 DATA CHICAGO,64000,14280,5250
260 DATA AUSTIN,33500,10270,2600
270 DATA SEATTLE,59200,17200,4290
280 DATA MONTREAL,52000,15000,5100
399 DATA END,0,0,0
400 REM
410 GOTO 1000                        'Display menu.
420 REM
430 REM ********************************
440 REM *    OPTION SELECTION SECTION    *
450 REM ********************************
460     PRINT
470     PRINT "OPTION NUMBER ";         'Select option.
480     INPUT OP
490     IF OP<0 OR OP>255 THEN OP=0    'Avoid possible crash.
500     ON OP GOTO 1000,2000,3000,4000
510 IF OP<>2 THEN 460                 'Was End Picked?
520 GOTO 9999                         'Yes. Stop.
530 REM
540 REM **************************************************
550 REM *       PROGRAM SEGMENTS TO CARRY OUT OPTIONS       *
560 REM **************************************************
570 REM
1000 REM **************************************************
1010 REM       OPTION 1:   DISPLAY MENU
1020 PRINT
1030 PRINT "AVAILABLE OPTIONS:"
1040 PRINT
1050 PRINT "     1    DISPLAY THIS MENU."
1060 PRINT "     2    END THE PROGRAM."
1070 PRINT "     3    DISPLAY THIS MONTH'S REPORT."
1080 PRINT "     4    DISPLAY SALES/PAYROLL RATIOS."
1200 REM
1210 GOTO 510                          'Return
```

```
1220 REM
2000 REM *****************************************************
2010 REM          OPTION 2:  END OPTION
2020 PRINT
2030 PRINT "PROGRAM TERMINATED."
2040 GOTO 510                              'Return
2050 REM
3000 REM *****************************************************
3010 REM          OPTION 3:  MONTHLY REPORT
3020 PRINT
3030 PRINT "            CURRENT MONTHLY REPORT"
3040 PRINT
3050 PRINT " LOCATION     SALES      PAYROLL     MAINTENANCE"
3060 LET F$=" ########  ######      #####        ####"
3070 PRINT
3080 READ L$,S,P,M
3090 WHILE L$<>"END"
3100    PRINT USING F$,L$,S,P,M
3110    READ L$,S,P,M
3120 NEXT   (or WEND)
3130 RESTORE
3140 GOTO 510                              'Return
3150 REM
4000 REM *****************************************************
4010 REM          OPTION 4:  SALES/PAYROLL REPORT
4020 PRINT
4030 PRINT "SALES/PAYROLL RATIOS"
4040 PRINT
4050 PRINT " LOCATION        RATIO"
4060 LET G$=" ########       ##.##"
4070 PRINT
4080 READ L$,S,P,M
4090 WHILE L$<>"END"
4100    PRINT USING G$,L$,S/P
4110    READ L$,S,P,M
4120 NEXT   (or WEND)
4130 RESTORE
4140 GOTO 510                              'Return
9999 END
```

We ran this program for the Options 3, 4, and 2, in that order, and obtained the following output:

```
PROGRAM TO EXAMINE MONTHLY REPORT OF:

        SALES
        PAYROLL
        MAINTENANCE


AVAILABLE OPTIONS:

   1    DISPLAY THIS MENU.
   2    END THE PROGRAM.
   3    DISPLAY THIS MONTH'S REPORT.
   4    DISPLAY SALES/PAYROLL RATIOS.


OPTION NUMBER ? 3

        CURRENT MONTHLY REPORT

LOCATION     SALES      PAYROLL     MAINTENANCE

MIAMI        45620      15600         3400
ORLANDO      27000      16000         2540
CHICAGO      64000      14280         5250
AUSTIN       33500      10270         2600
SEATTLE      59200      17200         4290
MONTREAL     52000      15000         5100
```

```
        OPTION NUMBER ? 4

        SALES/PAYROLL RATIOS

        LOCATION        RATIO

        MIAMI           2.92
        ORLANDO         1.69
        CHICAGO         4.48
        AUSTIN          3.26
        SEATTLE         3.44
        MONTREAL        3.47

        OPTION NUMBER ? 2

        PROGRAM TERMINATED.
```

■ **REMARK 1**   Each time a new task is added to this program, you must include a RESTORE statement that will be executed after the data have been read. If it is forgotten, the program will produce an out of data error when carrying out the next task. To ensure that this doesn't happen, you can include the line

```
        495 RESTORE
```

to restore the data pointer each time the user selects an option. No other RESTORE statement is needed.

■ **REMARK 2**   In addition to reserving line numbers for new tasks (lines 5000 on), we have reserved line numbers for possible new DATA statements (lines 290–390) and for future additions to the menu (lines 1090–1190).

☐

■ 10.4 Problems

1. Show the output of each program.

   a.
   ```
   10 LET I=2
   20 WHILE I<=6
   30     READ Y
   40     PRINT Y
   50     LET I=I+2
   60 NEXT (or WEND)
   65 RESTORE
   70 DATA 9,3,5,8,12
   80 END
   ```

   b.
   ```
   100 FOR I=1 TO 4
   110     READ X
   120     IF X=5 THEN RESTORE
   130     PRINT X
   140 NEXT I
   150 DATA 3,5,8,9,6
   160 END
   ```

   c.
   ```
   10 READ A$,B$,C$
   20 RESTORE
   30 READ D$
   40 PRINT B$;C$;D$
   50 DATA HEAD,ROB,IN,HOOD
   60 END
   ```

   d.
   ```
   10 READ A1,A2,A3
   20 PRINT A1,A2,A3
   30 RESTORE
   40 READ A3,A2,A1
   50 PRINT A3,A2,A1
   60 DATA 10,20,30
   70 END
   ```

In Problems 2–8, write a program to carry out each task described.

2. Allow a user to input several words and determine whether they appear in the DATA lines. For each word input, display the message IS IN THE LIST or IS NOT IN THE LIST, whichever is appropriate. Let the user end the run by typing DONE. Try your program by using the following DATA statements (you may wish to add to the data list):

   ```
   500 REM SOME CONJUNCTIONS
   510 DATA ALTHOUGH,AS,BUT,HOWBEIT,HOWEVER
   520 DATA IF,OR,SINCE,THOUGH,YET
   599 DATA END-OF-DATA
   ```

3. Several pairs of values are included in DATA lines. The first value in each pair represents an item code, and the second represents the current selling price. Allow a user to type several item codes to obtain the current selling prices. If an incorrect code is typed, an appropriate message should be displayed. Allow the user to end the run by typing DONE. Use the following data lines:

```
500 REM ITEMS WITH PRICES
510 DATA X100,12.39,X110,17.97,X120,23.55,X130,20.50
520 DATA Y100,72.60,Y110,85.00,Y120,97.43
530 DATA XXX,0
```

4. A list of numbers appears in DATA lines in ascending order. Allow a user to type a number. If the number appears in the list, all numbers in the list up to but not including it should be displayed. If it doesn't appear, a message to that effect should be displayed. In either case let the user enter another number. If 0 is typed, the run should terminate. Use the following DATA lines and inform the user that the numbers are in the range 1 to 50.

```
500 DATA 1,3,6,9,13,18,24,31,39,48
510 DATA 0
```

5. A wholesale firm has two warehouses, designated A and B. During a recent inventory, the following data were compiled:

Item	Warehouse	Quantity on hand	Average cost/unit
6625	A	52,000	$1.954
6204	A	40,000	3.126
3300	B	8,500	19.532
5925	A	22,000	6.884
0220	B	6,200	88.724
2100	B	4,350	43.612
4800	A	21,500	2.741
0077	A	15,000	1.605
1752	B	200	193.800

Prepare a separate inventory report for each warehouse. Each report is to contain the given information and show the total cost represented by the inventory of each item.

6. Use the inventory data shown in Problem 5 to prepare an inventory report for the warehouse whose entire stock represents the greater cost to the company.

7. The O'Halloran Shoe Company wants to know the average monthly income for its retail store and the number of months in which the income exceeds this average. Carry out this task with the following DATA lines, which give the 12 monthly income amounts:

```
500 DATA 13200.57,11402.48,9248.23,9200.94
510 DATA 11825.50,12158.07,11028.40,22804.22
520 DATA 18009.40,12607.25,19423.36,24922.50
```

8. I. M. Good, a candidate for political office, conducted a preelection poll. Each voter polled was assigned a number from 1 to 5 as follows:

```
1 = will vote for Good
2 = leaning toward Good but still undecided
3 = will vote for Shepherd, Good's only opponent
4 = leaning toward Shepherd but still undecided
5 = all other cases
```

The results of the poll are included in DATA lines as follows:

```
500 DATA 1,1,2,5,3,5,1,2
510 DATA 5,5,2, . . .
        .
        .
        .
998 DATA 0
```

Write a program that displays two tables as follows:

```
            TABLE 1
                    FOR    LEANING
    GOOD             -       -
    SHEPHERD         -       -
            TABLE 2
                    FOR OR    PERCENTAGE OF TOTAL
                    LEANING   NUMBER OF PEOPLE POLLED
    GOOD             -                -
    SHEPHERD         -                -
    OTHERS           -                -
```

In Problems 9–12, write a menu-driven program to carry out the specified tasks. Be sure to write each program so that it is a simple matter to add new tasks at a later time.

9. Below are last year's monthly income figures for the Garruga Dating Service. Include these data in DATA lines for a program that allows the user to obtain one or more of the following:
   a. A two-column table showing precisely the given information.
   b. The total income for last year.
   c. A two-column table showing each month and the amount by which the income for the month exceeds the average monthly income. (Some of these amounts will be negative.)

January	18,000	July	20,000
February	13,500	August	22,650
March	11,200	September	18,500
April	16,900	October	12,500
May	20,500	November	9,250
June	22,200	December	11,300

10. First write a program as specified in Problem 9 and run it to make sure it works. Then modify the program so that the user also can obtain a list of the months for which the income amount exceeds a value that is entered by the user.

11. Below is a table containing information about employees of the Mendosa Publishing Company. Include this information in DATA lines for a program that will carry out, at the request of the user, any of the following tasks:
    a. Display precisely the given information.
    b. Display the names of all employees who have been with the company for at least Y years. (Have the program request a value for Y *after* this option has been selected.)

Name	Age	Years of service
Lia Brookes	22	1
Mary Crimmins	27	3
Lee Marston	46	18
Joe Nunes	58	9
Paul Reese	23	2
Jean Saulnier	34	12
Jesse Torres	68	21
Mara Walenda	32	7

12. First write a program as specified in Problem 11 and run it to make sure it works. Then modify the program so that it will also carry out, at the request of the user, the following additional tasks:
    c. Display the names of all employees.
    d. Display the average age and average years of service of all employees.

■ 10.5 Review True-or-False Quiz

1. The READ and DATA statements provide the means to present data to the computer without having to type them during program execution.　　　　**T　F**
2. DATA statements must follow the READ statements that read the data values.　　**T　F**
3. If READ A,B,C,D is used to read data from the line

    ```
    300 DATA 5,1234E-03,7+3,12
    ```

    the variables A, B, C, and D will be assigned the respective values 5, 1.234, 10, and 12.　　**T　F**
4. A *pointer* is a special value appearing in a data list.　　**T　F**
5. It is not necessary to read an entire data list before the first value can be read a second time.　　**T　F**
6. At most one RESTORE statement may be used in a BASIC program.　　**T　F**
7. The READ and DATA statements can be useful when no interaction between the computer and the user is required.　　**T　F**
8. When we include a string in a DATA statement, quotation marks are sometimes necessary.　　**T　F**
9. It is sometimes useful to assign values to both string variables and numerical variables using the same READ statement.　　**T　F**

11 Subroutines

All but very simple programming applications involve carrying out several subtasks. As illustrated in many of the worked-out examples, these subtasks are coded as program segments, which are combined, as specified in an algorithm, to give the required program. BASIC subroutines, the topic of this chapter, provide a convenient way to include such program segments in your programs. By using subroutines as described in this chapter, you can write programs that are easy to read, to debug, and to modify, should that be required.

A BASIC subroutine is a program segment written in such a way that it can be referenced (that is, executed) from any part of the program, with program control returning to the BASIC statement following the one that caused the subroutine to be executed. Thus, if the same sequence of programming lines is needed in two or more places in a program you can code it once, as a subroutine, and reference it whenever it must be executed.

In Section 11.1 we describe the RETURN statement, which allows you to write subroutines, and the GOSUB statement, which allows you to execute these subroutines. In Section 11.3 we describe the ON GOSUB statement, which allows you to execute selectively any one of two or more subroutines.

■ 11.1 The GOSUB and RETURN Statements

The statement

GOSUB **ln**

transfers control to the subroutine at line **ln**. This subroutine can be any sequence of programming lines, but it must contain at least one RETURN statement. A RETURN statement will transfer control back to the statement that follows GOSUB **ln.**

Here is a subroutine to display a row of dashes:

```
500 REM ***SUBROUTINE TO DISPLAY 24 DASHES***
510 FOR I=1 TO 24
520    PRINT "-";
530 NEXT I
540 PRINT
550 RETURN
```

Program control is transferred to this subroutine each time the statement GOSUB 500 is encountered during program execution. In a program that contains this subroutine, the lines

```
200 GOSUB 500
210 PRINT "TODAY'S STARTING LINE-UP"
220 GOSUB 500
230 (program continuation)
```

will cause the output

```
--------------------------
TODAY'S STARTING LINE-UP
--------------------------
```

Line 200 transfers control to line 500 (the subroutine) and a row of dashes is displayed. The RETURN statement in line 550 then transfers control back to line 210, the first line following the GOSUB statement just used. When line 220 is encountered, control again passes to the subroutine and another row of dashes is displayed. This time the RETURN statement transfers control back to line 230.

EXAMPLE 1   **Here is a program to illustrate the GOSUB and RETURN statements.**

```
100 PRINT "THIS PROGRAM DISPLAYS THE AVERAGE"
110 PRINT "OF ANY TWO NUMBERS YOU TYPE AND"
120 PRINT "ALSO THE AVERAGE OF THEIR SQUARES."
130 PRINT
140 PRINT "FIRST NUMBER";
150 INPUT A
160 PRINT "SECOND NUMBER";
170 INPUT B
180 REM --- DISPLAY THEIR AVERAGE ---
190 GOSUB 300
200 PRINT
210 LET A=A*A
220 LET B=B*B
230 PRINT "FIRST SQUARE:";A
240 PRINT "SECOND SQUARE:";B
250 REM --- DISPLAY THEIR AVERAGE ---
260 GOSUB 300
270 GOTO 999
300 REM ***********************
310 REM * SUBROUTINE TO DISPLAY *
320 REM *  AVERAGE OF A AND B.  *
330 REM ***********************
340 REM
350 LET M=(A+B)/2
360 PRINT "THEIR AVERAGE IS";M
370 RETURN
999 END
RUN

THIS PROGRAM DISPLAYS THE AVERAGE
OF ANY TWO NUMBERS YOU TYPE AND
ALSO THE AVERAGE OF THEIR SQUARES.

FIRST NUMBER? 3
SECOND NUMBER? 4
THEIR AVERAGE IS 3.5

FIRST SQUARE: 9
SECOND SQUARE: 16
THEIR AVERAGE IS 12.5
```

For the run shown, lines 150 and 170 assign the input values 3 and 4 to A and B, respectively, and line 190 transfers control to the subroutine, which displays 3.5, the average of

A and B. The RETURN statement then transfers control back to line 200, the line following the GOSUB statement just used. Lines 210–240 assign the squares (9 and 16) to A and B, and display these values. When line 260 is encountered, a second transfer is made to the subroutine, and 12.5, the average of 9 and 16, is displayed. This time the RETURN statement transfers control back to line 270, which in this program terminates execution.

■ **REMARK 1**   The GOTO statement (line 270) ensures that the subroutine is entered only under the control of a GOSUB statement.

■ **REMARK 2**   When the GOSUB statement in line 190 or line 260 is executed, we say that the subroutine has been *called*.

■ **REMARK 3**   The GOSUB statement differs from the GOTO statement in that it causes the computer to "remember" which statement to execute next when it encounters a RETURN statement. As described, this is the statement immediately following the GOSUB statement used to call the subroutine.

■ **REMARK 4**   Note that we used M (for mean)—not A (for average)—in the subroutine. If line 350 is changed to

```
350 LET A=(A+B)/2
```

the original value of A will be lost during the first subroutine call, and incorrect results will be displayed. Thus, when writing subroutines make sure that the variable names you use do not conflict with variable names used in other parts of the program for different purposes.

The general forms of the GOSUB and RETURN statements are as follows:

ln₁ GOSUB ln₂   (**ln₂** is the line number of the first statement of the subroutine.)
ln RETURN

Line **ln₁** transfers control to line **ln₂**, and program execution continues as usual. When the first RETURN statement is encountered, control transfers back to the line following line **ln₁**.

EXAMPLE 2   **Each of Parts a–c shows a subroutine that can be used to process these data:**

```
1000 REM FOR EACH ITEM IN STOCK, THESE DATA SHOW:
1010 REM
1020 REM    ITEM CODE, ITEM DESCRIPTION, ITEM PRICE
1030 REM
1040 DATA Y222, YARDSTICK, 6.79
1050 DATA S955, SAW-RIP, 12.88
1060 DATA S457, SAW-CROSSCUT, 14.00
1070 DATA T12, 12 FOOT TAPE, 7.66
1080 DATA T16, 16 FOOT TAPE, 9.95
1090 DATA C777, CROWBAR, 13.52
1990 DATA END,END,0
```

Although we begin and end each subroutine with a RESTORE statement, you will not always need to do this.

```
a. 2000 REM SUBROUTINE TO COUNT DIFFERENT ITEMS
   2010 REM IN STOCK AND DISPLAY THIS COUNT.
   2020 REM
   2030 REM VALUE RETURNED BY SUBROUTINE: COUNT
   2040 REM
   2050 RESTORE
   2060 LET COUNT=0
   2070 READ CODE$,ITEM$,PRICE
```

```
2080 WHILE CODE$<>"END"
2090    LET COUNT=COUNT+1
2100    READ CODE$,ITEM$,PRICE
2110 NEXT   (or WEND)
2120 PRINT "NUMBER OF DIFFERENT ITEMS:";COUNT
2130 RESTORE
2140 RETURN
```

If a program contains this subroutine and the given data, the line

```
200 GOSUB 2000            'Find and display item count.
```

will produce the display:

```
NUMBER OF DIFFERENT ITEMS: 6
```

In the next subroutine, we'll assume that line 200 has been executed. This will allow us to use COUNT to simplify coding the loop that reads and processes the data.

```
b. 3000 REM SUBROUTINE TO DISPLAY ITEM CODES AND DESCRIPTIONS
   3010 RESTORE
   3020 PRINT
   3030 PRINT "ITEM CODE", "DESCRIPTION"
   3040 PRINT "---------", "--------------------"
   3050 FOR N=1 TO COUNT
   3060    READ CODE$,ITEM$,PRICE
   3070    PRINT CODE$,ITEM$
   3080 NEXT N
   3090 PRINT
   3100 RESTORE
   3110 RETURN
```

For the given data, the statement

```
300 GOSUB 3000            'Display codes and descriptions.
```

will produce the output:

```
ITEM CODE       DESCRIPTION
---------       --------------------
Y222            YARDSTICK
S955            SAW-RIP
S457            SAW-CROSSCUT
T12             12 FOOT TAPE
T16             16 FOOT TAPE
C777            CROWBAR
```

```
c. 4000 REM SUBROUTINE TO FIND PRICE FOR ANY ITEM
   4010 REM WHOSE CODE IS ENTERED AT THE KEYBOARD.
   4010 REM
   4020 PRINT "ITEM CODE";
   4030 INPUT CODE$
   4040 REM ------ SEARCH DATA FOR CODE --------
   4080 RESTORE
   4090 READ C$,I$,P
   4100 WHILE C$<>CODE$ AND C$<>"END"
   4110    READ C$,I$,PRICE
   4120 NEXT   (or WEND)
   4130 IF C$<>"END" THEN PRINT USING "PRICE $$###.##";P
   4140 IF C$="END" THEN PRINT CODE$;" IS AN INVALID CODE."
   4150 RESTORE
   4160 RETURN
```

The programming line

```
400 GOSUB 4000            'Find price for a code.
```

will produce the display:

```
ITEM CODE?
```

If you enter S457, the display will be

```
ITEM CODE? S457
PRICE:   $14.00
```

If you enter T24, the display will be

```
ITEM CODE? T24
T24 IS AN INVALID CODE.
```

A subroutine may be called from within another subroutine. Following is a schematic representation of a program that does this. The action of the program is indicated by the arrows labeled a, b, c, and d.

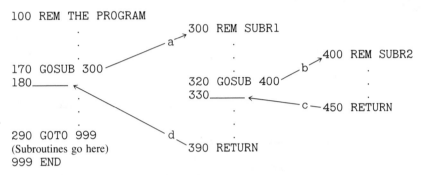

```
100 REM THE PROGRAM
          .                          300 REM SUBR1
          .                  a                 .
          .                                    .                    400 REM SUBR2
170 GOSUB 300                              320 GOSUB 400       b             .
180_____                                  330_____     ←              .
          .                                                   c—450 RETURN
          .
290 GOTO 999                    d
(Subroutines go here)              390 RETURN
999 END
```

Following are two examples that further illustrate the use of subroutines. The program in Example 3 uses a subroutine that calls another subroutine. Example 4 shows an application for an airline charter service.

EXAMPLE 3

Here is a program to display a short report for each employee whose name and annual salary are included in DATA lines. Two subroutines are used. The first displays the report for one employee. The second displays an output delimiter and is called by the first subroutine.

THE PROGRAM

```
100 REM ----- SALARY REPORT PROGRAM ----
110 REM PRODUCE SALARY REPORTS FROM DATA
120 REM GIVEN IN DATA LINES 300 TO 398.
130 REM
140 REM N$ = EMPLOYEE'S NAME
150 REM A  = ANNUAL SALARY OF N$
160 REM
170 REM ***************************
180 REM READ DATA & DISPLAY REPORTS.
190 REM
200 READ N$,A
210 WHILE N$<>"END-OF-DATA"
220    REM DISPLAY REPORT FOR N$.
230    PRINT
240    GOSUB 400
250    PRINT
260    READ N$,A
270 NEXT (or WEND)
280 GOTO 999
290 REM
300 REM ******************
310 REM      D   A   T   A
320 REM
330 DATA S.J.BRYANT,18500
340 DATA T.S.ENDICOTT,25700
398 DATA END-OF-DATA,0
```

FIRST SUBROUTINE

```
400 REM ******************************
410 REM SUBROUTINE TO DISPLAY ONE REPORT
```

```
420 REM
430 REM WK=ROUNDED WEEKLY SALARY FOR N$
440 REM
450 GOSUB 600
460 LET WK=A/52
470 LET WK=INT(100*WK+.5)/100
480 PRINT "EMPLOYEE NAME: ";N$
490 PRINT "ANNUAL SALARY:";A
500 PRINT "WEEKLY SALARY:";WK
510 GOSUB 600
520 RETURN
600 REM ******************************
610 REM SUBROUTINE TO DISPLAY 30 DASHES
620 REM
630 FOR N=1 TO 30
640    PRINT"-";
650 NEXT N
660 PRINT
670 RETURN
999 END
```

SECOND SUBROUTINE

For the given DATA lines (330–398), this program produces the following output:

```
------------------------------
EMPLOYEE NAME: S.J. BRYANT
ANNUAL SALARY: 18500
WEEKLY SALARY: 355.77

------------------------------


------------------------------
EMPLOYEE NAME: T.S. ENDICOTT
ANNUAL SALARY: 25700
WEEKLY SALARY: 494.23
------------------------------
```

■ **REMARK 1**   Line 470 uses the BASIC function INT to round the weekly salary WK to the nearest cent. The INT function is described in Section 12.1.

■ **REMARK 2**   Note that the first subroutine is called only from line 240. This means that we can delete the line

```
240 GOSUB 400
```

and in its place insert the BASIC code included in lines 400–510 that displays a single salary report. The resulting program will be two lines shorter but not necessarily better. By using a subroutine, we do not force a person reading the program to read through the details of how a report is produced. The REM statement in line 220 tells the reader that a report will be produced but leaves out the details. A reader who needs more details would simply look down to line 400 and read the subroutine.

■ **REMARK 3**   Programming applications calling for lengthy reports are not uncommon. If confronted with such a programming task, examine the requirements carefully to see if the long report in fact consists of several short reports that are to be repeated several times. Program segments that produce such short reports are often ideal candidates for subroutines.

■ **REMARK 4**   An important advantage in using subroutines is that your programs can be modified more easily should a change be needed. For instance, if the program shown must be altered to display other information about each employee, only the subroutine in lines 400–520 needs to be changed. You may sometimes find that a method used to carry out a particular task is inefficient and needs to be improved. If the task is coded as a subroutine, the entire subroutine can be replaced with more efficient code with no need to modify, or even debug, the rest of the program.

EXAMPLE 4   **Charter service example—an illustration of subroutines.**

An airline charter service estimates that ticket sales of $1,000 are required to break even on a certain excursion. It thus makes the following offer to an interested organization. If 10 people sign up, the cost will be $100 per person. For each additional person, the cost per person will be reduced by $3. Produce a table showing the cost per customer and the profit to the airline for N = 10, 11, 12, . . . , 30 customers. In addition, display a message giving the maximum possible profit for the airline and the number of customers that gives this profit. Use column headings underlined by a row of dashes and a row of dashes before and after the final message.

PROBLEM ANALYSIS

The problem statement says to produce a three-column table showing the number of customers, the corresponding cost per customer, and the corresponding profit to the airline. Thus, for each value of N from 10 to 30 (the number of custumers) we must calculate two values:

C = cost per person (C = 130 − 3 × N)
P = profit to the airline (P = N × C − 1000)

The problem statement also specifies that the three-column cost and profit table be followed by a message giving two values:

NMAX = number of people yielding a maximum profit to the airline
PMAX = the maximum profit

The following algorithm describes one way to produce the required output.

THE ALGORITHM

a. Display column headings.
b. Start with PMAX = 0
c. For N = 10 to 30, do the following:
   c1. Determine C and P.
   c2. Display N, C, and P in the table.
   c3. Adjust NMAX and PMAX, if necessary.
d. Display a message showing NMAX and PMAX.
e. Stop.

Step (c3) is included to determine NMAX and PMAX. To carry out this step, we will compare the profit P for N customers with PMAX, the largest profit obtained to that point. If P is larger than PMAX, we will assign P to PMAX and N to NMAX. To keep the main part of the program as uncluttered as possible, we'll do this in a subroutine (see lines 600–660). The problem statement specifies that three rows of dashes are to be displayed. To avoid writing this code three times, we'll use another subroutine for this purpose (see lines 500–540).

THE PROGRAM

```
100 REM--------------CHARTER SERVICE PROGRAM--------------------
110 REM PRODUCE TABLE OF AIRLINE EXCURSION RATES AND FIND
120 REM THE MAXIMUM POSSIBLE PROFIT FOR THE AIRLINE.
130 REM
140 REM     N=NUMBER OF PASSENGERS (10 TO 30)
150 REM     C=COST PER PERSON (N PASSENGERS)
160 REM     P=AIRLINE PROFIT (N PASSENGERS)
170 REM PMAX=MAXIMUM AIRLINE PROFIT
180 REM NMAX=PASSENGER COUNT FOR MAX PROFIT
190 REM
200 REM DISPLAY COLUMN HEADINGS AND CHOOSE OUTPUT FORMAT F$.
210 PRINT   "PASSENGERS       COST/PERSON      AIRLINE PROFIT"
220 LET F$= "    ##            ###.##            ####.##     "
230 GOSUB 500
240 REM DISPLAY TABLE VALUES AND FIND MAXIMUM PROFIT.
250 LET PMAX=0
```

```
260 FOR N=10 TO 30
270     LET C=130-3*N
280     LET P=N*C-1000
290     PRINT USING F$,N,C,P
300     REM CHECK FOR NEW MAXIMUM PROFIT AMOUNT.
310     GOSUB 600
320 NEXT N
330 REM DISPLAY MESSAGE SHOWING NMAX AND PMAX.
340 GOSUB 500
350 PRINT NMAX;"PASSENGERS YIELD A MAXIMUM PROFIT OF";PMAX;"DOLLARS."
360 GOSUB 500
370 GOTO 999
500 REM SUBROUTINE ------- DISPLAY A ROW OF DASHES.
510 FOR K=1 TO 49
520     PRINT "-";
530 NEXT K
540 RETURN
600 REM SUBROUTINE ----- CALCULATE MAXIMUM PROFIT.
610 REM     PMAX=MAXIMUM P (PROFIT) VALUE
620 REM     NMAX=NUMBER OF CUSTOMERS FOR MAXIMUM PROFIT
630 IF P<=PMAX THEN 660
640 LET PMAX=P
650 LET NMAX=N
660 RETURN
999 END
RUN
```

PASSENGERS	COST/PERSON	AIRLINE PROFIT
10	100.00	0.00
11	97.00	67.00
12	94.00	128.00
13	91.00	183.00
14	88.00	232.00
15	85.00	275.00
16	82.00	312.00
17	79.00	343.00
18	76.00	368.00
19	73.00	387.00
20	70.00	400.00
21	67.00	407.00
22	64.00	408.00
23	61.00	403.00
24	58.00	392.00
25	55.00	375.00
26	52.00	352.00
27	49.00	323.00
28	46.00	288.00
29	43.00	247.00
30	40.00	200.00

```
22 CUSTOMERS YIELD MAX PROFIT OF 408 DOLLARS.
```

■ **REMARK**

If at a later date the airline decides to offer a different excursion package, you can simply change lines 270 and 280, which determine the cost per customer C and the profit to the airline P. If you suspect that the airline will be offering many different excursion packages, you should consider using a subroutine to determine C and P. If you do this, any method specified by the airline for determining C and P, even complex methods that may require many programming lines, can be handled simply by replacing the subroutine with a new one. No change would be required in the rest of the program.

□

A common application of subroutines is in menu-driven programs. You code the program segments that carry out the options as subroutines and use GOSUB statements rather than GOTO statements to carry out these options. By coding options as subroutines rather than program segments, you will avoid several GOTOs that can make the action of the program difficult to follow—the GOTOs that transfer control to the program segments and those that transfer control back from these program segments. Example 5 illustrates the use of subroutines in menu-driven programs.

EXAMPLE 5   **A menu-driven program.**

Consider the following DATA lines given in Example 2:

```
1000 REM FOR EACH ITEM IN STOCK, THESE DATA SHOW:
1010 REM
1020 REM    ITEM CODE, ITEM DESCRIPTION, ITEM PRICE
1030 REM
1040 DATA Y222, YARDSTICK, 6.79
1050 DATA S955, SAW-RIP, 12.88
1060 DATA S457, SAW-CROSSCUT, 14.00
1070 DATA T12, 12 FOOT TAPE, 7.66
1080 DATA T16, 16 FOOT TAPE, 9.95
1090 DATA C777, CROWBAR, 13.52
1990 DATA END,END,0
```

Parts a–c of Example 2 show subroutines for these three tasks:

(Line 2000): Display a count of how many items are included and return this count as the value of COUNT.
(Line 3000): Display item codes and descriptions.
(Line 4000): Display the price for any item whose code is entered at the keyboard.

Here is a menu-driven program that includes these three tasks as options. The program allows the user to select from this menu:

```
1   END THE PROGRAM
2   DISPLAY COUNT OF DIFFERENT ITEMS
3   DISPLAY ITEM CODES AND DESCRIPTIONS
4   FIND PRICE OF ANY ITEM
```

```
100 REM          MENU-DRIVEN PROGRAM
110 REM
120 GOSUB 2000                        'Find and display item count.
130    PRINT
140    PRINT "AVAILABLE OPTIONS:"
150    PRINT
160    PRINT "    1  END THE PROGRAM
170    PRINT "    2  DISPLAY COUNT OF DIFFERENT ITEMS
180    PRINT "    3  DISPLAY ITEM CODES AND DESCRIPTIONS
190    PRINT "    4  FIND PRICE OF ANY ITEM
200    PRINT
210    PRINT "OPTION";
220    INPUT OP
230    IF OP=1 THEN GOSUB 5000
240    IF OP=2 THEN GOSUB 2000
250    IF OP=3 THEN GOSUB 3000
260    IF OP=4 THEN GOSUB 4000
270 IF OP<>1 THEN 130
280 GOTO 9999
```

    .
    .   (The given DATA lines at lines 1000–1990 and the subroutines
    .   at lines 2000, 3000, and 4000 given in Example 2 go here.)
    .

```
5000 REM      END SUBROUTINE
5010 REM
5020 PRINT "PROGRAM TERMINATED"
5030 RETURN
9999 END
```

■ **REMARK 1**   Line 120, which calls the count subroutine, is needed in case the user specifies option 3 (which uses the value of the variable COUNT) before specifying option 2.

■ **REMARK 2**   In Section 11.3, we describe the ON GOSUB statement that can be used in place of lines 230–260 to cause execution of the selected subroutine.

The examples in this section illustrate several important points that should be summarized since they must be understood if subroutines are to be used effectively. The following comments summarize the rules that govern the use of subroutines (comments 1–4), point out common practices used while coding subroutines (comments 5–7), and suggest situations in which subroutines can be used to advantage (comments 8–10).

1. A subroutine must contain one or more RETURN statements.
2. A subroutine must be entered only by using a GOSUB statement. This may require using a GOTO statement, as we did in each example program, to avoid entering a subroutine inadvertently.
3. An exit from a subroutine must be made only by the execution of a RETURN statement. Do not use a GOTO statement to jump out of a subroutine.
4. A subroutine can contain a GOSUB statement transferring control to another subroutine. However, a subroutine should not call itself.
5. The first line (or lines) of a subroutine should describe the task being performed. You should include these REM statements in addition to the REM statement or statements used to explain the GOSUB that executes the subroutine.
6. It is a common, but not universal, practice to place all subroutines together near the end of a program. We did this in each of the example programs and will continue to do so in subsequent examples.
7. Do not write excessively long subroutines. Many professional programmers try to keep their subroutines to 50 or fewer lines. For beginners, a maximum of about 20 is suggested.
8. If the same sequence of programming lines is needed in two or more parts of a program, you should consider coding it as a subroutine.
9. A subroutine should be used if it will make your program easier to read and understand, even if it is referenced in only one programming line. This is a common practice. Indeed, the programs in Examples 3, 4, and 5 contain such subroutines.
10. A subtask that you anticipate will need to be modified at a later date is an ideal candidate for a subroutine.

■ 11.2 Problems

1. Show the output of each program.

   a.
   ```
   100 READ X,Y
   110 WHILE X<>0
   120    GOSUB 170
   130    PRINT X;Y;Z
   140    READ X,Y
   150 NEXT  (or WEND)
   160 DATA 4,2,3,-7,0,8
   170 LET Z=3*X+2*Y
   180 RETURN
   190 END
   ```

   b.
   ```
   100 READ A,B
   110 WHILE A<>B
   120    IF A<B THEN GOSUB 200
   130    IF A>B THEN GOSUB 190
   140    READ A,B
   150 NEXT  (or WEND)
   160 DATA 2,4,8,6,5,5
   170 PRINT A
   ```

```
180 GOTO 220
190 PRINT A-B
200 PRINT B-A
210 RETURN
220 END
```

c.
```
100 FOR I=1 TO 4
110    GOSUB 200
120    PRINT I;S
130 NEXT I
140 GOTO 999
200 LET S=0
210 FOR J=1 TO I
220    LET S=S+J
230 NEXT J
240 RETURN
999 END
```

d.
```
110 LET M=1
120 GOSUB 300
130 PRINT M
140 GOTO 500
300 LET M=M+1
310 GOSUB 400
320 RETURN
400 LET M=(M+1)*(M+1)^2
410 RETURN
500 END
```

In problems 2–12 write a subroutine to carry out each task. In each case, test your subroutine by writing a short program that uses it. The lines you add to do this are called a **program stub.**

2. For any number N, assign OK to C$ if N is in the range 0–100 and assign BAD DATA to C$ in every other case.

3. Determine the sum S of the next N values appearing in DATA lines. (You may assume that only numbers appear in DATA lines.)

4. For any numbers A, B, and C, display the largest of the three values $(A + B + C)/3$, $(A + B + 2 * C)/4$, and $(B + C)/2$.

5. For any string C$, assign a value to U as in the following table:

C$	U
ONE	1
TWO	2
THREE	3
FOUR	4
Anything else	0

6. Given data organized as in lines 1000–1990, the subroutine should produce a two-column table showing each job classification code with the hourly pay rate for that job classification:

```
1000 REM EACH DATA LINE GIVES THESE THREE VALUES:
1010 REM
1020 REM    A JOB CLASSIFICATION CODE,
1030 REM    THE CORRESPONDING HOURLY PAY RATE,
1040 REM    THE NUMBER OF EMPLOYEES WITH THIS JOB CLASSIFICATION
1050 REM
1060 DATA A1101, 6.75, 12
1070 DATA A1343, 7.85, 8
1080 DATA F4423, 9.25, 23
     .
     .
     .
1990 DATA END,0,0
```

7. Given data as in Problem 6, the subroutine should display a count of the total number of employees and return this count.

8. Given data as in Problem 6, the subroutine should determine and display the total annual payroll for the firm. You may assume a 40-hour week for each employee.

9. Given data as in Problem 6, the subroutine should display the hourly pay rate for any job classification whose code is entered at the keyboard. If the code entered is not a valid job classification code, an appropriate message should be displayed.

10. N! (read "N factorial") is defined as the product

$$N! = 1 \times 2 \times 3 \times \cdots \times N$$

if N is a positive integer and as 1 if N = 0. For any integer N $\geq$ 0, assign the value N! to the variable FACT. When you test your subroutine, run it for several input values to determine the largest for which the subroutine gives correct answers. Also find the largest input value that does not cause a fatal error.

11. Determine the greatest common divisor (GCD) of the two positive integers A and B. Use the following algorithm (and convince yourself that it works):
    a. Start with GCD = smaller of A and B.
    b. If GCD is a factor of both A and B, RETURN.
    c. Subtract 1 from GCD and repeat Step (b).

12. Use the following algorithm to find the GCD of two positive integers A and B:
    a. Let R = integer remainder when A is divided by B.
    b. If R = 0, let GCD = B and RETURN.
    c. Assign B to A and R to B.
    d. Repeat Step (a).

    The algorithm in Problem 11 can be slow for large numbers; this algorithm, the so-called Euclidean algorithm, is very fast.

In Problems 13–20, write a program for each task specified.

13. A data list contains many sets of scores S1, S2, and S3. The three values 0, 0, 0 are used to terminate the data list. Produce a four-column report: the three scores are to appear in the first three columns; the fourth is to contain the larger of the two values (S1 + S2 + S3)/3 and (S1 + S2 + 2 * S3)/4. Use a subroutine to find the two "averages" and to determine which is larger. The subroutine is to contain no PRINT statements.

14. The following DATA lines show the names and annual salaries of all employees in a small firm:

```
1000 DATA SAUL JACOBS,23500,PAUL WINFIELD,29000
1010 DATA MARIA KARAS,30000,SILVIA STORM,26400
1020 DATA RAOUL PARENT,31400,RICHARD KELLY,28000
1030 DATA PATTY SAULNIER,22000,MARTHA BRADLEY,31400
1040 DATA XXX,0
```

Calculate and display the total annual payroll of the firm, and then display a report showing the names and salaries of those whose salary exceeds the average annual salary for all employees. Use a subroutine to determine the total annual payroll—it is to have no PRINT statements. Use another subroutine to produce the specified report.

15. Include the data in Problem 14 in a program that displays a two-column table showing precisely the given information and displays after this table a message telling which employee (or employees) has the highest salary. Use a subroutine to display the two-column table—the subroutine is to do nothing else. Use another subroutine to find the highest salary amount—this subroutine also is to do nothing else. Use a third subroutine that displays the concluding message. This subroutine should search for employees with the highest salary.

16. An apple orchard occupying 1 acre of land now contains 25 apple trees, and each tree yields 450 apples per season. For each new tree planted, the yield per tree will be reduced by 10 apples per season. How many additional trees should be planted so that the total yield is as large as possible? Produce a table showing the yield per tree and the total yield if N = 1, 2, 3, . . . , 25 additional trees are planted. Use column headings underlined by a row of dashes. Separate the message telling how many additional trees to plant from the table by a row of

dashes. Use a subroutine to keep track of the greatest total yield and the number of additional trees that give this greatest yield.

17. An organization can charter a ship for a harbor cruise for $9.75 a ticket provided that at least 200 people agree to go. However, the ship's owner agrees to reduce the cost per ticket by 25¢ for each additional 10 people signing up. Thus if 220 people sign up, the cost per person will be $9.25. Write a program to determine the maximum revenue the ship's owner can receive if the ship's capacity is 400 people. Moreover, prepare a table showing the cost per person and the total amount paid for N = 200, 210, 220, . . . , 400 people. Use column headings underlined by a row of dashes. The maximum revenue the ship's owner can receive should be displayed following the table and separated from it by a row of dashes. Use a subroutine to display the rows of dashes and another to keep track of the greatest revenue amount and the number of passengers that give this greatest revenue.

18. A merchant must pay the fixed price of $1 a yard for a certain fabric. From experience, the merchant knows that 1000 yards will be sold each month if the material is sold at cost and also that each 10¢ increase in price means that 50 fewer yards will be sold each month. Write a program to produce a table showing the merchant's profit for each selling price from $1 to $3 in increments of 10¢. Also display a message giving the selling price that will maximize the profit. Use a subroutine to keep track of the greatest profit amount and the selling price that gives this greatest profit.

19. Given data as described in Problem 6, write a menu-driven program to allow the user to specify any of the following tasks:
   a. Produce a report showing precisely the information given in DATA lines.
   b. Display a list of all job classification codes.
   c. Display the hourly pay rate for any job classification whose code is entered at the keyboard.

20. First write a menu-driven program as specified in Problem 19. Then modify it by including these two additional options:
   d. Display the equivalent annual salary for any job classification whose code is entered at the keyboard.
   e. Display the total weekly payroll for the firm. Assume a 40-hour week for each employee.

■ 11.3 The ON GOSUB Statement

The ON GOSUB statement is used to execute one of several subroutines selectively. It selects subroutines in exactly the same way that ON GOTO selects line numbers. For example, if a program contains subroutines at lines 500, 600, and 800, the statement

```
ON X GOSUB 500,800,600,800
```

will execute the subroutine at

line 500 if X = 1
line 800 if X = 2
line 600 if X = 3
line 800 if X = 4

The general form of the ON GOSUB statement is

ln ON **e** GOSUB **ln₁,ln₂,** . . . **,ln_k**

where **e** denotes a BASIC numerical expression and **ln₁,ln₂,** . . . **,ln_k** denote line numbers at which subroutines begin. On execution, **e** is evaluated and rounded (truncated on some systems) to an integer. If this integer is 1, the subroutine at line **ln₁** is executed, if it is 2 the subroutine at line **ln₂** is executed, and so on. What happens if this integer is less than 1 or greater than **k** is system dependent. The following actions, however, are common to many BASIC systems:

1. If the integer obtained from the expression **e** is 0 or a number from **k** + 1 to 255, no subroutine is called and control passes to the statement following the ON GOSUB statement.

2. If the integer obtained from **e** is less than 0 or greater than 255, a fatal error occurs. To avoid this fatal error, we will precede each ON GOSUB statement with an IF statement that assigns 0 to **e** whenever **e** is not in the range 0 to 255.

EXAMPLE 6   **Here is a program that uses ON GOSUB to execute one or more of three subroutines.**

```
100 PRINT "TYPE 1 WHEN DONE."
110    PRINT
120    PRINT "ENTER 1,2, OR 3 ";
130    INPUT V
140    IF V<0 OR V>255 THEN V=0
150    ON V GOSUB 200,300,400
160 IF V<>1 THEN 110
170 GOTO 999
200 REM ------ SUBROUTINE 1 ------
210 PRINT
220 PRINT "THIS IS A CONCLUDING SUBROUTINE."
230 PRINT "THE PROGRAM IS ABOUT TO HALT."
240 RETURN
300 REM ------ SUBROUTINE 2 ------
310 PRINT
320 PRINT "THIS IS THE SECOND SUBROUTINE."
330 RETURN
400 REM ------ SUBROUTINE 3 ------
410 PRINT
420 PRINT "THIS IS THE THIRD SUBROUTINE."
430 RETURN
999 END
RUN

TYPE 1 WHEN DONE.

ENTER 1,2, OR 3 ? 3

THIS IS THE THIRD SUBROUTINE.

ENTER 1,2, OR 3 ? 1

THIS IS A CONCLUDING SUBROUTINE.
THE PROGRAM IS ABOUT TO HALT.
```

For the run shown, 3 and then 1 were entered in response to the INPUT statement. With $V = 3$, the ON GOSUB statement causes the subroutine at line 400, the third listed line number, to be executed. With $V = 1$, the ON GOSUB statement executes the subroutine at line 200, the first listed line number. In each case, control returns to the IF statement following the ON GOSUB statement (line 160). The second time this happens, the condition V<>1 is false, so control passes to the next line (line 170), which terminates the program.

A common application of the ON GOSUB statement is in menu-driven programs. You code the various options the program can carry out as subroutines and use an ON GOSUB statement to select the subroutine corresponding to the option specified by the user. Thus, if a menu-driven program has three options carried out in subroutines at lines 500, 600, and 700, and if OP denotes the selected option number, you can transfer control to the correct subroutine by using the statement

```
ON OP GOSUB 500,600,700
```

You should not interpret the preceding paragraph as a suggestion that you always use ON GOSUB in menu-driven programs. Sometimes, especially if there are few options, you can effectively use IF statements to execute subroutines. For example, you can use either

```
ON OP GOSUB 500,600,700
```

or the three lines

```
IF OP=1 THEN GOSUB 500
IF OP=2 THEN GOSUB 600
IF OP=3 THEN GOSUB 700
```

to execute the appropriate subroutine. Both methods represent good ways to do this. Their action is easy to follow because subroutines are used to carry out the options, rather than program segments that end with GOTOs.

The program in Example 6 illustrates how ON GOSUB can be used in menu-driven programs. Indeed, if we replace the statements

```
120 PRINT "ENTER 1,2, OR 3 ";
130 INPUT V
```

by lines that also display a menu—for instance, by

```
120 PRINT "SELECT OPTIONS FROM THIS MENU:"
122 PRINT
124 PRINT "    1    TO END THE PROGRAM"
126 PRINT "    2    TO CARRY OUT ....."
128 PRINT "    3    TO CARRY OUT ....."
130 PRINT
132 PRINT "YOUR CHOICE ";
134 INPUT V
```

the program becomes menu-driven. Although the program will perform no useful task, it illustrates precisely how menu-driven programs can be coded by using ON GOSUB.

In every example of a menu-driven program considered to this point, we included option numbers in the menu and required the user to select options by typing option numbers. It isn't necessary to do this. You can use descriptive words, instead of numbers, to label the menu options and allow the user to choose options by typing these descriptive words. If you do this, you will need BASIC code to determine the option numbers corresponding to words entered by the user. The option numbers are needed for the ON GOSUB statement. The following example illustrates a simple way to determine option numbers for word options typed by the user.

EXAMPLE 7 **Here is a menu-driven program that allows the user to specify options by typing words instead of option numbers.**

This program contains DATA statements (lines 9000 on) giving the name, weight in pounds, height in inches, and sex for each child born during the current month. The program allows the user to specify options by entering NAMES, LENGTH, or END as described in the menu displayed by lines 130–160. Program lines 200–230 determine the option numbers OP.

THE PROGRAM

```
100 PRINT "THIS PROGRAM ALLOWS YOU TO OBTAIN BIRTH"
110 PRINT "INFORMATION FOR THE CURRENT MONTH."
120     PRINT
130     PRINT "SELECT ONE OF THESE OPTIONS:"
140     PRINT "    NAMES      LIST OF NAMES"
150     PRINT "    LENGTH     AVG. LENGTH BY SEX"
160     PRINT "    END        TO END THE PROGRAM"
170     PRINT "YOUR CHOICE ";
180     INPUT C$
190     REM ------ FIND OPTION NUMBER ------
200     LET OP=0
210     IF C$="END" THEN OP=1
220     IF C$="NAMES" THEN OP=2
230     IF C$="LENGTH" THEN OP=3
240     REM
250     REM -- CARRY OUT SPECIFIED OPTION --
260     REM
270     ON OP GOSUB 1000,2000,3000
280     IF OP=0 THEN PRINT "?BAD OPTION - TRY AGAIN."
290 IF C$<>"END" THEN 120
```

```
300 GOTO 9999
310 REM
1000 REM *****************************
1010 REM *        END SUBROUTINE        *
1020 REM *****************************
1030 RETURN
2000 REM *****************************
2010 REM *       NAMES SUBROUTINE       *
2020 REM *****************************
2030 PRINT
2040 PRINT "LIST OF NEWBORN NAMES:"
2050 READ N$,W,L,S$
2060 WHILE N$<>"EOD"
2070     PRINT N$
2080     READ N$,W,L,S$
2090 NEXT (or WEND)
2100 RESTORE
2110 RETURN
3000 REM *****************************
3010 REM *      LENGTH SUBROUTINE       *
3020 REM *****************************
3030 REM
3040 REM FIND AND DISPLAY AVERAGE LENGTH BY SEX.
3050 REM
3060 LET MTOT=0           'Male total length
3070 LET FTOT=0           'Female total length
3080 LET MCOUNT=0         'Male count
3090 LET FCOUNT=0         'Female count
3100 READ N$,W,L,S$
3110 WHILE N$<>"EOD"
3120     IF S$="M" THEN 3170
3130     REM - FEMALE -
3140     LET FTOT=FTOT+L
3150     LET FCOUNT=FCOUNT+1
3160     GOTO 3200
3170     REM - MALE -
3180     LET MTOT=MTOT+L
3190     LET MCOUNT=MCOUNT+1
3200     READ N$,W,L,S$
3210 NEXT  (or WEND)
3220 PRINT
3230 PRINT "AVERAGE LENGTH (F):";FTOT/FCOUNT
3240 PRINT "AVERAGE LENGTH (M):";MTOT/MCOUNT
3250 RESTORE
3260 RETURN
9000 REM *****************************
9010 REM *     D   A   T   A         *
9020 REM *****************************
9030 REM (NAME,WEIGHT,LENGTH,SEX)
9040 DATA SUE COREY,6.9,19.5,F
9050 DATA LIA TSAO,7.2,18.8,F
9060 DATA JUAN MENDOSSA,8.9,23.0,M
9070 DATA CANDY FOBES,7.6,20.0,F
9080 DATA ADAM PROUST,8.0,22.0,M
9090 DATA MARCO SANTOS,7.4,20.3,M
9998 DATA EOD,0,0,X
9999 END
```

The following output was produced when we specified the LENGTH option, the improper option LIST, and the END option.

```
THIS PROGRAM ALLOWS YOU TO OBTAIN BIRTH
INFORMATION FOR THE CURRENT MONTH.

SELECT ONE OF THESE OPTIONS:
    NAMES      LIST OF NAMES
    LENGTH     AVG. LENGTH BY SEX
    END        TO END THE PROGRAM
YOUR CHOICE ? LENGTH
```

```
AVERAGE LENGTH (F): 19.43333
AVERAGE LENGTH (M): 21.76667

SELECT ONE OF THESE OPTIONS:
    NAMES      LIST OF NAMES
    LENGTH     AVG. LENGTH BY SEX
    END        TO END THE PROGRAM
YOUR CHOICE ? LIST
?BAD OPTION - TRY AGAIN.

SELECT ONE OF THESE OPTIONS:
    NAMES      LIST OF NAMES
    LENGTH     AVG. LENGTH BY SEX
    END        TO END THE PROGRAM
YOUR CHOICE ? END
```

■ REMARK 1

Lines 200–230 ensure that OP will be 0 or one of the valid option numbers, 1, 2, or 3. Thus the ON GOSUB statement (line 270) will either execute one of the subroutines or, if OP = 0, simply pass control to line 280. Each time OP is 0—that is, each time the user enters an invalid option name—line 280 displays ?BAD OPTION—TRY AGAIN. and control passes back to line 120 to display the menu and again prompt the user.

■ REMARK 2

It is a simple matter to include a new option in this program. Suppose, for example, that you want an option SHOW that displays a four-column table showing precisely the information given in the DATA lines. To do this you could code the needed subroutine so that it begins in line 4000 and then make these three changes:

```
152    PRINT "  SHOW        DISPLAY EVERYTHING"
232    IF C$="SHOW" THEN OP=4
270 ON OP GOSUB 1000,2000,3000,4000
```

Line 152 displays SHOW in the menu, line 232 assigns 4 to OP when the user enters the new option SHOW, and line 270 allows the ON GOSUB statement to execute the new subroutine as well as the other three.

■ REMARK 3

You may have noticed that the END subroutine (lines 1000–1030) does nothing. No harm is done, and it is there to use if needed in the future. Although this subroutine can be removed, we don't recommend it. Several changes will be needed to do so, and you will probably end with a program that is more difficult to read. If subroutines that do nothing seem confusing, you might add a line as this one:

```
1025 REM RESERVED FOR POSSIBLE FUTURE USE.
```

In the preceding example we used the statements

```
200 LET OP=0
210 IF C$="END" THEN OP=1
220 IF C$="NAMES" THEN OP=2
230 IF C$="LENGTH" THEN OP=3
```

to assign to OP the option numbers of the menu options END, NAMES, and LENGTH, and to assign 0 to OP for any improper keyboard entry. For a longer menu, we could use the same method and include a similar IF statement for each menu item. Although this is a good way to determine option numbers, especially for small menus, there are other methods that you may find useful. For example, if your menu includes options labeled END, TOT, AVE, LIST, SHOW, PLOT, and INFO, you might want to include them in one or more DATA statements and use a loop to determine option numbers. If these DATA statements will be the only DATA statements in the program, you can use the following subroutine to assign option numbers:

```
1000 REM ----- OPTION SUBROUTINE -----
1010 REM FIND OPTION NUMBER OP FOR C$.
1020 REM RETURN OP=0 FOR INVALID C$.
1030 RESTORE
1040 LET OP=0
1050    READ X$
1060    LET OP=OP+1
1070 IF X$<>C$ AND X$<>"EOD" THEN 1050
1080 IF X$="EOD" THEN OP=0
1090 DATA END,TOT,AVE,LIST,SHOW,PLOT,INFO
1100 DATA EOD
1110 RETURN
```

If C$ is a valid menu item, this subroutine assigns to OP the integer from 1 to 7 that gives the position of C$ in the data list. You will discover other ways to determine option numbers as you learn more about the BASIC language.

■ 11.4 Problems

1. Show the output of each program.
   a.
   ```
   100 FOR I=1 TO 2
   110    ON I GOSUB 160,190
   120    PRINT S
   130 NEXT I
   140 GOTO 220
   150 DATA 5,3,7
   160 READ A
   170 LET S=A/I
   180 RETURN
   190 READ A,B
   200 LET S=(A+B)/I
   210 RETURN
   220 END
   ```
   b.
   ```
   10 READ A$,X
   20 ON X GOSUB 50,70
   30 IF X>0 THEN 10
   40 GOTO 99
   50 PRINT A$;" IS A CONJUNCTION."
   60 RETURN
   70 PRINT A$;" IS AN ARTICLE."
   80 RETURN
   90 DATA A,2,AND,1,BUT,1,OR,1
   95 DATA THE,2,EOD,0
   99 END
   ```

In Problems 2–9, write a program for each task specified.

2. While studying the current day's receipts, a bookkeeper must often perform calculations to answer these questions:
   a. What is the selling price of an item whose list price and discount percent are known?
   b. What is the discount percent for an item whose list and selling prices are known?
   c. What is the list price of an item whose selling price and discount percent are known?
   Write a program to help the bookkeeper obtain answers to these questions.

3. An investor must carry out several different calculations while assessing the performance of the family's current stock portfolio. These include finding the equity (paper value) given the number of shares and the current price and finding the profit (or loss) for a holding given the total price paid for all shares, the number of shares owned, and the current selling price. In addition, the investor must often add lists of numbers. Write a program to help the investor carry out these calculations.

4. The table shown below describes an investor's stock portfolio. Include this information in DATA lines for a menu-driven program that allows the user to obtain one or more of these reports: a four-column report showing precisely the given information; a three-column report showing each stock name with its current value (numbers of shares × current price) and its value at the close of business last month; a short report showing the name and current value of the stock whose current value is greatest.

Name of stock	Number of shares	Last month's closing price	Current closing price
STERLING DRUG	800	16.50	16.125
DATA GENERAL	500	56.25	57.50
OWEN ILLINOIS	1200	22.50	21.50
MATTEL INC	1000	10.75	11.125
ABBOTT LAB	2000	33.75	34.75
FED NATL MTG	2500	17.75	17.25
IC GEN	250	43.125	43.625
ALO SYSTEMS	550	18.50	18.25

5. First write a menu-driven program as described in Problem 4. Then modify the program so that it will also display a simple list showing only the names of the companies in which stock is owned.

6. The table shown below contains information about employees of the Libel Insurance Company. Include this information in DATA lines for a menu-driven program that allows the user to obtain one or more of these reports: a five-column report showing precisely the given information; a two-column report showing the name and years of service of each person who has been with the company for at least Y years (the subroutine that produces this report should prompt the user for Y); and a short report showing the total payroll amount for men and that for women.

Name	Sex	Age	Years of service	Annual salary
J. R. Adamson	M	47	13	20,200.00
P. M. Martell	F	33	6	14,300.00
J. D. Carlson	F	41	15	23,900.00
S. T. Chang	M	22	2	21,400.00
R. T. Richardson	M	59	7	29,200.00
M. E. Thompson	F	25	3	13,000.00
C. B. Rado	M	33	13	21,500.00
O. L. Lawanda	F	28	4	33,400.00
C. Hartwick	M	68	30	25,500.00
C. Cleveland Barnes	M	35	6	14,300.00
M. L. Chou	F	21	3	19,200.00

7. First write a menu-driven program as described in Problem 6. Then modify the program so that it will display two additional options: one to display a list of employee names and another to display the average age of all employees.

8. A menu-driven program is desired that will allow students to practice addition, multiplication, or taking powers. The student should choose addition by typing the letter A, multiplication by typing M, and powers by typing P. If addition is chosen, have the computer prompt the student for two numbers and then ask for their sum. If the correct answer is typed, have the computer say so. If the answer is not correct, display the correct answer. In either case, allow the student to try another addition or to return to the menu. Handle multiplication (of two numbers) the same way. If the student chooses to practice powers, have the computer ask for a number whose powers are to be found. If the student types 3, have the computer display, in order,

```
WHAT IS 3 TO THE POWER 2?
WHAT IS 3 TO THE POWER 3?
WHAT IS 3 TO THE POWER 4?
       .
       .
       .
WHAT IS 3 TO THE POWER 10?
```

Ask each question, however, only if the previous answer is correct. If an answer is incorrect, display the correct answer. Congratulate a student successful to high powers, perhaps in a way reflective of how high the power. In any case, allow the student to try powers of another number or to return to the menu.

9. First write a menu-driven program as described in Problem 8. Then modify it by changing the addition option so that the student practices summing three numbers instead of two.

■ 11.5 Review True-or-False Quiz

1. A program need not contain the same number of GOSUB statements as RETURN statements.   **T F**

2. The GOSUB statement is really unnecessary, since the GOTO statement will accomplish the same thing.   **T F**

3. If one subroutine calls a second subroutine, the first must appear in the program before the second.   **T F**

4. Subroutines should be used only when a group of statements is to be performed more than once.   **T F**

5. Subroutines can be useful even if their only purpose is to improve a program's readability.   **T F**

6. The following statement contains a syntax error:

    ```
    200 ON A GOSUB 500,600,500,500,600
    ```
                                                                            T F

7. Execution of the two lines

    ```
    200 LET S=2.3
    201 ON S GOSUB 300,400,500
    ```

    will necessarily result in an error.   **T F**

8. If a program will selectively execute one or more of several subroutines, you will have to use an ON GOSUB statement.   **T F**

12 Numerical Functions

BASIC is designed to assist you in manipulating both numerical and string data. For this reason, the language includes several functions, called **built-in functions,** to carry out automatically certain common calculations with numbers and operations with strings. In addition, BASIC allows you to define your own functions—functions that you may need but that are not part of the language. These are called **user-defined functions.**

In this chapter we consider only numerical functions. Section 12.1 describes and illustrates the built-in functions SQR, ABS, and INT. Also included is a description of the built-in numerical functions that are common to most BASIC systems. In Sections 12.3 and 12.4 we show how you can write your own functions and illustrate common ways in which such user-defined functions are used.

The BASIC functions used with string data are described in Chapter 13. These two chapters on functions can be taken up in either order.

■ 12.1 Built-In Numerical Functions

A list of the most common BASIC numerical functions is given in Table 12.1. These functions are an integral part of the BASIC language and can be used in any BASIC program. In this section we illustrate typical ways in which the functions SQR, ABS, and INT are used. The RND function (which is used somewhat differently from the other numerical

Table 12.1 The most common BASIC numerical functions

Function	Purpose
ABS(x)	Gives the absolute value of x.
INT(x)	Gives the greatest integer less than or equal to x.
SGN(x)	Returns the value 1 if x is positive, -1 if x is negative, and 0 if x is zero.
SQR(x)	Calculates the principal square root of x if $x \geq 0$; results in an error if x is negative.
RND(x)	Returns a pseudorandom number between 0 and 1 (see Chapter 17).
SIN(x)	Calculates the sine of x, where x is in radian measure.
COS(x)	Calculates the cosine of x, where x is in radian measure.
TAN(x)	Calculates the tangent of x, where x is in radian measure.
ATN(x)	Calculates the arctangent of x; $-\pi/2 < \text{ATN}(x) < \pi/2$.
LOG(x)	Calculates the natural logarithm $\ln(x)$; x must be positive.
EXP(x)	Calculates the exponential e^x, where $e = 2.71828 \ldots$ is the base of the natural logarithms.

functions) is considered in Chapter 16. The first sections of the RND chapter are written so that the material can be taken up at this time, should that be desired.

The Numerical Function SQR

SQR is called the **square root function.** Instead of writing N^0.5 to evaluate the square root of N, you can write SQR(N). The principal advantage in doing this is that your programs will be easier to read—SQR(N) is English-like, whereas N^0.5 is not. For instance, to evaluate the algebraic expression

$$\sqrt{\frac{S}{N-1}}$$

you can write

SQR(S/(N − 1))

instead of

(S/(N − 1))^0.5

From left to right, the SQR form of the expression reads evaluate the square root of S/(N − 1), whereas the exponential reads evaluate S/(N − 1) to the one-half power. (See Problem 12 in the next problem set for an application of the expression $\sqrt{S/(N-1)}$.)

EXAMPLE 1   **Here is an illustration of the SQR function.**

```
10 PRINT "NUMBER","SQUARE ROOT"
20 PRINT "------","-----------"
30 FOR N=10 TO 20
40    PRINT N,SQR(N)
50 NEXT N
60 END
RUN

NUMBER          SQUARE ROOT
------          -----------
  10            3.162278
  11            3.316625
  12            3.464102
  13            3.605551
  14            3.741657
  15            3.872984
  16            4
  17            4.123106
  18            4.242641
  19            4.358899
  20            4.472136
```

The Numerical Function ABS

ABS is the **absolute value function:** for example, ABS(−3) = 3, ABS(7) = 7, and ABS(4 − 9) = 5. In general, if **e** denotes a BASIC numerical expression, then ABS(**e**) is the absolute value of the value of the expression **e**.

EXAMPLE 2   **Here is an illustration of the ABS function.**

```
100 REM PROGRAM TO FIND THE ABSOLUTE VALUE
110 REM OF THE SUM OF ANY TWO INPUT VALUES.
120 REM
130 PRINT "ENTER TWO VALUES PER LINE."
140 PRINT "TYPE 0,0 TO STOP."
```

```
150 PRINT
160 PRINT "FIRST PAIR";
170 INPUT X,Y
180 WHILE X<>0 OR Y<>0
190     LET Z=ABS(X+Y)
200     PRINT "ABSOLUTE VALUE OF SUM:";Z
210     PRINT
220     PRINT "NEXT PAIR";
230     INPUT X,Y
240 NEXT    (or WEND)
250 END
RUN

ENTER TWO VALUES PER LINE.
TYPE 0,0 TO STOP.

FIRST PAIR? 7,3
ABSOLUTE VALUE OF SUM: 10

NEXT PAIR? 5,-9
ABSOLUTE VALUE OF SUM: 4

NEXT PAIR? 0,-92.7
ABSOLUTE VALUE OF SUM: 92.7

NEXT PAIR? 0,0
```

This program could have been written without using the ABS function. For example, if line 190 were replaced by the two lines

```
190 LET Z=X+Y
195 IF Z<0 THEN Z=-Z
```

the resulting program would work in the same way as the original. The first version is more desirable—its logic is transparent, whereas the logic of the second version is somewhat obscure. As a general rule, you should use the built-in functions supplied with your system. Not only will your programs be easier to code, but they will also be easier to understand and hence simpler to debug or modify, if required.

A common application of the ABS function is in problems that require examining numerical data to determine how they deviate from a specified number. The following example illustrates this use of the ABS function.

EXAMPLE 3

A data list contains two items for each of 10 retail stores: the current week's sales figure preceded by the store's identification code. Let's write a program to identify those stores whose sales deviate from the average sales by more than 20% of the average sales amount.

PROBLEM ANALYSIS

The problem statement specifies the following input and output:

Input: Identification code and current sales for each store.

Output: A report identifying those stores whose sales deviate from the average sales by more than 20% of the average sales figure. Let's prepare a two-column report with title and column headings as follows:

```
STORES WITH SIGNIFICANTLY
HIGH OR LOW SALES FOR THE WEEK.

STORE CODE      WEEK'S SALES
----------      ------------
    .               .
    .               .
    .               .
```

To determine if a store should be included in this report, we must compare the store's sales with the average sales of all stores. Thus, before attempting to prepare the report, we should first find the average sales figure. The following algorithm contains few details but shows precisely what must be done. In the algorithm, we use these variable names:

CODE$ Identification code of a store
SALES   Current sales for store with code CODE$
AVG   Average sales of all stores
DEV   20% of AVG

**THE
ALGORITHM**

a. Determine AVG and DEV.
b. Prepare a report showing CODE$ and SALES for each store whose current sales (SALES) differs from AVG by more than DEV.

To find the deviation of SALES from AVG, we could subtract SALES from AVG or AVG from SALES, depending on whether AVG is larger or smaller than SALES. Since we are interested only in how close SALES is to AVG, not which is larger, we will simply examine the absolute value of SALES − AVG (the two expressions SALES − AVG and AVG − SALES differ only in their signs). Thus, CODE$ and SALES for a particular store will be included in the report only if the logical expression

```
ABS(SALES−AVG)>DEV
```

is true.

**THE
PROGRAM**

```
100 REM PROGRAM TO PRODUCE REPORT SHOWING RETAIL
110 REM STORES WITH SIGNIFICANTLY HIGH OR LOW SALES.
120 REM
130 REM    STORECOUNT     NUMBER OF STORES
140 REM        CODE$      IDENTIFICATION CODE OF A STORE
150 REM        SALES      CURRENT SALES FOR STORE CODE$
160 REM          AVG      AVERAGE SALES OF ALL STORES
170 REM          DEV      20% OF AVG
180 REM
190 REM *************************************
200 REM * READ DATA TO DETERMINE AVG AND DEV *
210 REM *************************************
220 LET SUM=0
230 READ STORECOUNT
240 FOR N=1 TO STORECOUNT
250    READ CODE$,SALES
260    LET SUM=SUM+SALES
270 NEXT N
280 LET AVG=SUM/STORECOUNT
290 LET DEV=.2*AVG            'Specify 20% deviation.
300 RESTORE
310 REM ******************************
320 REM * PRODUCE THE SPECIFIED REPORT *
330 REM ******************************
340 REM
350 PRINT "STORES WITH SIGNIFICANTLY"
360 PRINT "HIGH OR LOW SALES FOR THE WEEK."
370 PRINT
380 PRINT "STORE CODE","WEEK'S SALES"
390 PRINT "----------","------------"
400 READ STORECOUNT
410 FOR N=1 TO STORECOUNT
420    READ CODE$,SALES
430    IF ABS(SALES−AVG)>DEV THEN PRINT CODE$,SALES
440 NEXT N
450 REM *******************
460 REM *  D   A   T   A   *
470 REM *******************
480 DATA 10
490 DATA BX14,21000,AX17,16000,BX19,12500
```

```
500 DATA BY12,25740,AY33,14480,AX11,28700
510 DATA BX09,20400,AY04,14200,BX27,10200
520 DATA AY22,17850
530 END
RUN

STORES WITH SIGNIFICANTLY
HIGH OR LOW SALES FOR THE WEEK.
```

STORE CODE	WEEK'S SALES
BX19	12500
BY12	25740
AY33	14480
AX11	28700
AY04	14200
BX27	10200

The Numerical Function INT

If INT(**e**) is used in a BASIC program, its value is the greatest integer less than or equal to the value of the expression **e**. For example, INT(2.6) = 2, INT(7) = 7, INT(7 − 3.2) = 3, and INT(−4.35) = −5. For this reason INT is called the **greatest-integer function.**

If a program requires integer input, you can use INT to detect input values that are not integers. This common use of INT is illustrated in the following example.

EXAMPLE 4   **Here is a program segment to reject numerical input values that are not integers.**

```
300 PRINT "HOW MANY APPLES HAVE YOU";
310 INPUT C
320 IF C<>INT(C) THEN 300
```

If the user types a number that is not an integer, the condition C<>INT(C) will be true, and control will pass back to line 300 so that another number can be entered.

■ REMARK   To inform the user why the prompt

```
HOW MANY APPLES HAVE YOU
```

is displayed a second time (the user may be thinking fruit instead of computers), and also to reject meaningless negative input values, you could use lines such as these:

```
300 PRINT "HOW MANY APPLES HAVE YOU";
310 INPUT C
320 WHILE C<>INT(C) OR C<0
330    PRINT "PLEASE ENTER A COUNT."
340    PRINT "HOW MANY APPLES HAVE YOU";
350    INPUT C
360 NEXT   (or WEND)
```

Should the user now enter an improper number, the message in line 330 will be displayed before the user is prompted a second time. Note that 0 as an input value is allowed and meaningful.

Another common use of INT is in rounding off numbers. To illustrate, let's suppose that X satisfies the inequalities

$$36.5 \leq X < 37.5$$

and we want to round X to the nearest integer. By adding 0.5 to each value we get

$$37 \leq X+0.5 < 38$$

and it follows that

$$INT(X+0.5) = 37$$

That is, to round a number X to the nearest integer, use the BASIC expression

```
INT(X+0.5)
```

A slight modification of this method of rounding to the nearest integer can be used to round to any decimal position. We illustrate by rounding the number X = 67.387 to the nearest hundredth to obtain 67.39.

Expression	Value	Comment
X	67.387	Number to be rounded
100*X	6738.7	Move decimal point to the right
INT(100*X+0.5)	6739	Round to nearest integer
INT(100*X+0.5)/100	67.39	Move decimal point back

Thus, to round X to the nearest hundredth, use the BASIC expression

```
INT(100*X+0.5)/100
```

If you change 100 in this expression to 1000, X will be rounded to three decimal positions, if you use 10000 it will be rounded to four, and so on. You are limited only because each computer keeps a fixed number of significant digits.

For more work with rounding numbers, see Section 12.2, Problem 5.

EXAMPLE 5 **Here is a program that uses INT to round the values 1/7, 2/7, 3/7, . . . , 6/7 to five decimal places.**

```
10 PRINT " N","   N/7"
20 PRINT
30 FOR N=1 TO 6
40    PRINT N,INT(100000*N/7+.5)/100000
50 NEXT N
60 END
RUN

N                N/7

1                .14286
2                .28571
3                .42857
4                .57143
5                .71429
6                .85714
```

In Example 4 we saw that the condition C = INT(C) is true if C is an integer and false if it is not. Thus, if N is any integer, the condition

$$N/2 = INT(N/2)$$

will be true precisely when N/2 is an integer—that is, when N is divisible by 2. Similarly, if N and D are any integers (with D not 0), the condition

$$N/D = INT(N/D)$$

is true precisely when N/D is an integer—that is, when N is divisible by D.

Relational expression	Truth value
63/7 = INT(63/7)	true
6/4 = INT(6/4)	false
INT(105/15) = 105/15	true
INT(100/8) <> 100/8	true

CAUTION

In BASIC, the condition

$$N/D = INT(N/D)$$

is used to determine whether N/D is an integer only if both N and D are integers. If either is not an integer, you may get unexpected results. A computer stores numbers and does arithmetic in the binary number system. This means that a calculation involving a number that cannot be represented exactly as a binary number may be only approximate; hence, exact comparisons may not be possible. The same situation occurs in the decimal number system. For instance, if you use a calculator to divide 1 by 3 and then multiply by 6, you will get

$$1/3 = .33333333$$

$$6*(1/3) = 1.9999999$$

not 2, which is the correct result. Just as 1/3 cannot be represented exactly as a decimal, the number 1/10 (among others) cannot be represented exactly as a binary number. Thus, although the correct value of 1/.1 is 10, BASIC will give you only a close approximation of 10. Specifically, in BASIC the condition

$$1/.1 = INT(1/.1)$$

is false. The value on the left is approximately but not exactly 10. The value on the right will depend on the computer being used. It will be 9 if the approximation of 1/.1 is slightly less than 10, and 10 if the approximation is slightly more than 10.

In the next example, we use a condition of the form $N/D = INT(N/D)$ to control the number of output values per line.

EXAMPLE 6   **Here is a program to display a rectangular array of asterisks.**

```
100 FOR N=1 TO 45
110     PRINT "*";
120     IF N/15=INT(N/15) THEN PRINT
130 NEXT N
140 END
RUN

* * * * * * * * * * * * * * *
* * * * * * * * * * * * * * *
* * * * * * * * * * * * * * *
```

On each pass through the loop, line 110 displays an asterisk. The semicolon in line 110 suppress the RETURN that usually occurs after a PRINT statement is executed. Then line 120 tests whether N is divisible by 15. If it is, the PRINT statement causes a RETURN to be executed so that subsequent output will appear on the next line.

■ REMARK   If line 120 is changed to

```
120 IF N/5=INT(N/5) THEN PRINT
```

the program will display nine rows with five asterisks per row.

□

The INT function has many applications. We have illustrated its use in validating user input (Example 4), in rounding numbers (Example 5), and in controlling the number of output values per line by testing divisibility of one number by another (Example 6). As you work through the examples and problems in this and subsequent chapters, you will find that the INT function is a valuable programming tool that can be used to simplify many programming tasks.

In the next example we give a detailed analysis for a prime number program. The example illustrates the use of the SQR and INT functions and also discusses simple ways to speed up program execution, should that be important.

EXAMPLE 7 **Write a program to tell whether an integer typed at the keyboard is a prime number.**

PROBLEM ANALYSIS

Let N denote the number to be tested. A number N is prime if it is an integer greater than 1 whose only factors are 1 and N. To determine whether a number N is prime, you can divide it successively by 2, 3, . . . , N − 1. If N is divisible by none of these, then N is a prime. It is not necessary to check all the way to N − 1, however, but only to the square root of N. Can you see why? We will use this fact.

Let's construct a flowchart to describe this process in detail. Since all primes are at least as large as 2, we will reject any input value that is less than 2. Thus we can begin our flowchart as follows:

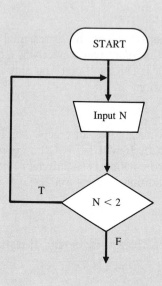

Next we test all integers from 2 to $\sqrt{N}$ as possible factors of N. If we test them in the order D = 2, 3, 4, and so on, we can stop testing when D > $\sqrt{N}$ or when D is a factor of N. Thus we can add the following segment to our partial flowchart:

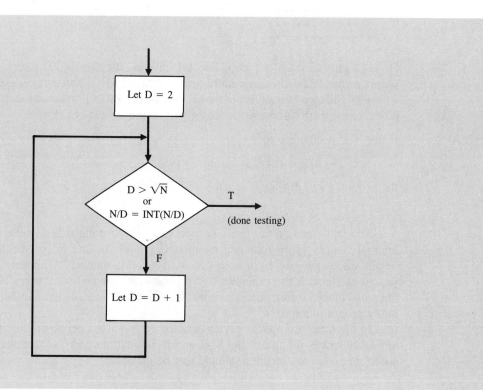

When we are done testing, we can be sure that N is prime if the last D value satisfies the condition $D > \sqrt{N}$, since this means that no factor less than or equal to $\sqrt{N}$ was found. On the other hand, if this last D value does not satisfy the condition $D > \sqrt{N}$, then it must satisfy the only other condition, $N/D = INT(N/D)$, that can get us out of the loop. This means that D is a factor of N that lies between 2 and $\sqrt{N}$, inclusive; that is, N is not prime. Thus we can now complete the flowchart as follows.

**PRIME
NUMBER
FLOWCHART**

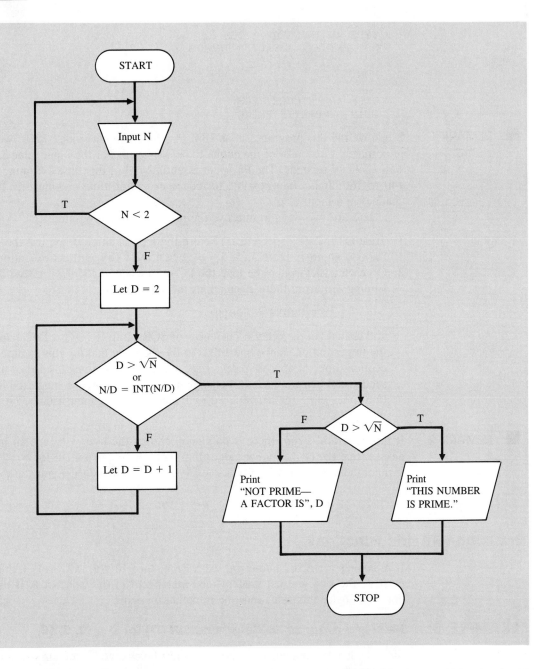

■ REMARK   It is tempting to say that N is not a prime if the last value of D is a factor of N—that is, if $N/D = INT(N/D)$ is true. If you use this condition (instead of the condition $D > \sqrt{N}$) to complete the flowchart, you will find that you have a bug. You should find it. (*Suggestion:* When debugging a program, test it for *extreme* values of any input variables.

In this problem, the smallest value that the program will actually test is N = 2, so 2 is an extreme value here.)

THE PROGRAM

```
100 PRINT "TYPE AN INTEGER";
110 INPUT N
120 IF N<2 THEN 100
130 LET D=2
140 WHILE D<=SQR(N) AND N/D<>INT(N/D)
150     LET D=D+1
160 NEXT    (or WEND)
170 IF D>SQR(N) THEN PRINT "THIS NUMBER IS PRIME."
180 IF D<=SQR(N) THEN PRINT "NOT PRIME - A FACTOR IS";D
190 END
RUN

TYPE AN INTEGER? 37769
NOT PRIME - A FACTOR IS 179

RUN

TYPE AN INTEGER? 765767
THIS NUMBER IS PRIME.
```

■ REMARK 1

When we ran this program (on an IBM PC) for the input value 37769, we had to wait approximately 4 seconds for the output to be displayed. For the input value 765767 we had to wait about 17 seconds. The PC spent essentially all of this time executing the loop in lines 140 to 160. It is often possible to reduce execution time significantly by making small changes in a loop.

Here are two ways to improve the prime number program:

1. Treat D = 2 as a special case before the loop is entered and use the loop to test only the odd numbers D = 3, 5, 7, . . . , SQR(N). This will cut execution time in half.
2. On each pass through the loop the PC must calculate SQR(N) anew. This is time consuming. To avoid these calculations include the line

```
125 LET ROOTN = SQR(N)
```

and change all the other occurrences of SQR(N) to ROOTN. The change in line 140 is the important one since line 140 is in the loop. By making this change we obtained execution times of approximately 3 seconds and 11 seconds instead of 4 seconds and 17 seconds. When we made this change in addition to the one suggested in (1), the execution times were further reduced to 1 second for the input value 37769 and 6 seconds for 765767.

■ REMARK 2

If this program is run, there is no guarantee that the user will type an integer. Line 110 ensures that the prime number algorithm will not be carried out for N < 2, but if 256.73 is input the algorithm will produce a silly result. To avoid this, you can make this change:

```
120 IF N<2 OR N<>INT(N) THEN 100
```

The Trigonometric Functions

If **e** denotes a BASIC numerical expression, then SIN(**e**), COS(**e**), TAN(**e**), and ATN(**e**) evaluate the sine, cosine, tangent, and arctangent of the value of **e.** If the value of **e** denotes an angle, this value must be in radian measure.

EXAMPLE 8

Here is a program to determine SIN (D) for D = 0, 5, 10, . . . , 45°.

Since D denotes an angle in degrees, it must be changed to radian measure. Recalling the correspondence

1 degree = $\pi/180$ radians

we must multiply D by $\pi/180$ to convert to radian measure.

```
100 PRINT   "DEGREES          SINE"
110 PRINT   "-------          ----"
120 LET F$="   ##            #.####"
130 LET PI=3.14159
140 FOR D=0 TO 45 STEP 5
150    LET Y=SIN(PI/180*D)
160    PRINT USING F$,D,Y
170 NEXT D
180 END
RUN

DEGREES       SINE
-------       ----
    0        0.0000
    5        0.0872
   10        0.1736
   15        0.2588
   20        0.3420
   25        0.4226
   30        0.5000
   35        0.5736
   40        0.6428
   45        0.7071
```

EXAMPLE 9

Given side a and angles A and B in degrees, use the law of sines to determine side b of the following triangle:

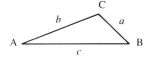

PROBLEM ANALYSIS

The law of sines states that

$$\frac{a}{\sin A} = \frac{b}{\sin B}$$

Solving for b, we obtain

$$b = \frac{a \sin B}{\sin A}$$

Since the angles A and B will be given in degrees, they must be changed to radian measure as required by the BASIC function SIN. In the following program, A1 and B1 denotes the sides a and b, respectively.

THE PROGRAM

```
100 PRINT "LAW OF SINES PROGRAM"
110 PRINT
120 LET PI=3.14159
130 REM
140 REM ***********************************
150 REM             KEYBOARD INPUT
160 REM
170 PRINT "ANGLE A IN DEGREES";
180 INPUT A
190 PRINT "ANGLE B IN DEGREES";
200 INPUT B
210 PRINT "SIDE OPPOSITE ANGLE A";
220 INPUT A1
230 REM ***********************************
240 REM CONVERT A AND B TO RADIANS AND FIND
250 REM LENGTH B1 OF SIDE OPPOSITE ANGLE B.
260 REM
```

```
270 LET A=PI/180*A
280 LET B=PI/180*B
290 LET B1=A1*SIN(B)/SIN(A)
300 PRINT
310 PRINT "SIDE OPPOSITE ANGLE B HAS LENGTH";B1
320 END
RUN

LAW OF SINES PROGRAM

ANGLE A IN DEGREES? 28
ANGLE B IN DEGREES? 42
SIDE OPPOSITE ANGLE A? 2

SIDE OPPOSITE ANGLE B HAS LENGTH 2.85057
```

■ 12.2 Problems

1. Evaluate the following BASIC expressions.
   a. ABS(3*(2-5))   b. ABS(-3*(-2))
   c. ABS(2-30/3*2)   d. INT(26.1+0.5)
   e. INT(-43.2+0.5)   f. INT(10*2.37+0.5)/10
   g. 100*INT(1235.7/100+0.5)   h. ABS(INT(-3.2))
   i. INT(ABS(-3.2))

2. Evaluate the following with A = −4.32, B = 5.93, and C = 2864.7144.
   a. INT(ABS(A))   b. ABS(INT(A))
   c. INT(B+0.5)   d. INT(A+0.5)
   e. INT(C+0.5)   f. 10*INT(C/10+0.5)
   g. 100*INT(C/100+0.5)   h. 1000*INT(C/1000+0.5)
   i. INT(1000*C+0.5)/1000

3. Show the output for each program.
   a.
```
100 FOR N=0 TO 4
110     LET X=N*(N-1)
120     LET Y=ABS(X-8)
130     PRINT N,Y
140 NEXT N
150 END
```
   b.
```
100 LET X=1.1
110 LET Y=X
120 WHILE Y<=1.5
130     LET Z=INT(Y)
140     PRINT Y,Z
150     LET Y=X*Y
160 NEXT  (or WEND)
170 END
```
   c.
```
10 FOR X=3 TO 10
20     PRINT "X";
30     IF X/4=INT(X/4) THEN PRINT
40 NEXT X
50 END
```
   d.
```
100 LET N=63
110 LET D=2
120 WHILE D<=N/2
130     IF N/D=INT(N/D) THEN PRINT D
140     LET D=D+1
150 NEXT  (or WEND)
160 END
```
   e.
```
10 LET M=24
20 FOR D=2 TO 23 STEP 3
30     PRINT "*";
40     IF M/D=INT(M/D) THEN PRINT
50 NEXT D
60 END
```

f.
```
100 LET S=13.99
110 WHILE S<=14
120    LET R=INT(100*S+0.5)/100
130    PRINT USING "##.### ##.##";S,R
140    LET S=S+0.003
150 NEXT  (or WEND)
160 END
```

4. Write a *single* BASIC statement for each task:
   a. For any two numbers A and B, display EQUAL if the absolute value of their sum is equal to the sum of their absolute values.
   b. For any two positive integers M and N, display DIVISIBLE if M is divisible by N.
   c. Display OK if X is a positive integer. (All you know about X is that it is a number.)
   d. Add 1 to COUNT if the integer K is divisible by either 7 or 11.
   e. Cause a RETURN to be executed if the integer L is even and also divisible by 25.
   f. For any integers A, B, and C, display OK if C is a factor of both A and B.

5. Using the INT function, write a single BASIC statement that will round off the value of X:
   a. to the nearest hundredth   b. to the nearest thousandth
   c. to the nearest millionth   d. to the nearest hundred
   e. to the nearest thousand   f. to the nearest million

In Problems 6–17 write a program for each task specified. For tasks that require keyboard input, allow the user to try different input values without having to rerun the program.

6. Find the sum of the values and the sum of the absolute values of any input list. Display the number of values in the list as well as the two sums.

7. The deviation of a number N from a number M is defined to be ABS(M − N). Find the sum of the deviations of the numbers 2, 5, 3, 7, 12, −8, 43, −16 from M = 6. (All of these values are to be input during program execution.)

8. Find the sum of the deviations of numbers X from INT(X) where the X's are input.

9. For any input list, sums S1 and S2 are to be found. S1 is the sum of the numbers, and S2 is the sum of the numbers each rounded to the nearest integer. Display both sums and the number of values in the list.

10. Determine all positive factors of a positive integer N typed at the keyboard. (Include the factors 1 and N.)

11. A list of integers is to be input. Any integer less than 1 serves as the EOD tag. Display the sum and a count of the even input values and the sum and count of the odd ones.

12. Find the mean M and standard deviation D of a set of numbers contained in DATA lines. Use the following method to compute D. If the numbers are x_1, x_2, x_3, . . . , x_n, then

    $D = \sqrt{S2/(n-1)}$, where

    $$S2 = (x_1 - M)^2 + (x_2 - M)^2 + \cdots + (x_n - M)^2$$

13. If a, b, and c are any three numbers with $a \neq 0$, the quadratic equation

    $$ax^2 + bx + c = 0$$

    can be solved for x by using the formula

    $$x = \frac{-b \pm \sqrt{b^2 - 4ac}}{2a}$$

    If $b^2 - 4ac > 0$, the formula gives two solutions; if $b^2 - 4ac = 0$, it gives one solution. If $b^2 - 4ac < 0$, however, there are no real solutions. Write a program to solve the quadratic equation for any input values, a, b, and c, with $a \neq 0$.

14. Include the following information in DATA lines for a program to determine the batting average and slugging percentage for each player. In the table, 1B indicates a single, 2B a double, 3B a triple, HR a homerun, and AB the number of times a player has been at bat.

$$\text{Batting average} = \frac{\text{number of hits}}{\text{AB}} \qquad \text{Slugging percentage} = \frac{\text{total bases}}{\text{AB}}$$

Player	1B	2B	3B	HR	AB
Gomez	100	22	1	14	444
Boyd	68	20	0	3	301
Jackson	83	15	8	7	395
O'Neil	68	22	1	8	365
Struik	65	11	3	6	310
McDuffy	54	11	4	0	256
Vertullo	78	18	1	15	418
Ryan	25	1	1	0	104
Torgeson	49	15	0	11	301
Johnson	54	5	2	0	246

Your program is to produce two tables: the first showing the players with their batting averages in adjacent columns, and the second showing the players with their slugging percentages. Each table is to have a title and each column a heading. The batting averages and slugging percentages are to be shown rounded to three decimal places.

15. Last year's sales report of the RJB Card Company reads as follows:

January	$32,350	July	$22,000
February	$16,440	August	$43,500
March	$18,624	September	$51,400
April	$26,100	October	$29,000
May	$30,500	November	$20,100
June	$28,600	December	$27,500

Display the average monthly sales and a short report showing the month and the monthly sales for those months for which the sales deviate from the average by more than P percent. Have the user enter a value for P.

16. Display the exact change received from a purchase of P dollars if an amount D is presented to the salesclerk. Assume that D is at most $100. The change should be given in the largest possible denominations of bills and coins, but $50 and $2 bills are not to be used. If P = 26.68 and D = 100, for example, the change D − P = 73.32 would be

   3 $20 bills, 1 $10 bill, 3 $1 bills, 1 quarter, 1 nickel, and 2 pennies

Suggestion: If C denotes the change in pennies, then N = INT(C/2000) gives the number of $20 bills. You would then subtract 2000 ∗ N from C and proceed to the next lower denomination. Because computers store some numbers only approximately, you must not use the statement LET C=100∗(D−P) to get C. Rather, you must use the statement LET C=INT(100∗(D−P)+0.1) and explain the reason for adding 0.1.

17. The Apex Gas Station is running a special on cut glassware regularly costing $3.29. The sale price of the glassware is determined by the number of gallons of gasoline purchased according to this table:

Number of gallons purchased	Sale price of glassware
Less than 10	Regular price
From 10 to 15	Twenty percent is deducted from regular price for each whole numbered gallon over the minimum of 10
15 or more	Free

Apex sells four grades of gasoline:

Grade	Code	Price per gallon
Regular leaded	R	80.9¢
Premium leaded	P	91.9¢
Regular unleaded	U	84.9¢
Premium unleaded	S	98.9¢

Write a program that prompts the user to enter the code for the grade of gasoline and the number of gallons purchased. Then have it display the sale price of the glassware and ask the user (Y or N) whether the glassware will be purchased. After the user enters a response, display the cost of the gasoline purchase and the total cost of the transaction.

In Problems 18–27, write a program for each task specified. (These are for the mathematically inclined reader.)

18. Determine all prime numbers that do not exceed N. N is to be input.
19. Determine all prime numbers between A and B. A and B are to be input and are to be rejected if either is not a positive integer.
20. Display the prime factorization of any positive integer greater than 1 typed at the keyboard. For example, if 35 is input, the output should be $35 = 5 * 7$; if 41 is input, the output should be 41 IS PRIME; if 90 is input, the output should be $90 = 2 * 3 * 3 * 5$.
21. Write a program to input a decimal constant containing fewer than five fractional digits, and display it as a quotient of two integers. For example, if 23.79 is input, the output should be $2379/100$. (Remember, the computer may store only a close approximation of the input value. Be sure that your program works in all cases.)
22. Write a program to input a decimal constant as in Problem 21 and display it as a quotient of two integers that have no common factors. For example, if 4.40 is input, the output should be $22/5$.
23. The distance d of a point (x, y) in the xy-plane from the line $ax + by + c = 0$ is given by

$$d = \frac{|ax + by + c|}{\sqrt{a^2 + b^2}}$$

Write a program to input the coefficients a, b, and c, and compute the distance d for any number of points (x, y) typed at the keyboard. Be sure that all input requests and all output values are labeled. End the program when $a = 0$ and $b = 0$.
24. Produce a two-column table showing the value of X and the cotangent of X for all values of X from zero to $\pi/2$ in increments of 0.05. (The case $X = 0$ must get special treatment.)
25. Referring to the diagram in Example 9, write a program to determine side c if sides a and b and angle C are given. [Use the law of cosines: $c^2 = a^2 + b^2 - 2ab \cos (C)$.]
26. An object moves so that its distance d from a fixed point P at time t is

$$d = \frac{1}{1 - 0.999 \cos t}$$

Produce a table (with column headings) of the d values for t between zero and 2π in increments of 0.1.

■ 12.3 User-Defined Functions: The DEF FN Statement

In addition to providing the built-in functions, BASIC allows you to define and name your own functions. These functions, called **user-defined functions,** can be referenced in any part of your program just as the built-in functions are referenced. We'll illustrate how functions are defined and used with a simple example. The statement

```
100 DEF FNR(X)=INT(100*X+0.5)/100
```

defines a function whose *name* is R (also called FNR) and whose value for any number X is X rounded to the nearest hundredth (recall that the expression INT(100*X+0.5)/100 rounds X to two decimal places). The keyword DEF is an abbreviation for *define* and FN stands for *function*. The variable X is called a **formal parameter**—it serves only to define the function. To reference (or *call*) this function, you must use the form

> FNR(**argument**)

where **argument** denotes any numerical expression whose value is to be substituted for X in the function definition. Thus, if the expression FNR(943.828) appears in a program, its value will be 943.83. Similarly, if Y has the value 943.828, then FNR(Y) will again have the value 943.83. The following short program uses this user-defined function to round calculated values before they are displayed.

EXAMPLE 10   **Here is a program to illustrate the DEF FN statement.**

```
100 REM ****************************
110 REM      FUNCTION DEFINITION
120 REM
130 DEF FNR(X)=INT(100*X+.5)/100
140 REM
150 REM ****************************
160 REM
170 PRINT "ENTER AN AMOUNT (0 TO STOP ) ";
180 INPUT AMT
190 WHILE AMT<>0
200     PRINT "ENTER A PERCENT ";
210     INPUT PCT
220     LET RESULT=(PCT/100)*AMT
230     PRINT PCT;"PERCENT OF";AMT;"IS";FNR(RESULT)
240     PRINT
250     PRINT "ENTER AN AMOUNT (0 TO STOP ) ";
260     INPUT AMT
270 NEXT  (or WEND)
280 END
RUN

ENTER AN AMOUNT (0 TO STOP ) ? 100
ENTER A PERCENT ? 12.625
 12.625 PERCENT OF 100 IS 12.63

ENTER AN AMOUNT (0 TO STOP ) ? 154.49
ENTER A PERCENT ? 7
 7 PERCENT OF 154.49 IS 10.81

ENTER AN AMOUNT (0 TO STOP ) ? 0
```

There are several advantages in defining your own functions:

1. A program containing a user-defined function is easily modified to treat different functions. For instance, if you change line 130 in the preceding program to

```
130 DEF FNR(X)=INT(1000*X+0.5)/1000
```

values will be rounded to three decimal places.

2. The expression defining a function is written only once even though it may be used several times in a program.
3. By assigning a name to an expression, you can often write programs so that they are easier to read and their logic is simpler to follow.

   A program can contain any number of user-defined functions. In the next example we use two: a function to calculate a bonus amount and another to round values to the nearest whole dollar.

EXAMPLE 11   **Salaried employees are to receive an end-of-year bonus of $400 plus 1% of their annual salaries. The following program calculates the bonus amounts for any salary figures entered at the keyboard.**

```
100 REM *************************
110 REM       FUNCTION DEFINITIONS
120 REM
130 DEF FNBONUS(X)=400+.01*X
140 DEF FNROUND(X)=INT(X+.5)
150 REM
160 REM ***************************
170 REM   DISPLAY USER INSTRUCTIONS.
180 REM
190 PRINT "THIS PROGRAM DETERMINES BONUSES FOR"
200 PRINT "ANNUAL SALARY AMOUNTS YOU SPECIFY."
210 PRINT "(ENTER 0 WHEN DONE.)"
220 PRINT
230 REM *******************************
240 REM  FIND BONUS B FOR ANY SALARY S.
250 REM
260 PRINT "ANNUAL SALARY";
270 INPUT S
280 WHILE S<>0
290    LET B=FNBONUS(S)        'Find bonus.
300    LET B=FNROUND(B)        'Round it.
310    PRINT "YEAR-END-BONUS:";B
320    PRINT
330    PRINT "ANNUAL SALARY";
340    INPUT S
350 NEXT   (or WEND)
360 END
RUN

THIS PROGRAM DETERMINES BONUSES FOR
ANNUAL SALARY AMOUNTS YOU SPECIFY.
(ENTER 0 WHEN DONE.)

ANNUAL SALARY? 23028
YEAR-END-BONUS: 630

ANNUAL SALARY? 22560
YEAR-END-BONUS: 626

ANNUAL SALARY? 18500
YEAR-END-BONUS: 585

ANNUAL SALARY? 0
```

■ **REMARK 1**   The two statements

```
290 LET B=FNBONUS(S)
300 LET B=FNR(B)
```

can be replaced by the single statement

```
290 LET B=FNR(FNBONUS(S))
```

■ **REMARK 2**

The variable name X used as the formal parameter in the function definition (line 130) could have been any simple numerical variable name. As we have mentioned, formal parameters serve only to define functions. They have no meaning outside the function definition. If the DEF FN statement in line 130 is changed to

```
130 DEF FNBONUS(S)=400+0.01*S
```

the program will behave just as before. No conflict will arise because of the appearance of the variable S elsewhere in the program.

Many BASIC systems allow you to use the DEF FN statement to define functions of more than one variable. For example, the statement

```
10 DEF FNINTEREST(P,R)=P*R/100
```

defines a function whose value for any numbers P and R is P*R/100. If the expression FNINTEREST(2000,10) is used in the program, its value will be 2000*10/100 = 200. Similarly, if the variables A and B have the values 2000 and 10, respectively, then FNINTEREST(A,B) will again have the value 200.

EXAMPLE 12

Charges at a car-rental agency are $14 a day plus 32¢ a mile. The following program calculates the total charge if the number of days D and the total mileage M are typed at the keyboard.

```
100 DEF FNC(D,M)=14*D+(0.32)*M
110 PRINT "HOW MANY DAYS";
120 INPUT D
130 PRINT "HOW MANY MILES";
140 INPUT M
150 PRINT "CHARGE:";FNC(D,M)
160 END
RUN

HOW MANY DAYS? 3
HOW MANY MILES? 523
CHARGE: 209.36
```

The functions FNR, FNBONUS, FNROUND, and FNC used in Examples 10–12 are called **single-statement functions**; each is defined by using one BASIC statement. The examples in this section illustrate the use of single-statement functions to evaluate numerical expressions. User-defined functions involving string data are considered in Section 13.8. Many versions of BASIC also allow *multiple-statement functions*, which are defined by using more than one BASIC statement. These are considered in Section 12.4.

The general form of the DEF FN statement for single-statement functions is

ln DEF FN**name(parameters)** = **e**

where **name** denotes a simple variable name, **parameters** denotes a list of simple variable names separated by commas, and **e** denotes a BASIC expression defining a function of these simple variables. The function is referenced by using this form:

FN**name(arguments)**

where **arguments** denotes a list of BASIC expressions separated by commas. These expressions supply values for the parameters in the function definition.

The following rules govern the use of the DEF FN statement and user-defined functions:

1. Place function definitions near the beginning of the program and before any statements that reference the functions. Although this is not required in some systems, it is a common practice.

2. A function that has been defined by a DEF FN statement may be used anywhere in the program, in the same way that the built-in BASIC functions are used.
3. The expression **e** used in a DEF statement may contain variables other than the formal parameters. When such a function is referenced, the current values of these variables are used in the evaluation. Thus, if a function is defined by

```
100 DEF FNEVAL(S)=5*S+T
```

the programming lines

```
200 LET T=1000
210 PRINT FNEVAL(7)
```

will display the value 1035 [FNEVAL (7)=5*7+1000 = 1035].
4. The expression **e** used in a DEF FN statement may involve built-in functions and user-defined functions. Thus the two lines

```
100 DEF FNY(X)=X+3
110 DEF FNZ(S)=S*FNY(S)
```

are admissible. The reference FNZ(4) will have the value 28:

```
(FNZ(4)=4*FNY(4)=4*(4+3)=28)
```

■ 12.4 Multiple-Statement Functions

The user-defined functions discussed in Section 12.3 must be completely defined by using only one BASIC statement. Some versions of BASIC, including Vax BASIC and BASIC-PLUS, allow you to write **multiple-statement functions** by using the DEF and FNEND(end of function) statements.

Multiple-statement functions can be used in program design much as subroutines are used. You will recall that subtasks indentified in an algorithm often can be coded effectively as subroutines. If the purpose of such a subtask is to determine a single value, you can alternatively code it as a multiple-statement function as explained in this section.

EXAMPLE 13   **Here is a program to display the smaller of any two numbers typed at the keyboard.**

```
100 DEF FNMIN(X,Y)
110    IF X<Y THEN FNMIN=X ELSE FNMIN=Y
120 FNEND
130 PRINT "ENTER TWO NUMBERS";
140 INPUT A,B
150 LET S=FNMIN(A,B)
160 PRINT "SMALLER IS";S
170 END
RUN

ENTER TWO NUMBERS? 7,3
SMALLER IS 3
```

Execution of this program begins at line 130. Lines 100–120 define the function FNMIN but cause no action until the function is referenced in line 150. When the function reference FNMIN(A,B) in line 150 is encountered, A and B supply values for the X and Y appearing in the function definition. The line between the DEF and FNEND statements is then executed, assigning the smaller of X and Y (equivalently of A and B) to FNMIN. This value, FNMIN, is the value of the expression FNMIN(A,B) in line 150.

■ **REMARK 1**   As shown in line 110, a value must be assigned to FNMIN before the FNEND statement is encountered.

■ **REMARK 2**

In the function definition, FNMIN can appear to the left of the equals sign in a LET statement, but in no other way. Thus, it would *not* be correct to replace line 110 with the lines

```
110 LET FNMIN=X
115 IF Y<FNMIN THEN FNMIN=Y    (Syntax error)
```

The use of FNMIN in the relational expression Y<FNMIN is not allowed.

The following two examples illustrate how multiple-statement functions can be used effectively in program design. As you work through the examples, notice that the advantages of using multiple-statement functions are not unlike those provided by the subroutine structure. The general form of multiple-statement functions and rules governing their use are summarized at the end of the section.

EXAMPLE 14   **Here is a program to display the week's pay for any salesperson whose total sales amount is entered at the keyboard.**

```
100 REM PROGRAM TO DETERMINE WEEK'S PAY
110 REM
130 DEF FNPAY(SALES)
140     REM THIS FUNCTION FINDS THE LARGER OF THE
150     REM VALUES RATE*SALES AND BASE.
170     LET BASE=250
180     LET RATE=0.10
190     LET COMM=RATE*SALES
200     IF COMM>BASE THEN FNPAY=COMM ELSE FNPAY=BASE
210 FNEND
220 REM **************************
230 REM *  EXECUTION BEGINS HERE. *
240 REM **************************
250 REM
260 PRINT "SALES (0 WHEN DONE)";
270 INPUT S
280 WHILE S<>0
290     PRINT "PAY FOR THE WEEK:";FNPAY(S)
300     PRINT
310     PRINT "SALES (0 WHEN DONE)";
320     INPUT S
330 NEXT  (or WEND)
340 END
RUN

SALES (0 WHEN DONE)? 3200
PAY FOR THE WEEK: 320

SALES (0 WHEN DONE)? 500
PAY FOR THE WEEK: 250

SALES (0 WHEN DONE)? 0
```

Lines 130–210 define and describe the function FNPAY. Each time the user types a value for S, line 290 causes the program segment between the DEF and FNEND statements to be executed, with the input value S supplying a value for the formal parameter SALES. As with subroutines, we say that the expression FNPAY(S) *calls* the function.

■ **REMARK**

Note that the method used to calculate the pay FNPAY(S) for the sales amount S is completely defined in the function definition (lines 130–210). To use a different method of calculating FNPAY(S), simply change this function definition. There is no need to tamper with the rest of the program.

EXAMPLE 15   **A program is desired for the following game. Two players alternate in typing a whole number from 1 to 5. The computer assigns a point value (unknown to the players) for each number typed according to the table given. The first player to accumulate a total of 15 points or more wins.**

Number chosen	Point value
1	3
2	2
3	2
4	1
5	2
Any other	0

PROBLEM ANALYSIS

The input and output values for this problem are as follows:

Input: A sequence of numbers alternately typed by two players.

Output: The scores of the two players when one of them has achieved a score of 15 or more.

It isn't difficult to devise an algorithm for this task if we leave out the details. In the following algorithm we use these variable names:

FIRST Accumulated score of the first player
SECOND Accumulated score of the second player

THE ALGORITHM

  a. Display game instructions.
  b. Set FIRST and SECOND to 0.
  c. Repeat the following until FIRST or SECOND is at least 15.
      c1. Input the first player's choice and add its point value to FIRST.
      c2. If FIRST < 15, input the second player's choice and add its point value to SECOND.
  d. Display the results and stop.

In coding this algorithm, only Steps (c1) and (c2) may be troublesome. Since the point value of a keyboard entry is the same whether the entry is made by the first or second player, we'll use a multiple-statement function to determine point values. The following function definition is easy to understand, and easy to modify should we wish to associate different point values with the keyboard entries. The function calculates the point value FNPT(KB) of any keyboard entry KB.

```
DEF FNPT(KB)
    LET FNPT=0
    IF KB=1 THEN FNPT=3
    IF KB=2 THEN FNPT=2
    IF KB=3 THEN FNPT=2
    IF KB=4 THEN FNPT=1
    IF KB=5 THEN FNPT=2
FNEND
```

With this multiple-statement function, the required program can be coded directly from the algorithm. The only difficulty remaining is deciding how to carry out Step (a), which says to display game instructions. This task is left as an exercise (see Problem 16 in Section 12.5).

The general form of a multiple-statement function is

ln DEF FN**name**(**parameters**)

(Statements to be executed when the function is referenced.)

ln FNEND

As with single-statement functions, **name** denotes a simple variable name and **parameters** denotes a list of simple variable names separated by commas. The function is referenced by using the form

FNname(**arguments**)

in exactly the same way that single-statement functions are referenced.

The following rules govern the use of multiple-statement functions:

1. The variables appearing in the DEF statement are formal parameters used only to define the function (X and Y in Example 13, SALES in Example 14, and KB in Example 15). They can be used elsewhere in the program for some other purpose with no conflict arising.
2. Variables other than the formal parameters may be used between the DEF and FNEND statements. Unlike the formal parameters, however, these variables will have the same meaning wherever they appear in the program. It is an excellent programming practice to avoid variable names in function definitions that are used elsewhere in the program. (The names selected for formal parameters are an exception.)
3. The function name must be assigned a value before the FNEND statement is encountered. This must be done with a LET statement.
4. The function name can be used between the DEF and FNEND statements only as explained in item (3).
5. The only way the program statements in a function definition can be executed is by referencing the function. A GOTO or IF statement must not transfer control from outside a function definition to a line in the definition. Similarly, a GOTO or IF statement appearing in a function definition must not transfer control to a statement outside the function definition.
6. Functions are defined near the beginning of a program before they are referenced.

■ 12.5 Problems

1. Each of these short programs contains an error—either a syntax error that will cause an error message to be printed or a programming error that the computer will not recognize but that will cause incorrect results. In each case, find the error and tell which of the two types it is.

   a.
   ```
   10 REM DISPLAY 6 PERCENT
   20 REM OF ANY NUMBER.
   30 DEF FNZ(U)=0.06*U
   40 INPUT X
   50 LET V=FNZ(U)
   60 PRINT V
   70 END
   ```

   b.
   ```
   10 REM A TABLE OF SQUARES
   20 DEF FNS(I)=X^2
   30 FOR I=1 TO 9
   40    LET S=FNS(I)
   50    PRINT I,S
   60 NEXT I
   70 END
   ```

   c.
   ```
   10 REM BONUS CALCULATION
   20 DEF FCN(S)=200+0.02*S
   30 PRINT "SALARY";
   40 INPUT S
   50 LET B=FCN(S)
   60 PRINT "BONUS IS";B
   70 END
   ```

   d.
   ```
   10 REM DISPLAY RECIPROCALS
   20 REM OF 1,2,3, . . . ,10
   30 DEF FNR(X)=X/N
   40 LET X=1
   50 FOR N=1 TO 10
   60    PRINT FNR(N)
   70 NEXT N
   80 END
   ```

2. Show the output of each program:

   a.
   ```
   10 DEF FNR(X)=100*INT(X/100+0.5)
   20 FOR I=1 TO 3
   30    READ S
   40    PRINT FNR(S)
   50 NEXT I
   60 DATA 227.376,1382.123,7.125
   70 END
   ```

b.
```
10 DEF FNY(X)=1+1/X
20 LET X=2
30 FOR I=1 TO 3
40     LET X=FNY(X)-1
50     PRINT X;
60 NEXT I
70 END
```

c.
```
10 DEF FNQ(A)=A+1
20 DEF FNR(A)=A+2
30 FOR X=0 TO 3
40     LET A=FNR(FNQ(X))
50     PRINT X;A
60 NEXT X
70 END
```

d.
```
10 DEF FNA(X,Y)=X/Y
20 FOR I=1 TO 2
30     FOR J=1 TO 4
40         PRINT FNA(J,I);
50     NEXT J
60     PRINT
70 NEXT I
80 END
```

e.
```
10 DEF FNI(P,R,T)=P*R/100*T
20 LET T=1/2
30 LET P=1000
40 FOR R=2 TO 5
50     PRINT FNI(P,R,T)
60 NEXT R
70 END
```

f.
```
100 DEF FNM(X,Y)
110     IF X<Y THEN FNM=Y
120     IF X>=Y THEN FNM=X
130 FNEND
140 READ A
150 READ B
160 WHILE B<>9999
170     LET A=FNM(A,B)
180     READ B
190 NEXT (or WEND)
200 PRINT A
210 DATA 3,5,1,7,4,9,2,9999
220 END
```

g.
```
100 DEF FNA(X,Y)=SQR(X^2+Y^2)
110 DEF FNB(X,Y)=X+Y
120 DEF FNC(X,Y)
130     IF FNA(X,Y)<FNB(X,Y) THEN FNC=FNA(X,Y)
140     IF FNA(X,Y)>=FNB(X,Y) THEN FNC=FNB(X,Y)
150 FNEND
160 FOR I=1 TO 3
170     READ A,B
180     PRINT FNC(A,B)
190 NEXT I
200 DATA 2,-1,3,4,5,12
210 END
```

3. Write a single-statement function that:

   a. gives the total cost of an article listed at L dollars if the sales tax is 5%.

   b. gives the simple interest earned in 3 months on $100 at an annual rate of R percent.

   c. gives the cost of covering a floor whose length and width (in feet) are L and W, respectively, if the covering costs $12.95 per square yard.

   d. gives the excise tax on a car assessed at E dollars if the tax rate is $27/$1,000.

   e. converts degrees Celsius to degrees Fahrenheit [F = (9/5)C + 32].

   f. converts degrees Fahrenheit to degrees Celsius.

   g. converts feet to miles.

   h. converts kilometers to miles (1 mi = 1609.3 m).

i. converts miles to kilometers.

j. rounds X to the third decimal place.

k. gives the average speed in miles per hour for a trip of D miles that takes T hours.

l. gives the selling price if an article whose list price is X dollars is selling at a discount of Y percent.

m. gives the cost in dollars of a trip of X miles in a car that averages 15 mph if gasoline costs Y cents per gallon.

n. gives the area of a circle of radius R.

o. gives the volume of a sphere of radius R.

p. gives the sine of an angle of A degrees.

4. Write a multiple-statement function to determine each value specified. In each case, test your function by writing a short program that uses it.

   a. Determine the gross salary for an H-hour week if the hourly wage is D dollars and if time and a half is earned for all hours worked over 32.

   b. The cost for an order of 2-quart syrup containers is determined as follows:

Quantity	Price per container
1–49	99¢
50–99	89¢
100–199	75¢
200 or more	62¢

   Determine the cost for an order of QTY containers. Write the function so that it is a simple matter to change the four price-per-container amounts (see Example 14).

   c. For any three numbers A, B, and C, determine the largest of the weighted averages $(A + B + C)/3$, $(A + B + 2C)/4$, and $(2A + 2B + 3C)/7$.

   d. The semester's tuition for full-time students at Bayside Community College is determined as follows: students taking 12 or more credit hours are charged a flat rate of $1,300, and students taking less than 12 hours pay $110 per credit hour. Determine the tuition given the number of credit hours. Write your function so that it is a simple matter to change the credit hour and flat rate charges (see Example 14.)

   e. For any number NUM, return the value 1 if NUM is a positive integer, 2 if it is a negative integer, 3 if it is 0, and 4 if it is not an integer.

In Problems 5–15 write a program to perform each task specified.

5. Produce a three-column table showing the conversions from feet F to miles and then to kilometers for the values F = 1,000, 2,000, 3,000, . . . , 20,000. All output values are to be rounded to three decimal places. Write user-defined functions to perform the two conversions required and to do the rounding.

6. Produce a three-column table showing the conversions from grams G to ounces and then to pounds (1 oz = 28.3495 g) for G = 20, 40, 60, . . . , 400. All output values are to be rounded to three decimal places. Employ a user-defined function to do the rounding.

7. Produce a four-column table as follows. The first column is to contain the mileage figures 10 miles, 20 miles, . . . , 200 miles. The second, third, and fourth columns are to give the time in minutes required to travel these distances at the respective speeds 45 mph, 50 mph, and 55 mph. All output values are to be rounded to the nearest minute. Write user-defined functions to calculate the times and to do the rounding.

8. Following is the weekly inventory report of a sewing-supply wholesaler:

Item	Batches on hand Monday	Batches sold during week	Cost per batch	Sales price per batch
Bobbins	220	105	8.20	10.98
Buttons	550	320	5.50	6.95
Needles—1	450	295	2.74	3.55
Needles—2	200	102	7.25	9.49
Pins	720	375	4.29	5.89
Thimbles	178	82	6.22	7.59
Thread—A	980	525	4.71	5.99
Thread—B	1424	718	7.42	9.89

Produce a three-column report showing the item names, the number on hand at the end of the week, and the income per item. Denoting the markup by M and the quantity sold by Q, use a function FNP(M,Q) to calculate the income figures.

9. Using the inventory report shown in Problem 8, produce a five-column report showing the item names, the cost per batch, the sales price per batch, the dollar markup per batch, and the percent markup per batch. Denoting the markup by M and the cost by C, use a function FNA(M,C) to calculate the percent figures in the fifth column (M/C $\times$ 100 gives the required percentage). In addition, use a function to round the percentages to the nearest whole number.

10. Each salesperson for the Mod Dress Company is paid $140 a week plus 4.875% of all sales. Using the following sales figures, produce a five-column report showing the name, total sales, base pay, commission, and gross pay for each salesperson. All money amounts are to be rounded to the nearest cent.

Name	Total sales for the week	
	Type-1 items	Type-2 items
Barnes, James	$ 726.28	$1198.42
Colby, Irene	415.92	2092.50
Cole, Bruce	2606.95	700.40
Drew, Nancy	350.42	301.27
Hilton, Lynn	1300.23	1521.32
Moore, Warren	268.92	399.92
Rich, Steven	2094.50	227.03
Skinner, Kerry	1102.37	303.52

11. Assume that a salesperson for the Mod Dress Company is paid $230 a week plus a commission of 3.125% on all Type-1 sales and 5.875% on all Type-2 sales. However, a salesperson whose total sales do not exceed $700 receives only the base pay of $230. Using the sales figures given in Problem 10, produce a five-column report showing the name, base pay, Type-1 commission, Type-2 commission, and gross pay for each salesperson. All money amounts are to be rounded to the nearest cent.

12. Produce a three-column table showing the values of t, x, and y for $t = 0, 1, 2, \ldots, 10$, where $x = 5(1 + t)$ and $y = \sqrt{x^2 + 1}$. Determine x and y with user-defined functions.

13. Determine the area in square centimeters of any rectangle whose length and width in inches are typed by the user. Use a function to convert inches to centimeters.

14. Write a user-defined function AC to determine the area of a circle with circumference L. Also write a function AS to determine the area of a square with perimeter L. Use these two functions in a program to produce a three-column table showing L and the values of AC and AS for $L = 1, 2, 3, \ldots, 10$. The values of AC and AS are to be rounded to three decimal places.

15. A thin wire of length L is cut into two pieces of lengths L1 and L2. One piece is bent into the shape of a circle and the other into a square. Decide how the wire should be cut if the sum of the two enclosed areas is to be as small as possible. (Use the functions AC and AS described in Problem 14.) How should the wire be cut if the sum of the areas is to be as large as possible?

16. Code the algorithm given in Example 15.

■ 12.6 Review True-or-False Quiz

1. If a BASIC function exists that performs a needed task, you should use it even if it is a simple matter to write your own programming lines to perform this task. **T F**
2. INT(5/2)<>5/2. **T F**
3. ABS(INT(-2.3)) = INT(ABS(-2.3)). **T F**
4. If A = ABS(INT(A)), then A is a positive integer. **T F**
5. If N and D are positive numbers but not necessarily integers, BASIC allows you to use the logical expression INT(N/D) = N/D to determine whether dividing N by D gives an integer. **T F**
6. The relational expression INT(N) = N is true if N is either 0 or a positive integer and is false in all other cases. **T F**
7. If the statement 1 DEF FNC(P) = 2*P + 2 appears in a program, then the function FNC may be referenced as often as desired and in exactly the same way as any built-in function is referenced. **T F**
8. If the variable Y is used as the formal parameter in a DEF statement, then Y may be used elsewhere in the program for a different purpose. **T F**
9. If FNF(X) is defined in a program, we may also define the function FNC(X) = 2 + FNF(X). **T F**
10. Any variable appearing between the DEF and FNEND statements of a multiple-statement function definition can appear elsewhere in the program for any purpose whatever. **T F**
11. The expression SIN(37 * 3.14159/180) may be used to find the sine of 37 degrees. **T F**
12. When defining a multiple-statement function, you must assign a value to the function name before the FNEND statement is encountered. **T F**

13 More on Processing String Data

S tring processing is now a major application area for computers. For this reason, modern programming languages are designed to simplify tasks that require processing string data. In this chapter we describe the BASIC functions and operations used with string data.

In Sections 13.1–13.3 we show how programming tasks that require examining parts of strings or combining given strings to build new ones can be carried out by using substring qualifiers, the string functions LEFT\$, RIGHT\$, and MID\$, the string-related functions LEN and INSTR, and the concatenation operator +. In Section 13.5 we discuss how computers store string data and explain how this knowledge allows you to give meaning to string comparisons involving the relational operators $<$, $<=$, $>$, and $>=$. To this point, strings have been compared only to determine if they are equal ($=$) or not equal ($<>$). In Section 13.7 we describe the BASIC conversion functions CHR\$, ASC, STR\$, and VAL and show how they can be used effectively for many programming tasks that would otherwise be difficult. In Section 13.8 we return to the topic of user-defined functions begun in Chapter 12 and show how you can use the DEF FN statement to write your own string and string-related functions.

■ 13.1 String and String-Related Functions

Four of the most useful functions included in the BASIC language are described in this section. The first determines the length of a string, and the other three are used to examine individual characters or groups of characters in a string.

The Length Function LEN

If **s** denotes a string, then LEN(**s**), read length of **s,** is the number of characters contained in **s.** Thus, LEN ("STOCKS AND BONDS") has the value 16. And if Z\$ = "STOCKS AND BONDS", then LEN(Z\$) also has the value 16. As always, blanks are counted as characters. The **s** in LEN(**s**) is called the **argument** of the function and must be enclosed in parentheses as shown.

EXAMPLE 1 **Here is a program to display only the strings that contain exactly three characters.**

```
10 FOR I=1 TO 6
20    READ X$
30    IF LEN(X$)=3 THEN PRINT X$
40 NEXT I
```

```
50 DATA "THE","I DO","ONE","OLD ","THREE","127"
60 END
RUN

THE
ONE
127
```

Note that "I DO" has four characters—three letters and an embedded blank. Similarly, "OLD " has a trailing blank character.

EXAMPLE 2   **Here is a program to display a column of words lined up on the right.**

```
100 PRINT "12345678901234567890"
110 REM READ AND DISPLAY WORDS RIGHT JUSTIFIED.
120 READ A$
130 WHILE A$<>"XXX"
140    PRINT TAB(15-LEN(A$));A$
150    READ A$
160 NEXT   (or WEND)
170 DATA A,SHORT,LIST,OF,WORDS,XXX
180 END
RUN

12345678901234567890
        A
    SHORT
     LIST
       OF
    WORDS
```

The TAB function tabs to position 15−1 for the letter A, to position 15−5 for SHORT, and so on. This spacing effectively displays the column of words with the last character of each word in column position 14.

The String Function LEFT$

If **s** denotes a string and **n** an integer from 1 to LEN(**s**), then LEFT$(**s**,**n**) is the string consisting of the first **n** characters of **s**. Thus, LEFT$("STOCKS AND BONDS",6) has the value STOCKS. IF A$ = "STOCKS AND BONDS" and N = 6, the expression LEFT$(A$,N) also has the value STOCKS.*

Your system may use a **substring qualifier** **s(i:j)** to indicate the substring in the **i**th through the **j**th positions of the string **s**. If so you would use A$(1:4) instead of LEFT$(A$,4). This substring qualifier is included in the BASIC standard and is used in several versions of BASIC including BASIC on Cyber computers.

EXAMPLE 3   **Here is a program that extracts strings with the LEFT$ function.**

```
10 LET Y$="SEVEN"
20 FOR N=1 TO LEN(Y$)
30    PRINT LEFT$(Y$,N)
40 NEXT N
50 END
RUN

S
SE
SEV
SEVE
SEVEN
```

On systems that use the substring qualifier, use Y$(1:N) in place of LEFT$(Y$,N).

---

* In Vax BASIC and BASIC-PLUS the three string functions LEFT$,RIGHT$, and MID$ described in this section are written LEFT, RIGHT, and MID.

EXAMPLE 4 Here is a program that displays only those words that begin with whatever prefix is typed by the user.

```
100 PRINT "TYPE A PREFIX ";
110 INPUT P$
120 PRINT
130 PRINT "WORDS BEGINNING WITH THE PREFIX ";P$;":"
140 PRINT
150 FOR K=1 TO 13
160    READ A$
170    IF LEFT$(A$,LEN(P$))=P$ THEN PRINT TAB(6);A$
180 NEXT K
190 DATA ENABLE,ENACT,ENGAGE,ENSURE,ENDORSE
200 DATA HYPERACTIVE,HYPERMYSTICAL,HYPERNEUROTIC,HYPERPURE
210 DATA UNAFRAID,UNDO,UNEVEN,UNFOLD
220 END
RUN

TYPE A PREFIX ? UN

WORDS BEGINNING WITH THE PREFIX UN:

      UNAFRAID
      UNDO
      UNEVEN
      UNFOLD
```

On systems that use the substring qualifier, replace LEFT$(A$,LEN(P$)) in line 170 by A$(1:LEN(P$)).

REMARK 1 If you enter the prefix HYPER for P$, the condition

```
LEFT$(A$,LEN(P$))=P$
```

in line 170 says to compare the first five characters of A$ with HYPER. But when the value UNDO is read for A$, A$ will have only *four* characters. As we explain following this example, LEFT$("UNDO",5) is the four-character string UNDO. Thus, with P$ = "HYPER" and A$ = "UNDO", the condition in line 170 is false and UNDO is not displayed, as it shouldn't be. Thus, the program will work for any prefix you enter, not only for prefixes with fewer letters than the words in the DATA lines.

REMARK 2 In each pass through the loop, the computer determines the length LEN(P$) anew. Since P$ does not change in the loop, its length should be determined once, before the loop is entered. To do this, add the line

```
115 LET L=LEN(P$)
```

and change LEN(P$) in line 170 to L.

We have explained how the computer assigns to LEFT$(**s**,**n**) a substring of **s** in cases in which the value of **n** is an integer from 1 to LEN(**s**). What happens if **n** does not evaluate to one of these integers is system dependent. All versions of BASIC, however, evaluate LEFT$("UNDO",5) as the four-character string UNDO. Indeed, if **n** in the expression LEFT$(**s**,**n**) is greater than LEN(**s**) but not greater than the longest integer your version of BASIC allows in LEFT$ expressions, the value of LEFT$(**s**,**n**) will be **s.** A similar comment applies to **n** in the substring qualifier **s** (1:**n**).

The String Function RIGHT$

If **s** denotes a string and **n** a positive integer, the string value of RIGHT$(**s**,**n**) will be either

1. All characters of **s** from the **n**th character on. For instance, the value of RIGHT$("STOCKS AND BONDS",12) is BONDS and the value of RIGHT$("STOCKS AND BONDS",20) is the empty string (there is no 20th character).

2. The last **n** characters of **s.** For instance, the value of RIGHT$("STOCKS AND BONDS",5) is BONDS. This second method is used in many versions of BASIC implemented on personal computers.

EXAMPLE 5

This example illustrates the two methods that are used to extract string values with the RIGHT$ function.

RIGHT$ evaluated by using Method 1

```
10 LET Y$="SEVEN"
20 FOR N=1 TO LEN(Y$)
30    PRINT RIGHT$(Y$,N)
40 NEXT N
50 END
RUN

SEVEN
EVEN
VEN
EN
N
```

On systems that use the substring qualifier, replace RIGHT$(Y$,N) by Y$(N:LEN(Y$)).

RIGHT$ evaluated by using Method 2

```
10 LET Y$="SEVEN"
20 FOR N=1 TO LEN(Y$)
30    PRINT RIGHT$(Y$,N)
40 NEXT N
50 END
RUN

N
EN
VEN
EVEN
SEVEN
```

On systems that use the substring qualifier, replace RIGHT$(Y$,N) by Y$(LEN(Y$) − N + 1:LEN(Y$)).

The String Function MID$

There are two forms of the MID$ function: If **s** denotes a string and **m** and **n** denote integers, then

1. MID$(**s,m,n**) is the string of **n** characters from **s** beginning with the **m**th character of **s**.
2. MID$(**s,m**) is the string consisting of all characters in **s** from the **m**th character on.

In the following illustration, A$ = "STOCKS AND BONDS"

Expression	Its value	Length of its value
MID$(A$,8,3)	AND	3
MID$(A$,8)	AND BONDS	9
MID$(A$,8,9)	AND BONDS	9
MID$(A$,8,1)	A	1
MID$(A$,8,0)	nullstring	0

EXAMPLE 6

Here is a program to illustrate the two forms of the MID$ function.

```
10 LET Y$="ABCD"
20 FOR K=1 TO LEN(Y$)
30    PRINT MID$(Y$,K,1),MID$(Y$,K)
40 NEXT K
50 END
RUN

A          ABCD
B          BCD
C          CD
D          D
```

On systems that use the substring qualifier, replace line 30 by

```
30    PRINT Y$(K:K),Y$(K:LEN(Y$)−K+1)
```

EXAMPLE 7   **Here is a program to count the number of A's in a string A\$ of any length.**

```
100 LET C=0
110 PRINT "TYPE ANY STRING";
120 INPUT A$
130 FOR K=1 TO LEN(A$)
140    IF MID$(A$,K,1)="A" THEN C=C+1
150 NEXT K
160 PRINT "NUMBER OF A'S IS";C
170 END
RUN

TYPE ANY STRING? ABRACADABRA
NUMBER OF A'S IS 5
```

On systems that use the substring qualifier, replace line 140 with

```
140    IF A$(K:K)="A" THEN C=C+1
```

☐

■ 13.2 Combining Strings (Concatenation)

The **concatenation operator** + allows you to combine two or more strings into a single string. Thus the statement

```
LET X$="PARA"+"MEDIC"
```

assigns the string "PARAMEDIC" to the variable X\$. Similarly, if A\$ = "PARA" and B\$ = "MEDIC" the statement

```
LET X$=A$+B$
```

does exactly the same thing.

EXAMPLE 8   **Here is a program to illustrate the concatenation operator.**

```
10 LET X$="BIOLOGY"
20 LET Y$="ELECTRONICS"
30 LET Z$=LEFT$(X$,3)+MID$(Y$,8)
40 PRINT Z$
50 END
RUN

BIONICS
```

On systems that use the substring qualifier, replace line 30 with

```
30 LET Z$=X$(1:3)+Y$(8:LEN(Y$))
```

Using only the functions LEFT\$ and MID\$, we could have caused BIONICS to be displayed by the statement

```
PRINT LEFT$(X$,3);MID$(Y$,8)
```

but we could not have assigned the string BIONICS to the variable Z\$.

☐

EXAMPLE 9   **Here is a program to interchange the first and last names given in the string "EMILY DICKINSON".**

```
100 LET A$="EMILY DICKINSON"
110 PRINT A$
120 REM FIND THE POSITION P OF THE BLANK IN A$.
130 LET P=1
```

```
140 WHILE P<=LEN(A$) AND MID$(A$,P,1)<>"  "
150    LET P=P+1
160 NEXT    (or WEND)
170 IF P<=LEN(A$) THEN 200
180    PRINT "NAME HAS NO BLANK."
190    GOTO 250
200 REM STORE FIRST NAME IN F$ AND LAST NAME IN L$.
210 LET F$=LEFT$(A$,P-1)
220 LET L$=MID$(A$,P+1)
230 LET A$=L$+", "+F$
240 PRINT A$
250 END
RUN

EMILY DICKINSON
DICKINSON, EMILY
```

On systems that use the substring qualifier, use A$(P:P) in line 140, A$(1:P − 1) in line 210, and A$(P + 1:LEN(A$)) in line 220.

■ **REMARK 1**   In an actual application, it isn't likely that you would use

```
100 LET A$="EMILY DICKINSON"
```

to assign a value to A$. Instead you might include names in DATA lines and use READ. It is for such a situation that we included lines 170–190; they will flag names that contain no separating blank, rather than allowing meaningless output to be displayed.

■ **REMARK 2**   The technique illustrated in this example has two immediate applications: it gives you additional control over the precise form of your output, and it allows you to alphabetize a list of names, even if first names are given first (simply interchange first and last names, and then use a standard sorting algorithm to alphabetize your list). See Section 14.5.

☐

EXAMPLE 10   **Here is a program to assign the contents of A$ to B$, but in reverse order. Thus, if A$ = "AMNZ", then B$ will contain "ZNMA".**

```
100 LET A$="RORRIM"
110 REM B$ IS THE EMPTY STRING.
120 LET B$=""
130 REM USING THE CONCATENATION OPERATOR,
140 REM APPEND EACH OF THE CHARACTERS OF A$ TO B$.
150 FOR I=LEN(A$) TO 1 STEP -1
160    LET B$=B$+MID$(A$,I,1)   [B$=B$+A$(I:I)]
170 NEXT I
180 PRINT A$;" IN REVERSE ORDER IS ";B$
190 END
RUN

RORRIM IN REVERSE ORDER IS MIRROR
```

The string constant " " appearing in line 120 denotes a string containing no characters. Thus, the statement LET B$ = " " ensures that we will enter the FOR loop that appends letters to B$ with nothing in B$.

■ **REMARK 1**   The MID$ function allows you to display a given string in reverse order. The concatenation operator is what allows you to assign the new string to B$.

■ **REMARK 2**   A string containing no characters is called the **null (empty) string;** its length is 0. Thus, if B$ = " ", then LEN(B$) = 0. The program shown in this example illustrates the principal reason that programming languages such as BASIC allow the null string. When you wish to determine a numerical sum by adding a list of numbers, you begin with a sum of 0; when you wish to build a new string by concatenating a list of characters or strings, you begin with the empty string.

☐

■ 13.3 The Search Function INSTR

In Example 9 we used the following loop to determine the position P of the blank in the string A$ = "EMILY DICKINSON":

```
130 LET P=1
140 WHILE P<=LEN(A$) AND MID$(A$,P,1)<>" "
150    LET P=P+1
160 NEXT   (or WEND)
```

Searching a string for a specific character or sequence of characters is a common programming task. For this reason many versions of BASIC (including Vax BASIC, BASIC-PLUS, and Microsoft BASIC) provide the INSTR function to search one string for another automatically. If your system allows the INSTR function, you can use

```
LET P=INSTR(1,A$," ")
```

to determine the position P of the blank in A$. The number 1 instructs the computer to begin the search with the first character in A$.

The general form of the INSTR function is

INSTR(**n,s,t**)

where **s** and **t** denote strings and **n** denotes a positive integer. The expression INSTR(**n,s,t**) has an integer value determined as follows. The string **s** is searched, beginning at position **n,** for the first occurrence of the string **t.**

1. If **t** is found, INSTR returns the first position in **s** at which the match occurs. Thus INSTR(1, "STOCKS AND BONDS", "ND") has the value 9—the search for ND begins in position 1 and is successful at position 9. The expression INSTR(10, "STOCKS AND BONDS", "ND") has the value 14—the search for ND begins in position 10 and is successful at position 14.
2. If **t** is not found, INSTR returns the value 0.
3. If **n** > LEN(**s**), INSTR returns the value 0.

EXAMPLE 11 **Here is a program to search the words in DATA lines for any string typed at the keyboard.**

```
100 PRINT "FOR WHAT STRING ARE YOU LOOKING";
110 INPUT S$
120 PRINT "THESE WORDS CONTAIN THE SPECIFIED STRING:"
130 READ W$
140 WHILE W$<>"XXX"
150    IF INSTR(W$,S$)>0 THEN PRINT TAB(10);W$
160    READ W$
170 NEXT   (or WEND)
180 DATA THEORIZE,GUESS,HYPOTHESIZE,CONJECTURE
190 DATA XXX
200 END
RUN

FOR WHAT STRING ARE YOU LOOKING? THE
THESE WORDS CONTAIN THE SPECIFIED STRING:
         THEORIZE
         HYPOTHESIZE
```

EXAMPLE 12 **Here is a program to count the number of A's in any input string.**

```
100 LET C=0
110 PRINT "TYPE ANY STRING";
120 INPUT A$
130 LET P=INSTR(1,A$,"A")
140 WHILE P>0
150    LET C=C+1
160    LET P=INSTR(P+1,A$,"A")
170 NEXT   (or WEND)
```

```
180 PRINT "NUMBER OF A'S IS";C
190 END
RUN

TYPE ANY STRING? ABRACADABRA
NUMBER OF A'S IS 5
```

Line 130 gives the position P of the first A in the input string A\$. If P is not 0—that is, if a letter A is found—lines 150 and 160 are executed. Line 150 adds 1 to the counter C, and line 160 searches A\$ for the next A—the search begins at position P + 1, the position after the A just counted. This process is repeated until P = 0. This happens when the search for the letter A is not successful. Control then passes out of the loop to line 180, which displays the count C.

■ **REMARK**

The program in Example 7 counts the number of A's in A\$ by using the statement

```
IF MID$(A$,K,1)="A" THEN C=C+1
```

to compare each character in A\$ with the letter A. By using INSTR, any necessary comparisons are carried out automatically. It is worth mentioning that INSTR is very efficient; it will carry out the necessary comparisons faster than can be achieved by writing IF statements. Thus, if your system allows INSTR, you should not hesitate to use it.

□

EXAMPLE 13

This example shows how INSTR can be used to allow abbreviations for input values.

```
10 REM S$ CONTAINS A LIST OF ALLOWED WORDS.
20 LET S$=" APPLE  BANANA LEMON  PEACH  PLUM  "
30 PRINT "ENTER AN ABBREVIATION";
40 INPUT A$
50 LET P=INSTR(1,S$," "+A$)
60 IF P>0 THEN PRINT A$;" STANDS FOR ";MID$(S$,P+1,6)
70 END

RUN
ENTER AN ABBREVIATION? LE
LE STANDS FOR LEMON

RUN
ENTER AN ABBREVIATION? PLU
PLU STANDS FOR PLUM

RUN
ENTER AN ABBREVIATION? P
P STANDS FOR PEACH
```

[On systems using the substring qualifier, replace MID\$(S\$,P + 1,6) by S\$(P + 1:P + 6).]

Each word in S\$ is preceded by a blank. Since line 50 searches S\$ for the string " " + A\$, the leading blank ensures that the abbreviation that's typed will only match the beginnings of words included in S\$. For instance, LE is matched with the LE in LEMON and not with the first occurrence of LE in APPLE.

Each word in S\$ uses exactly seven positions: the leading blank, the letters in the word, and the trailing blanks if needed. This ensures that the string MID\$(S\$,P + 1,6) displayed by line 60 will give the entire word corresponding to the abbreviation typed by the user.

Note that the input value P gives PEACH, the first word in S\$ that begins with P. To ensure that abbreviations are unique, you can require abbreviations with more than one letter.

■ 13.4 Problems

1. Show the output of each program (for systems that use LEFT$, RIGHT$, and MID$).

   a.
   ```
   10 LET A$="CYBERNETIC"
   20 PRINT LEFT$(A$,LEN(A$)/2)
   30 END
   ```

   b.
   ```
   10 LET B$="A TO Z"
   20 PRINT MID$(B$,6);" TO ";LEFT$(B$,1)
   30 END
   ```

   c.
   ```
   10 LET A$="CONSTRUCTION"
   20 LET B$="SULTAN OF SWAT"
   30 LET C$=LEFT$(A$,3)+LEFT$(B$,5)+MID$(A$,9)
   40 PRINT C$
   50 END
   ```

   d.
   ```
   10 LET A$="BIOLOGY"
   20 LET B$="PHYSICS"
   30 LET C$=LEFT$(A$,3)
   40 FOR I=1 TO LEN(B$)
   50    LET C$=C$+MID$(B$,I,1)
   60 NEXT I
   70 PRINT C$
   80 END
   ```

2. Show the output of each program (for systems that use the substring qualifier).

   a.
   ```
   10 LET A$="CYBERNETIC"
   20 PRINT A$(1:LEN(A$)/2)
   30 END
   ```

   b.
   ```
   10 LET B$="A TO Z"
   20 PRINT B$(6:6);" TO ";B$(1:1)
   30 END
   ```

   c.
   ```
   10 LET A$="CONSTRUCTION"
   20 LET B$="SULTAN OF SWAT"
   30 LET C$=A$(1:3)+B$(1:5)+A$(9:LEN(A$))
   40 PRINT C$
   50 END
   ```

   d.
   ```
   10 LET A$="BIOLOGY"
   20 LET B$="PHYSICS"
   30 LET C$=A$(1:3)
   40 FOR I=1 TO LEN(B$)
   50    LET C$=C$+B$(I:I)
   60 NEXT I
   70 PRINT C$
   80 END
   ```

3. Show the output of each program (for systems that use the INSTR function).

   a.
   ```
   100 LET S$=" "
   110 READ X$
   120 LET A=1
   130 LET B=INSTR(A,X$,S$)
   140 WHILE B>0
   150     PRINT MID$(X$,A,B-A)
   160     LET A=B+1
   170     LET B=INSTR(A,X$,S$)
   180 NEXT    (or WEND)
   190 PRINT MID$(X$,A)
   200 DATA "GREAT SALT LAKE DESERT, UTAH"
   210 END
   ```

   b.
   ```
   10 LET S$="-ADD -LIST-STEP-STOP "
   20 FOR K=1 TO 7
   30     READ C$
   40     IF LEN(C$)<3 THEN 70
   50     LET P=INSTR(1,S$,"-"+C$)
   60     IF P>0 THEN PRINT MID$(S$,P+1,4)
   70 NEXT K
   80 DATA ADD,LIST,STOP,START,S,ST,STE
   90 END
   ```

```
c. 10 LET S$="-ADD -LIST-STOP-STOP"
   20 FOR K=1 TO 4
   30     READ C$
   40     LET P=INSTR(1,S$,"-"+C$)
   50     LET N=1+(P-1)/5
   60     PRINT N;C$
   70 NEXT K
   80 DATA STEP,LIST,STOP,ADD
   90 END
```

4. Write a *single* program statement to perform each of the following tasks.

   a. Display the first character of A$.

   b. Display the second character of A$.

   c. Display the last character of A$.

   d. Display the first three characters of A$.

   e. Display the last three characters of A$.

   f. Display the first and last characters of A$.

   g. Increase N by 1 if A$ and B$ have the same number of characters.

   h. Display the first character in A$ only if it's the same as the last character in A$.

   i. Assign the string SAME to X$ if the first two characters in A$ are the same.

   j. Assign the first N characters of A$ to B$.

   k. A$ is a two-letter string. Interchange these letters to obtain the string B$.

   l. Interchange the first two characters in S$ to obtain T$.

   m. Create a string F$ consisting of the first three characters of G$ and the last three characters of H$.

   n. Display the string OK if the first character of A$, the second character of B$, and the third character of C$ spell YES.

   o. Display the string COMMA if A$ contains a comma. (Use INSTR.)

   p. Display the string NO SPACES if A$ contains no spaces. (Use INSTR.)

In Problems 5–17, write a program for each task specified.

5. Display any five-character string typed at the keyboard in reverse order. If the string does not contain exactly five characters, display nothing. Allow the user to try many strings, and stop the program when the user types DONE.

6. Display any string typed at the keyboard in reverse order. Stop the program when the user types DONE.

7. Examine all strings appearing in DATA lines to determine and display those that begin with whatever letter is input. Allow the user to try different letters during a single run, and stop the program when ∗ is typed.

8. The user types two five-letter words. Compare them letter by letter. If two corresponding letters are different, display a dollar sign. Otherwise display the letter. If CANDY and CHIDE are typed, for example, the output should be C$$D$.

9. The user types two words to obtain a listing of those letters in the second word that are also in the first. If the user types STRING and HARNESS, for example, the output should be RNSS, since these four letters in the second word HARNESS are also in the first word STRING.

10. The user types a string containing two words separated by a comma. Display the two words in reverse order without the comma. If the user types "PUCKETT,KIRBY", for example, the output should be KIRBY PUCKETT. Stop the program only when the user types DONE.

11. Include a list of names, with last names last, in DATA lines. Produce a listing of the names with last names first followed by a comma. Run your program with the given DATA lines. Note that

```
BRICE, MARY ELLEN
```

is how MARY ELLEN BRICE should be displayed. You may assume, however, that *last* names contain no blanks.

```
DATA MARY ELLEN BRICE,MARK BRONSON,MARIA MANDELA
DATA LIZ WALKER,LI-JUAN WEI,SUE ANN TILTON
DATA ART ROBELLO,RONALD MACDONALD
DATA END-OF-DATA
```

12. Input a string and change all occurrences of the letter Y to the letter M.

13. Read a list of words from DATA lines to determine the average number of letters per word.

14. Read a list of words from DATA lines, and display only the words with exactly N letters. N is to be input by the user, who should be allowed to try several different values for N during a single program run.

15. Read a list of strings appearing in DATA lines to determine how many times a particular letter or other character appears in this list. The letter or character is to be input by the user, who should be allowed to try several different characters during the same run. Stop the program if the user types END.

16. Display the words appearing in an English sentence, one per line. You may assume that words are separated by exactly one space, that the sentence ends with a period, and that no other punctuation is used. The sentence is to be input into a string variable. Stop the program only when the user types DONE. If the input sentence does not contain a period, inform the user of this fact. Try your program with the sentences

```
ALL GAUL IS DIVIDED INTO THREE PARTS.
WHERE IS THE PERIOD?
```

17. Carry out the task described in Problem 16 with the following difference: words may be separated by more than one space and may be followed by a comma, semicolon, or colon, and sentences may end with a period or a question mark. Inform the user if a sentence does not end with a period or question mark. Try your program with these sentences:

```
ALLOWED COMMANDS ARE ADD, LIST, STEP, AND STOP.
YOU MAY USE THE FOLLOWING: ADD, LIST, AND STOP.
IS ALL GAUL DIVIDED INTO THREE PARTS?
THERE IS NO PERIOD
```

■ 13.5 The BASIC Character Set

BASIC allows several operations with string data that we have yet to explain. For instance, although we have used relational expressions such as A\$ = B\$ and A\$ <> B\$ to determine if two strings are identical or not, we have not compared strings by using the other relational operators <, <=, >, and >=. As we explain shortly, there are many programming situations that require making such string comparisons. To understand these, and other operations with strings described in Section 13.7, you will need some knowledge of how a computer stores string data in memory.

Whenever a program requires the use of a string, each character of the string is assigned a numerical value called its **numeric code.** It is these numerical values that are compared. As we would expect, the numeric code for the letter A is smaller than that for B, the numeric code for B is smaller than that for C, and so on. But it is not only letters that can be compared; each BASIC character has its own unique numeric code so that any two characters may be compared. One BASIC character is less than a second character if the numeric code of the first is less than the numeric code of the second.

The **ordering sequence** (or **collating sequence**) of numeric codes for the BASIC character set as given by the American Standard Code of Information Interchange (ASCII) is presented in Table 13.1. These are called the ASCII codes and are used in

Table 13.1 ASCII numeric codes for the BASIC character set

Numeric code	Character	Numeric code	Character	Numeric code	Character	Numeric code	Character
032	(space)	056	8	080	P	104	h
033	!	057	9	081	Q	105	i
034	"	058	:	082	R	106	j
035	#	059	;	083	S	107	k
036	$	060	<	084	T	108	l
037	%	061	=	085	U	109	m
038	&	062	>	086	V	110	n
039	'	063	?	087	W	111	o
040	(	064	@	088	X	112	p
041	)	065	A	089	Y	113	q
042	*	066	B	090	Z	114	r
043	+	067	C	091	[	115	s
044	,	068	D	092	\	116	t
045	–	069	E	093	]	117	u
046	.	070	F	094	^	118	v
047	/	071	G	095	–	119	w
048	0	072	H	096	'	120	x
049	1	073	I	097	a	121	y
050	2	074	J	098	b	122	z
051	3	075	K	099	c	123	{
052	4	076	L	100	d	124	¦
053	5	077	M	101	e	125	}
054	6	078	N	102	f	126	~
055	7	079	O	103	g	127	

many versions of BASIC including Vax BASIC, BASIC-PLUS, Microsoft BASIC, and Applesoft BASIC. In the examples that follow, we assume that ASCII codes are used.*

Using this ASCII ordering sequence, we have:

"G" < "P"	since 71 < 80
"4" < "Y"	since 52 < 89
"$" < "^"	since 36 < 94
"8" < "?"	since 56 < 63
"M" < "m"	since 77 < 109
"Z" < "a"	since 90 < 97

If strings containing more than one character are to be compared, they are compared character by character beginning at the left. Strings consisting of uppercase letters of the alphabet are ordered just as they would appear in a dictionary, as are strings consisting only of lowercase letters. Here are some relational expressions and their truth values:

Relational expression	Truth value
"AMA" > "AM"	True
"Bat" <="BAT"	False
"13N" < "14N"	True
"M24" < "M31"	True
"B2" < "A59"	False
"sect" > "Zen"	True
"BEAL TOM" < "BEALS TOM"	True

*If you are using a Cyber computer you may find that a different ordering sequence, one that does not allow lowercase letters, is used. If so, try issuing the system command ASCII as soon as you log into the system. This command instructs the computer to use ASCII codes as shown in Table 13.1.

In the last expression, the fifth character in "BEAL TOM" is the blank character (ASCII code 32), whereas the fifth character in "BEALS TOM" is S (ASCII code 83). Since 32 < 83, the relational expression is true. Note that "sect" > "Zen" is true even though sect appears before Zen in the dictionary. The comparison of words that contain both upper- and lowercase letters is considered in Section 13.7.

EXAMPLE 14
Here is a program to display the words appearing in a data list that begin with a letter from D to M.

```
100 PRINT "WORDS WITH FIRST LETTER D TO M:"
110 READ W$
120 WHILE W$<>"END OF LIST"
130    IF W$>="D" AND W$<"N" THEN PRINT TAB(5);W$
140    READ W$
150 NEXT (or WEND)
500 DATA WHITE,BLACK,YELLOW,RED,BLUE,ORANGE,GREEN
510 DATA PINK,GRAY,MAGENTA,BEIGE,BROWN,VIOLET,LIME
998 DATA END OF LIST
999 END
RUN

WORDS WITH FIRST LETTER D TO M:
     GREEN
     GRAY
     MAGENTA
     LIME
```

Each word from the data list is read into W$ and compared with the EOD tag END OF LIST. (This EOD tag is not a member of the list being searched.) If W$ < "D", W$ is not displayed since its first letter must be an A, B, or C. Similarly, if W$ > ="N", W$ is rejected because its first letter must be N,O,P, . . . , or Z.

■ **REMARK** If words with lowercase as well as uppercase letters are included in the data list, you can insert the line

```
135 IF W$>="d" and W$<"n" THEN PRINT TAB(5);W$
```

EXAMPLE 15
Here is a program segment to display the value of W$ if it contains only letters of the alphabet and to display an informative message if it doesn't.

```
300 REM FLAG IS SET TO 1 IF A CHARACTER
310 REM OTHER THAN A LETTER IS FOUND IN W$.
320 LET FLAG=0
330 REM P DENOTES THE CURRENT POSITION IN W$.
340 LET P=0
350 REM TEST EACH CHARACTER IN W$.
360 WHILE P<LEN(W$) AND FLAG=0
370    LET P=P+1
380    LET L$=MID$(W$,P,1)                [or L$ = W$(P:P)]
390    IF L$<"A" OR L$>"Z" THEN FLAG=1
400 NEXT    (or WEND)
410 REM
420 IF FLAG=0 THEN PRINT W$
430 IF FLAG=1 AND L$=" "  THEN PRINT W$;" CONTAINS A SPACE."
440 IF FLAG=1 AND L$<>" " THEN PRINT W$;" CONTAINS ";L$
```

Line 380 assigns the Pth character of W$ to L$, and line 390 sets FLAG to 1 if this character is not a letter. Line 360 causes an exit from the loop when all characters in W$ have been tested or when one that is not a letter is encountered, whichever event occurs first.

■ **REMARK 1** If W$ can contain lowercase as well as uppercase letters, replace line 390 by

```
390 IF L$<"A" OR (L$>"Z" AND L$<"a") OR L$>"z" THEN FLAG=1
```

■ **REMARK 2**   Rather than having the computer evaluate LEN(W$) on each pass through the loop, you could include a line such as

> 355 LET L=LEN(W$)

and change LEN(W$) in line 360 to L.

■ **REMARK 3**   If it is important that all data processed by a program consist entirely of letters, lines 300 □ to 400 might be coded as a subroutine and used to test each data value.

EXAMPLE 16   **Here is a program segment to interchange the word contents of W1$ and W2$ if they are not in alphabetical order.**

```
200 IF W1$<=W2$ THEN 240
210 LET T$=W1$
220 LET W1$=W2$
230 LET W2$=T$
240 (Program continuation)
```

A program segment that interchanges two words when they are not in alphabetical order can be used in larger program segments (or subroutines) to alphabetize lists of any length. Before doing this you will need to understand how long lists can be stored conveniently. □   This topic is covered in Chapter 14.

■ 13.6 Problems

1. Show the output of each program:
   a. ```
   10 FOR I=1 TO 3
   20   READ A$,B$
   30   IF A$<=B$ THEN PRINT A$
   40 NEXT I
   50 DATA M,MO,A,AA,M,KANT
   60 END
   ```
   b. ```
   10 FOR J=1 TO 3
   20     READ C$,D$
   30     IF C$>D$ THEN C$=D$
   40     PRINT C$;D$
   50 NEXT J
   60 DATA CAT,DOG,7,10,MAN,BEAST
   70 END
   ```
   c. ```
   10 LET M$="MIDDLE"
   20 FOR N=1 TO 4
   30   READ A$
   40   IF A$>M$ AND A$<"ZZZ" THEN A$="LAST"
   50   PRINT A$
   60 NEXT N
   70 DATA HARRY,ALICE,PAUL,ROSE
   80 END
   ```

*In Problems 2–6, write a program for each task specified.*

2. Include a list of English words in DATA lines. First display those words beginning with a letter from A to M; then display the rest. If your system allows lowercase letters, be sure that the program works whether the words begin with a lowercase or an uppercase letter.

3. Write a program that contains the following DATA lines:

```
800 DATA 9
810 DATA MARIAN EVANS,JAMES PAYN,JOSEPH CONRAD
820 DATA EMILY DICKINSON,HENRY THOREAU,JOHN PAYNE
830 DATA JOHN FOX,MARY FREEMAN,GEORGE ELIOT
```

Read the names twice. On the first pass, display only those names with a last name beginning with a letter from A to M. Display the remaining names on the second pass.
```

4. For any string typed at the keyboard, display THE FIRST CHARACTER IS A LETTER or THE FIRST CHARACTER IS NOT A LETTER, whichever message is correct. Allow the user to type many strings during a single program run, and stop the program when $ is typed. If your system allows lowercase letters, be sure that the program works with whatever input values the user types.

5. Include a list of English words in DATA lines. Allow a user to type any two words to obtain a listing of all words alphabetically between them. Stop the program when both input words are the same. If your system allows lowercase letters, do not use them in the DATA lines and instruct the user to use only uppercase letters.

6. Repeat Problem 5 but this time assume that the words are in alphabetical order and make use of this fact.

■ 13.7 BASIC Conversion Functions

A conversion function is a function that converts values from one data type to another. In this section we describe two functions that are used to convert between characters and their numeric codes and two functions that convert between strings whose contents denote numbers and their corresponding numerical values. As illustrated in the examples, conversion functions provide a convenient way to code several string-related programming tasks.

The Character Function CHR$

The CHR$ function converts numeric codes to their corresponding characters. Thus, in light of Table 13.1, CHR$(65) = "A" and CHR$(43) = "+".

EXAMPLE 17   **This example illustrates the CHR$ function.**

```
100 PRINT "THE SEQUENCE OF CHARACTERS CORRESPONDING TO THE"
110 PRINT "NUMERIC CODES CONTAINED IN THE DATA LINES IS:"
120 PRINT
130 READ N
140 WHILE N<>0
150    PRINT CHR$(N);
160    READ N
170 NEXT (or WEND)
180 DATA 42,42,42,72,79,87,68,89,42,42,42
190 DATA 0
200 END
RUN

THE SEQUENCE OF CHARACTERS CORRESPONDING TO THE
NUMERIC CODES CONTAINED IN THE DATA LINES IS:

***HOWDY***
```

EXAMPLE 18   **Here is a program to display the English alphabet.**

```
10 FOR K=65 TO 90
20    PRINT CHR$(K);
30 NEXT K
40 END
RUN

ABCDEFGHIJKLMNOPQRSTUVWXYZ
```

■ REMARK   If your version of BASIC allows lowercase letters, you can change line 20 to

```
20 PRINT CHR$(K);CHR$(K+32);
```

to obtain the output

AaBbCcDdEeFfGgHhIiJjKkLlMmNnOoPpQqRrSsTtUuVvWwXxYyZz

As shown in Table 13.1, the ASCII codes for the lowercase letters are 97 to 122—each is 32 more than the code for the corresponding uppercase letter.

The Numeric Code Functions ASC, ASCII, and ORD

The ASC function converts the first character in a string to its numeric code. For example, ASC("BROOK") = 66, the numeric code for B, and ASC(" BROOK") = 32, the numeric code for the space character. When ASC is used with a one-character string, it converts the character to its numeric code. Thus, ASC("A") = 65 and ASC(" ") = 32.

Instead of ASC, your system may require ASCII or ORD. Vax BASIC and BASIC-PLUS use ASCII; versions of BASIC on Cyber computers use ORD; most other versions of BASIC use ASC (Microsoft BASIC, Applesoft BASIC, BASIC on TRS-80 computers, and others). In the following examples, change ASC to ASCII or ORD if necessary. The programs will work as described.

EXAMPLE 19 **Here is a program to find the position in the alphabet of letters typed at the keyboard.**

```
100 REM FIND THE POSITION OF A CAPITAL LETTER IN THE ALPHABET.
110 PRINT "TYPE A CAPITAL LETTER ";
120 INPUT L$
130 WHILE L$>="A" AND L$<="Z"
140     LET N=ASC(L$)-ASC("A")+1
150     PRINT "ITS POSITION IN ALPHABET IS";N
160     PRINT
170     PRINT "NEXT LETTER ";
180     INPUT L$
190 NEXT (or WEND)
200 PRINT "NOT A CAPITAL LETTER"
210 END
RUN

TYPE A CAPITAL LETTER ? C
ITS POSITION IN ALPHABET IS 3

NEXT LETTER ? Z
ITS POSITION IN ALPHABET IS 26

NEXT LETTER ? +
NOT A CAPITAL LETTER
```

The numeric codes for the letters A, B, C, . . . , Z are 65, 66, 67, . . . , 90, respectively. Thus, if L\$ = "C", then ASC(L\$) = 67, so that line 130 gives N = 67 − 65 + 1 = 3.

■ **REMARK 1** Since the numeric codes for A and Z are 65 and 90, respectively, it is correct to replace line 130 with

```
130 WHILE ASC(L$)>=65 AND ASC(L$)<=90
```

■ **REMARK 2** To guard against the user's typing more than one character, you can change line 130 to

```
130 WHILE L$>="A" AND L$<="Z" AND LEN(L$)=1
```

■ **REMARK 3** If your system allows lowercase letters, you can make the following changes so that the program will work for lowercase as well as uppercase letters:

```
130 WHILE (L$>="A" AND L$<="Z") OR (L$>="a" AND L$<="z")
135     IF L$<="Z" THEN N=ASC(L$)-ASC("A")+1
140     IF L$>="a" THEN N=ASC(L$)-ASC("a")+1
```

The parentheses in line 130 are for readability—they are not required.

EXAMPLE 20 **Here is a program to display a partial ordering sequence for any BASIC system.**

```
100 REM ----- ASSIGN LIST OF CHARACTERS TO A$ -------
110 LET A$="ABCDEFGHIJKLMNOPQRSTUVWXYZ0123456789:;<>=?!#$"
120 REM
130 REM ----- DISPLAY COLUMN HEADINGS AND ASSIGN OUTPUT FORMAT ----
140 PRINT "   CHAR   CODE   CHAR   CODE   CHAR   CODE"
150 LET F$= "    #     ##  "
160 PRINT
170 REM ------------ DISPLAY CHARACTERS WITH CODES -------------
180 FOR K=1 TO LEN(A$)
190    LET C$=MID$(A$,K,1)
200    PRINT USING F$,C$,ASC(C$);
210    REM CAUSE A RETURN AFTER EVERY THIRD CHARACTER.
220    IF K/3=INT(K/3) THEN PRINT
230 NEXT K
240 END
RUN
```

CHAR	CODE	CHAR	CODE	CHAR	CODE
A	65	B	66	C	67
D	68	E	69	F	70
G	71	H	72	I	73
J	74	K	75	L	76
M	77	N	78	O	79
P	80	Q	81	R	82
S	83	T	84	U	85
V	86	W	87	X	88
Y	89	Z	90	0	48
1	49	2	50	3	51
4	52	5	53	6	54
7	55	8	56	9	57
:	58	;	59	<	60
>	62	=	61	?	63
!	33	#	35	$	36

Here are changes you may have to make for your version of BASIC:

1. Your system may require ASCII or ORD instead of ASC.
2. If your system uses substring qualifiers, change MID$(A$,K,1) to A$(K:K).
3. With Microsoft BASIC, change the first comma in line 200 to a semicolon.

On systems that allow lowercase letters it is sometimes important to convert lowercase letters to uppercase or uppercase letters to lowercase. Two such situations are as follows:

1. If a list of words containing only uppercase letters must be alphabetized, standard sorting algorithms such as shown in Chapters 14 and 17 can be used. If the words contain both upper- and lowercase letters, the necessary comparisons can be very awkward. When sorting lists of strings, it is common practice to convert strings that must be compared to uppercase before making comparisons.
2. If an input string must be compared with other strings for equality, the comparisons are easily made if only uppercase letters are used. For example, if a program contains the lines

```
300 INPUT C$
310 IF C$="DONE" THEN 999
```

control will transfer to line 999 only if the user types *DONE*. Although it is unlikely that the user will type *doNE* or *DoNE*, it is quite likely that *Done* or *done* will be typed. By converting all lowercase letters in C$ to uppercase before the comparison C$ = "DONE" is made, the difficulty vanishes.

Some versions of BASIC contain a string function to convert all lowercase letters in a string to uppercase automatically. In Vax BASIC or BASIC-PLUS you can use

```
LET B$=CVT$$(A$,32)
```

to assign the string A$ to B$, but with each lowercase letter converted to uppercase. With recent versions of BASIC on Cyber computers, you can do the same thing by using

```
LET B$=UPRC$(A$)
```

Unfortunately, many versions of BASIC do not have such a conversion function. The next two examples show how you can use the functions ASC and CHR$ to accomplish lowercase to uppercase conversions.

EXAMPLE 21   **Here is a program segment to convert a single lowercase letter to uppercase.**

```
200 PRINT "Type a letter";
210 INPUT L$
220 IF L$>="a" AND L$<="z" THEN L$=CHR$(ASC(L$)-32)
```

The ASCII code for each lowercase letter is 32 more than the code for the corresponding uppercase letter. Thus, if L$ is a lowercase letter, ASC(L$) − 32 gives the numeric code for the corresponding uppercase letter, and CHR$(ASC(L$) − 32) gives the uppercase letter itself.

EXAMPLE 22   **Here is a subroutine to change all lowercase letters in X$ to uppercase letters.**

```
800 REM SUBROUTINE: L.C. TO U.C. CONVERSION
810 REM   X$  STRING TO BE CONVERTED
820 REM   Y$  USED TO BUILD U.C. STRING
830 LET Y$="" 'Null string
840 FOR N=1 TO LEN(X$)
850    LET C$=MID$(X$,N,1)   [or C$ = X$(N:N)]
860    REM CONVERT CHARACTER C$ TO UPPERCASE IF NECESSARY.
870    IF C$>="a" AND C$<="z" THEN C$=CHR$(ASC(C$)-32)
880    LET Y$=Y$+C$
890 NEXT N
900 REM REPLACE X$ BY U.C. STRING Y$.
910 LET X$=Y$
920 RETURN
```

Line 850 assigns the Nth character of X$ to C$ and line 870 converts this character to uppercase if it happens to be a lowercase letter. Line 880 then appends C$, whether it was converted or not, to Y$. Thus, Y$ starts as the empty string (line 830), and we use it to build the converted string, character by character. Finally, Y$ is assigned to X$ so that the converted string is returned as X$.

REMARK 1   If you require the user of a program to respond to the prompt

```
PRINT "NAME(TYPE DONE WHEN FINISHED)";
INPUT N$
```

you can use

```
LET X$=N$
GOSUB 800
```

to transform N$ to X$ with only uppercase letters in X$. If you then compare X$ (instead of N$) with DONE, the user can repond in lowercase letters, uppercase letters, or a mixture of the two.

REMARK 2   In many programming applications, you must include strings typed at the keyboard in your output. By using conversion subroutines such as the one in this example, you can control the exact form of the output and don't have to rely on the user to be consistent in how letters are typed.

The Value Function VAL

The VAL function converts a string whose contents represent a number to its numerical form. The statement

```
LET A=VAL("537.2")
```

for example, assigns the number 537.2 to the numerical variable A. Similarly,

```
LET B=VAL("5372E-1")
```

assigns the number $5372E-1 = 537.2$ to B.

EXAMPLE 23   **This example illustrates the VAL function.**

```
100 REM DETERMINE TOTAL NUMBER T OF TOOLS.
110 LET T=0
120 READ X$
130 WHILE X$<>"XXX"
140     LET C$=MID$(X$,9,3)   [or C$ = X$(9:11)]
150     LET T+T+VAL(C$)
160     READ X$
170 NEXT   (or WEND)
180 PRINT "TOTAL NUMBER OF TOOLS: ";T
200 REM *******************
210 REM    D    A    T    A
220 REM   12345678901234567890
230 DATA HAMMERS 320 SHELF X
240 DATA PLIERS  100 SHELF L
250 DATA SAWS     57 SHELF B
260 DATA XXX
270 END
RUN

TOTAL NUMBER OF TOOLS: 477
```

Line 120 reads the first datum

```
HAMMERS 320 SHELF X
```

for X$, and line 140 assigns to C$ the string consisting of the characters in positions 9, 10, and 11 of X$. This gives C$ = "320". Line 150 converts this numeric string to the numerical value 320 and adds it to T. Line 160 reads the next datum, and the process is repeated until XXX is read.

□

The String Function STR$

The function STR$ reverses the process just described for VAL—it converts a numerical value to a string. For example, the two statements

```
LET A$=STR$(23.6)
LET B$=STR$(-23.6)
```

assign the four-character string 23.6 to A$ and the five-character string -23.6 to B$. (Some versions of BASIC include a leading blank in the string representation of positive numbers.)

If you need to display a positive numerical value X without the leading blank, you can use STR$(X). For instance, the three lines

```
150 LET A=15.37
160 LET B=10
170 PRINT STR$(A);"+";STR$(B);"=";STR$(A+B)
```

produce the output

```
15.37+10=25.37
```

with no blank spaces, as there would be if we had used

```
60 PRINT A;"+";B;"=";A+B
```

[If your system includes the leading blank in STR$(X), you can use MID$(STR$(X),2) to eliminate the blank.]

EXAMPLE 24   **Here is a program to display the individual digits in any number, positive or negative.**

```
100 PRINT "TYPE A NUMBER";
110 INPUT X
120 LET X$=STR$(X)
130 PRINT "THE DIGITS IN";X;"ARE ";
140 FOR K=1 TO LEN(X$)
150    LET D$=MID$(X$,K,1)  [or D$= X$(K:K)]
160     IF D$<>"-" AND D$<>"." THEN PRINT D$;" ";
170 NEXT K
180 END
RUN

TYPE A NUMBER? -102.9
THE DIGITS IN -102.9 ARE 1 0 2 9

RUN

TYPE A NUMBER? 123456
THE DIGITS IN 123456 ARE 1 2 3 4 5 6
```

If your system includes the leading blank in STR$(X) for positive X values, you would include the condition D$<>" " in line 160, or you could start the K loop with 2 instead of 1 and simplify line 160 to

```
160 IF D$<>"." THEN PRINT D$;" ";
```

Examining the individual characters that make up a number is not simply an academic exercise. In Example 25 we'll show how this capability can be used to test if values intended as numerical input are correctly formed. To this point we have tested if numerical input values are integers or if they lie in specified ranges, but we have not been able to test if they are correctly formed numbers. For instance, if a user types 52L6 instead of 5216 in response to the statements

```
PRINT "ENTER THE COUNT";
INPUT X
```

your computer might display

```
ENTER THE COUNT? 52L6
TYPE MISMATCH
```

and terminate your program. By using STR$ and VAL you can prevent this from happening. The idea is to assign a numerical input value to a string variable, rather than to a numerical variable, and to validate the contents of this string variable. If no errors are found, VAL would be used to convert the input to a numerical value for subsequent processing. If an error is found, it would be handled in whatever way the program was written to do so. Example 25 illustrates the method.

EXAMPLE 25   **Here is a program segment to validate that a numerical input value consists entirely of the digits 0 to 9, a possible decimal point, and a possible leading + or − sign.**

THE PROGRAM

```
300 PRINT "TYPE A NUMBER ";
310 INPUT N$
320 REM ******************************
330 REM STORE N$ IN C$ AND THEN STRIP
340 REM OFF ANY LEADING + OR - FROM C$.
```

```
350 REM
360 LET C$=N$
370 LET L$=LEFT$(C$,1)
380 IF L$="+" OR L$="-" THEN C$=MID$(C$,2,LEN(C$))
390 REM
400 REM *****************************
410 REM CHECK THAT C$ CONTAINS ONLY
420 REM DIGITS WITH AT MOST 1 PERIOD.
430 REM
440 LET FLAG=0                          'Set to 1 on bad data.
450 LET D=0                             'Decimal point counter
460 LET P=0                             'Position in C$
470 WHILE P<LEN(C$) AND FLAG=0
480     LET P=P+1
490     LET L$=MID$(C$,P,1)
500     IF L$="." THEN D=D+1
510     IF (L$<"0" OR L$>"9") AND L$<>"."  THEN FLAG=1
520     IF D=2 THEN FLAG=1
530 NEXT    (or WEND)
540 REM
550 REM ************************
560 REM  ASSIGN N$ TO N, IF N$ OK.
570 REM IF NOT OK, FLAG THE ERROR.
580 REM
590 IF FLAG=0 THEN N=VAL(N$)
600 IF FLAG=1 THEN PRINT "BAD DATA: ";N$
610 (Program continuation)
```

[On systems using the substring qualifier, replace LEFT$(C$,1) by C$(1:1), MID$(C$,2,LEN(C$)) by C$(2:LEN(C$)), and MID$(C$,P,1) by C$(P:P).]

If the user enters a value that does not conform to the specifications described, the loop in lines 500–550 will assign 1 to FLAG and line 620 will display the message BAD DATA: followed by the improper input value. If the input value has the form specified, the loop will not assign 1 to FLAG, so FLAG will retain the value 0 assigned in line 470. Then line 610 will assign the numerical value VAL(N$) to N, and program execution will continue uninterrupted.

■ 13.8 User-Defined Functions Involving String Data

Many versions of BASIC allow you to use the DEF FN statement to define your own string and string-related functions. To illustrate, the statement

```
DEF FNNAME$(A$,B$)=A$+" "+B$
```

defines a function called NAME$ (also called FNNAME$) whose value for any two strings A$ and B$ is the concatenation of the strings with a separating blank. To reference (or *call*) this function, you must use the form

FNNAME$(**string1,string2**)

where **string1** and **string2** denote string expressions whose values are to be substituted for A$ and B$ in the function definition. Thus, if FIRST$ = "MAGIC" and LAST$ = "JOHNSON", the statement

```
PRINT FNNAME$(FIRST$,LAST$)
```

will display

```
MAGIC JOHNSON
```

An example of a user-defined string-related function is

```
DEF FNP(L$) = ASC(L$)-ASC("A")+1
```

This statement defines a numerical function that gives the position in the alphabet of any uppercase letter L$. (See Example 19, Section 13.7.)

The general forms of user-defined functions given in Sections 12.3 (single-statement functions) and 12.4 (multiple-statement functions) apply to both numerical and string functions. The following examples illustrate how some of the programming tasks considered previously might be coded by using user-defined functions.

EXAMPLE 26   **Here is a program to display the names read from DATA lines in two ways, first name first and last name first.**

```
100 REM ****** FUNCTION DEFINITIONS ******
110 REM
120 REM DEF FNFIRSTLAST$(A$,B$)=B$+" "+A$
130 REM DEF FNLASTFIRST$(A$,B$)=A$+", "+B$
140 REM
150 PRINT "FIRST LAST";TAB(30);"LAST FIRST"
160 PRINT "----------";TAB(30);"----------"
170 READ C$,D$
180 WHILE C$<>"XXXX"
190    PRINT FNFIRSTLAST$(C$,D$);TAB(30);FNLASTFIRST$(C$,D$)
200    READ C$,D$
210 NEXT    (or WEND)
220 DATA WORTHY,JAMES
230 DATA THOMPSON,MYCHAL
240 DATA GREEN,A.C.
250 DATA SCOTT,BYRON
260 DATA JOHNSON,MAGIC
270 DATA XXXX,ZZZZ
280 END
RUN

FIRST LAST                    LAST FIRST
----------                    ----------
JAMES WORTHY                  WORTHY,JAMES
MYCHAL THOMPSON               THOMPSON,MYCHAL
A.C. GREEN                    GREEN,A.C.
BYRON SCOTT                   SCOTT,BYRON
MAGIC JOHNSON                 JOHNSON,MAGIC
```

EXAMPLE 27   **Here is a program to display the letters of the alphabet.**

```
100 DEF FNLETTER$(N)=CHR$(N+ASC("A")-1)
110 REM
120 FOR P=1 TO 26
130    PRINT FNLETTER$(P)
140 NEXT P
150 END
RUN

ABCDEFGHIJKLMNOPQRSTUVWXYZ
```

To display the alphabet in lowercase letters, simply change ASC("A") in the function definition to ASC("a").

EXAMPLE 28   **Here is a multiple-statement function that can be used when lowercase letters in a string must be converted to uppercase.**

```
1000 REM **********************************
1010 REM * FUNCTION TO CONVERT L.C. TO U.C. *
1020 REM **********************************
1030 REM
1040 REM    OBJECT STRING IS X$.
1050 REM    Y$ IS USED TO BUILD U.C. STRING.
1060 REM
```

```
1070 DEF FNCONVERT$(X$)
1080    LET Y$=""              'Null string
1090    FOR N=1 TO LEN(X$)
1100       LET C$=MID$(X$,N,1)
1110       REM CONVERT C$ TO UPPERCASE IF NECESSARY.
1120       IF C$>="a" AND C$<="z" THEN C$=CHR$(ASC(C$)-32)
1130       LET Y$=Y$+C$
1140    NEXT N
1150    FNCONVERT$=Y$
1160 FNEND
```

If this multiple-statement function is included in a program, you can convert all lowercase letters in a string ST$ to uppercase by using the statement

```
LET ST$=FNCONVERT$(ST$)
```

To display the string ST$ in uppercase without actually changing it, you can use the statement

```
PRINT FNCONVERT$(ST$)
```

■ **REMARK 1**   Note that the function definition uses Y$ to build the uppercase string and then, in line 1150, assigns this uppercase string to FNCONVERT$. We could not have used the name FNCONVERT$ to build the uppercase string. Doing so would require a statement such as

```
LET FNCONVERT$=FNCONVERT$+C$
```

to append characters to FNCONVERT$. But, as explained in Chapter 12, the name of the function being defined (FNCONVERT$ in this example) can appear only to left of the equals sign in a LET statement.

■ **REMARK 2**   In Example 22, we included the statements in lines 1090 to 1140 in a subroutine to perform the lower- to uppercase conversion. Since the result of the conversion is a single value (the converted string), the conversion task is suitable for coding as a user-defined function.

☐

EXAMPLE 29   **Here is a multiple-statement function to determine option numbers for the menu options REPT, NAME, MENU, and DONE.**

```
1000 REM *************************************
1010 REM * FUNCTION TO FIND THE OPTION NUMBER *
1020 REM * OPNUM FOR THE WORD OPTION C$.       *
1030 REM *************************************
1040 REM
1050 DEF FNOPNUM(C$)
1060    LET OPNUM=0
1070    IF C$="REPT" THEN OPNUM=1
1080    IF C$="NAME" THEN OPNUM=2
1090    IF C$="MENU" THEN OPNUM=3
1100    IF C$="DONE" THEN OPNUM=4
1110 FNEND
```

To assign the option number corresponding to the input value OP$ to OP, you would use the statement

```
LET OP=FNOPNUM(OP$)
```

☐

■ 13.9 Problems

1. Show the output of each program.

a.
```
10 LET A$="31"
20 LET B$="31"
30 PRINT A$;"+";B$;"=";
40 PRINT VAL(A$)+VAL(B$)
50 END
```

b.
```
10 LET L$="E"
20 LET N=ASC(L$)-ASC("A")+1
30 PRINT L$;N
40 END
```

c.
```
10 LET D$="7"
20 LET N=ASC(D$)-ASC("0")
30 PRINT D$;N
40 END
```

d.
```
10 FOR K=48 TO 58
20    PRINT CHR$(K);
30 NEXT K
40 END
```

e.
```
10 REM W=NUMBER OF WINS
20 REM G=NUMBER OF GAMES PLAYED
30 LET W=42
40 LET G=63
50 LET B$=STR$(W)+" WINS AND "
60 LET C$=STR$(G-W)+" LOSSES GIVES A PERCENTAGE OF "
70 LET D$=STR$(INT(1000*W/G+0.5)/1000)
80 PRINT B$;C$;D$
90 END
```

f.
```
10 DEF FNXT$(D$)=CHR$(ASC(D$)+1)
20 FOR N=1 TO 7
30    READ X$
40    PRINT FNXT$(X$);
50 NEXT N
60 DATA B,N,Q,Q,D,B,S
70 END
```

g.
```
10 DEF FNPRE$(X$)=CHR$(ASC(X$)-1)
20 LET L$=":"
30 FOR N=1 TO 10
40    LET L$=FNPRE$(L$)
50    PRINT L$;
60 NEXT N
70 END
```

h.
```
100 DEF FNV(X$)
110    LET V$=LEFT$(X$,2)     [or V$=X$(1:2)]
120    LET FNV=VAL(V$)
130 FNEND
140 LET COUNT=0
150 FOR N=1 TO 3
160    READ A$
170    LET COUNT=COUNT+FNV(A$)
180 NEXT N
190 PRINT "COUNT:";COUNT
200 DATA 12 DUCKS
210 DATA 15 GEESE
220 DATA 20 GULLS
230 END
```

In Problems 2–7, write a program for each task specified.

2. For any input string, display two columns. The first column is to contain the characters in the string and the second their numeric codes. Allow the user to try many strings during a single program run.

3. Input any decimal number and display its digits backward. For example, if 764.38 is typed, the output should be 83467; if −124.6 is typed, the output should be 6421.

4. Display any input string other than DONE but only after converting all lowercase letters to uppercase. Stop the program only when the user types DONE.

5. Display any word typed at the keyboard with its first letter uppercase and all other letters lowercase. However, if a character other than a letter is included, display nothing and allow the user to enter another word. Stop the program only when the user types DONE.

6. Each of the following DATA lines includes a person's name, the hours worked this week, and the hourly wage. (Line 800 is for reference only and line 899 contains the EOD tag.)

```
800 REM   123456789012345678901234567890
810 DATA HARRY SMITHSON      36    8.25
820 DATA SUSAN COREY         25    6.00
830 DATA ABIGAIL ADAMS       32    6.85
840 DATA BERT REGIS          32    7.00
850 DATA EMERSON FOSDICK     40    9.50
860 DATA BART BARTLETT       20    5.25
899 DATA END-OF-DATA
```

Produce a four-column report showing the name, hours worked, hourly rate, and gross pay of each person. Time and a half is earned for all hours over 32.

7. Input two positive integers A and B for which A < B. The program should display the decimal expansion of A/B to N places where the positive integer N is also input during program execution. For example, if 1, 8, and 10 are input for A, B, and N, respectively, the output should be .1250000000.

■ 13.10 Review True-or-False Quiz

1. If A is any number, LEN(A) will give the number of digits in A.   **T   F**
2. If LEN(X$) = LEN(Y$), then X$ = Y$.   **T   F**
3. LEN(X$ + Y$) = LEN(X$) + LEN(Y$).   **T   F**

(4–6 are for systems that use LEFT$, RIGHT$, and MID$.)

4. B$ = LEFT$(B$,LEN(B$)).   **T   F**
5. Although it may be convenient to use the functions LEFT$ and RIGHT$, they are
   not necessary. The function MID$ can always be used in their place.   **T   F**
6. If X$ = "MADAM", then MID$(X$,3,3) has the value "D".   **T   F**

(7–9 are for systems that use the substring qualifiers.)

7. B$ = B$(1:LEN(B$)).   **T   F**
8. IF Y$ = "SEVEN", then Y$(3:3) has the value "V".   **T   F**
9. If A$ = "CYBER72", then A$(6:2) has the value "72".   **T   F**
10. The BASIC statement

```
IF A$>="A" AND A$<="Z" THEN PRINT "OK"
```

will display OK whenever the first character in A$ is an uppercase letter of the
alphabet.   **T   F**
11. The BASIC statement PRINT CHR$(1) will display the letter A.   **T   F**
12. ASC("Z") − ASC("A") = 25   **T   F**
13. ASC("3") = ASC("2") + 1   **T   F**
14. ASC(CHR$(32)) = 32   **T   F**
15. VAL(STR$(55.23)) = 55.23   **T   F**
16. CHR$(ASC("a") + 32) = "A"   **T   F**

14 Arrays

In this chapter you will encounter several programming situations for which the numerical and string variables we have been using are inadequate. To illustrate, suppose that many words are contained in a data list and you must determine counts of the number of A's, of B's, of C's, and so on, so that these counts can be used later in the program. If only the numerical variables considered to this point were available, you would need 26 different variable names, one for each of the 26 counts. If instead of words the data list contains integers in the range 1 to 100 and you must determine counts of the number of 1s, of 2s, of 3s, and so on, you would need 100 different variables, one for each of the 100 counts. Certainly, writing a program with 100 (or even 26) different variable names would be a long and tedious task and the program would be unwieldy.

To be useful, a programming language must provide the means for handling such problems efficiently. BASIC meets this requirement with the inclusion of the **array** data structure. As you work through the material in this chapter, you will learn how an array can be used to store an entire collection of values under a single name and how the values stored in an array are referenced simply by specifying their positions in the array. The array data structure not only provides the means to resolve the difficulties cited, but it also provides a way to simplify significantly many programming tasks involving both large and small quantities of data.

In Sections 14.1 and 14.2 we explain how data are placed into arrays, how these data are referenced, and illustrate how arrays can be used in programming tasks that involve lists of numbers or lists of strings. The application of arrays in programming tasks that involve tables of values (other than lists) is taken up in Sections 14.3 and 14.7. In Section 14.5 we describe a sorting algorithm that can be used to rearrange string data into alphabetical order or numerical data into either ascending or descending order.

■ 14.1 One-Dimensional Arrays

A **one-dimensional array,** or list, is an ordered collection of items in the sense that there is a first item, a second item, and so on. For example, if you took five quizzes during a semester and received grades of 71, 83, 96, 77, and 92, you have a list in which the first grade is 71, the second grade is 83, and so forth. In mathematics we might use the following subscripted notation:

$$g_1 = 71$$
$$g_2 = 83$$
$$g_3 = 96$$
$$g_4 = 77$$
$$g_5 = 92$$

Since the BASIC character set does not include such subscripts, the notation is changed to the following:

$$G(1) = 71$$
$$G(2) = 83$$
$$G(3) = 96$$
$$G(4) = 77$$
$$G(5) = 92$$

We say that the *name* of the array is G, that G(1), G(2), G(3), G(4), and G(5) are **subscripted variables,** and that 1, 2, 3, 4, and 5 are the *subscripts* of G. G(1) is read **G sub 1,** and in general G(N) is read **G sub N.** G(1), G1, and G are all different variables and can be used in the same program; the computer has no problem distinguishing among them, even though we might.

The array G can be visualized as follows:

	1	2	3	4	5
G	71	83	96	77	92

The name of the array appears to the left, the subscripts are above each entry, and the entries are inside, just below their subscripts. Names that are acceptable for simple variables are also admissible array names.

To declare to the computer that your program will use the subscripted variables G(1) through G(5), you would include the DIM (for **dimension**) statement

```
DIM G(5)
```

so that it is encountered before any of the subscripted variables are referenced. If instead you include the statement

```
DIM G(100)
```

your program can reference any or all of the subscripted variables G(1) through G(100). The DIM statement is explained in greater detail in Section 14.2.

The value of a subscripted variable—that is, an entry in an array—is referenced in a program just as values of simple variables (variables with no subscripts) are referenced. For example, the two LET statements

```
LET G(1)=71
LET G(2)=G(1)+12
```

assign 71 to the subscripted variable G(1) and 83 to G(2); that is, 71 and 83 are assigned as the first and second entries of array G. To allow the user to enter a value for G(1) at the keyboard, you can use the statement

```
INPUT G(1)
```

The principal advantage in using subscripted variables is that the subscripts can be specified by using variables or other numerical expressions, rather than just integer constants. For instance, if N has the value 3, then G(N) refers to G(3), G(2 * N) refers to G(6), and G(2 * N − 1) refers to G(5). It is common practice to refer to *subscript expressions* such as N, 2 * N, and 2 * N − 1 as the subscripts, even though the actual subscripts are the integer values of these expressions.

EXAMPLE 1   **Here is a program segment to assign values to G(1), G(2), G(3), G(4), and G(5).**

```
100 DIM G(5)
110 FOR J=1 TO 5
120    READ G(J)
130 NEXT J
140 DATA 71,83,96,77,92
```

On each pass through the loop, the index J of the loop serves as the subscript. The first time through the loop, J has the value 1, so line 120 assigns the first data value 71 to G(1). Similarly, G(2) through G(5) are assigned their respective values during the remaining four passes through the loop.

■ REMARK 1

To allow the user to enter the five array values at the keyboard, you can use

```
110 FOR J=1 TO 5
120    INPUT G(J)
130 NEXT J
```

■ REMARK 2

Having assigned five values to array G—that is, to the subscripted variables G(1) through G(5)—you can process these values just as you process any other numerical variables. For instance, if you need to find and display the sum of the five entries in G, you can continue the program by writing

```
150 LET SUM=0
160 FOR J=1 TO 5
170    LET SUM=SUM+G(J)
180 NEXT J
190 PRINT "SUM OF THE 5 QUIZ SCORES:";SUM
```

■ REMARK 3

Note that we use the same control variable (J) for the FOR loops beginning at lines 110 and 160. Although we could have used different control variables, there is no good reason for doing so. There is reason, however, for using the same one. In each loop, J serves the *same* purpose—it provides subscripts for array G; hence the program will be easier to read if the *same* name is used.

Just as with simple variables, values assigned to subscripted variables are retained until they are changed in another programming line. Thus, individual entries in an array can be changed without affecting the rest of the array. For instance, if G has been assigned values as in Example 1

	1	**2**	**3**	**4**	**5**
G	71	83	96	77	92

the statement

```
200 LET G(1)=G(5)
```

will assign the value 92 of G(5) to G(1) but will not change G(5). The modified array will be as follows [note that the previous value 71 of G(1) is lost]:

	1	**2**	**3**	**4**	**5**
G	92	83	96	77	92

EXAMPLE 2

Here is a program segment that modifies each entry of the array G and then stores the resulting values in a second array M, but in the reverse order.

```
200 REM INCREASE ARRAY G ENTRIES BY 2.
210 FOR K=1 TO 5
220    LET G(K)=G(K)+2
230 NEXT K
240 REM CREATE ARRAY M.
250 DIM M(5)
260 FOR K=1 TO 5
270    LET M(K)=G(6-K)
280 NEXT K
```

Let's assume that before the execution of this program segment, values are read into array G as in Example 1. Pictorially,

	1	2	3	4	5
G	71	83	96	77	92

The first FOR loop adds 2 to each entry in G:

	1	2	3	4	5
G	73	85	98	79	94

The second FOR loop creates a new array M. For $K = 1$, the assignment statement is LET $M(1) = G(5)$; for $K = 2$, LET $M(2) = G(4)$; and so on. Thus, after execution of this second loop, M is as follows:

	1	2	3	4	5
M	94	79	98	85	73

REMARK 1 The two DIM statements

```
100 DIM G(5)
250 DIM M(5)
```

can be combined into the single statement

```
100 DIM G(5),M(5)
```

REMARK 2 Creating new arrays that are modifications of existing arrays is a common programming task. In this example, the entries in the array M are a rearrangement of the entries in array G. Note that the creation of array M by the second FOR loop in no way modifies the existing array G.

REMARK 3 Although it is common practice to refer to the symbols $G(K)$, $M(K)$, and $G(6 - K)$ as variables, remember that the actual variable names are $G(1)$, $G(2)$, $G(3)$, and so on. Each time the LET statements are executed, K has a particular value indicating which of these variables is being referenced.

The subscript expression that appears within the parentheses to indicate the position in an array (K and $6 - K$ in Example 2 and J in Example 1) can be any BASIC numerical expression. Thus the following are all admissible:

```
A(7)       X(I+1)
B(7+3/2)   Z(100-N)
```

When the computer encounters a subscript, the subscript is evaluated; if it is not an integer, it is rounded or truncated to an integer, depending on the version of BASIC being used. In this book we will use only subscript expressions whose values are integers.

The smallest subscript allowed is 0 or 1, depending on the version of BASIC being used. Some systems allow you to specify the smallest subscript by using one of the statements

```
OPTION BASE 0
OPTION BASE 1
```

or some similar statement as described in your BASIC manual. The largest subscript allowed is the subscript specified in the DIM statement. A subscript not in the range specified will cause a fatal SUBSCRIPT OUT OF RANGE error condition.

BASIC allows string arrays for storing strings as well as numerical arrays for storing numbers. The only difference is that string array names must end with a $. The use of subscripts is the same as for numerical arrays.

EXAMPLE 3   **Here is a program to read string values into the string array DAY$.**

```
100 DIM DAY$(7)
110 FOR N=1 TO 7
120    READ DAY$(N)
130 NEXT N
140 DATA SUNDAY,MONDAY,TUESDAY,WEDNESDAY
150 DATA THURSDAY,FRIDAY,SATURDAY
```

When N is 1, the first datum SUNDAY is read into DAY$(1), when N is 2, MONDAY is read into DAY$(2), and so on. At this point we can use the string values stored in DAY$—that is, the values of the subscripted variables DAY$(1) through DAY$(7)—just as the values of any string variables can be used. For instance, if we follow line 150 with the statements

```
160 PRINT "ENTER DAY OF WEEK (1-7)";
170 INPUT D
180 PRINT "YOU SELECTED ";DAY$(D);"."
```

and later enter 7 in response to the INPUT statement, the computer will display

```
ENTER DAY OF WEEK (1-7)? 7
YOU SELECTED SATURDAY.
```

■ **REMARK 1**   Since the variable D in lines 170 and 180 represents a day of the week (1–7), we could have used the more descriptive name DAY. Had we done this, line 180 would have been written

```
180 PRINT "YOU SELECTED ";DAY$(DAY);"."
```

The computer has no difficulty with the expression DAY$(DAY). It correctly interprets DAY as the name of a simple numerical variable whose value gives the position (subscript) of an entry in the string array DAY$. Thus, with DAY = 7, DAY$(DAY) refers to DAY$(7).

■ **REMARK 2**   The array DAY$ can be pictured as shown previously for array G:

	1	2	3	4	5	6	7
DAY$	SUNDAY	MONDAY	TUESDAY	WEDNESDAY	THURSDAY	FRIDAY	SATURDAY

There is no special significance in the placement of the array entries along a line. You may find it more convenient to think of the array as follows:

DAY$

1	SUNDAY
2	MONDAY
3	TUESDAY
4	WEDNESDAY
5	THURSDAY
6	FRIDAY
7	SATURDAY

□   The two diagrams contain the same information.

In each of Examples 1–3, we used a FOR loop to read values into an array. If you know exactly how many values are to be stored in an array, a FOR loop provides the most convenient way to do it. Thus, if a table of values to be read into one or more arrays appears in DATA statements and if the DATA are preceded by a data count, you would read the count into a simple numerical variable and use its value as the terminal value of a FOR loop that reads the data into the array or arrays.

The next example illustrates a common method used to store data in arrays when the data are given in DATA lines that end with an EOD tag rather than being preceded with a count.

EXAMPLE 4   **Here is a program segment to read a table of flight numbers and arrival times into arrays. The data are presented in DATA lines terminated with the EOD tag XXX.**

```
100 REM LOAD FLIGHT NUMBERS AND ARRIVAL TIMES.
110 REM
120 REM     COUNT     NUMBER OF FLIGHTS
130 REM     FLIGHT$   ARRAY OF FLIGHT NUMBERS
140 REM     ARR$      ARRAY OF ARRIVAL TIMES
150 REM
160 DIM FLIGHT$(50),ARR$(50)
170 LET COUNT=1
180 READ FLIGHT$(COUNT),ARR$(COUNT)
190 WHILE FLIGHT$(COUNT)<>"XXX" AND COUNT<50
200    LET COUNT=COUNT+1
210    READ FLIGHT$(COUNT),ARR$(COUNT)
220 NEXT   (or WEND)
230 REM
240 REM SUBTRACT ONE TO GET ACTUAL DATA COUNT.
250 LET COUNT=COUNT-1
260 REM
270   (Program continuation)
      .
      .
      .
5000 REM ********************
5010 REM * ARRIVAL TIME DATA *
5030 REM ********************
5040 REM
5050 REM FLIGHT, ARRIVAL TIME
5030 DATA 53, "8:15 AM"
5040 DATA 172, "9:20 AM"
5050 DATA 122, "11:30 AM"
5060 DATA 62, "2:20 PM"
5070 DATA 303, "4:45 PM"
5080 DATA 291, "6:15 PM"
5999 DATA XXX,XXX
9999 END
```

The variable COUNT provides the successive subscripts 1, 2, 3, and so on, for the statement

```
READ FLIGHT$(COUNT),ARR$(COUNT)
```

Each time values are read into the arrays FLIGHT$ and ARR$ by this statement, the FLIGHT$ value is compared with the EOD tag XXX. If FLIGHT$(COUNT) is not XXX (and if 50 flight numbers have not yet been read), the WHILE loop is entered: line 200 increases COUNT by 1 and line 210 reads the next flight number and arrival time into the next array positions. When the EOD tag is read, we have FLIGHT$(COUNT) = "XXX" and the WHILE statement transfers control to the line following NEXT (or WEND). At this point, COUNT, FLIGHT$, and ARR$ are as follows (notice that the EOD tag XXX is in position COUNT of array FLIGHT$):

COUNT=7   (One more than the number of flights)

	FLIGHTS	ARR$
1	53	8:15 AM
2	172	9:20 AM
3	122	11:30 AM
4	62	2:20 PM
5	303	4:45 PM
6	291	6:15 PM
7	XXX	XXX

Line 250 then decreases COUNT by 1 so that it specifies the number of values read into each array, exclusive of the EOD tag XXX. In any subsequent processing of arrays FLIGHT$ and ARR$, we can use COUNT to denote their length. For example, to display a simple list of flight numbers, we could use the FOR loop

```
FOR F=1 TO COUNT
   PRINT FLIGHT$(F)
NEXT F
```

■ **REMARK 1** Since line 160 specifies that the largest subscript allowed for FLIGHT$ and ARR$ is 50 and since XXX is stored in both FLIGHT$ and ARR$, the program can handle only up to 49 flights. If data for 50 or more flights are included in DATA lines, the program will read the data for the first 50 flights and simply ignore the others; it will never get to the EOD tag. Moreover, the user will not be aware that this has happened. If we insert the lines

```
222 IF FLIGHT$(COUNT)="XXX" THEN 250
224   PRINT "TOO MUCH DATA!"
226   GOTO 9999
```

any attempt to include more data than the program is designed to handle will cause the computer (during a trial run) to halt after displaying the message

```
TOO MUCH DATA!
```

The person entering the data would understand this message or would seek help from a programmer.

■ **REMARK 2** The quotation marks used in the DATA statements are not required unless your system uses the colon (:) as a separator when two or more BASIC statements are included in a single programming line.

■ 14.2 The DIM Statement (Declaring Arrays)

As illustrated in the preceding examples, the DIM statement specifies the names and dimensions (sizes) of arrays. An array for which only one subscript is specified (variables with more than one subscript are considered in Section 14.5) is called a **one-dimensional** array. Thus, the statement

```
DIM G(5),DAY$(7)
```

specifies a one-dimensional numerical array G with 5 as the largest allowed subscript and a one-dimensional string array DAY$ with 7 as the largest subscript. It is common terminology to say that the arrays G and DAY$ have been **declared,** or that they have been **dimensioned.**

The general form of the DIM statement, as it applies to one-dimensional arrays (lists), is

ln DIM **a(e),b(f), . . . ,c(g)**

where **a,b,c** denote array names and **e,f,g** denote positive-integer constants or, as will be explained, shortly, numerical expressions. The following points concerning the use of arrays should be understood:

1. BASIC requires that you use DIM statements to declare only those arrays whose subscripts exceed 10. If any of the subscripted variables A(1) through A(10) is referenced in a program that does not declare A in a DIM statement, BASIC, by default, will declare A as if the program included the statement

```
DIM A(10)
```

Thus, the DIM statements in Examples 1–3 are not actually required. It is an excellent programming practice, however, to use DIM statements to declare all arrays. Doing so will make your programs easier to read since DIM statements explicitly establish which variable names represent arrays and indicate their sizes.

2. A DIM statement must be executed before any reference is made to the array (or arrays) being dimensioned. The customary practice is to place DIM statements near the beginning of a program.

3. An array can be declared only once. If an array has been declared, either explicitly with a DIM statement or implicitly by usage, a subsequent DIM statement that includes the array name will cause a fatal error condition.

4. When coding a program, you must see to it that your DIM statements specify array sizes large enough to accommodate all the values to be stored in the arrays. Thus, if you know in advance that your program will never be required to read more than 1000 values into an array A, the statement

```
DIM A(1000)
```

will suffice. This statement, however, actually reserves space in the computer's memory for the 1000 variables A(1) to A(1000); that is, your program will tie up this memory space whether or not a particular run of the program uses it. This means that you must not only specify array sizes that are large enough, but you should keep them as small as possible.

5. As noted in Chapter 1, every BASIC system uses either a compiler (an *entire* program is translated into machine code before it is executed) or an interpreter (each BASIC statement is translated into machine code each time it is executed). Essentially all systems that use interpreters allow **dynamic storage allocation** for arrays. This means that sizes for arrays can be determined during program execution. For example, if a list of words included in DATA lines is to be stored in an array WORDS$, you can precede the data list with a word count and use the statements

```
READ COUNT
DIM WORDS$(COUNT)
```

to declare the array WORDS$. You can then be sure that WORDS$ is just the right size, provided only that the word count is correct. Dynamic storage allocation can also be used if you end the data list with an EOD tag rather than precede it with a word count. Indeed, if the EOD tag is XXX, you can use a program segment such as the following, first to count the words and then to declare and read the words into the array WORDS$:

```
100 REM ********************
110 REM DETERMINE WORD COUNT.
120 REM
130 LET COUNT=0
140 READ W$
150 WHILE W$<>"XXX"
160    LET COUNT=COUNT+1
170    READ W$
180 NEXT  (or WEND)
190 RESTORE
200 REM *************************
```

```
210 REM READ DATA INTO ARRAY WORDS$.
220 REM
230 DIM WORDS$(COUNT)
240 FOR N=1 TO COUNT
250    READ WORDS$(N)
260 NEXT N
```

At the outset of this chapter we mentioned that arrays can be used effectively in programming tasks that require us to determine many counts. The following example illustrates this use of arrays.

EXAMPLE 5

A list of integers, all between 1 and 100, is contained in DATA lines. Let's write a program to determine how many of each integer are included. We assume that 9999 terminates the list.

PROBLEM ANALYSIS

We must determine 100 counts: the number of 1s, the number of 2s, and so on. Let's use C(1), C(2), . . . , C(100) to store these counts. Each value appearing in the DATA lines must be read to determine which of the 100 integers it is. If it is 87, then C(87) must be increased by 1; if it is 24, then C(24) must be increased by 1. Using X to denote the value being read, we can write the following algorithm:

THE ALGORITHM

   a. Initialize: C(N) = 0 for N = 1 to 100.
   b. Read a value for X.
   c. Repeat the following until X = 9999.
      c1. Add 1 to C(X).
      c2. Read next value for X.
   d. Display the results and stop.

In the following program we display two columns showing N and the corresponding count C(N) but suppress the output if C(N) = 0—that is, if N is not in the given list.

THE PROGRAM

```
100 REM INITIALIZE COUNTERS.
110 DIM C(100)
120 FOR N=1 TO 100
130    LET C(N)=0
140 NEXT N
150 REM READ X AND ADD 1 TO C(X) UNTIL
160 REM THE EOD TAG 9999 IS ENCOUNTERED.
170 READ X
180 WHILE X<>9999
190    LET C(X)=C(X)+1
200    READ X
210 NEXT   (or WEND)
220 REM DISPLAY THE FREQUENCY TABLE.
230 PRINT "DATUM","FREQUENCY"
240 PRINT "-----","---------"
250 FOR N=1 TO 100
260    IF C(N)>0 THEN PRINT N,C(N)
270 NEXT N
500 DATA 80,80,80,80,80,60,60,50
510 DATA 50,50,45,45,50,50,50,32
998 DATA 9999
999 END
RUN
```

DATUM	FREQUENCY
32	1
45	2
50	6
60	2
80	5

■ 14.3 Table Processing

Several of the examples considered in previous chapters involved processing data given in tabular form. In each case, we used READ statements to read the data into simple variables for processing and RESTORE statements to allow us to reuse the data. Although this method can be used for many programming tasks, there are times when the method is inadequate, or at least very inconvenient. The examples in this section illustrate how the array data structure sometimes can provide a useful and convenient alternative to this method of processing tabular data.

EXAMPLE 6   **The hourly pay rate of each employee in a certain business is determined by the employee's job classification. We are to produce a report showing the week's gross pay for each employee.**

PROBLEM ANALYSIS

We need more information. We need to know the name, job classification, and hours worked for each employee as well as the hourly pay rates for the job classifications. Let's assume this information is given to us in two tables as shown and that time and a half is paid for all hours over 32.

Hours-worked table

Name	Job class	Hours
Jane Arcus	3	40
Jonathan Beard	6	45
Sandra Carlson	3	32
Susan Dahlberg	1	24
Thomas Farrell	5	29
Heidi Graves	1	40
.	.	.
.	.	.
.	.	.

Hourly-rate table

Job class	Rate of pay
1	$ 4.00
2	4.75
3	5.75
4	7.00
5	8.50
6	10.75

To produce the required report, we must look up the job class and hours worked for each employee from the Hours-Worked Table and the corresponding rate of pay from the Hourly-Rate Table. There is a difference in how these two tables should be used. In particular, the Hourly-Rate Table is needed each time the week's pay for an employee is being calculated—that is, each time we process a line from the Hours-Worked Table. Thus, the data in the Hourly-Rate Table must be accessed many times whereas the data in the Hours-Worked Table is needed only once. For this reason, we will read the Hourly-Rate Table into an array. If we name this array PAYRATE and if JOB denotes a job class (1 through 6), the rate of pay corresponding to job class JOB will be PAYRATE(JOB).

The discussion in the preceding paragraph allows us to give a precise description of the input data and how they should be organized. (The output is simply a two-column report showing the name and gross pay for each employee.)

Input: Six hourly pay rates corresponding to job classes 1–6.
The name, job class, and hours worked for each employee.

All input data will be included in DATA statements. Since the Hourly-Rate Table will be read into an array for use in determining the week's pay for each employee, the six hourly rate amounts should be first, before the data given in the Hours-Worked Table. To avoid having to count the employees, we will end this latter table with XXX,0,0, and use XXX to detect the end of the data. Since each employee's name, job class, and hours worked will be read and immediately processed, there is no need to read these data into arrays.

At this point, it should not be difficult to write an algorithm for the task specified in the problem statement. To keep our algorithm concise, we will use these descriptive variable names:

PAYRATE = Array of hourly rates for job classes 1–6
EMPNAME\$ = An employee's name
JOB = Job classification for EMPNAME\$
HOURS = Hours worked this week by EMPNAME\$
GROSSPAY = Week's gross pay for EMPNAME\$

THE ALGORITHM

a. Read hourly rates for job classes 1–6 into array PAYRATE.
b. Display report title and column headings.
c. Read EMPNAME\$, JOB, and HOURS.
d. Repeat the following as long as (while) EMPNAME\$ is not XXX:
   d1. Calculate GROSSPAY for EMPNAME\$.
   d2. Display EMPNAME\$ and GROSSPAY.
   d3. Read EMPNAME\$, JOB, and HOURS.
e. Stop

Note that Step (d1) does not explain how to calculate GROSSPAY. Recalling that time and a half is paid for all hours over 32, we can rewrite this step as follows:

d1.1 Let RATE = PAYRATE(JOB)
d1.2 Let GROSSPAY = HOURS $*$ RATE
d1.3 If HOURS $>$ 32, add (HOURS $-$ 32) $*$ RATE/2 to GROSSPAY.

THE PROGRAM

```
100 REM ************************************************
110 REM * LOAD HOURLY-RATE TABLE INTO ARRAY PAYRATE *
120 REM ************************************************
130 REM
140 DIM PAYRATE(6)
150 FOR JOBCLASS=1 TO 6
160    READ PAYRATE(JOBCLASS)
170 NEXT JOBCLASS
180 REM
190 REM ********************************************
200 REM * DISPLAY REPORT TITLE AND COLUMN HEADERS. *
210 REM ********************************************
220 REM
230 PRINT "SALARIES FOR THE CURRENT WEEK"
240 PRINT
250 PRINT  "EMPLOYEE'S NAME          GROSS PAY"
255 LET F$="##############          ####.##"
260 PRINT
270 REM ********************************************
280 REM * READ HOURS-WORKED DATA TO DETERMINE AND *
290 REM * DISPLAY NAMES AND GROSS SALARY AMOUNTS. *
300 REM ********************************************
310 REM
320 READ EMPNAME$,JOB,HOURS
330 WHILE EMPNAME$<>"XXX"
340    LET RATE=PAYRATE(JOB)
350    LET GROSSPAY=HOURS*RATE
360    IF HOURS>32 THEN GROSSPAY=GROSSPAY+(HOURS-32)*RATE/2
370    PRINT USING F$, EMPNAME$,GROSSPAY
380    READ EMPNAME$,JOB,HOURS
390 NEXT   (or WEND)
400 REM
410 REM ----------------------------------
420 REM    DATA FROM HOURLY-RATE TABLE
430 REM
440 DATA 4.00, 4.75, 5.75, 7.00, 8.50, 10.75
450 REM
460 REM ----------------------------------
470 REM    DATA FROM HOURS-WORKED TABLE
480 REM
```

```
490 REM NAME, JOB CLASS, HOURS WORKED
500 DATA JANE ARCUS,3,40
510 DATA JONATHAN BEARD,6,45
520 DATA SANDRA CARLSON,3,32
530 DATA SUSAN DAHLBERG,1,24
540 DATA THOMAS FARRELL,5,29
550 DATA HEIDI GRAVES,1,40
560 DATA XXX,0,0
570 END
RUN

   SALARIES FOR THE CURRENT WEEK

EMPLOYEE'S NAME          GROSS PAY

JANE ARCUS                 253.00
JONATHAN BEARD             553.63
SANDRA CARLSON             184.00
SUSAN DAHLBERG              96.00
THOMAS FARRELL             246.50
HEIDI GRAVES               176.00
```

■ **REMARK**   It is worth noting that we decided on the organization of the input data by considering how the data were to be used, not by the form in which the data were given. Specifically, we decided to store the Hourly-Rate Table in an array because the information it contains must be used each time an employee's pay is to be calculated. Also, we decided not to store the Hours-Worked Table in arrays because the information it contains needs to be processed only once, in the order given. In other programming tasks involving exactly the same data, you may find it convenient to use a different organization of these data. To illustrate, suppose you must produce listings of employees whose job class numbers are typed at the keyboard. If you read the entire Hours-Worked Table into arrays EMP$, JOBCLASS, and HRS and use the simple variable CLASSNUM to store the job class number typed at the keyboard, it is a simple matter to produce the required listing. The following subroutine does this:

```
1000 REM SUBROUTINE TO LIST ALL EMPLOYEES
1010 REM WITH A SPECIFIED JOB CLASS NUMBER.
1020 REM
1030 REM    CLASSNUM    THE SPECIFIED JOB CLASS NUMBER
1040 REM    EMP$        ARRAY OF THE EMPLOYEE NAMES
1050 REM    JOBCLASS    CORRESPONDING ARRAY OF JOB CLASSES
1060 REM    COUNT       COUNT OF ALL EMPLOYEES
1070 PRINT
1080 PRINT "LIST OF EMPLOYEES IN JOB CLASS";CLASSNUM;":"
1090 FOR N=1 TO COUNT
1100    IF JOBCLASS(N)=CLASSNUM THEN PRINT EMP$(N)
1110 NEXT N
1120 RETURN
```

Each time the program in Example 6 references the array PAYRATE, it does so by specifying a position in the array. This happens because the integers 1 through 6 are used to specify both job class numbers and the positions of the corresponding pay rates in the array—PAYRATE(1) is the pay rate for job class 1, PAYRATE(2) is the pay rate for job class 2, and so on. Tabular data, however, are not often so conveniently stored in arrays. In most programming applications, two or more arrays are used to store a single table, and the positions of the table items that are needed must be determined by searching one or more of these arrays for a specified value or values (called **search arguments**). The remark following the program of Example 6 illustrates the use of multiple arrays to store a single table; we used three arrays—EMP$, JOBCLASS, and HRS—to store the Hourly-Rate Table. Moreover, the table was searched for all employees with job class number CLASSNUM (the *search argument*) by comparing the value of CLASSNUM with each entry (or *table argument*) in the array JOBCLASS. The program in the next example further illustrates the use of multiple arrays to store a single table. The program also shows how a search argument can be used in a table look-up application.

EXAMPLE 7 Here is a program to display information about incoming flights whose flight numbers are entered at the keyboard. The REM statements in lines 130, 280, and 290 describe the purpose and action of the program.

```
100 REM ------ AIRLINE FLIGHT INFORMATION PROGRAM ------
110 REM
120 REM ***************************************************
130 REM *     LOAD INCOMING FLIGHT DATA INTO ARRAYS.     *
140 REM ***************************************************
150 REM
160 REM     COUNT          COUNT OF INCLUDED FLIGHTS
170 REM     FLIGHTNUM      ARRAY OF FLIGHT NUMBERS
180 REM     ORIGIN$        ARRAY SHOWING ORIGINATION POINTS
190 REM     ARRIVE$        ARRAY OF ARRIVAL TIMES
200 REM
210 DIM FLIGHTNUM(50),ORIGIN$(50),ARRIVE$(50)
220 READ COUNT
230 FOR F=1 TO COUNT
240    READ FLIGHTNUM(F),ORIGIN$(F),ARRIVE$(F)
250 NEXT F
260 REM
270 REM ***********************************************
280 REM * DISPLAY AVAILABLE FLIGHT INFORMATION FOR *
290 REM * FLIGHT NUMBERS ENTERED AT THE KEYBOARD.  *
300 REM ***********************************************
310 REM
320 PRINT "FLIGHT NUMBER (0 WHEN DONE)";
330 INPUT FLIGHT
340 WHILE FLIGHT<>0
350    REM --- SEARCH ARRAY FLIGHTNUM FOR FLIGHT.---
360    LET F=1
370    WHILE FLIGHTNUM(F)<>FLIGHT AND F<COUNT
380       LET F=F+1
390    NEXT  (or WEND)
400    IF FLIGHTNUM(F)=FLIGHT THEN 430
410       PRINT FLIGHT;" IS NOT A LISTED FLIGHT NUMBER."
420       GOTO 460
430    PRINT "AVAILABLE INFORMATION ON FLIGHT";FLIGHT
440    PRINT "   ORIGINATION POINT:        ";ORIGIN$(F)
450    PRINT "   EXPECTED TIME OF ARRIVAL: ";ARRIVE$(F)
460    PRINT
470    PRINT "FLIGHT NUMBER (0 WHEN DONE)";
480    INPUT FLIGHT
490 NEXT  (or WEND)
500 REM
510 REM -----------------------------------------------
520 REM            D   A   T   A
530 REM -----------------------------------------------
540 REM      FLIGHT INFORMATION TABLE - INCOMING
550 REM
560 REM FLIGHT COUNT FOLLOWS - UP TO 50 ALLOWED.
570 DATA 6
575 REM FLIGHTNUMBER,POINT OF ORIGIN,ARRIVAL TIME
580 REM
590 DATA 53,MIAMI,"8:15 AM"
600 DATA 172,ATLANTA,"9:20 AM"
610 DATA 122,NEW YORK,"11:30 AM"
620 DATA 62,MONTREAL,"2:20 PM"
630 DATA 303,HOUSTON,"4:45 PM"
640 DATA 291,CHICAGO,"6:15 PM"
650 END
```

The following display was produced when we ran this program with the keyboard input value 62, 281 (an incorrect flight number), and 291:

```
FLIGHT NUMBER (0 WHEN DONE)? 62
AVAILABLE INFORMATION ON FLIGHT 62
```

```
          ORIGINATION POINT:           MONTREAL
          EXPECTED TIME OF ARRIVAL: 2:20 PM

FLIGHT NUMBER (0 WHEN DONE)? 281
 281  IS NOT A LISTED FLIGHT NUMBER.

FLIGHT NUMBER (0 WHEN DONE)? 291
AVAILABLE INFORMATION ON FLIGHT 291
          ORIGINATION POINT:           CHICAGO
          EXPECTED TIME OF ARRIVAL: 6:15 PM

FLIGHT NUMBER (0 WHEN DONE)? 0
```

REMARK   The loop in lines 370–390 compares the input value FLIGHT (the search argument) with the successive table arguments FLIGHTNUM(1), FLIGHTNUM(2), and so on, until a match is found or the last entry of array FLIGHTNUM is reached, whichever occurs first. Since FLIGHT is compared with the entries of array FLIGHTNUM *in order*, that is, *sequentially*, this method of searching an array for a specified value is called a **sequential search.**

■ 14.4 Problems

1. Show the output of each program.
   a.
   ```
   100 DIM X(4)
   110 LET I=2
   120 READ X(I),X(1)
   130 FOR I=1 TO 2
   140    PRINT X(I)
   150 NEXT I
   160 DATA 4,5,7,3
   170 END
   ```
   b.
   ```
   100 DIM X$(7)
   110 LET N=1
   120 READ X$(N)
   130 WHILE X$(N)<>"."
   140    PRINT " ";X$(N);
   150    LET N=N+1
   160    READ X$(N)
   170 NEXT   (or WEND)
   180 PRINT X$(N)
   190 DATA TO,BE,OR,NOT,TO,BE,.
   200 END
   ```
   c.
   ```
   100 DIM M(7)
   110 READ J
   120 FOR J=5 TO 7
   130    READ M(J)
   140 NEXT J
   150 READ B,C
   160 FOR K=B TO C
   170    PRINT M(K);
   180 NEXT K
   190 DATA 2,9,8,4,6,6,3
   200 END
   ```
   d.
   ```
   100 DIM A$(4)
   110 FOR J=1 TO 4
   120    READ X$
   130    IF X$<>"HAT" THEN A$(J)=X$
   140 NEXT J
   150 FOR J=1 TO 4 STEP 2
   160    PRINT A$(J);
   170 NEXT J
   180 DATA IRAN,TOP,GATE,HAT
   190 END
   ```

e.
```
100 DIM F$(4),L$(4)
110 FOR J=1 TO 4
120     READ F$(J),L$(J)
130 NEXT J
140 FOR I=4 TO 1 STEP -1
150     PRINT L$(I);", ";F$(I)
160 NEXT I
170 DATA JOHN,CASH,ELTON,JOHN
180 DATA JOHN,DENVER
190 DATA JOHN,PAYCHECK
200 END
```

f.
```
100 DIM A$(5)
110 FOR I=1 TO 5
120     READ A$(I)
130 NEXT I
140 FOR I=1 TO 5
150     LET N=LEN(A$(I))
160     LET J=1
170     WHILE MID$(A$(I),J,1)<>"S" AND J<N
180         LET J=J+1
190     NEXT (or WEND)
200     IF MID$(A$(I),J,1)="S" THEN PRINT A$(I)
210 NEXT I
220 DATA SAM,HARRY,JESS,SANDI,OLIVER
230 END
```

2. Explain what is wrong with each of the following.

a.
```
10 FOR A=9 TO 12
20     READ M(A)
30     PRINT M(A);
40 NEXT A
50 DATA 7,3,5,2,9,1,-3,-2
60 END
```

b.
```
10 READ A(1),A(2),A(3)
20 PRINT A(3),A(2),A(1)
30 DIM A(2)
40 READ A(1),A(2)
50 PRINT A(2),A(1)
60 DATA 1,2,3,4,5
70 END
```

c.
```
300 REM PROGRAM SEGMENT TO REVERSE THE
310 REM ORDER IN AN ARRAY L$ OF LENGTH 10
320 FOR K=1 TO 10
330     LET L$(11-K)=L$(K)
340 NEXT K
```

d.
```
400 REM PROGRAM SEGMENT TO FIND THE LARGEST
410 REM NUMBER L IN AN ARRAY A OF LENGTH 10.
420 FOR J=1 TO 10
430     IF L<A(J) THEN A(J)=L
440 NEXT J
```

In Problems 3–8, write a program for each task specified. In each program use a single numerical array or a single string array.

3. Input a list of numbers of undetermined length, and display the values in reverse order. Use an EOD tag to terminate the input list. (You may assume that the input list will contain fewer than 20 numbers.)

4. Input a list of words of undetermined length, and display them in reverse order. Use an EOD tag to terminate the input list. (You may assume that the input will contain fewer than 20 words.)

5. First read a list of words from DATA lines into a string array. Then allow the user to enter letters, one at a time, to obtain a list of those words that begin with the letter typed. The program should halt only when the user types DONE.

6. Input five numbers into an array B as follows: assign the first value to B(1) and B(10), the second to B(2) and B(9), and so on. Then display the array B and input five more values in the same manner. Continue this process until the user types 0. When this happens, stop program execution with no further output.

7. Input a list of numbers of undetermined length into array A and display three columns as follows: Column 1 contains the input list in the order typed; Column 2 contains them in reverse order; and Column 3 contains the averages of the corresponding numbers in Columns 1 and 2. You may assume that the input list will contain fewer than 20 numbers.

8. Produce the following designs. Begin each program by reading the needed strings A, B, C, and so on, into an array from DATA lines. Use the arrays to produce the designs.

   a. A
      BB
      CCC
      DDDD
      EEEEE
      FFFFFF

   b. ABCDEFG
      BCDEFG
      CDEFG
      DEFG
      EFG
      FG
      G

   c. A A A A
      B B B
      C C C C
      D D D
      E E E E

   d. A
      BBB
      CCCCC
      DDDDDDD
      EEEEEEEEE

In Problems 9–24, write a program for each task specified. Use one or more arrays in each program.

9. The following DATA lines show the annual salaries of all the employees in Division 72 of the Manley Corporation. The last value (72) is an EOD tag.

   ```
   500 DATA 14000, 16200, 10195, 28432, 13360
   510 DATA 19300, 16450, 12180, 25640, 18420
   520 DATA 18900, 12270, 13620, 12940, 31200
   530 DATA 72
   ```

   Read these data into an array S, and then create a new array T as follows. For each subscript I, obtain T(I) by subtracting the average of all the salaries from S(I). Then display arrays S and T as a two-column table with appropriate headings.

10. Use the salary data shown in Problem 9 to create two arrays as follows. Array A is to contain all salaries less than $14,000 and B is to contain the rest. Display arrays A and B in adjacent columns with appropriate headings.

11. Input an undetermined number of values into arrays P and N so that array P contains those that are positive and N contains those that are negative. Ignore zeros and let 999 serve as the EOD tag. When the EOD tag is encountered, display the two lists in adjacent columns with the headings POSITIVES and NEGATIVES.

12. Read a list of words from DATA lines into arrays A$ and B$. Have array A$ contain all words beginning with a letter from A to M. Put the other words into B$. Display the contents of the two arrays in adjacent columns with appropriate column headings.

13. The following DATA lines show a name and four scores for each student in a psychology class:

    ```
    700 DATA ARDEN MARK,72,79,91,70
    710 DATA AUDEN WINN,95,92,86,82
    720 DATA BRICE SALLY ANN,90,80,70,84
    730 DATA BRANT EMILY,75,62,43,65
    740 DATA RANDALL TONY,52,54,50,33
    750 DATA RANDOLPH KIM,82,72,80,79
                      .
                      .
                      .
    799 DATA XXX
    ```

    Create arrays S$ and A so that S$ contains the names and A contains the corresponding average scores. Then display two reports as follows. The first is to show the names and averages for students whose average is at least 60. The other students and their averages should be shown in the second report. Each report is to have an appropriate title and column headings.

14. Create arrays S$ and A exactly as described in Problem 13. Then allow the user to enter a string with one or more letters to obtain the names and averages of all students whose names begin with the letters typed.

15. Write a program as described in Problem 14. This time assume the names in DATA lines are in alphabetical order, and use this fact to reduce the number of string comparisons that must be made.

16. Letter grades for students in the psychology class mentioned in Problem 13 are determined by specifying four cutoff values for the four passing grades A, B, C, and D. Write a program to display the names and letter grades of all students. Include the four cutoff values, as well as the student names and scores shown in Problem 13, in DATA statements. (Determine how to organize the data by considering how they are to be used. For this, you may wish to reread Example 6.)

17. The names and precinct numbers of all residents of the town of Plymouth who voted in the last election are included in DATA lines in alphabetical order. Here are the first two DATA lines:

```
1000 DATA ALDEN JOHN,1,ALDEN PRISCILLA,1
1010 DATA BARTON JONATHAN,4,BARTON MARY,2
```

Plymouth has four precincts. You are to read the names into four arrays according to precinct, and then display the four lists as follows:

```
    PRECINCT 1              PRECINCT 2
---------------        ---------------

ALDEN JOHN             BARTON MARY
ALDEN PRISCILLA              .
      .                      .
      .                      .

    PRECINCT 3              PRECINCT 4
---------------        ---------------
      .                BARTON JONATHAN
      .                      .
      .                      .
```

The names in each precinct should be in alphabetical order, as are the names in the DATA lines.

18. A produce wholesaler uses the given price table while preparing invoices. A typical invoice is shown following the price table:

Current price table

Item	Item code	Price per crate
Artichokes	ART	8.50
Carrots	CAR	5.20
Cabbage	CAB	5.40
Collard Greens	COL	5.90
Cucumbers	CUK	11.00
Lettuce-Iceberg	LET1	14.00
Lettuce-Romaine	LET3	12.75
Lettuce-Boston	LET7	10.50
Turnips	TUR	3.75

```
                NORTH END PRODUCE, INC.
        CUSTOMER: RAINBOW VEGETABLE STAND
        DESCRIPTION       QUANTITY   PRICE     AMOUNT
        ----------------------------------------------
        CABBAGE              3        5.40      16.20
        ARTICHOKES          10        8.50      85.00
        LETTUCE-ICEBERG     10       14.00     140.00
        ----------------------------------------------
        TOTALS              23                 241.20
```

Write a program to prepare an invoice for each produce order included in the following DATA statements. (The first of these contains the order for the invoice shown.)

```
DATA RAINBOW VEGETABLE STAND,CAB,3,ART,10,LET1,10,X,0
DATA WEST END MARKET,TUR,1,LET3,1,COL,3,X,0
DATA CASEY'S PUB,ART,1,CUK,1,LET7,1,LET1,1,X,0
        .
        .   (additional orders go here)
        .
DATA END-OF-ORDERS
```

The pair X, 0 would be used to indicate the end of each order, and END-OF-ORDERS would be used to indicate that all invoices have been completed. (If it is not obvious to you how the price information and order data should be organized, you may wish to reread Example 6.)

19. Write a program to produce invoices as in Problem 18 but with the produce orders typed at the keyboard rather than being included in DATA lines. A suitable display created while typing the order whose invoice is shown would be

```
CUSTOMER? RAINBOW VEGETABLE STAND
(ENTER X FOR ITEM WHEN ORDER IS COMPLETE)

ITEM? CAB
CRATES? 3
ITEM? ART
CRATES? 10
ITEM? LET1
CRATES? 10
ITEM? X
```

(A complete order must be entered before any part of the invoice is displayed. Thus, you will need either two arrays to store the order information as it is entered or one or more arrays to store the invoice as it is generated. Either method is appropriate.)

20. A number of scores, each lying in the range from 0 to 100, are given in DATA lines. Use these scores to create an array C so that

$C(1)$ = a count of scores S satisfying $S \leq 20$
$C(2)$ = a count of scores S satisfying $20 < S \leq 40$
$C(3)$ = a count of scores S satisfying $40 < S \leq 60$
$C(4)$ = a count of scores S satisfying $60 < S \leq 80$
$C(5)$ = a count of scores S satisfying $80 < S \leq 100$

Display the results in tabular form as follows:

Interval	Frequency	
0–20	C(1)	*[actually the value of C(I)]*
20–40	C(2)	
40–60	C(3)	
60–80	C(4)	
80–100	C(5)	

21. Problem 20 asks for a count of the number of scores in each of five equal-length intervals. Instead of using five intervals, allow a user to type a positive integer N to produce a similar frequency table using N equal-length intervals.

22. A correspondence between *x* and *y* is given by the following table. (Each *y* entry corresponds to the *x* entry just above it.)

x	0	2	4	6	8	10	12	14	16	18	20
y	−5	3	27	67	123	195	283	387	507	643	795

Write a menu-driven program for this menu:

1. To end the program.
2. To find the *y* value for any *x* value entered at the keyboard.
3. To use linear interpolation to find a *y* value for any *x* value entered at the keyboard.

In option 2, display NOT FOUND if the value typed is not in the table. In option 3, display VALUE IS OUT OF THE INTERPOLATION RANGE if *x* is less than 0 or greater than 20. The interpolation formula is

$$y = y_1 + \frac{x - x_1}{x_2 - x_1}(y_2 - y_1)$$

where x_1 and x_2 are successive values in the list of *x* values, with *x* lying between them; y_1 and y_2 are the corresponding *y* values.

23. For any input string, display two columns. In the first show the letters appearing in the string; in the second display how many times these letters occur in the string. For example, if the string constant "BOB,ROB,OR BO" is typed (quotation marks are included because of the commas), the output should be

```
B 4
O 4
R 2
```

If the string "Bob, Rob, or Bo" is typed, the output should be the same. Use F(1) to store the count of A's, F(2) for the B's, and so on, up to F(26). The method used in Example 19 of Section 13.7 to find the position in the alphabet of any letter, can be used here to find the appropriate subscript for any letter in the input string. It isn't necessary to use a second array to hold the letters of the alphabet. You may check that the letter whose count is stored in F(K) is CHR$(ASC("A") + K − 1).

24. Each of many DATA lines contains a single string (it may be long.) The last string is the EOD tag END-OF-DATA. Produce a two-column table as described in Problem 23 for all letters appearing in all DATA lines but the last. Label the columns LETTER and FREQUENCY. Run your program with the following DATA lines:

```
800 DATA "BASIC IS FUN! ESPECIALLY WHEN I MUST CONVERT"
810 DATA "STRINGS TO NUMBERS AND NUMBERS TO STRINGS,"
820 DATA "AND SO ON, AND SO ON, AND SO ON,..."
899 DATA END-OF-DATA
```

25. A list of words terminated with an EOD tag is contained in DATA lines. Determine how many of the words begin with the letter A, how many begin wih B, and so on. Display these counts in a two-column frequency table as described in Problem 24.

■ 14.5 Sorting

Many programming tasks require sorting (arranging) arrays according to some specified order. When lists of numbers are involved, this usually means arranging them according to size—from smallest to largest or from largest to smallest. For example, you may be required to produce a salary schedule in which salaries are displayed from largest to smallest. When lists of names are involved, you may wish to arrange them in alphabetical order. In this section we'll describe the bubble sort and show how it can be used in applications that require sorting numerical arrays in ascending or descending order, or string arrays in alphabetical order.

The bubble sort algorithm described in this section is very inefficient (slow) when used to sort large arrays, but for small arrays (up to about 30 entries) it will execute as rapidly as most sorting algorithms. Moreover, the bubble sort algorithm is easy to understand and easy to code. Thus it serves as an excellent introduction to the topic of sorting. A more comprehensive treatment of this topic is included in Chapter 17.

The idea behind the bubble sort is to compare adjacent array entries beginning with the first pair and ending with the last pair. If two values being compared are in the proper order, we leave them alone. If not, we interchange them. Thus to sort the short numerical array

	1	**2**	**3**	**4**
A	6	5	8	3

into ascending order, we begin the bubble sort by comparing the values in positions 1 and 2. Since these values (6 and 5) are not in order, they are swapped:

6 5 8 3   becomes   **5 6** 8 3

Next we compare the values in positions 2 and 3 in the same manner:

5 **6 8** 3   remains   5 **6 8** 3

Then we compare the values in positions 3 and 4:

5 6 **8 3**   becomes   5 6 **3 8**

The effect of these three comparisons is to move the largest value to the last position. If we repeat exactly the same process for the modified array

	1	**2**	**3**	**4**
A	5	6	3	8

the array entries will be rearranged as follows:

5 6 3 8	remains	**5 6** 3 8
5 **6 3** 8	becomes	5 **3 6** 8
5 3 **6 8**	remains	5 3 **6 8**

The effect of these three comparisons is to move the next-to-largest value (6) to the next-to-last position. Repeating the process a third time will move the third-from-largest value (5) to the third-from-last position and the array will be in order:

5 3 6 8	becomes	**3 5** 6 8
3 **5 6** 8	remains	3 **5 6** 8
3 5 **6 8**	remains	3 5 **6 8**

You probably noticed that several of the comparisons shown are unnecessary. After the first three comparisons are made (we'll refer to these three comparisons as *a pass through the array*), we can be sure that the largest array value is in the last position. Hence, it isn't necessary to make further comparisons involving the last array entry. Similarly, after the second pass through the array, it isn't necessary to make further comparisons involving the next-to-last array entry. If we include these unnecessary comparisons, however, it is a simple matter to code the process described. Indeed, since the three statements

```
LET T=A(I)
LET A(I)=A(I+1)
LET A(I+1)=T
```

interchange the values of the adjacent entries A(I) and A(I + 1), we can cause a single pass through the array A of size 4, swapping values that are not in order, with a FOR loop of the form

```
      FOR I=1 TO 3
         IF A(I)<=A(I+1) THEN ln
            LET T=A(I)
            LET A(I)=A(I+1)
            LET A(I+1)=T
ln NEXT I
```

If the array A is of size N, we would simply change the FOR statement to

```
FOR I=1 TO N-1
```

The number of passes that must be made to sort an array depends on the array size and the array values. For an array of size N, at most N − 1 passes are required because on each pass another array value is moved to its proper position. But it isn't always necessary to make N − 1 passes through the array. For instance, to sort the four-element array

	1	**2**	**3**	**4**
A	5	3	8	6

we make one pass through the array to move the largest entry to the last position:

5 3 8 6	becomes	3 **5** 8 6
3 **5** 8 6	remains	3 **5** 8 6
3 5 **8** 6	becomes	3 5 **6 8**

Thus, for this array, one pass is enough. Rather than attempting to keep count of how many passes have been made, we'll simply repeat the process described until a pass is made in which no array entries are swapped—this will happen only if the array is in order. The subroutine shown in Figure 14.1 accomplishes this by using the variable FLAG. Just before each pass through the array (that is, through the FOR loop), FLAG is set to 0. If a swap occurs in the loop, FLAG is set to 1. If the loop is completed with FLAG = 1, another pass is made; but if FLAG = 0 the array is sorted.

```
500 REM BUBBLE SORT TO ARRANGE THE N TERMS
510 REM OF ARRAY A INTO ASCENDING ORDER.
520 REM
530 LET FLAG=1    'Force a pass through WHILE loop.
540 WHILE FLAG=1
550    LET FLAG=0
560    FOR I=1 TO N-1
570       IF A(I)<=A(I+1) THEN 620
580       LET T=A(I)
590       LET A(I)=A(I+1)
600       LET A(I+1)=T
610       LET FLAG=1
620    NEXT I
630 NEXT  (or WEND)
640 RETURN
```

Figure 14.1 Subroutine to perform a bubble sort.

The bubble sort algorithm shown in Figure 14.1 can be used in any program to sort, in ascending order, any one-dimensional array A of size N. If you need to sort array A into descending rather than ascending order, simply change line 570 to

```
570 IF A(I)>=A(I+1) THEN 620
```

As we explained in the preceding analysis, the bubble sort we have devised makes many unnecessary comparisons. Even so, it is only a bit slower than a bubble sort that includes extra statements to avoid these comparisons. If speed is essential, you would not try to improve the bubble sort. Rather, you would use a different and faster algorithm. Two very fast sorting algorithms (called Shellsort and Heapsort) are given in Chapter 17.

Any sorting algorithm used to sort numerical arrays is easily modified to sort string arrays. To use the bubble sort in Figure 14.1 to sort strings, simply change the array name A to A$ or to any other string array name, and change the variable T to T$.

EXAMPLE 8 **Here is a program to alphabetize lists of names typed at the keyboard.**

```
100 REM       BUBBLE SORT AS APPLIED TO STRINGS
110 REM
120 REM **********************************************
130 REM            D A T A   E N T R Y
140 REM
150 DIM A$(51)
160 PRINT "ENTER UP TO 50 NAMES TO BE ALPHABETIZED."
170 PRINT "USE ONLY UPPERCASE. TYPE FINI WHEN DONE."
180 PRINT
190 LET N=1                        'Name count
200 PRINT "NAME";N;                'Prompt for name
210 INPUT A$(N)
```

```
220 WHILE A$(N)<>"FINI" AND N<51
230    LET N=N+1
240    PRINT "NAME";N;
250    INPUT A$(N)
260 NEXT  (or WEND)
270 LET N=N-1                        'Actual name count
280 REM
290 REM ****************************************
300 REM ALPHABETIZE THE N ENTRIES OF ARRAY A$.
310 REM
320 GOSUB 500
330 REM
340 REM **********************************
350 REM DISPLAY THE ALPHABETIZED ARRAY A$.
360 PRINT
370 PRINT "THE ALPHABETIZED LIST:"
380 PRINT
390 FOR I=1 TO N
400    PRINT A$(I)
410 NEXT I
420 GOTO 999
430 REM --------------------------------
500 REM     BUBBLESORT SUBROUTINE
510 REM ALPHABETIZE THE N ENTRIES OF A$.
520 REM
530 LET FLAG=1 'Force a pass through WHILE loop.
540 WHILE FLAG=1
550    LET FLAG=0
560    FOR I=1 TO N-1
570       IF A$(I)<=A$(I+1) THEN 620
580       LET T$=A$(I)
590       LET A$(I)=A$(I+1)
600       LET A$(I+1)=T$
610       LET FLAG=1
620    NEXT I
630 NEXT  (or WEND)
640 RETURN
999 END
RUN

ENTER UP TO 50 NAMES TO BE ALPHABETIZED.
USE ONLY UPPERCASE. TYPE FINI WHEN DONE.

NAME 1? LINCOLN
NAME 2? JOHNSON
NAME 3? GRANT
NAME 4? HAYES
NAME 5? GARFIELD
NAME 6? FINI

THE ALPHABETIZED LIST:

GARFIELD
GRANT
HAYES
JOHNSON
LINCOLN
```

■ **REMARK 1** A list of words to be alphabetized should contain all uppercase or all lowercase letters. Otherwise, as you can see by referring to Table 13.1,

"CRANSTON" < "Carlson"

even though Carlson should precede CRANSTON in an alphabetical listing.

■ **REMARK 2** If you must alphabetize an array A$ that contains both upper-and lowercase letters, you can use the lowercase-to-uppercase conversion subroutine given in Example 22 of Section 13.7. A common way to do this is to create a second array B$ containing the entries of A$ with each lowercase letter changed to uppercase. Then to sort A$ you would sort B$, being sure to swap entries in array A$ whenever the corresponding entries in B$ are swapped. If A$ contains N entries, the following loop will give you B$ (the conversion subroutine begins at line 800 and converts lowercase letters in X$ to uppercase):

```
FOR K=1 TO N
    LET X$=A$(K)
    GOSUB 800
    LET B$(K)=X$
NEXT K
```

You may have noticed that you don't have to create a new array B$ as described. One way to avoid B$ is to make the lowercase-to-uppercase conversions in array A$. You may not want to do this, however, if array A$ is needed for another purpose—for instance, to produce output containing both lower-and uppercase letters. Another way to avoid the use of a second array B$ would be to make conversions only as they are needed. For instance, to make a comparison involving A$(I), you could use the BASIC statements

```
LET X$=A$(I)
GOSUB 800
LET Y$=X$
```

to assign A$(I) to Y$, but with lowercase letters converted to uppercase, and then make the comparison by using Y$ instead of A$(I). Although this method saves memory space by avoiding the use of the second array B$, it is not recommended. Each time a comparison involving A$(I) must be made—many comparisons may be needed for each A$(I)—Y$ must be determined anew. This is very time consuming and can slow program execution significantly.

Many applications requiring arrays to be sorted involve more than one array. For example, suppose NAME$ and SAL denote one-dimensional arrays with each pair NAME$(I),SAL(I) giving a person's name and salary. If the contents of these two arrays must be displayed in a two-column report with the salaries appearing from largest to smallest, the list of pairs NAME$(I),SAL(I) must be sorted so that the entries in SAL are in descending order. This is easily accomplished by modifying a bubble sort that sorts array SAL. Simply insert statements to interchange NAME$(I) and NAME$(I+1) whenever SAL(I) and SAL(I+1) are interchanged. If a second two-column report must be displayed with the names in alphabetical order, you would modify a bubble sort that alphabetizes NAME$ by inserting statements to swap SAL(I) and SAL(I+1) whenever NAME$(I) and NAME$(I+1) are swapped. The next example demonstrates this procedure.

EXAMPLE 9

Several pairs of numbers are included in DATA lines. The first of each pair is a quality point average (QPA), and the second gives the number of students with this QPA. Write a program to produce a table with the column headings QPA and FREQUENCY. The frequency counts in the second column are to appear in descending order.

PROBLEM ANALYSIS

Two lists are given in the DATA lines. Let's use Q to denote QPAs and F to denote the frequency counts. The following algorithm shows the three subtasks that must be performed:

   a. Read arrays Q and F.
   b. Sort the two arrays so that the frequencies appear in descending order.
   c. Display the two arrays as a two-column table and stop.

To code Step (a), we must remember that the lists are presented in DATA lines as pairs of numbers. Thus, we will read values for Q(I) and F(I) for I = 1, 2, and so on, until all pairs have been read. We'll use the dummy pair 0, 0 as the EOD tag.
   To code Step (b), we will use a bubble sort to sort array F in descending order. How-

ever, since a pair Q(I), F(I) must not be separated, we will interchange Q values whenever the corresponding F values are interchanged.

In the following program, note that the REM statements at lines 110, 240, and 290 correspond to Steps (a), (b), and (c) of the algorithm.

THE PROGRAM

```
100 REM ************************************
110 REM        READ ARRAYS Q AND F AND
120 REM        FIND COUNT (N) OF PAIRS.
130 REM
140 DIM Q(50),F(50)
150 LET N=1
160 READ Q(N),F(N)
170 WHILE NOT (Q(N)=0 AND F(N)=0)
180    LET N=N+1
190    READ Q(N),F(N)
200 NEXT  (or WEND)
210 LET N=N-1      'Actual data count
220 REM
230 REM ************************************
240 REM        SORT ARRAYS Q AND F.
250 REM
260 GOSUB 500
270 REM
280 REM ************************************
290 REM        DISPLAY ARRAYS Q AND F.
300 REM
310 PRINT "   QPA      FREQUENCY"
320 PRINT "  -----     ---------
330 LET F$="   #.##         ###"
340 FOR I=1 TO N
350    PRINT USING F$,Q(I),F(I)
360 NEXT I
370 GOTO 999
380 REM ------------------------------------------------
500 REM SUBROUTINE TO SORT ARRAYS Q AND F SO THAT
510 REM ARRAY F ENTRIES ARE IN DESCENDING ORDER.
520 REM REM
530 LET FLAG=1              'Force a pass through loop.
540 WHILE FLAG=1
550    FLAG=0
560    FOR I=1 TO N-1
570       IF F(I)>=F(I+1) THEN 650
580       LET T=F(I)
590       LET F(I)=F(I+1)
600       LET F(I+1)=T
610       LET T=Q(I)
620       LET Q(I)=Q(I+1)
630       LET Q(I+1)=T
640       LET FLAG=1
650    NEXT I
660 NEXT  (or WEND)
670 RETURN
999 END
RUN
```

QPA	FREQUENCY
2.30	352
2.00	280
2.75	162
3.00	92
1.70	81
3.40	41
3.20	38
1.50	27
3.75	16
4.00	2

Lines 610–630 are inserted in the bubble sort that sorts F so that Q values will be interchanged whenever the corresponding F values are interchanged.

■ 14.6 Problems

In Problems 1–20, write a program to perform each task specified.

1. Display, in ascending order, any five input values L(1),L(2),L(3),L(4), and L(5). Have your program process many such sets of five numbers during a single run. Test your program with the following input data:

5	4	3	2	1
5	1	2	3	4
−1	−2	−3	−4	−5
2	1	4	3	5
15	19	14	18	10
1	2	3	4	5

2. Modify your program for Problem 1 so that each group of five integers is displayed in descending order. (Only one line needs to be changed.)

3. Display any list of numbers typed at the keyboard in ascending order. Use the value 9999 to indicate that the entire list has been entered.

4. Read a list of numbers to obtain a two-column table with the column headings ORIGINAL LIST and SORTED LIST. Have the first column contain the list values in the order in which they are read and the second column contain the same values displayed from largest to smallest. Use the following algorithm:

   a. Read the list values into identical arrays A and B.
   b. Sort array A into descending order.
   c. Display the two-column table as described.

   Try your program using the following DATA lines:

   ```
   500 DATA 80,70,40,90,95,38,85,42,60,70
   510 DATA 40,60,70,20,18,87,23,78,85,23
   998 DATA 9999
   ```

5. Read several numbers, ranging from 0 to 100, and store them in two arrays A and B. Let array A contain numbers less than 50 and array B the others. Then sort arrays A and B in descending order and display them side by side with the column headings LESS THAN 50 and 50 OR MORE. Test your program by using the data shown in Problem 4.

6. A study of Tidy Corporation's annual reports for 1980–1988 yielded the following statistics:

Year	Gross sales in thousands	Earnings per share
1981	18,000	−0.84
1982	18,900	0.65
1983	20,350	0.78
1984	24,850	1.05
1985	24,300	0.68
1986	27,250	0.88
1987	34,000	2.05
1988	51,000	1.07
1989	46,500	0.22

   Include the first and third columns of this table in DATA lines for a program to produce a two-column report with the same headings as those shown. However, have the earnings-per-share figures appear in ascending order.

7. Include all three columns given for the Tidy Corporation (Problem 6) in DATA lines for a program to produce a three-column table with the same headings. However, have the gross sales figures appear in descending order.

8. Compute the semester averages for all students in a psychology class. A separate DATA line should be used for each student and should contain the student's name and five grades. A typical DATA line might read

```
700 DATA LINCOLN JOHN,72,79,88,97,90
```

Produce the output in tabular form with the column headings STUDENT and SEMESTER AVERAGE. Have the names appear in alphabetical order.

9. Modify Problem 8 as follows: round averages to the nearest integer and give letter grades according to this table:

Average	Grade
90–100	A
80–89	B
70–79	C
60–69	D
Below 60	E

Read the five strings A, B, C, D, and E into an array. Produce the output in tabular form with the column headings STUDENT, SEMESTER AVERAGE, and LETTER GRADE. Have the names appear in alphabetical order.

10. Following is the weekly inventory report of a sewing-supply wholesaler:

Item	Batches on hand Monday	Batches sold during week	Cost per batch	Sales price per batch
Bobbins	220	105	$8.20	$10.98
Buttons	550	320	5.50	6.95
Needles—1	450	295	2.74	3.55
Needles—2	200	102	7.25	9.49
Pins	720	375	4.29	5.89
Thimbles	178	82	6.22	7.59
Thread—A	980	525	4.71	5.99
Thread—B	1424	718	7.42	9.89

Include all five columns in DATA lines by using one DATA statement for each item. Have your program produce a three-column report showing the item names and, for each item, the number of batches on hand at the end of the week and the income generated by that item. Have the income column appear in descending order.

11. Using the inventory report shown in Problem 10, produce a five-column report showing the item names, the cost per batch, the sales price per batch, the dollar markup per batch, and the percent markup per batch. Have the figures in the last column appear in descending order. [The percentages in the fifth column are given by (M/C)*100, where M denotes the markup and C denotes the cost.]

12. A program is to contain the following DATA lines.

```
800 DATA 9
810 DATA MARIAN EVANS, JAMES PAYN, JOSEPH CONRAD
820 DATA EMILY DICKINSON, HENRY THOREAU, JOHN PAYNE
830 DATA JOHN FOX, MARY FREEMAN, GEORGE ELIOT
```

Use the following algorithm to alphabetize the list of names:

a. Read the names into an array A$.

b. Create a new array B$ containing the names in A$ but with last names first.

c. Sort B$ into alphabetical order. When a swap is made in B$, make the corresponding swap in A$.

13. A program is to contain the following DATA lines.

```
800 DATA 9
810 DATA MARIAN, EVANS, JAMES, PAYN, JOSEPH, CONRAD
820 DATA EMILY, DICKINSON, HENRY, THOREAU, JOHN, PAYNE
830 DATA JOHN, FOX, MARY, FREEMAN, GEORGE, ELIOT
```

(Note that these are the names given in Problem 12 but with first names and last names included as separate strings.) Have your program produce an alphabetical listing with each name appearing in the form

```
LAST, FIRST
```

with a space after the comma as shown. (*Suggestion:* Use the concatenation operator + to place the names in a single string array with each name in the form specified for the output. Then simply sort and display this array. No other arrays are needed.)

14. A list of English words is presented in DATA lines. The last datum is the EOD tag XXX. The user should be allowed to issue any of the following commands: LIST, to display the list in the order given in the DATA lines; SORT, to display the list in alphabetical order; and DONE, to terminate the run. After any command other than DONE, the user should be allowed to issue another command. The command LIST must produce the list in the order given in DATA lines, even after SORT has been carried out. You should avoid lowercase letters in the DATA lines and instruct the user to use only uppercase when typing LIST, SORT, or DONE.

15. Display a list of words as described in Problem 14 in two adjacent columns with the column headings A–M and N–Z. Have the words in each column appear in alphabetical order.

16. Write a program as specified in Problem 14, but allow both lower-and uppercase letters in the DATA lines and in the keyboard input.

17. If a set of N scores is arranged in either increasing or decreasing order, the *median* score is the middle score when N is odd and the average of the two "middle" scores when N is even. Thus the sixth score is the median for a set of 11 scores, whereas the average of the fifth and sixth scores is the median for a set of 10 scores. Determine the median for an undetermined number of scores typed at the keyboard.

18. Read N pairs of numbers so that the first of each pair is in array A and the second is in array B. Sort the pairs A(I), B(I) so that $A(1) \leq A(2) \leq \cdots \leq A(N)$ and so that $B(I) \leq B(I + 1)$ whenever $A(I) = A(I + 1)$. Display the modified arrays in two adjacent columns with the headings LIST A and LIST B. [*Hint:* If $A(I) > A(I + 1)$, a swap is necessary; if $A(I) < A(I + 1)$, no swap is necessary; otherwise—that is, if $A(I) = A(I + 1)$—swap only if $B(I) > B(I + 1)$.]

19. English prose can be written in DATA lines by representing each line of text as a string occupying a single DATA line:

```
500 DATA "WHEN IN THE COURSE OF HUMAN EVENTS,"
501 DATA "IT BECOMES NECESSARY FOR ONE PEOPLE"
502 DATA "TO DISSOLVE THE POLITICAL"
    .
    .
    .
998 DATA "END-OF-TEXT"
```

Write a program to determine some or all of the following statistics:

a. A count of the number of words of text.

b. A count of the number of N-letter words for N = 1,2,3, ...

c. A two-column table giving each word used and its frequency. The column of words should be in alphabetical order.

d. A two-column table showing the number of sentences with one word, the number with two words, and so on.

e. A count of the number of words used from a list of words you include in DATA lines. For instance, to determine the number of times the author uses articles and conjunctions, your list might include A, AN, AND, BUT, HOWEVER, NOR, OR, THE, and others. If you were studying an author's use of color imagery, your list might be one of colors.

Avoid lowercase letters in the DATA lines and instruct the user to use only uppercase at the keyboard.

20. Write a program as specified in Problem 19, but allow both lower-and uppercase letters in the DATA lines and in the keyboard input.

■ 14.7 Higher-Dimensional Arrays

Each array used to this point is one dimensional, a term indicating that the array entries are referenced by using a single subscript. As illustrated in Sections 14.1–14.3, programming tasks involving tables represent an important application of one-dimensional arrays. There are some table-processing applications, however, for which the one-dimensional array structure is inadequate. For example, consider the following table that summarizes the responses of 10 families to a product survey:

Product survey table

	Key to table entries									
	Rating		**Survey response**							
	0		POOR							
	1		FAIR							
	2		GOOD							
	3		VERY GOOD							
	4		EXCELLENT							
	Family number									
	1	2	3	4	5	6	7	8	9	10
1	0	1	1	2	1	2	2	1	0	1
2	2	3	3	0	3	2	2	3	4	1
3	1	3	4	4	4	1	4	2	3	2
4	3	4	2	4	3	1	3	4	2	4
5	0	1	3	2	2	2	1	3	0	1
6	4	4	4	3	2	1	4	4	1	1
7	1	3	1	3	2	4	1	4	3	4
8	2	2	3	4	2	2	3	4	2	3

Product number appears to the left of rows 1–8.

To store these data in one-dimensional arrays, we could use a string array to store the table of responses (POOR, FAIR, and so on) corresponding to the rating keys 0 through 4, but it would not be convenient to use one-dimensional arrays to store the larger table of numerical ratings. Doing so would require eight numerical arrays if a separate array is used for each product or ten arrays if an array is used for each family. The program would be unnecessarily complicated (each array would have a different name) and very difficult to modify to handle other than eight products and ten families.

What is needed is a convenient way to store such tables. BASIC provides this capability by allowing you to declare arrays whose entries are referenced by using two subscripts. First, we will introduce some terminology to make it easier to refer to arrays used to store tables such as the Product Survey Table. To keep things as simple as possible, however, we will use the following smaller table for illustration. The data in this table summarize the responses of college students to a hypothetical opinion poll concerning the abolition of grades.

Class	In favor of abolishing grades	Not in favor of abolishing grades	No opinion
Freshmen	207	93	41
Sophomores	165	110	33
Juniors	93	87	15
Seniors	51	65	8

A **two-dimensional array** is a collection of items arranged in a rectangular fashion. That is, there is a first (horizontal) row, a second row, and so on, and a first (vertical) column, a second column, and so on. An array with *m* rows and *n* columns is called an *m-by-n array* (also written **m × n array**). Thus the opinion-poll data are presented as a 4-by-3 array.

An item in a two-dimensional array is specified by giving its row number and column number. For example, the item in the third row and second column of the opinion-poll table is 87. By convention, the row number is specified first. Thus, in the opinion-poll table, 33 is in the 2,3 position and 51 is in the 4,1 position. In mathematical notation we could write

$$P_{1,1} = 207, P_{1,2} = 93, P_{1,3} = 41$$

to indicate the values in the first row of our table. Since the BASIC character set does not include such subscripts, this notation is changed as it was for one-dimensional arrays. Thus, the values in the opinion-poll table would be written as follows:

P(1,1) = 207	P(1,2) = 93	P(1,3) = 41
P(2,1) = 165	P(2,2) = 110	P(2,3) = 33
P(3,1) = 93	P(3,2) = 87	P(3,3) = 15
P(4,1) = 51	P(4,2) = 65	P(4,3) = 8

We say that P is the **name** of the array, that P(1,1),P(1,2), . . . , are **doubly subscripted variables,** and that the numbers enclosed in parentheses are the *subscripts* of P. The symbol P(I,J) is read **P sub I comma J** or simply **P sub IJ.**

The 4-by-3 array P can be visualized as follows:

```
                      (Column)
            P  |   1     2     3
            ___|_____
            1  |  207    93    41
            2  |  165   110    33
  (Row)     3  |   93    87    15
            4  |   51    65     8
```

This schematic displays the array name P, the row number for each item, and the column numbers.

To declare to the computer that your program will use the 4-by-3 array P, you would include the statement

```
DIM P(4,3)
```

so that it is encountered before any of the doubly subscripted variables P(1,1),P(1,2), and so on, are referenced. If instead you include the statement

```
DIM P(100,100)
```

your program can reference any or all of the subscripted variables P(R,C) with R and C integers in the range 1 to 100—there are 10,000 such subscript assignments.

The value of a doubly subscripted variable—that is, an array entry—is referenced in a program just as values of singly subscripted variables are referenced. The subscripts can be integer constants, variables, or expressions. For example, the FOR loop

```
FOR C=1 TO 3
   LET P(1,C)=5*C
NEXT C
```

assigns the values 5, 10, and 15 to the first row, P(1,1),P(1,2),P(1,3), of P. Similarly,

```
LET C=1
FOR R=1 TO 4
   LET P(R,C)=P(R,C)+6
NEXT R
```

adds 6 to each entry in the first column, P(1,1), P(2,1), P(3,1), P(4,1), of P.

EXAMPLE 10 **Here is a program segment to read the college students opinion-poll data into an array P.**

```
100 REM READ VALUES FOR THE 4-BY-3 ARRAY P.
110 DIM P(4,3)
120 FOR R=1 TO 4
130    REM READ VALUES FOR THE RTH ROW OF P.
140    FOR C=1 TO 3
150       READ P(R,C)
160    NEXT C
170 NEXT R
500 DATA 207,93,41
510 DATA 165,110,33
520 DATA 93,87,15
530 DATA 51,65,8
```

When the first FOR statement (line 120) is executed, R is assigned the initial value 1. The C loop then reads the first three data values 207, 93, and 41 for the variables P(1,1), P(1,2), and P(1,3), respectively. That is, when R = 1, values are read into the first row of P. Similarly, when R = 2, values are read into the second row, P(2,1), P(2,2), P(2,3), of P, and so on, until all 12 values have been assigned to P.

■ REMARK 1 The data do not have to be given in four lines as shown here. The single line

```
500 DATA 207,93,41,165,110,33,93,87,15,51,65,8
```

could replace lines 500 through 530. The order in which they appear is all that matters.

■ REMARK 2 We used the following five lines to assign values to P:

```
FOR R=1 TO 4
   FOR C=1 TO 3
      READ P(R,C)
   NEXT C
NEXT R
```

Some BASIC systems allow you to accomplish the same thing with a single statement called a MAT (matrix) statement. (**Matrix** is another name for an array of values.) Proper use of MAT statements can shorten your programs and make them easier to understand. MAT statements are described in Chapter 18.

□

EXAMPLE 11 **Let's use the program segment of Example 10 in a program to count the number of students in each class who participated in the opinion-poll survey.**

PROBLEM ANALYSIS

The following algorithm describes one way to carry out the specified task.

    a. Read the opinion-poll data into array P (done in Example 10).
    b. Determine and display how many students in each class participated in the survey.

Since all three entries in any one row of P correspond to students in one of the four classes, the task in Step (b) is to add the three entries in each row of P and display these four sums. Let's use S(1) to denote the sum of the entries in the first row and S(2),S(3), and S(4) for the other three row sums. These sums can be determined as follows:

```
LET S(1)=P(1,1)+P(1,2)+P(1,3)
LET S(2)=P(2,1)+P(2,2)+P(2,3)
LET S(3)=P(3,1)+P(3,2)+P(3,3)
LET S(4)=P(4,1)+P(4,2)+P(4,3)
```

However, note that S(R), for R = 1, 2, 3, and 4, is obtained by summing P(R,C) for C = 1, 2, and 3. This is exactly the order of subscripts determined by the nested FOR loops

```
FOR R=1 TO 4
   FOR C=1 TO 3
       .
       .
       .
   NEXT C
NEXT R
```

The following program can now be written. Lines 100–170, which carry out Step (a) of the algorithm, are the program segment shown in Example 10. To this we add lines 180–330, which represent one way to code Step (b) of the algorithm.

THE PROGRAM

```
100 REM READ VALUES FOR THE 4-BY-3 ARRAY P.
110 DIM P(4,3)
120 FOR R=1 TO 4
130    REM READ VALUES FOR THE RTH ROW OF P.
140    FOR C=1 TO 3
150       READ P(R,C)
160    NEXT C
170 NEXT R
180 REM DETERMINE AND DISPLAY THE ROW SUMS OF P.
190 PRINT "PARTICIPATION IN SURVEY BY CLASS."
200 PRINT "----------------------------------"
210 FOR R=1 TO 4
220    LET S(R)=0
230 NEXT R
240 FOR R=1 TO 4
250    FOR C=1 TO 3
260       LET S(R)=S(R)+P(R,C)
270    NEXT C
280    IF (R=1) THEN PRINT "FRESHMEN",
290    IF (R=2) THEN PRINT "SOPHOMORES",
300    IF (R=3) THEN PRINT "JUNIORS",
310    IF (R=4) THEN PRINT "SENIORS",
320    PRINT S(R)
330 NEXT R
500 DATA 207,93,41
510 DATA 165,110,33
520 DATA 93,87,15
530 DATA 51,65,8
999 END
RUN

PARTICIPATION IN SURVEY BY CLASS.
----------------------------------
FRESHMEN          341
SOPHOMORES        308
JUNIORS           195
SENIORS           124
```

■ REMARK

This program could have been written with only one pair of nested FOR loops by inserting appropriate lines in the program segment

```
100 REM READ VALUES FOR THE 4-BY-3 ARRAY P.
110 DIM P(4,3)
120 FOR R=1 TO 4
130    REM READ VALUES FOR THE RTH ROW OF P.
140    FOR C=1 TO 3
150       READ P(R,C)
160    NEXT C
170 NEXT R
```

that was used to carry out Step (a) of the algorithm. Specifically, inserting the line

```
125 LET S(R)=0
```

serves to initialize the counters S(1),S(2),S(3), and S(4). Also, if the line

```
155 LET S(R)=S(R)+P(R,C)
```

is included, the required row sums S(1),S(2),S(3), and S(4) will be calculated. The lines that display the caption

```
PARTICIPATION IN SURVEY BY CLASS.
---------------------------------
```

can be placed anywhere before line 120 and, finally, the lines that display the counts S(R) with the identifying labels can be placed just after S(R) is determined—that is, between lines 160 and 170.

Although these changes result in a shorter program, it is not necessarily better. In the program as given, each of the two subtasks [Steps (a) and (b)] in the algorithm occupies its own part of the program. (The REM statements in lines 100 and 180 identify these program segments.) That the resulting program may not be the shortest possible is of little consequence. The longer program obtained by segmenting is easier to read and certainly easier to modify, should that be required. The axiom "the shorter the better" is not always valid in programming.

Many programming applications involve rearranging the entries in two-dimensional arrays. The same methods used with one-dimensional arrays apply. The next two examples illustrate the rearrangement of entries of two-dimensional arrays.

EXAMPLE 12   **Here is a program segment to interchange rows K and L of an N-by-N array A.**

```
200 FOR C=1 TO N
210    LET T=A(K,C)
220    LET A(K,C)=A(L,C)
230    LET A(L,C)=T
240 NEXT C
```

When C = 1, the three statements in the range of the loop interchange A(K,1) and A(L,1), the first entries in the Kth and Lth rows of A. When C = 2, the second entries A(K,2) and A(L,2) are interchanged. Similarly statements apply for C = 3, 4, . . . , N.

EXAMPLE 13   **Here is a self-explanatory program.**

```
100 REM ****************************************
110 REM * READ VALUES FOR ARRAY A, ROW BY ROW *
120 REM ****************************************
130 REM
140 DIM A(4,4)
150 FOR ROW=1 TO 4
160    FOR COL=1 TO 4
170       READ A(ROW,COL)
180    NEXT COL
190 NEXT ROW
200 REM -------------------------
210 REM      DATA FOR ARRAY A
220 REM
230 DATA 22.25, 21.75, 28.63, 29.00
```

```
240 DATA 61.23, 55.47, 59.50, 62.33
250 DATA 33.35, 42.00, 39.25, 48.62
260 DATA 44.45, 43.20, 27.62, 39.40
270 REM
280 REM ******************************
290 REM * DISPLAY ARRAY A, ROW BY ROW *
300 REM ******************************
310 REM
320 PRINT "ORIGINAL ARRAY:"
330 PRINT
340 GOSUB 700                      'Display A.
350 PRINT
360 REM ********************************
370 REM * FIND THE ROW NUMBER K OF THE ROW *
380 REM *  WITH LARGEST FIRST VALUE A(K,1) *
390 REM ********************************
400 REM
410 LET K=1
420 FOR ROW=2 TO 4
430    IF A(ROW,1)>A(K,1) THEN K=ROW
440 NEXT ROW
450 REM
460 REM ********************************
470 REM * INTERCHANGE FIRST ROW AND ROW K *
480 REM ********************************
490 REM
500 FOR COL=1 TO 4
510    LET T=A(K,COL)
520    LET A(K,COL)=A(1,COL)
530    LET A(1,COL)=T
540 NEXT COL
550 REM
560 REM ****************************************
570 REM * DISPLAY MODIFIED ARRAY A, ROW BY ROW *
580 REM ****************************************
590 REM
600 PRINT "MODIFIED ARRAY:"
610 PRINT
620 GOSUB 700                      'Display A.
630 PRINT
640 GOTO 999                       'Program exit
650 REM
700 REM ----------------------------------------
710 REM  SUBROUTINE TO DISPLAY A 4-BY-4 ARRAY A
720 REM
730 FOR ROW=1 TO 4
740    FOR COL=1 TO 4
750       PRINT USING "###.## ",A(ROW,COL);
760    NEXT COL
770    PRINT
780 NEXT ROW
790 RETURN
800 REM ----------------------------------------
999 END
RUN

ORIGINAL ARRAY:

 22.25  21.75  28.63  29.00
 61.23  55.47  59.50  62.33
 33.35  42.00  39.25  48.62
 44.45  43.20  27.62  39.40

MODIFIED ARRAY:

 61.23  55.47  59.50  62.33
 22.25  21.75  28.63  29.00
 33.35  42.00  39.25  48.62
 44.45  43.20  27.62  39.40
```

BASIC does not restrict you to one or two subscripts. For example, the statement

```
DIM A(2,2,2)
```

specifies a three-dimensional array whose entries can be referenced by using A(I,J,K), where the subscripts I, J, and K can be any of the integers 0, 1, or 2. Similarly,

```
DIM B(3,3,3,3,3)
```

specifies a five-dimensional array whose entries can be referenced by B(I,J,K,L,M), where the five subscripts can be any of the values 0, 1, 2, or 3.

Arrays with more than two dimensions are sometimes used in technical engineering and mathematical applications, but they are rarely used in nontechnical programming tasks. For this reason, they are not illustrated here.

We conclude this section with three points concerning the use of two-dimensional arrays that were not specifically mentioned or illustrated in this section:

1. Every higher-dimensional array should be declared in DIM statements. As with one-dimensional arrays, however, failure to do so will cause a fatal error only if you use a subscript that's not in the range 1 to 10 (0 to 10, on many systems).

2. Both one-and higher-dimensional arrays can be declared with the same DIM statement. The following DIM statement properly declares a one-dimensional numerical array A with largest subscript 5, a two-dimensional 5-by-2 array B, and a one-dimensional string array M$ with largest subscript 25:

```
100 DIM A(5),B(5,2),M$(25)
```

3. Higher-dimensional string arrays are permitted. At the beginning of this section we showed an 8-row-by-10 column Product Survey Table. Each entry in the table is a numerical rating whose meaning is as follows:

Key to table entries

Rating	Survey response
0	POOR
1	FAIR
2	GOOD
3	VERY GOOD
4	EXCELLENT

Thus, to store the given Product Survey Table in the two-dimensional array PRODUCT, we could declare PRODUCT as follows:

```
DIM PRODUCT(8,10)
```

If we wanted to store the actual responses (POOR,FAIR, and so on) rather than the corresponding rating numbers in a table, we would specify a string array as follows:

```
DIM PRODUCT$(8,10)
```

■ 14.8 Problems

1. Show the output of each program.
   a.
   ```
   100 DIM M(4,4)
   110 FOR R=1 TO 4
   120    FOR C=1 TO 4
   130       LET M(R,C)=R*C
   140    NEXT C
   150 NEXT R
   160 FOR K=1 TO 4
   170    PRINT M(K,K);
   180 NEXT K
   190 END
   ```

b.
```
100 DIM A(3,2),B(2,3)
110 FOR R=1 TO 3
120     FOR C=1 TO 2
130         READ A(R,C)
140         LET B(C,R)=A(R,C)
150     NEXT C
160 NEXT R
170 PRINT B(2,1);B(2,2);B(2,3)
180 DATA 1,2,3,4,5,6,7,8,9
190 END
```

c.
```
100 DIM S(3,3)
110 FOR K=1 TO 3
120     FOR L=1 TO K
130         READ S(K,L)
140         LET S(L,K)=S(K,L)
150     NEXT L
160 NEXT K
170 FOR N=1 TO 3
180     PRINT S(N,2);
190 NEXT N
200 DATA 1,2,3,4,5,6
```

d.
```
100 DIM YESNO$(4,4)
110 FOR R=1 TO 4
120     FOR C=1 TO 4
130         IF R>C THEN A$="N" ELSE A$="Y"
140         LET YESNO$(R,C)=A$
150     NEXT C
160 NEXT R
170 FOR R=1 TO 4
180     FOR C=1 TO 4
190         PRINT YESNO$(R,C);
200     NEXT C
210     PRINT
220 NEXT R
230 END
```

e.
```
100 DIM T$(3),P$(3,4)
110 FOR N=1 TO 3
120     READ T$(N)
130     FOR P=1 TO 4
140         READ P$(N,P)
150     NEXT P
160 NEXT N
170 FOR N=1 TO 3
180     PRINT T$(N);":",
190 NEXT N
200 PRINT
210 FOR P=1 TO 4
220     FOR N=1 TO 3
230         PRINT P$(N,P),
240     NEXT N
250     PRINT
260 NEXT P
270 DATA DEVILS,ED,JANE,JOHN,SUE
280 DATA HOOFERS,ANN,JIM,RON,RUTH
290 DATA SAINTS,DEB,DOT,RUSS,TIM
300 END
```

2. Find and correct the errors in the following program segments. Assume that values have already been assigned to the 5-by-5 array A.

a.
```
200 REM DISPLAY THE SUM S OF EACH ROW OF A.
220 LET S=0
230 FOR R=1 TO 5
240     FOR C=1 TO 5
250         LET S=S+A(R,C)
260     NEXT C
270     PRINT S
280 NEXT R
```

b.
```
200 REM INTERCHANGE ROWS R1 AND R2 OF ARRAY A.
210 FOR C=1 TO 5
220     LET A(R1,C)=A(R2,C)
230     LET A(R2,C)=A(R1,C)
240 NEXT C
```

In Problems 3–16, write a program to perform each task specified.

3. Read 16 values into the 4×4 array M. Then display the array. Further, display the four column sums below their respective columns.

4. Repeat Problem 3 for an $N \times N$ array M in which N can be any integer up to 6.

5. Read 16 values into the 4×4 array M. Then display the array. Have row sums appear to the right of their respective rows and column sums below their respective columns.

6. Repeat Problem 5 for an $N \times N$ array M in which N can be any number up to 6.

7. Read values into an $N \times N$ array A. Then display the sum of the entries in the upper-left to lower-right diagonal of A. This sum is called the *trace* of array A. (Input N before the array values are read. Assume that N will never exceed 6.)

8. The *transpose* B of an $N \times N$ array A is the $N \times N$ array whose rows are the columns of A in the same order. Read the entries of A from DATA lines, and display the transpose B. (Assume that N will be less than 6.)

9. The *sum* S of two $N \times N$ arrays A and B is the $N \times N$ array whose entries are the sums of the corresponding entries of A and B. Read A and B from DATA lines, and display arrays A, B, and S. (Assume that N will be less than 6.)

10. Create the following 5×5 array N

```
  0    1    1    1    1
 -1    0    1    1    1
 -1   -1    0    1    1
 -1   -1   -1    0    1
 -1   -1   -1   -1    0
```

Determine the values N(I,J) during program execution without using READ or INPUT statements. Display array N. [*Hint:* The value to be assigned to N(I,J) can be determined by comparing I with J.]

11. A manufacturing company sends a package consisting of eight new products to each of ten families and asks each family to rate each product. Here are the survey results:

Product survey table

	Key to table entries								
	Rating	Survey response							
	0	POOR							
	1	FAIR							
	2	GOOD							
	3	VERY GOOD							
	4	EXCELLENT							

Family number

Product number		1	2	3	4	5	6	7	8	9	10
	1	0	1	1	2	1	2	2	1	0	1
	2	2	3	3	0	3	2	2	3	4	1
	3	1	3	4	4	4	1	4	2	3	2
	4	3	4	2	4	3	1	3	4	2	4
	5	0	1	3	2	2	2	1	3	0	1
	6	4	4	4	3	2	1	4	4	1	1
	7	1	3	1	3	2	4	1	4	3	4
	8	2	2	3	4	2	2	3	4	2	3

Write a menu-driven program that will carry out any or all of the tasks listed. (Have your program read the given data into arrays. You may find it convenient to use a string array to store the possible responses POOR, FAIR, and so on, and a two-dimensional array to store the data given in the table of numerical ratings.)

1. Display the entire Product Survey Table essentially as shown.
2. Display a two-column report showing the average rating for each product.
3. Display a two-column report as follows: the first column gives the product numbers receiving at least six ratings of 3 or better; the second gives the number of these ratings obtained.
4. Display a two-column table showing how many times each of the five possible responses (POOR, FAIR, and so on) were made.

12. An N × N array of numbers is called a *magic square* if the sums of each row, each column, and each diagonal are all equal. Test any N × N array in which N will never exceed 10. Values for N and array values should be input. Be sure to display and identify all row, column, and diagonal sums, the array itself, and a message indicating whether or not the array is a magic square. Try your program on the following arrays:

a. 1 1
    1 1

b.
11	10	4	23	17
18	12	6	5	24
25	19	13	7	1
2	21	20	14	8
9	3	22	16	15

c.
4	139	161	26	174	147
85	166	107	188	93	12
98	152	138	3	103	157
179	17	84	165	184	22
183	21	13	175	89	170
102	156	148	94	8	143

13. Input five numbers to produce a five-column table as follows. The first column is to contain the five numbers in the order they are input. The second column is to contain the four differences of successive values in the first column. For example, if the first column contains 2, 4, 8, 9, 3, the second column will contain 2, 4, 1, −6. In the same way, each of columns three through five is to contain the differences of successive values in the column before it. If the values 1,5,9,6,12 are input, the output should be

1	4	0	−7	23
5	4	−7	16	
9	−3	9		
6	6			
12				

In the following suggested algorithm, M denotes a 5 × 5 array:

   a. Input the first column of M.
   b. Generate the remaining four columns of M as specified in the problem statement.
   c. Display the table as specified.

14. Input N numbers to produce a table of differences as described in Problem 13. Assume that N is an integer from 2 to 10.

15. Read values into a 5 × 3 array N. Then display the subscripts corresponding to the largest entry in N. If this largest value appears in N more than once, more than one pair of subscripts must be displayed. Use the following algorithm:

   a. Read values for array N.
   b. Determine M, the largest number in array N.
   c. Display all subscripts I,J for which N(I,J) = M.

16. Read values into a 5 × 3 array N. Display the row of N with the smallest first entry. If this smallest value is the first entry in more than one row, display only the first of these rows. Then interchange this row with the first row and display the modified array N. Use the following algorithm:

a. Read values for array N.
b. Find the first K such that row K has the smallest first entry.
c. Display row K.
d. Interchange rows 1 and K.
e. Display the modified array N.

■ 14.9 Review True-or-False Quiz

1. The two programming lines

   ```
   100 DIM A(25)
   110 LET A=0
   ```

   will assign the value 0 to all 25 positions in the array A.   **T   F**

2. Once array L is assigned values in a program, the statement PRINT L is sufficient to cause the entire array to be displayed.   **T   F**

3. If arrays A and B are declared by using DIM A(20),B(20), then the statement LET A = B will replace all entries of A by the corresponding entries of B.   **T   F**

4. The programming line

   ```
   50 LET A(I)=7
   ```

   can cause an error message to be displayed.   **T   F**

5. The statement LET A(7) = 25 can never cause an error message to be displayed.   **T   F**

6. Array values may be assigned by READ, INPUT, or LET statements.   **T   F**

7. The statement LET G = 5 may appear in a program that contains the statement DIM G(100).   **T   F**

8. If both one-dimensional and two-dimensional arrays are to be used in a program, two DIM statements must be used.   **T   F**

9. Two or more arrays are sometimes needed to store a single table of values.   **T   F**

10. If a program is needed to process data given in tabular form, it is always best to store the data by using one or more arrays.   **T   F**

15

Data Files

In the preceding chapters, all data to be processed by programs were included in DATA lines or entered at the keyboard, and all output was directed to the display screen or a printer. Although these methods of handling I/O are adequate for many programming applications, situations often arise for which they are inadequate. For example, the output values of one program might be required as the input values of another program, or even of several other programs. Also, it might be necessary to store extensive output for printing at a later time when the computer isn't otherwise being used—long reports can be generated very quickly by computers, but by comparison printers are very slow. To make all of this possible, BASIC allows for input data to come from a source external to the program (other than a keyboard) and for the output to be stored on secondary storage devices for later use. This is accomplished with data files.

A **data file** is a named collection of related data that can be referenced by a BASIC program.

Every BASIC statement used for file processing is one of the following types:

1. Statements to establish a communication link between a program and any files to be used as input or output files. The files named in such statements are said to have been "opened."
2. Statements to read information from a file or write information to a file.
3. Statements to position a file at its beginning.
4. Statements to "close" a file—that is, to terminate any communication between a program and a file.

The data files considered in this book are called **sequential files** because their contents are ordered in sequence; that is, there is a first entry, a second entry, a third, and so on. Thus, it makes sense to talk about statements to position a file at its beginning. Associated with each sequential file is a conceptual *pointer*. If the file is used as an input file, the pointer is positioned at the next input value; if it is used as an output file, the pointer is positioned just after the most recent output value.

Methods for creating and reading data files and the BASIC statements needed to perform these tasks are described in this chapter. You should be forwarned, however, that BASIC systems vary in the form of the statements used to manipulate files. Although the file statements for your system may closely resemble those described in this chapter, you should consult your BASIC manual for the precise forms required. In what follows, we have not attempted to point out all of the differences in how BASIC systems handle files. Our objectives are to indicate those applications for which files are appropriate and to illustrate programming techniques you can use for file processing on any system. Only major differences in BASIC systems are discussed.

■ 15.1 File Statements

Let's assume that a file named SCORES contains the following six lines (the use of the term "lines" as it applies to files will be explained shortly):

```
NICKLAUS
206
MILLER
208
WATSON
205
```

In Example 1 we show how a BASIC program can access the data contained in this file, and in Example 2 we show how the file SCORES can be created.

EXAMPLE 1

Here are two programs that use the data contained in the file SCORES.

Program A	*Program B*
100 OPEN "SCORES" FOR INPUT AS FILE 1	100 FILE#1="SCORES"
110 FOR N=1 TO 3	110 FOR N=1 TO 3
120 INPUT#1,A$	120 INPUT#1,A$
130 INPUT#1.S	130 INPUT#1,S
140 PRINT A$,S	140 PRINT A$,S
150 NEXT N	150 NEXT N
160 END	160 END
RUN	RUN
NICKLAUS 206	NICKLAUS 206
MILLER 208	MILLER 208
WATSON 205	WATSON 205

In each program, line 100 specifies SCORES as the name of the file to be used. In addition, line 100 assigns the integer 1 as the **file designator** (also called the **file ordinal** or **channel number**) for this file.* Whenever the file is used in the program, it is referenced by its designator, not by its name. As shown in lines 120 and 130, this is accomplished by using INPUT#1 instead of INPUT. Each time the INPUT# statements at lines 120 and 130 are executed, values for A$ and S are obtained from the file SCORES. Line 140 displays these two values as shown in the output.

■ **REMARK 1**   File designators can be unsigned integer constants from 1 up to the number allowed on your BASIC system. On most BASIC systems you can use variables to specify file designators.

■ **REMARK 2**   In line 100 we used the string constant "SCORES" to specify the name of the file being opened. On most BASIC systems you can use string variables for this purpose. For example, the three lines

```
10 PRINT "FILE NAME";
20 INPUT A$
30 OPEN A$ FOR INPUT AS FILE 1
```

or

```
10 PRINT "FILE NAME";
20 INPUT A$
30 FILE#1=A$
```

allow the user to specify, during program execution, the name of the file to be opened.

■ **REMARK 3**   The keywords FOR INPUT in the OPEN statement are required only on some BASIC systems.

---

* Information is transmitted to and from a computer over one or more communications channels. The file designator specifies which of these channels is to be used for the file named in the OPEN or FILE# statement.

◼ REMARK 4
☐
If your system uses the FILE# statement shown in Program B, you may have to type a system command such as GET,SCORES before you type the RUN command.

EXAMPLE 2   **Here are two programs that can be used to create the file SCORES.**

PROGRAM A

```
100 OPEN "SCORES" FOR OUTPUT AS FILE 1
110 REM
120 PRINT "USE NAME=END TO STOP."
130 PRINT
140 PRINT "NAME";
150 INPUT N$
160 WHILE N$<>"END"
170     PRINT#1,N$
180     PRINT "SCORE";
190     INPUT S
200     PRINT#1,S
210     PRINT "NAME";
220 NEXT    (or WEND)
230 CLOSE 1
240 END
RUN

USE NAME=END TO STOP.

NAME? NICKLAUS
SCORE? 206
NAME? MILLER
SCORE? 208
NAME? WATSON
SCORE? 205
NAME? END
```

PROGRAM B

```
100 FILE#1="SCORES"
110 REM
120 PRINT "USE NAME=END TO STOP."
130 PRINT
140 PRINT "NAME";
150 INPUT N$
160 WHILE N$<>"END"
170     PRINT #1,N$
180     PRINT "SCORE";
190     INPUT S
200     PRINT#1,S
210     PRINT "NAME";
220 NEXT    (or WEND)
230 RESTORE#1
240 END
RUN

USE NAME=END TO STOP.

NAME? NICKLAUS
SCORE? 206
NAME? MILLER
SCORE? 208
NAME? WATSON
SCORE? 205
NAME? END
```

In each program, line 100 designates a file with ordinal 1 and name SCORES. (The keywords FOR OUTPUT in the OPEN statement are required only on some BASIC systems.)

Each time an INPUT statement is executed, we type a name or a score as shown in the display produced when the program was run. The PRINT# statements in lines 170 and

200 transmit these values to file 1 (that is, to the file SCORES), rather than to the screen or printer. When a PRINT# statement transmits a value to a file, we say that it *writes* the value or that the value is *written*.

The statement CLOSE 1 in line 230 (Program A) terminates any communication between the program and the file SCORES. It also ensures that the files SCORES will be saved for later use. Any files used in a program should be closed before the run terminates.

The statement RESTORE#1 in line 230 (Program B) restores the file pointer to the beginning of the file before program execution terminates. The reasons for including this final RESTORE# statement differ for different systems. Although it is not always required, it is a good (and safe) policy to restore all files with the RESTORE# statement just before the program run terminates.

■
□ **REMARK**

If your system uses the FILE# statement, you may have to type a command such as SAVE,SCORES, or REPLACE,SCORES if you wish to preserve the data file for later use.

In the preceding example, each time either of the statements PRINT#1,N$ or PRINT#1,S is executed, a single value is transmitted to the file SCORES. Moreover, since these two PRINT# statements do not have a final semicolon or comma, each also transmits a RETURN character to the output file. Following is a schematic representation of the six values stored in the file:

NICKLAUS	↻	206	↻	MILLER	↻	208	↻	WATSON	↻	205	· · ·

It is customary to visualize this file as containing the six distinct lines

```
NICKLAUS
 206
MILLER
 208
WATSON
 205
```

Note that we have included a blank in front of each numerical value. The PRINT# statement writes exactly the same information on a file as would be displayed if PRINT were used. If you replace lines 170 and 200 of the program in Example 2 with the single line

```
200 PRINT#1,N$;S
```

the program would create file SCORES with these three lines:

```
NICKLAUS 206
MILLER 208
WATSON 205
```

If the intent is to save the file for later printing, you may want this form, but if the file is intended only as an input file, you may find it inconvenient. For instance, if SCORES has this form, the statement

```
INPUT#1,N$
```

will give

```
N$="NICKLAUS 206"
```

and you will have to use string functions as explained in Chapter 13 to separate the string NICKLAUS from the number 206.

As illustrated in the foregoing discussion, special care must be taken when using PRINT# to create files that will be used as input files. In particular, INPUT# statements obtain values from the lines of a file in exactly the same way that ordinary INPUT statements obtain values from lines typed at the keyboard. Thus, if two or more values on one line of a file are to be read into distinct variables by an INPUT# statement, the values must be separated by commas. To write the values of the variables A$ and S on one line of file 1, you would use the statement

```
PRINT#1,N$;",";S
```

That is, the comma is actually written on the file. When the file is used later as an input file, the computer recognizes the comma as separating two distinct input values.

If you modify the program in Example 2 by replacing the lines

```
170 PRINT#1,N$
200 PRINT#1,S
```

with the single line

```
200 PRINT#1,N$;",";S
```

the output file SCORES will consist of three distinct lines, as follows:

```
NICKLAUS, 206
MILLER, 208
WATSON, 205
```

Any program that uses this file as an input file should use INPUT# statements that are consistent with this data structure. The statement INPUT#1,N$,S would be appropriate.

Note the use of semicolons in the statement

```
PRINT#1,N$;",";S
```

When using a PRINT# statement to direct the output to a file that will be used later as an input file, the usual practice is to use semicolons, not commas, to separate any variables and constants included in the PRINT# statement. On some BASIC systems you *must* use semicolons.

CAUTION

If PRINT# is used to write a string that contains a comma to a file and if the file is used later as an input file, the computer will no longer recognize the comma as part of the string. Rather, it will recognize it as separating two distinct input values. For example, the programming lines

```
50 LET X$="NICKLAUS,JACK"
60 PRINT#1,X$
```

will create one line of a file containing

```
NICKLAUS,JACK
```

with the comma having become a separator rather than a part of the string. To read this line with the INPUT# statement, you can use

```
INPUT#1,X$,Y$
```

but not

```
INPUT#1,X$
```

The next example illustrates the use of commas in input files.

EXAMPLE 3   **Here is a program to create a short file and then read it.**

```
100 REM ****************************************
110 REM * CREATE FILE CITIES FROM DATA LINES. *
120 REM ****************************************
130 REM
140 OPEN "CITIES" FOR OUTPUT AS FILE 1    (or FILE#1="CITIES")
150 READ COUNT
```

```
160 FOR C=1 TO COUNT
170    READ CITY$,STATE$,ZIP$
180    PRINT#1,CITY$;",";STATE$;",";ZIP$
190 NEXT C
200 REM
210 REM **************************
220 REM * READ AND DISPLAY DATA  *
230 REM * STORED IN FILE CITIES. *
240 REM **************************
250 REM
260 CLOSE 1                               (or RESTORE#1)
270 OPEN "CITIES" FOR INPUT AS FILE 1     (not needed with FILE#)
280 FOR C=1 TO COUNT
290    INPUT#1,CITY$,STATE$,ZIP$
300    PRINT CITY$;", ";STATE$;" ";ZIP$
310 NEXT C
320 CLOSE 1                               (or RESTORE#1)
500 REM *****************
510 REM *  D   A   T   A  *
520 REM *****************
530 DATA 4
540 DATA MONTEREY,CA,93940
550 DATA BRIDGEWATER,MA,02324
560 DATA AUSTIN,TX,78731
570 DATA JOHNSON CITY,TN,37601
999 END
RUN

MONTEREY, CA 93940
BRIDGEWATER, MA 02324
AUSTIN, TX 78731
JOHNSON CITY, TN 37601
```

The action of the first program segment (lines 140–190) is as follows. Line 140 designates the ordinal number 1 for the file CITIES that is to be created. Then on each pass through the FOR loop, line 170 reads values from the DATA statements into the variables CITY\$, STATE\$, and ZIP\$, and line 180 transmits these values with separating commas to the output file CITIES. After execution of this program segment, the contents of file CITIES will be as follows:

```
MONTEREY,CA,93940
BRIDGEWATER,MA,02324
AUSTIN,TX,78731
JOHNSON CITY,TN,37601
```

The action of the second program segment (lines 260–320) is as follows. Lines 270 and 280 reposition the file CITIES so that its data can be accessed from the beginning. (On systems that use the FILE# statement, RESTORE#1 is all that is needed.) Then on each pass through the FOR loop, line 290 reads values from the file CITIES into the variables CITY\$, STATE\$, and ZIP\$, and line 300 displays them as shown in the output.

■ **REMARK 1** In some versions of BASIC, the awkward situation with commas in files can be avoided by using WRITE# instead of PRINT#. In Microsoft BASIC, the WRITE# statement automatically encloses all strings in quotation marks and inserts commas between output values. In versions of BASIC on Cyber computers, WRITE# writes data on a file in a compact binary form that uses neither commas nor RETURN characters as data separators. The data in such a binary file are stored as a single list of values and are read by using READ# (not INPUT#) in the same way that the ordinary READ statement reads values from the data list included in DATA statements.

■ **REMARK 2** If you change line 180 of the program to

```
180 PRINT#1,ZIP$;STATE$;CITY$
```

the data in the file CITIES will be organized as follows:

```
93940CAMONTEREY
02324MABRIDGEWATER
78731TXAUSTIN
37601TNJOHNSON CITY
```

Note that each zip code occupies positions 1–5, each state code appears in positions 6 and 7, and each city name begins in position 8. With this organization of file CITIES, you can use string functions to read the data. If your version of BASIC allows the LEFT$ and MID$ function, you can replace line 290 with these four lines:

```
290 INPUT#1,LINE$
292 LET ZIP$=LEFT$(LINE$,5)
294 LET STATE$=MID$(LINE$,6,2)
296 LET CITY$=MID$(LINE$,8)
```

If your system uses string qualifiers, you can use

```
290 INPUT#1,LINE$
292 LET ZIP$=LINE$(1:5)
294 LET STATE$=LINE$(6:7)
296 LET CITY$=LINE$(8:LEN(LINE$))
```

■ **REMARK 3** It is important to understand how the computer obtains data from files that contain commas. We do not suggest, however, that you always use commas to separate values stored in files. In Remark 2, we show how string functions can be used to avoid writing commas in files. If you are a beginning programmer, you may wish to avoid commas in files by using PRINT# and INPUT# statements that transmit only single values to and from files and by being sure never to include commas in string output values. To do this for the program shown, simply replace line 180 with

```
180 PRINT#1,CITY$
182 PRINT#1,STATE$
184 PRINT#1,ZIP$
```

and line 290 with

```
290 INPUT#1,CITY$
292 INPUT#1,STATE$
294 INPUT#1,ZIP$
```

The program will produce exactly the same output, but the file CITIES will be organized as follows:

```
MONTEREY
CA
93940
BRIDGEWATER
MA
02324
AUSTIN
TX
78731
JOHNSON CITY
TN
37061
```

□

■ 15.2 Detecting the End of a Sequential File

Each file contains a special **end-of-file mark** following its last datum. While reading data from a file, the computer senses the end-of-file mark. Any attempt to read information beyond this end-of-file mark results in an error diagnostic, and program execution terminates. Each version of BASIC, however, provides a way to avoid such fatal run-time errors. In this section we describe the most common BASIC statements and functions that are used for this purpose.

The End-of-File Functions EOF and END#

If file **n** is being used as an input file, the expression EOF(**n**) (END **n** with some versions of BASIC) is true if the end-of-file mark on file **n** has been reached; otherwise it is false. Thus, the statement

>   IF EOF(n) THEN **ln**

will transfer control to line number **ln,** but only if the end-of-file mark has been reached. Similarly, the statement

>   WHILE NOT EOF(1)

will cause looping to continue until EOF(1) is true—that is, until the end of the file has been reached.

EXAMPLE 4   **Here is a program segment to display the contents of a file named BIRTHS that contains these three lines:**

```
SUE COREY,2,4,90
ADAM JONES,2,15,90
CANDY FOBES,2,29,90

100 OPEN "BIRTHS" FOR OUTPUT AS FILE 1      (or FILE#1="BIRTHS")
110 LET C=0
120 WHILE NOT EOF(1)
130    INPUT#1,N$,M,D,Y
140    PRINT N$,M;"/";D;"/";Y
150    LET C=C+1
160 NEXT   (or WEND)
170 CLOSE 1                                 (or RESTORE#1)
180 PRINT
190 PRINT "THERE WERE";C;"BIRTHS THIS MONTH."
```

Output:

```
SUE COREY     2 / 4 / 90
ADAM JONES    2 / 15 / 90
CANDY FOBES   2 / 29 / 90

THERE WERE 3 BIRTHS THIS MONTH.
```

Line 120 checks whether more data are available on file 1. If the end of file mark has not been reached, NOT EOF(1) is true and the WHILE loop is entered. On each pass through this loop, lines 130 and 140 read and display one line of the file and line 150 increases the name count C by 1. After the last line of file BIRTHS has been processed by lines 130–150, the WHILE condition NOT EOF(1) is false; that is, the end of file mark has been sensed. The WHILE statement then transfers control out of the loop to line 170 and program execution continues from that point.

☐

The ON ERROR GOTO Statement

This BASIC statement is used to transfer control to a specified line number *after* a run-time error has occurred. As illustrated in Example 4, the EOF and END# functions are used to *avoid* a run-time error.

The two BASIC statements

>   ON ERROR GOTO **ln₁**
>   RESUME **ln₂**

have the following effect. Once the ON ERROR statement is executed, any fatal error—that is, any error that would otherwise cause can error message and halt program execution—will cause an immediate transfer to line **ln₁.** The statements beginning at line **ln₁** will be executed and when the RESUME statement is encountered, program execution will resume at line **ln₂.**

EXAMPLE 5   **Here is a program to display the contents of the file BIRTHS shown in Example 4.**

```
1 ON ERROR GOTO 1000
100 OPEN "BIRTHS" FOR OUTPUT AS FILE 1   (or FILE#1="BIRTHS")
110 LET C=0
120     INPUT#1,N$,M,D,Y
130     PRINT N$,M;"/";D;"/";Y
140     LET C=C+1
150 GOTO 120
160 CLOSE 1                              (or RESTORE#1)
170 PRINT
180 PRINT "THERE WERE";C;"BIRTHS THIS MONTH."
190 GOTO 1020
1000 REM *** HANDLE END-OF-FILE ERROR ***
1010 RESUME 160
1020 END
RUN

SUE COREY     2 / 4 / 90
ADAM JONES    2 / 15 / 90
CANDY FOBES   2 / 29 / 90
THERE WERE 3 BIRTHS THIS MONTH.
```

The loop in lines 120–150 looks like an infinite loop, but on the fourth pass through this loop the INPUT# statement attempts to read data beyond the end-of-file mark. Because of the ON ERROR GOTO statement, this run-time error causes control to pass to line 1000. The RESUME statement in line 1010 returns to line 160, and the final tally is displayed.

■ **REMARK 1**   To improve program readability, you should include a comment such as

```
115 REM LOOP UNTIL NO MORE DATA.
```

■ **REMARK 2**   Note the use of line 190 to transfer control around the error-handling lines 1000–1010. If
□   you omit line 190, the unintended execution of the RESUME statement will cause an error or an infinite loop, depending on the system being used.

   The method of handling errors illustrated in Example 5 is called **error trapping.** The error caused by the INPUT# statement is *trapped* by the computer's error-trapping facility. Error trapping is enabled (turned on) by the ON ERROR GOTO statement, is disabled (turned off) when an otherwise fatal run-time error occurs, and is enabled again when a RESUME statement is encountered.
   If you use the statements

ON ERROR GOTO **ln₁**
RESUME **ln₂**

to trap an error, the program statements from line **ln₁** up to the RESUME statement are used to handle the error—that is, to take any corrective action that is needed so that program execution can continue from line **ln₂**. These error-handling statements must contain no errors—the effect of the ON ERROR GOTO statement is canceled when the run-time error occurs and is not restored until the RESUME statement is encountered. Because of this, the programming lines that handle errors should be kept to a minimum. In Example 5, RESUME 160 was the only error-handling statement needed. We insert a REM statement

```
1000 REM *** HANDLE END-OF-FILE ERROR ***
1010 RESUME 160
```

to improve program readability.
   Any fatal run-time error can be trapped—not just those caused by attempts to read beyond the end of a file. A common practice, however, is to use the ON ERROR GOTO statement to trap only those errors that cannot conveniently be handled in another way. Thus, if your version of BASIC allows the end-of-file function EOF or the end-of-file specifier END#, you would use it to avoid the end-of-file error entirely. If your system

does not provide a way to detect when the end-of-file mark has been reached, you must allow the error to occur and handle it by using the ON ERROR GOTO statement.

Another error that you may have to trap involves the OPEN statement. If you use the lines

```
100 PRINT "ENTER NAME OF THE FILE";
110 INPUT F$
120 OPEN F$ FOR INPUT AS FILE 1
```

to allow the user to enter the name of an input file, there is no guarantee that the user will type the name of a file that actually exists. If F$ is not the name of an existing file, the OPEN statement will cause a fatal run-time error that must be handled by using the ON ERROR GOTO statement.

If F$ is an admissible file name, but not the name of an existing file, the error described in the preceding paragraph occurs only for OPEN statements that contain the keywords FOR INPUT. Other statements that open files, such as

```
OPEN F$ FOR OUTPUT AS FILE 1
OPEN F$ AS FILE 1
FILE#1=F$
```

will simply create an empty file named F$.

When writing a program that will trap errors, the common practice is to place the ON ERROR GOTO statement near the beginning of programs. We used

> 1 ON ERROR GOTO **ln**

Then, beginning at line **ln,** you would write program segments to handle all errors that might occur and end each of these program segments with an appropriate RESUME statement. To assist you in handling errors, BASIC provides two special error-handling functions:

ERL   gives the line number that caused the error. (Cyber computers use ESL.)

ERR   gives a number that indicates the type of the error. These error type numbers differ from system to system. (Cyber computers use ESM.)

The next example illustrates how a single program can handle several errors.

EXAMPLE 6   **Here is a partial program that handles more than one otherwise fatal run-time error. On Cyber computers, use ESL and ESM for ERL and ERR, respectively.**

```
  1 ON ERROR GOTO 1000
100 OPEN "NUMBERS" FOR INPUT AS FILE 1   (or FILE#1="NUMBERS")
110 DIM A(50)
120 LET K=0
130    LET K=K+1
140    INPUT#1,X
150    LET A(K)=X
160 GOTO 130
170 (program continuation)
     .
     .
     .
990 GOTO 2000
1000 IF ERL=140 THEN RESUME 170
1010 IF ERL<>150 THEN 1040
1020    PRINT "FILE TOO LARGE FOR THIS PROGRAM."
1030    GOTO 2000
1040 PRINT "UNEXPECTED ERROR AT LINE";ERL
1050 PRINT "ERROR TYPE IS";ERR
2000 END
```

Line 140 will cause an error when the INPUT# statement attempts to read beyond the end-of-file mark. This error transfers control to line 1000 with ERL = 140. The statement RESUME 170 in line 1000 handles the error by causing program execution to continue at line 170.

Line 150 will cause an error if the file contains more than 50 numbers. The DIM statement specifies 50 as the largest subscript for array A. This error transfers control to line 1000 with ERL = 150. Since the IF conditions in lines 1000 and 1010 are false, control passes to line 1020, which displays the message

```
FILE TOO LARGE FOR THIS PROGRAM.
```

Line 1030 then causes a jump to the END statement.

Any other fatal run-time error will transfer control to line 1000, with ERL equal to the line number that caused the error. Since ERL will not be 140 or 150, control will pass to line 1040, and the following display will be produced:

UNEXPECTED ERROR AT LINE **ln**
ERROR TYPE IS **et**

where **ln** denotes the line number that caused the error and **et** denotes the number your computer associates with the error type.

■ **REMARK 1**   If a file with the name NUMBERS does not exist, the statement

```
100 OPEN "NUMBERS" FOR INPUT AS FILE 1
```

will cause an error with ERL = 100, and the error-handling lines 1000–1050 will cause the display

```
UNEXPECTED ERROR AT LINE 100
ERROR TYPE IS et
```

To cause a more informative error message, you can insert these lines:

```
1002 IF ERL<>100 THEN 1010
1004    PRINT "THIS PROGRAM NEEDS A FILE NAMED NUMBERS."
1006    PRINT "IT CAN'T BE FOUND."
1008    GOTO 2000
```

■ **REMARK 2**   If you replace the two lines

```
140    INPUT#1,X
150    LET A(K)=X
```

with the single line

```
140    INPUT#1,A(K)
```

both the *end-of-file error* and the *subscript-out-of-range error* can occur in line 140. To handle two or more errors that can occur in the same programming line, you will need to know what numbers your system uses for the error-type function ERR. For instance, if your computer uses ERR = 11 for the end-of-file error, you can handle this error by using

```
IF ERL=140 AND ERR=11 THEN RESUME 170
```

■ **REMARK 3**   Special care should be taken in writing the error-handling section of a program. It is part of the program and should be readable and easily modified to handle previously unexpected errors, just as the rest of the program should be readable and easily modified. Use REM statements just as you would elsewhere in the program.

□

EXAMPLE 7   **Here is a program that can be used to display the contents of any sequential file.**

Instead of using INPUT#1 to read data from file 1, we will use

```
LINPUT#1,A$
```

This statement assigns an entire input line, including any commas, to the string variable A\$. Your version of BASIC may require one of the following equivalent statements:

```
LINE INPUT#1,A$
INPUT LINE#1,A$
```

THE
PROGRAM

```
1 ON ERROR GOTO 1000
100 PRINT "ENTER FILE NAME";
110 INPUT F$
120 OPEN F$ FOR INPUT AS FILE 1      (or FILE#1=F$)
130 PRINT
140 PRINT "CONTENTS OF FILE ";F$;":"
150 REM LOOP UNTIL END OF FILE.
160     LINPUT#1,A$
170     PRINT A$
180 GOTO 160
190 REM FILE HAS BEEN DISPLAYED.
200 CLOSE 1                           (or RESTORE#1)
210 GOTO 2000
1000 REM ****** ERROR HANDLING SECTION *******
1010 IF ERL<>120 THEN 1070
1020 REM --- HANDLE NON-EXISTENT FILE ---
1030     PRINT "I CAN'T FIND ";F$
1040     PRINT "ANOTHER FILE (Y OR N)";
1050     INPUT C$
1060     IF C$="Y" THEN RESUME 100 ELSE GOTO 2000
1070 REM --- HANDLE END-OF-FILE ERROR ---
1080     IF ERL=160 THEN RESUME 200
1090 REM --- HANDLE UNEXPECTED ERRORS ---
1100     PRINT "ERROR IN LINE";ERL
1110     PRINT "ERROR TYPE IS";ERR
2000 END
```

Line 1 specifies that any fatal run-time error will cause a transfer to line 1000. If the user enters a nonexistent file name for F$, the statement

```
OPEN F$ FOR INPUT AS FILE 1
```

in line 120 causes an error that transfers control to line 1000 with ERL = 120. Lines 1020–1060 handle this error. Note that the user is allowed to try another file name or to halt program execution by typing Y or N for C$ in line 1050. Without the option of halting program execution, the user would have to keep typing file names until an existing file name were typed. The only other way out of the program would be to stop it manually; but this should never be required of a user.

■ **REMARK 1**   This program traps the end-of-file error caused by the LINPUT# statement in line 160. As we mentioned previously, if your system allows the end-of-file function EOF(1) or the end-of-file specifier END#1, you should use it to *avoid* rather than *trap* this end-of-file error.

■ **REMARK 2**   On some BASIC systems, the statement

```
LINPUT#1,A$
```

will assign an entire input line to A$ and also include return and line feed characters as the last two characters of A$. If your version of BASIC does this, the program will display the contents of file F$ on alternating lines. To correct this, simply place a semicolon at the end of line 170:

□

```
170     PRINT A$;
```

The contents of a data file created as described in this chapter are stored as a sequence of BCD *(binary coded decimal)* characters. This means that a numerical value such as 38 is stored as two separate codes, one for 3 and one for 8, and not as the binary number representation (100110) of the number 38. Similarly, the information "SAM 31.7" is stored as a sequence of eight code numbers, one for each of the characters "S", "A", "M", " ", "3", "1", ".", and "7". Such files are referred to as BCD files or *text* files—text because their contents are stored as a sequence of characters.

As noted at the outset of this chapter, the files considered in this book are called *sequential files* because their contents are ordered in sequence; that is, there is a first entry, a second entry, a third, and so on. When reading from or writing to a sequential file, the following rules apply:

1. Data in a sequential file are accessed in order. Thus, to read a particular entry in the file, all entries preceding it must be read first, even though they may not be needed.
2. To modify an existing sequential file by changing values in the file, create a new copy of the entire file containing whatever changes are desired. The modification of existing files is referred to as *file maintenance* and is the subject of Section 15.4.
3. Some systems allow you to add data at the end of an existing sequential file. The common practice, however, is to make a new copy of any file whose contents are to be changed in any way.

■ 15.3 Problems

1. Here is a program to create a file GRADES (for systems that use EOF or END#):

```
100 OPEN "GRADES" FOR OUTPUT AS FILE 1      (or FILE#1="GRADES")
110 READ A$,N1,N2
120 WHILE A$<>"X"
130     PRINT#1,A$;",";N1;",";N2
140     READ A$,N1,N2
150 NEXT  (or WEND)
160 CLOSE 1                                 (or RESTORE#1)
300 DATA JOAN,80,90
310 DATA SAM,100,80
320 DATA GREG,80,40
330 DATA MARY,70,30
340 DATA MARK,50,90
350 DATA X,0,0
999 END
```

Show the output of each program in parts (a) and (b).

a.
```
10 OPEN "GRADES" FOR INPUT AS FILE 1     (or FILE#1="GRADES")
20 WHILE NOT EOF (1)
30     INPUT#1,B$,A,B
40     IF A>B THEN PRINT B$
50 NEXT (or WEND)
60 CLOSE 1                                (or RESTORE#1)
70 END
```

b.
```
10 OPEN "GRADES" FOR INPUT AS FILE 2     (or FILE#2="GRADES")
20 LET P$="PASS"
30 LET F$="FAIL"
40 WHILE NOT EOF(2)
50     INPUT#2,N$,X,Y
60     LET A=(X+2*Y)/3
70     IF A>65 THEN PRINT N$,P$ ELSE PRINT N$,F$
80 NEXT (or WEND)
90 CLOSE 2                                (or RESTORE#2)
99 END
```

2. Here is a program to create a file COMM (for systems that use ON ERROR GO):

```
100 OPEN "COMM" FOR OUTPUT AS FILE 1      (or FILE#1="COMM")
110 READ N$,S,Q
120 WHILE N$<>"XXX"
130     PRINT#1,N$;",";S;",";Q
140     READ N$,S,Q
150 NEXT (or WEND)
160 CLOSE 1                               (or RESTORE#1)
300 DATA J.D.SLOANE,13000,10000
310 DATA R.M.PETERS,5000,5000
320 DATA A.B.CARTER,7400,5000
330 DATA I.O.ULSTER,12000,10000
340 DATA XXX,0,0
999 END
```

Show the output of each program in parts (a) and (b).

a.
```
10 OPEN "COMM" FOR INPUT AS FILE 1        (or FILE#1="COMM")
20 ON ERROR GOTO 90
30     INPUT#1,N$,S,Q
40     IF S<=Q THEN 30
50     PRINT N$
60     PRINT "EXCESS: ";S-Q
70     PRINT
80 GOTO 30
90 CLOSE 1                                (or RESTORE#1)
99 END
```

b.
```
10 OPEN "COMM" FOR INPUT AS FILE 2        (or FILE#2="COMM")
20 ON ERROR GOTO 90
30     LET C=0
40     INPUT#2,A$,S,Q
50     IF S>Q THEN C=.10*(S-Q)
60     LET W=265+C
70     PRINT A$,W
80 GOTO 30
90 CLOSE 2                                (or RESTORE#2)
99 END
```

In Problems 3–24, write a program for each task specified.

3. Create a file named WORDS containing whatever English words are typed at the keyboard. The file is to contain one word per line. After WORDS has been created, display its contents, three words per line. The file is to be used as an input file for Problems 4 and 5.

4. Given the file WORDS described in Problem 3, display all words beginning with a letter A through M, and follow this list by two counts—a count of how many words are in the file and a count of how many words were displayed.

5. Given the file WORDS described in Problem 3, create two files—one containing all words beginning with a letter A through M and the other containing the remaining words. Use appropriate names for the two files. After the two new files have been created, display their contents with appropriate titles.

6. Create a file NAMES containing up to 50 names typed at the keyboard. If a name is typed a second time, display an appropriate message but do not store the name twice. If at any time LIST is typed, display all names entered to that point. If END is typed, halt program execution. (*Suggestion:* Input names into an array and create the file NAMES only after the user types END.)

7. Create two files named ALPHA and BETA. ALPHA is to contain all numbers from 1 to 200 that are multiples of either 2, 3, 5, or 7. The rest of the numbers from 1 to 200 go in file BETA. After the files have been created, display their contents with appropriate titles.

8. Create and display two files as in Problem 7. This time, however, include a first entry in each file telling how many numbers it contains.

9. The following table describes an investor's stock portfolio. Create a file STOCKS that contains this information. The file STOCKS is to be used as an input file in Problems 10–12.

Name of stock	Number of shares	Last week's closing price	Current week's closing price
STERLING DRUG	800	16.50	16.125
DATA GENERAL	500	56.25	57.50
OWEN ILLINOIS	1200	22.50	21.50
MATTEL INC	1000	10.75	11.125
ABBOTT LAB	2000	33.75	34.75
FED NATL MTG	2500	17.75	17.25
IC GEN	250	43.125	43.625
ALO SYSTEMS	550	18.50	18.25

10. Produce a report displaying precisely the information contained in the file STOCKS. Be sure to label each column and to give the report a title.

11. Produce a five-column report with the first four columns as in Problem 10 and a fifth column showing the percentage increase or decrease for each security.

12. Produce a four-column report showing the stock name, the equity at the close of business last week, the equity this week, and the dollar change in equity. End the report with a message showing the total net gain or loss for the week.

13. Create a file named LIBEL containing the following information about employees of the Libel Insurance Company. The file LIBEL is to be used as an input file in Problems 14–19.

ID	Sex	Age	Years of service	Annual salary
012-24-2735	M	47	13	25,200.00
024-18-2980	F	33	6	19,300.00
018-26-3865	F	41	15	28,900.00
035-14-4222	M	22	2	16,400.00
026-21-4740	M	59	7	24,200.00
024-25-5200	F	25	3	18,000.00
018-17-5803	M	33	13	26,500.00
016-24-7242	F	28	4	18,400.00
021-18-7341	M	68	30	30,500.00
021-25-8004	M	35	6	19,300.00
031-42-9327	F	21	3	14,200.00

14. Produce a five-column report with a title and appropriate column headings displaying the employee information contained in the file LIBEL. (The sex column is to contain MALE or FEMALE, not M or F.)

15. Produce two reports showing the employee information contained in LIBEL by sex. Give each report a title and four appropriately labeled columns.

16. Produce a report showing the ID numbers, years of service, and salaries of all employees who have been with the firm for more than 5 years.

17. Produce a two-column report showing ID numbers and annual salaries of all employees whose annual salary exceeds $15,000. In addition to column headings, be sure the report has an appropriate title.

18. Produce a two-column report as described in Problem 17 for all employees whose annual salaries exceed the average annual salary of all Libel employees. Following the report, display the total annual salary earned by these employees. The title of the report should include the average salary of all Libel employees. (Do not read the file contents into arrays. Rather, read through the file to determine the total annual salary and average annual salary figures; then read the file a second time to produce the report.)

19. Write a menu-driven program to perform some or all of the tasks specified in Problems 14–18.

20. Create a file INVTRY containing the following inventory data. The file INVTRY is to be used as an input file in Problems 21–24.

Item code	Item type	Units on hand	Average cost per unit	Sales price per unit
ITEM 1	A	20500	1.55	1.95
ITEM 2	A	54000	0.59	0.74
ITEM 3	B	8250	3.40	4.10
ITEM 4	B	4000	5.23	6.75
ITEM 5	A	15000	0.60	0.75
ITEM 6	A	10500	1.05	1.35
ITEM 7	B	6000	7.45	9.89
ITEM 8	B	7500	5.10	5.43
ITEM 9	B	15500	3.10	4.10

21. Produce a five-column report displaying exactly the information in INVTRY.
22. Produce two separate reports, the first displaying the given information for type-A items and the second for type-B items.
23. Produce a five-column report showing the item code, the number of units on hand, and the total cost, total sales price, and total income these units represent (income = sales − cost). Conclude the report with a message showing the total cost, total sales price, and total income represented by the entire inventory.
24. Write a menu-driven program to perform some or all of the tasks specified in Problems 21–23.

■ 15.4 File Maintenance

Updating existing data files is a common programming application. In this section we give two examples illustrating this practice. The first involves updating a short simplified inventory file and the second a short personnel file. It should be remarked, however, that data files usually are not short and require rather complicated programs to maintain them. Our objective is simply to show that file maintenance is possible. A complete discussion of the many techniques used in file-maintenance programs is beyond the scope of this introductory book.

EXAMPLE 8   **A file update example.**

A file named INVTRY contains the following data:

```
A10010, 2000
A10011, 4450
C22960, 1060
D40240, 2300
X99220, 500
X99221, 650
Y88000, 1050
Y88001, 400
```

The first entry in each line denotes an item code, and the second entry gives the quantity on hand. Our task is to write a program to allow a user to update INVTRY to reflect all transactions since the last update.

Let's assume that the user must specify, for each item to be changed, the item code, the number of units shipped since the last update, and the number of units received since the last update. Thus the user might come to the computer armed with a list like this:

Item code	Shipped	Received
A10010	1200	1000
A10011	1000	550
D40240	1800	2000
Y88000	300	0

A person carrying out this task by hand might proceed as follows:

a. Read an item code.
b. Search the file INVTRY for this code, and change the units-on-hand figure as required.
c. If more changes are to be made, go to Step (a).
d. Have the updated copy of INVTRY typed.

This algorithm is not suitable for a BASIC program. Step (b) says to change a *single* number appearing in the file INVTRY, and this is not done when using sequential files. We will first input the data from INVTRY into two arrays and then make the necessary changes in these arrays. After this has been done for each item requiring a change, Step (d) will involve creating a new copy of INVTRY. Before rewriting this algorithm in a form suitable for a BASIC program, let's choose variable names:

$$\begin{aligned}
\text{CODES\$} &= \text{array of item codes from file INVTRY} \\
\text{UNITS} &= \text{corresponding array of quantities from INVTRY} \\
\text{ITEMCOUNT} &= \text{number of lines in the file INVTRY} \\
\text{X\$} &= \text{item code to be typed} \\
\text{S} &= \text{quantity shipped} \\
\text{R} &= \text{quantity received}
\end{aligned}$$

In the following algorithm we require the user to type END after all changes have been made.

THE ALGORITHM

a. Input arrays CODES$ and UNITS from the file INVTRY.
b. Enter an item code X$.
c. While X$ is not END do the following:
    c1. Search for subscript K with CODES$(K) = X$.
    c2. If X$ is not found display an appropriate message, otherwise input quantities S and R for X$ and change UNITS(K) to UNITS(K) + R − S.
    c3. Enter next item code X$.
d. Make a new copy of INVTRY.
e. Stop.

Step (a) is easily coded. We simply open INVTRY as an input file and use a loop to read its contents into arrays CODES$ and UNITS.

Step (c) is also easily coded. We will include the code for Steps (c1)–(c3) in a loop that terminates when the input value X$ is END. Writing code for Steps (c1)–(c3) is not new to us and is relatively straightforward.

Code for Step (d) is also straightforward. We will position the file pointer to the beginning of the file INVTRY and then write the contents of the arrays CODES$ and UNITS in the file.

■ REMARK

You may have to change EOF(1) in lines 220 and 260 to END#1. If your version of BASIC does not allow EOF or END#, you can make these changes:

```
105 ON ERROR GOTO 900
220 REM ABORT EXECUTION
290 LET ITEMCOUNT=ITEMCOUNT-1
660 GOTO 999
900 RESUME 290
```

THE PROGRAM

```
100 REM ------------ INVENTORY UPDATE PROGRAM --------------------
110 REM
120 REM          CODES$ = ARRAY OF ITEM CODES
130 REM           UNITS = ARRAY OF QUANTITIES
140 REM       ITEMCOUNT = NUMBER OF ITEMS
150 REM
160 REM ************************************************************
170 REM    INPUT ARRAYS CODES$ AND UNITS FROM FILE INVTRY.
180 REM
190 OPEN "INVTRY" FOR INPUT AS FILE 1      (or FILE#1="INVTRY")
200 DIM CODES$(50),UNITS(50)
210 LET ITEMCOUNT=0
220 WHILE NOT EOF(1) AND ITEMCOUNT<50
230     LET ITEMCOUNT=ITEMCOUNT+1
240     INPUT#1,CODES$(ITEMCOUNT),UNITS(ITEMCOUNT)
250 NEXT   (or WEND)
260 IF EOF(1) THEN 290
270     PRINT "INADEQUATE ARRAY DIMENSIONS - SEE PROGRAMMER."
280     GOTO 650
290 REM
300 REM ************************************************************
310 REM    GET KEYBOARD INPUT AND UPDATE ARRAYS CODES$ AND UNITS.
320 REM
```

```
330 PRINT "TYPE END FOR ITEM CODE WHEN DONE."
340 PRINT
350 PRINT "ITEM CODE";
360 INPUT X$                                    'Keyboard input
370 WHILE X$<>"END"
380    REM
390    LET K=1                                  'Search array
400    WHILE CODES$(K)<>X$ AND K<ITEMCOUNT      'CODES$ for
410       LET K=K+1                             'item X$.
420    NEXT   (or WEND)
430    IF X$=CODES$(K) THEN 460
440       PRINT X$;" IS NOT A CORRECT ITEM CODE."
450       GOTO 515
460    REM --- X$ IS ITEM K ---
470    PRINT "UNITS SHIPPED";
480    INPUT S                                  'Keyboard input
490    PRINT "UNITS RECEIVED";
500    INPUT R                                  'Keyboard input
510    LET UNITS(K)=UNITS(K)+R-S                'Update array.
515    PRINT
520    PRINT "ITEM CODE";
530    INPUT X$                                 'Keyboard input
540 NEXT   (or WEND)
550 REM
560 REM ***************************************
570 REM    MAKE A NEW COPY OF FILE INVTRY.
580 REM
590 CLOSE 1                                  (or RESTORE#1)
600 OPEN "INVTRY" FOR OUTPUT AS FILE 1       (Not needed with FILE#)
610 FOR K=1 TO ITEMCOUNT
620    PRINT#1,CODES$(K);",";UNITS(K)
630 NEXT K
640 PRINT "INVTRY IS UPDATED."
650 CLOSE 1                                  (OR RESTORE#1)
999 END
```

We ran this program, with file INVTRY as shown in the problem statement, and obtained the following screen display:

```
TYPE END FOR ITEM CODE WHEN DONE.

ITEM CODE? A10010
UNITS SHIPPED? 1200
UNITS RECEIVED? 1000

ITEM CODE? A10011
UNITS SHIPPED? 1000
UNITS RECEIVED? 550

ITEM CODE? D40241
D40241 IS NOT A CORRECT ITEM CODE.

ITEM CODE? D40240
UNITS SHIPPED? 1800
UNITS RECEIVED? 2000

ITEM CODE? Y88000
UNITS SHIPPED? 300
UNITS RECEIVED? 0

ITEM CODE? END
INVTRY IS UPDATED.
```

■ **REMARK**   The last output value INVTRY IS UPDATED. is intended to reassure us that the file has been correctly updated. To see that this is so, we displayed its contents by using the program shown in Example 7 of Section 15.2 and obtained the following display:

```
ENTER FILE NAME? INVTRY
CONTENTS OF FILE INVTRY:
```

```
A10010, 1800
A10011, 4000
C22960, 1060
D40240, 2500
X99220, 500
X99221, 650
Y88000, 750
Y88001, 400
```

Note that the file as shown in the problem statement has been modified to reflect the changes made by the current run of the program.

EXAMPLE 9

The ID numbers and names of all employees of the Land Foundry Company are stored on the personnel file EMPLOY. Let's write a program to allow a user to add new employees to this file.

The following short file shows how data are stored in the file (5 is a count of how many employees are included):

```
5
23501 JOHN F. AHEARN
00266 SARAH ANN FIEDLER
01234 THOMAS VAN HEBERLING
15151 AMY ARMSTRONG
62155 ARNOLD DRINKWATER
```

PROBLEM ANALYSIS

Input: Data stored in the file EMPLOY
New names and ID numbers typed at keyboard

Output: File EMPLOY updated as specified in the problem statement

Each ID number typed at the keyboard must be different from those already in use. Thus, this programming task involves a search—the uniqueness of new ID numbers must be verified. For this purpose, we'll read the contents of the file into an array (or arrays) so that an array, rather than a file, can be searched. The following short algorithm identifies the essential subtasks that must be performed:

THE ALGORITHM

 a. Read the contents of the file EMPLOY into an array (or arrays).
 b. Store new employee data typed at the keyboard in the array (or arrays).
 c. Create an updated copy of the file EMPLOY.

Noting that the file EMPLOY begins with a data count, we can refine Step (a) as follows:

 a1. Open the file EMPLOY.
 a2. Read the employee count.
 a3. Read the employee data into an array (or arrays).

As we have mentioned, the ID numbers assigned to new employees must be compared with those ID numbers already in use. To simplify making these comparisons, we'll keep a separate array of ID numbers. Thus, with the variable names

COUNT = number of employees
 INFO\$ = array containing all employee data
   ID\$ = array of ID numbers

we can open the file EMPLOY and then carry out Steps (a2) and (a3) as follows:

```
INPUT#1,COUNT
FOR K=1 TO COUNT
    INPUT#1,INFO$(K)
    LET ID$(K)=LEFT$(INFO$(K),5)     [or ID$(K)=INFO$(1:5)]
NEXT K
```

Step (b) of the original three-step algorithm involves typing a name and ID number for each new employee and storing this information in the arrays INFO$ and ID$. Let's refine Step (b) as follows:

b. For each new employee
    b1. Enter the employee's name N$.
    b2. Select an ID number I$ not yet used.
    b3. Add 1 to the employee count COUNT.
    b4. Store the new data in arrays INFO$ and ID$.

To code this refinement of Step (b), we'll first prompt the user for a new employee's name N$—the user will be instructed to type END to end the input session. For Step (b2), we'll prompt the user for an ID number I$ and then compare it with the ID numbers stored in array ID$ to ensure that it is not already in use. If it is in use, we'll reject it and ask for another. For Step (b3), we simply add 1 to COUNT. Step (b4) requires that we store the new employee information in arrays INFO$ and ID$. Thus, we will assign the new ID number I$ to ID$(COUNT) and, noting that entries in array INFO$ have the same form as lines of the file, we will assign INFO$(COUNT) as follows:

```
LET INFO$(COUNT)=I$+" "+N$
```

Coding Step (c) of the original three-step algorithm is routine. The entries in array INFO$ are formatted exactly as they must appear in the file; thus, we will position the file pointer at the beginning of the file, write the value of COUNT on the file, and then use a FOR loop to write the contents of array INFO$ on the file.

THE PROGRAM

```
100 REM PROGRAM TO UPDATE THE FILE 'EMPLOY'
110 REM
120 REM    COUNT = EMPLOYEE COUNT
130 REM    INFO$ = ARRAY CONTAINING ALL EMPLOYEE DATA
140 REM    ID$   = ARRAY OF ID NUMBERS
150 REM
160 REM ********************************************
170 REM READ AND STORE CONTENTS OF FILE 'EMPLOY'.
180 REM
190 DIM INFO$(100),ID$(100)
200 OPEN "EMPLOY" FOR INPUT AS FILE 1    (or FILE#1="EMPLOY")
210 INPUT#1,COUNT
220 IF COUNT<=100 THEN 250
230    PRINT "INADEQUATE ARRAY DIMENSIONS."
240    GOTO 690
250 FOR K=1 TO COUNT
260    INPUT#1,INFO$(K)
270    LET ID$(K)=LEFT$(INFO$(K),5)       [or ID$=INFO$=(1:5)]
280 NEXT K
290 REM
300 REM ********************************************
310 REM GET NEW EMPLOYEE DATA FROM KEYBOARD, STORE
320 REM IN ARRAYS INFO$ AND ID$, AND ADJUST COUNT.
330 REM
340 PRINT "NAME (TYPE END WHEN DONE)";
350 INPUT N$
360 WHILE N$<>"END" AND COUNT<100
370    PRINT "ID NUMBER";
380    PRINT I$
390    REM -- SEARCH ARRAY ID$ FOR I$. --
400    LET K=1
410    WHILE ID$<>I$ AND K<COUNT
420       LET K=K+1
430    NEXT (or WEND)
440    IF ID$(K)<>I$ THEN 480
450       PRINT I$;"IS ALREADY BEING USED."
460       PRINT "RE-ENTER NAME WITH ANOTHER ID."
470       GOTO 530
```

```
480     REM -- STORE NEW EMPLOYEE INFORMATION --
490     LET COUNT=COUNT+1
500     LET ID$(COUNT)=I$
510     LET INFO$(COUNT)=I$+" "+N$
520     REM -- GET NEXT NAME (OR 'END') --
530     PRINT
540     PRINT "NAME (TYPE END WHEN DONE)";
550     INPUT N$
560 NEXT   (or WEND)
570 IF N$<>"END" THEN PRINT "NO MORE ROOM - SEE PROGRAMMER."
580 REM
590 REM ***********************
600 REM UPDATE THE FILE 'EMPLOY'.
610 REM
620 CLOSE 1                               (or RESTORE#1)
630 OPEN "EMPLOY" FOR OUTPUT AS FILE 1  (not needed with FILE#1)
640 PRINT#1,COUNT
650 FOR K=1 TO COUNT
660     PRINT#1,INFO$(K)
670 NEXT K
680 PRINT "FILE EMPLOY IS UPDATED."
690 CLOSE 1                               (or RESTORE#1)
999 END
```

Here is a run of this program for the file EMPLOY shown in the problem statement:

```
RUN

NAME (TYPE END WHEN DONE)? HEATHER A. MANN
ID NUMBER? 63341

NAME (TYPE END WHEN DONE)? SUSAN JACKSON
ID NUMBER? 23501
23501 IS ALREADY BEING USED.
RE-ENTER NAME WITH ANOTHER ID.

NAME (TYPE END WHEN DONE)? SUSAN JACKSON
ID NUMBER? 23502

NAME (TYPE END WHEN DONE)? END
FILE EMPLOY IS UPDATED.
```

■ **REMARK 1**   We used the program in Example 7 of Section 15.2 to display the file EMPLOY and obtained the following display:

```
ENTER FILE NAME? EMPLOY
CONTENTS OF FILE EMPLOY:

 7
23501 JOHN F. AHEARN
00266 SARAH ANN FIEDLER
01234 THOMAS VAN HEBERLING
15151 AMY ARMSTRONG
62155 ARNOLD DRINKWATER
63341 HEATHER A. MANN
23502 SUSAN JACKSON
```

Note that the two new employees are included, and the employee count has been increased by 2.

■ **REMARK 2**   A simple, but important, improvement needs to be made in this program. There is no guarantee that the user will correctly enter five-digit ID numbers. If the user inadvertently types fewer or more than five digits, the program will continue to execute as if no error was made, but the updated file will not have the required form shown in the problem statement. Subsequent use of the file EMPLOY may produce incorrect results. To correct the program, simply compare LEN(I$) with 5 as soon as I$ is input, and reject I$ if its length isn't 5.

■ 15.5 Problems

In Problems 1–16, write a program for each task specified.

1. The Hollis Investment Company maintains a file EMPLOY containing the name, age, years of service, and monthly salary of salaried employees. Include the following information in DATA lines for a program to create the file EMPLOY. The file will be used as an input file in Problems 2–5.

Name	Age	Years of service	Monthly salary
Murray George	53	21	2100.00
Ritchie Albert	41	13	1850.00
Galvin Fred	62	35	2475.00
Cummings Barbara	37	16	1675.00
Gieseler Norma	41	20	2200.00
Hughes Bette	52	18	2050.00
Meland Ralph	29	5	1550.00
Tibeau Betty	30	7	1340.00

2. A 5% across-the-board salary increase has been negotiated for all Hollis employees. Write a program to update the file EMPLOY to reflect this increase.

3. Write a program to remove an employee from the file or to add new employees. Use your program to delete Fred Galvin and add the following:

```
BING MELINDA 23 0 1200
DEREK SUSAN  24 0 1800
```

Suggestion: If you use an array to store the names, do not actually delete Fred Galvin. Rather, store a special value such as DELETE in place of the name. Then when you make an updated copy of the file EMPLOY, simply omit employees stored as DELETE.

4. Using the file EMPLOY as an input file, create a file EMPLOY1 that contains precisely the information in EMPLOY but with the names in alphabetical order. After EMPLOY1 has been created, display its contents. (*Suggestion:* Read the file contents into four arrays, sort the arrays so that the names are in alphabetical order, and then create EMPLOY1.)

5. Create a file EMPLOY2 that contains the same information as EMPLOY, but with monthly salaries in descending order. After EMPLOY2 has been created, display its contents.

6. A manufacturing company sends a package consisting of eight new products to each of ten families and asks each family to rate each product on the following scale:

    0 = poor   1 = fair   2 = good   3 = very good   4 = excellent

Here are the results in tabular form:

		1	2	3	4	5	6	7	8	9	10
						Family number					
	1	0	1	1	2	1	2	2	1	0	1
	2	2	3	3	0	3	2	2	3	4	1
	3	1	3	4	4	4	1	4	2	3	2
Product number	4	3	4	2	4	3	1	3	4	2	4
	5	0	1	3	2	2	2	1	3	0	1
	6	4	4	4	3	2	1	4	4	1	1
	7	1	3	1	3	2	4	1	4	3	4
	8	2	2	3	4	2	2	3	4	2	3

Create a file RATE containing the information in this table. Then use this file to produce a two-column report showing the product numbers and the average rating for each product. (The file RATE will be used as an input file in Problems 7–9.)

7. An error in the transcription of the numbers in the survey is discovered. The correct results for Families 1 and 7 are as follows:

Family 1	3	2	4	2	2	4	1	3
Family 7	2	3	4	4	2	4	3	2

Write a program to allow the user to change the eight ratings for any family. Use your program to correct the ratings for Family 1 and Family 7.

8. Use the file RATE to produce a report as in Problem 6. However, have the average ratings appear from smallest to largest.

9. Use the file RATE to produce a two-column report as follows: The first column is to give the product numbers receiving at least six ratings of 3 or better and the second column is to give the number of these ratings obtained.

10. The Sevard Company maintains files SST and WEEKLY. Create these two files so that they contain the following information. The files are to be used as input files in Problems 11–13.

File SST

Employee ID number	Year-to-date income	Hourly rate
024–25–5200	18240.00	12.00
018–26–2980	16800.00	10.50
021–18–7341	21150.50	14.25
031–42–9327	25600.00	16.00
035–14–4222	47250.00	25.00
026–21–1274	44980.00	23.00

File WEEKLY

Employee ID number	This week's hours
024–25–5200	42
018–26–2980	36
021–18–7341	32
031–42–9327	52
035–14–4222	50
026–21–1274	48

11. A Social Security tax deduction of 7.51% is taken on the first $45,000 earned by an employee. Once this amount is reached, no further deduction is made. Using the files SST and WEEKLY, produce a report giving the ID number, the current week's gross pay, and the current week's Social Security deduction for each employee.

12. Modify the program written for Problem 11 to update the year-to-date income in the file SST.

13. Using the files SST and WEEKLY, display a list of the ID numbers of all employees who have satisfied the Social Security tax requirement for the current year. With each ID number, give the year-to-date income figure.

14. Write a program to allow the user to create a mailing list file by typing its contents at the keyboard. Organize the file so that each entry occupies six lines as follows:

Line 1	Last Name
Line 2	First Name and Middle Initial
Line 3	Street Address
Line 4	City or Town
Line 5	State
Line 6	Zip Code

After the file has been created, display its contents by using a standard three-line address format.

15. Write a menu-driven program to allow the user to create a mailing list file as described in Problem 14 and also to maintain the file by specifying changes at the keyboard. Since the user can modify the mailing list, you should store all mailing list entries in arrays (for instance, six string arrays) and make any changes in these arrays. This means that the file will be opened in only two situations: when any previously entered data must be read into the arrays (at the outset), and when the user specifies that the file should be updated (see UPDATE option below). Following is a suggested menu:

ADD	To add new names and addresses.
DEL	To delete names from the mailing list. (To delete a name, you can change the array entry that stores the last name to a special string (for instance,

/////). Then, while using the array in any way, you would ignore any entries marked in this way.)

LIST   To display the current mailing list entries in a standard three-line address format.

UPDATE   To make a new copy of the mailing list file.

END   To end the program. (In the subroutine that carries out this option, remind the user that UPDATE is required to save the latest version of the mailing list. Then give the user the chance to cancel this option selection.)

16. First write a menu-driven program as described in Problem 15. Then modify it by adding some or all of the following options:

SEARCH   To display the address of any person whose last name is typed at the keyboard. (Display all names and addresses of persons with the specified last name.)

ZLIST   To display all addresses with a specified zip code.

SORT   To alphabetize the mailing list. (As explained in Problem 15, the array entries should be rearranged. The file will be sorted only after the UPDATE option.)

ZSORT   To sort the mailing list by zip codes.

■ 15.6 Review True-or-False Quiz

1. At most two files can be referenced in a program—one for input data and one for output data.   **T F**

2. If a program uses a file as an input file, then the program cannot also use this file as an output file.   **T F**

3. Input data to a program cannot be read from a file and also from DATA lines.   **T F**

4. An error will not necessarily occur if an attempt is made to open a nonexistent file.   **T F**

5. The term *line* has no meaning for sequential files.   **T F**

6. If a sequential file contains only words, you can change the first word simply by opening the file, writing the new word on the file, and then closing the file.   **T F**

7. Any attempt to read data from a file after the end-of-file mark has been detected by the computer will necessarily cause program execution to halt.   **T F**

8. The ON ERROR GOTO statement allows you to detect run-time errors before they occur.   **T F**

9. BCD is an acronym for the expression binary coded data.   **T F**

10. A number stored on a BCD file is stored as a sequence of codes, with each code representing a single character.   **T F**

16 Random Numbers and Their Applications

If you toss a coin several times, you'll obtain a sequence such as HTTHTHHHTTH, where H denotes a head and T a tail. We call this a **randomly generated sequence** because each letter is the result of an experiment (tossing a coin) and could not have been determined without actually performing the experiment. Similarly, if you roll a die (a cube with faces numbered 1 through 6) several times, you'll obtain a randomly generated sequence such as 5315264342. The numbers in such a sequence are called **random numbers.**

BASIC contains a built-in function called **RND** used to generate sequences of numbers that have the appearance of being randomly generated. Although these numbers are called random numbers, they are more accurately referred to as **pseudorandom numbers** because the RND function does not perform an experiment such as tossing a coin to produce a number; rather, it uses an algorithm carefully designed to generate sequences of numbers that emulate random sequences. This ability to generate such sequences makes it possible for us to use the computer in many new and interesting ways. Using "random number generators," people have written computer programs to simulate the growth of a forest, to determine the best location for elevators in a proposed skyscraper, to assist social scientists in their statistical studies, to simulate game playing, and to perform many other tasks.

In this chapter we describe the RND function and illustrate its use in several areas.

■ 16.1 The RND Function

The RND function is used somewhat differently from the other BASIC functions. For any number X, RND(X) has a value between 0 and 1:

$$0 < RND(X) < 1$$

The particular value assumed by RND(X) is unpredictable. It will appear to have been selected randomly from the numbers between 0 and 1.

EXAMPLE 1   **Here is a program to generate and display eight random numbers between 0 and 1.**

```
100 LET X=1
110 FOR I=1 TO 8
120    PRINT RND(X)
130 NEXT I
140 END
RUN
```

```
1.78311E-2
.597702
.986238
.526585
.302629
.619982
.899148
.184081
```

Observe that each time line 120 is executed a different number is displayed even though the same expression RND(X) is used.

The value of X in RND(X) has different meanings on different systems; in Example 1, we used X = 1. Your system may allow or even require you to use RND(0), RND(-1), or some other form of the RND function. On some systems, RND(X) will produce different random sequences for different values of X. Experiment! The BASIC standard specifies that the abbreviated form RND be used; we will adhere to this latter form in what follows.

☐

EXAMPLE 2

Here is a program to generate 1000 random numbers between 0 and 1 and determine how many are in the interval from 0.3 to 0.4.

```
10 LET C=0
20 FOR I=1 TO 1000
30    LET R=RND
40    IF R>0.3 AND R<0.4 THEN C=C+1
50 NEXT I
60 PRINT "OF 1000 NUMBERS GENERATED,"
70 PRINT C;"WERE BETWEEN 0.3 AND 0.4."
80 END
RUN

OF 1000 NUMBERS GENERATED,
 104 WERE BETWEEN 0.3 AND 0.4.
```

Each time line 30 is executed, RND takes on a different value, which is then assigned to R. The IF statement at line 40 determines whether R lies in the specified interval. In this example it was necessary to assign the value of RND to a variable R so that the comparisons could be made. If we had written

```
40 IF RND>0.3 AND RND<0.4 THEN C=C+1
```

the two occurrences of RND would have different values, which is not what was wanted in this situation.

☐

The numbers generated by the RND function are nearly uniformly distributed between 0 and 1. For example, if many numbers are generated, approximately as many will be less than .5 as greater than .5, approximately twice as many will be between 0 and $2/3$ as between $2/3$ and 1, approximately $1/100$th of the numbers will be between .37 and .38, and so on. The examples throughout the rest of this chapter illustrate how this property of random-number sequences can be put to use by a programmer.

EXAMPLE 3

Let's write a program to simulate tossing a coin 20 times. An H is to be displayed each time a head occurs and a T each time a tail occurs.

PROBLEM ANALYSIS

Since RND will be less than .5 approximately half the time, let's say that a head is tossed whenever RND is less than .5. We can now write the following program:

```
10 FOR I=1 TO 20
20    IF RND<.5 THEN PRINT "H"; ELSE PRINT "T";
30 NEXT I
40 END
RUN
HHTHTTTHTTHTHTHHHTTH
```

■ **REMARK**

If you wish to simulate tossing a bent coin that produces a head twice as often as a tail, you could say that a head is the result whenever RND < .66667. Thus, one change in line 20 allows the same program to work in this case.

Normally, if a program containing RND is run a second time, exactly the same sequence of random numbers is generated. Although this result can be useful during the debugging process, it does not reflect what actually happens in real-life situations. The BASIC statement RANDOMIZE is designed to cause different and unpredictable sequences to be generated each time a program is run.* Its form is

    ln RANDOMIZE

as illustrated in the following program.

EXAMPLE 4

Here are two "runs" of a program using RANDOMIZE.

```
100 RANDOMIZE
110 FOR I=1 TO 5
120     PRINT RND
130 NEXT I
140 END
RUN

 .182351
 .400231
 .909222
 .612347
 .338525

RUN

 .621112
 .121235
6.71728E-2
 .425276
 .882146
```

The next example shows how the RND function can be used to simulate a real-life situation.

EXAMPLE 5

A professional softball player has a lifetime batting average of .365. Assuming that the player will have four official times at bat (walks are not official at bats) in each of the next 100 games, estimate the number of games in which 0, 1, 2, 3, and 4 hits are made.

PROBLEM ANALYSIS

To simulate one time at bat, we will generate a number RND and concede a hit if RND < .365. For any one game we will compare four such numbers with .365. If in a particular game H hits are made ($0 \leq H \leq 4$), we will record this by adding 1 to the counter C(H). Thus, C(0) counts the number of hitless games, C(1) the games in which one hit is made, and so on.[†] This problem analysis suggests how to code Step(b) of the following algorithm. Steps (a) and (c) are routine.

THE ALGORITHM

a. Set counters C(0), C(1), . . . , C(4) to zero.
b. Repeat the following 100 times:
    Simulate one game to obtain the number H of hits.
    Add 1 to C(H).
c. Display the results C(0), C(1), . . . , C(4) and stop.

---

*Some systems do not allow the RANDOMIZE statement but do provide the means for causing different sequences of random numbers to be generated. The BASIC manual for your system will describe how to do this.
[†] Some versions of BASIC use 1 as the smallest subscript in arrays unless you specify that 0 is to be used. The statement OPTION BASE 0 (BASE 0 on some systems) accomplishes this.

THE PROGRAM

```
100 REM ****** SOFTBALL SIMULATION - 100 GAMES ******
110 REM
120 REM    H = NUMBER OF HITS IN A SINGLE GAME (0-4).
130 REM    G = GAME NUMBER (1-100).
140 REM    B = AT BAT NUMBER (1-4)  FOR EACH GAME.
150 REM    C = COUNTING ARRAY (C(H) COUNTS THE NUMBER
160 REM         OF GAMES IN WHICH H HITS ARE MADE.)
170 REM
180 REM INITIALIZE COUNTERS TO ZERO.
190 FOR H=0 TO 4
200    LET C(H)=0
210 NEXT H
220 REM SIMULATE 100 GAMES.
230 FOR G=1 TO 100
240    LET H=0
250    FOR B=1 TO 4
260       IF RND<.365 THEN H=H+1
270    NEXT B
280    LET C(H)=C(H)+1
290 NEXT G
300 REM DISPLAY THE RESULTS.
310 PRINT  "HITS PER GAME    FREQUENCY"
320 LET F$="        #               ##"
330 FOR H=0 TO 4
340    PRINT USING F$,H,C(H)
350 NEXT H
360 END
RUN

HITS PER GAME     FREQUENCY
      0               23
      1               32
      2               28
      3               15
      4                2
```

■ **REMARK 1**   This program is easily modified to handle different batting averages. Simply make these three changes:

```
175 PRINT "BATTING AVERAGE";
176 INPUT A
260 IF RND<A THEN H=H+1
```

■ **REMARK 2**   In this example, we concede a hit if the condition RND < 0.365 in line 260 is true. If we change this condition to RND <= 0.365, essentially the same results will occur; it is extremely unlikely that RND will ever take on the exact value 0.365. In fact, if A denotes any constant, it is extremely unlikely that RND will take on the exact value A. But even if it does, it will happen so rarely that no significant change in the simulation being carried out will occur.

□

■ 16.2 Problems

1. Approximately how many asterisks are displayed by each program segment?
   a.
   ```
   10 FOR I=1 TO 100
   20    IF RND<.8 THEN PRINT "*";
   30 NEXT I
   ```
   b.
   ```
   10 FOR J=1 TO 10
   20    IF RND=RND THEN PRINT "*";
   30 NEXT J
   ```
   c.
   ```
   10 FOR K=1 TO 100
   20    LET X=RND
   30    IF X<.4 OR X>.7 THEN PRINT "*";
   40 NEXT K
   ```

```
d. 10 FOR L=1 TO 100
   20    IF RND<>.5 THEN PRINT "*";
   30 NEXT L
```

2. Which of these logical expressions are always true? Which are always false? Which may be true or false?

   a. `RND>0`   **b.** `4*RND<4`
   c. `RND<RND`   **d.** `RND+RND<3*RND`
   e. `RND+1>RND`   **f.** `INT(RND)=0`

In Problems 3–12, write a program to perform each task specified.

3. Display approximately one-fourth of all values appearing in DATA lines. Make a decision to display or not to display as the number is read.

4. Display approximately 1% of all integers from 1000 to 9999, inclusive. Select the integers randomly.

5. Simulate tossing two coins 100 times. The output should be a count of the number of times each of the possible outcomes HH, HT, TH, and TT occurs.

6. Simulate tossing three coins ten times. The output should be a list of ten terms such as HHH, HTH, HHT, and so on.

7. Simulate tossing K coins N times. The output should be a list of N terms in which each term is a sequence of K H's and T's. N and K are to be input.

8. A game between players A and B is played as follows. A coin is tossed three times or until a head comes up, whichever occurs first. As soon as a head comes up, player A collects $1 from player B. If no head comes up on any of the three tosses, player B collects $6 from player A. In either case, the game is over. Have your program simulate this game 1000 times to help decide whether A or B has the advantage (or if it is a fair game).

9. Generate an array L of 500 random numbers between 0 and 1. Using L, determine an array C as follows. C(1) is a count of how many entries of L are between 0 and 0.1, C(2) a count of those between 0.1 and 0.2, and so on. Display a two-column table showing the intervals and the corresponding counts stored in array C.

10. The first three hitters in the Bears' batting order have lifetime batting averages of .257, .289, and .324, respectively. Simulate their first trip to the plate for the next 100 games, and tabulate the number of games in which they produce zero, one, two, and three hits. Allow the user to specify the three batting averages during program execution.

11. Jones and Kelley are to have a duel at 20 paces. At this distance Jones will hit the target on the average of two shots in every five, and Kelley will hit one in every three. Kelley shoots first. Who has the best chance of surviving? Use a FOR loop to run the program 20 times and display the results.

12. (Drunkard's Walk) A poor soul, considerably intoxicated, stands in the middle of a 10-foot-long bridge that spans a river. The inebriate staggers along, either toward the left bank or toward the right bank, but fortunately cannot fall off the bridge. Assuming that each step taken is exactly 1 foot long, how many steps will the drunkard take before a bank is reached? Assume that it is just as likely that a step will be toward the left bank as toward the right.

    You must do three things:

    a. Find how many steps are taken in getting off the bridge.

    b. Tell which bank is reached.

    c. Let the drunkard go out for several nights and arrive at the same point (the center) on the bridge. Find, on the average, how many steps it takes to get off the bridge.

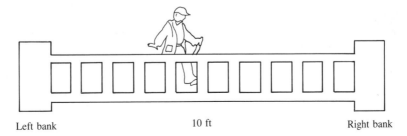

Left bank   10 ft   Right bank

■ 16.3 Random Integers

Many computer applications require generating **random integers** rather than just random numbers between 0 and 1. For example, suppose a manufacturer estimates that a proposed new product will sell at the rate of 10 to 20 units each week and wants a program to simulate sales figures over an extended period of time. To write such a program, you must be able to generate random integers from 10 to 20 to represent the estimated weekly sales. To do this, you can multiply RND, which is between 0 and 1, by 11 (the number of integers from 10 to 20) to obtain

$$0 < 11 * RND < 11$$

If many numbers are obtained using $11 * RND$, they will be nearly uniformly distributed between 0 and 11. This means that the value of $INT(11 * RND)$ will be one of the integers 0, 1, 2, . . . , 10. Thus, if you add 10 to this expression, you will get an integer from 10 to 20:

$$10 \le INT(11 * RND) + 10 \le 20$$

The important thing here is that integers generated in this manner will appear to have been chosen randomly from the set of integers {10, 11, 12, . . . , 20}.

In general, if A and B are integers with $A < B$,

$$INT((B - A + 1) * RND)$$

will generate an integer from 0 to $B - A$. (Note that $B - A + 1$ gives the number of integers between A and B, inclusive.) Thus, adding A to this expression, we obtain

$$INT((B - A + 1) * RND) + A$$

whose value is an integer chosen randomly from the set {A, A + 1, A + 2, . . . , B}. The following table illustrates how to obtain random integers within specified bounds:

Expression	Value of the expression
INT(10 * RND)	A random integer from 0 to 9
INT(N * RND)	A random integer from 0 to N − 1
INT(N * RND) + 1	A random integer from 1 to N
INT(51 * RND) + 100	A random integer from 100 to 150
INT(11 * RND) − 5	A random integer from −5 to 5

EXAMPLE 6

Let's write a program to generate 15 numbers randomly selected from the set {1, 2, 3, 4, 5}.

PROBLEM ANALYSIS

From the preceding discussion we know that the expression $INT(5 * RND)$ will be an integer from 0 to 4. Thus, $INT(5 * RND) + 1$ will be an integer from 1 to 5, as required.

```
10 FOR I=1 TO 15
20    PRINT INT(5*RND)+1;
30 NEXT I
40 END
RUN

   1  2  5  1  5  5  4  3  5  3  3  4  2  4  2
```

EXAMPLE 7

Let's write a program to generate 15 numbers randomly selected from the set {100, 101, 102, . . . , 199}.

PROBLEM ANALYSIS

The technique used in Example 6 is also applicable here. Since $INT(100 * RND)$ is an integer from 0 to 99, we add 100 to obtain an integer from the specified set. Thus, the program required is that of Example 6 with line 20 changed to

```
20 PRINT INT(100*RND)+100
```

■ 16.4 Simulation

Example 5 of Section 16.1 shows how the RND function can be used to simulate a ballplayer's future performance based on past performance. The example illustrates a major category of simulation problems encountered in computer programming—namely, the simulation of future events based on data obtained by observing the results of similar or related previous events. In this section we show how such a simulation can be used to advantage in a business setting.

EXAMPLE 8

A retail store will soon handle a new product. A preliminary market survey indicates that between 500 and 1,000 units will be sold each month. (The survey is no more specific than this.) Write a program to simulate sales for the first 6 months. The retail store management is to be allowed to experiment by specifying two values: the number of units to be purchased initially and the number to be purchased on the first of each subsequent month.

PROBLEM ANALYSIS

The input values are:

IPUR = initial inventory purchase
 PUR = inventory purchase for subsequent months

The problem statement does not specify the nature of the output. Let's agree to produce a four-column report showing the following items:

MONTH = month (1, 2, . . . , 6)
  SALES = estimated sales (500–1,000) for 1 month.
   FIRST = quantity on hand at beginning of month (initially, IPUR)
   LAST = quantity on hand at end of month

For each month we must generate a random integer SALES from 500 to 1000. There are 501 integers to choose from (501 = 1000 − 500 + 1). Thus, we can use the following expression to select an integer randomly from 500 to 1000:

```
INT(501*RND)+500
```

After the initial and periodic purchase quantities (IPUR and PUR) are input, we will display column headings and then assign the input value IPUR to FIRST so that the simulation can begin. The actual simulation of sales for each of the 6 months (MONTH = 1 to 6) can be carried out as follows:

1. Estimate sales for 1 month (SALES = INT(501 * RND) + 500).
2. Determine the quantity on hand at the end of the month
   (LAST = FIRST − SALES).
3. Display MONTH, SALES, FIRST, LAST.
4. Determine the quantity on hand at the start of the next month
   (FIRST = LAST + PUR).

Since the problem statement specifies that the store management is to be allowed to experiment, the program should generate different sequences of random numbers each time it is run. The RANDOMIZE statement in line 390 accomplishes this.

THE PROGRAM

```
100 REM              NEW PRODUCT SIMULATION
110 REM
120 REM        PUR = MONTHLY INVENTORY PURCHASE
130 REM      MONTH = MONTH (1,2,...,6)
140 REM      FIRST = ON HAND - BEGINNING OF MONTH
150 REM      SALES = SALES FOR ONE MONTH (500-1000)
160 REM       LAST = ON HAND - END OF MONTH
170 REM
180 REM ************************************************
190 REM              KEYBOARD INPUT
200 REM
```

```
210 PRINT "INITIAL INVENTORY PURCHASE";
220 INPUT IPUR
230 PRINT "SUBSEQUENT MONTHLY PURCHASE";
240 INPUT PUR
250 PRINT
260 REM *************************************************
270 REM DISPLAY HEADINGS AND ASSIGN OUTPUT FORMAT F$.
280 REM
290 PRINT "                        INVENTORY"
300 PRINT "                    ----------------------"
310 PRINT "MONTH     ESTIMATED    START OF    END OF"
320 PRINT "NUMBER      SALES       MONTH      MONTH"
330 LET F$=" ##       ####        #####      #####"
340 PRINT
350 REM
360 REM *************************************************
370 REM    SIMULATE AND DISPLAY SALES FOR SIX MONTHS.
380 REM
390 RANDOMIZE
400 LET FIRST=IPUR                      'On hand first month
410 FOR MONTH=1 TO 6
420     LET SALES=INT(501*RND)+500      'Sales for the month
430     LET LAST=FIRST-SALES            'On hand end-of-month.
440     PRINT USING F$,MONTH,SALES,FIRST,LAST
450     LET FIRST=LAST+PUR              'On hand start of month
460 NEXT MONTH
999 END
RUN

INITIAL INVENTORY PURCHASE? 1000
SUBSEQUENT MONTHLY PURCHASE? 900
```

```
                          INVENTORY
                    ----------------------
MONTH     ESTIMATED    START OF    END OF
NUMBER      SALES       MONTH      MONTH

  1         865         1000        135
  2         672         1035        363
  3         712         1263        551
  4         690         1451        761
  5         965         1661        696
  6         990         1596        606
```

■ **REMARK**

□

A user would run this program several times and use the results as a guide to determining a reasonable purchasing strategy. The increasingly larger values in the last two columns suggest that a monthly purchase of 900 units is excessive.

We wrote the new-product simulation program so that sales of 500 to 1,000 units would be selected with equal likelihood. We did this not because it is realistic, but because the preliminary market analysis gave no further information. A more careful market analysis would probably show that the number of units would range from 500 to 1,000—with sales near 750 more likely than sales near the extremes 500 to 1,000. We'll now show how random numbers that cluster about a specific number can be generated.

The subroutine

```
500 LET R=0
510 FOR K=1 TO 5
520     LET R=R+RND
530 NEXT K
540 LET R=R/5
550 RETURN
```

generates a random number R from 0 to 1 by averaging five random numbers RND. If many numbers R are generated by this subroutine, they will tend to cluster about the midpoint 0.5 of the interval 0 to 1, with fewer occurring toward the endpoints 0 to 1. If a number larger than 5 is used in the subroutine, the numbers generated will cluster more closely around the midpoint 0.5.

With R obtained from this subroutine, the statement

```
LET SALES=INT(501*R)+500
```

will generate random integers SALES from 500 to 1000. Since the R values will cluster about the midpoint 0.5 of the interval 0 to 1, the corresponding SALES values will cluster about the midpoint 750 of the interval 500 to 1000. The new-product simulation program given in Example 8 is easily modified to generate sales by this method. Simply insert the given subroutine and make these changes:

```
420 GOSUB 500
425 LET SALES=INT(501*R)+500
470 GOTO 999
```

Here is a run of the program after the changes were made:

```
INITIAL INVENTORY PURCHASE? 1000
SUBSEQUENT MONTHLY PURCHASE? 900
```

		INVENTORY	
MONTH NUMBER	ESTIMATED SALES	START OF MONTH	END OF MONTH
1	658	1000	342
2	757	1242	485
3	773	1385	612
4	720	1512	792
5	761	1692	931
6	778	1831	1053

Note that the estimated sales figures are nearer 750 than before. Note also that the figures in the last column give more evidence that purchasing 900 units per month is excessive.

■ 16.5 Problems

1. Write a single BASIC statement to display each of the following:
   a. A nonnegative random number (not necessarily an integer) less than 4
   b. A random number less than 11 but not less than 5
   c. A random number less than 3 but not less than −5
   d. A random integer between 6 and 12, inclusive
   e. A random number from the set {0, 2, 4, 6, 8}
   f. A random number from the set {1, 3, 5, 7, 9}

2. What values can be assumed by each of the following expressions? For each expression, tell whether the possible values are all equally likely to occur.
   a. INT(2*RND+1)   **b.** 3*INT(RND)
   c. INT(5*RND)−2   **d.** INT(2*RND+1)+INT(2*RND+1)
   e. INT(6*RND+1)+INT(6*RND+1)   **f.** INT(3*RND+1)*(INT(3*RND)+1)

3. If two coins are tossed, two heads, two tails, or one each may result. The following program was written to simulate tossing two coins a total of 20 times. If it is run, the output will not reflect what would happen if the coins were actually tossed. Explain why, and then write a correct program.

```
100 FOR I=1 TO 20
110     LET R=INT(3*RND)
120     IF R=0 THEN PRINT "TWO HEADS"
130     IF R=1 THEN PRINT "TWO TAILS"
140     IF R=2 THEN PRINT "ONE OF EACH"
150 NEXT I
160 END
```

In Problems 4–18, write a program to perform each task specified.

4. Display a sequence of 20 letters that are selected randomly from the word RANDOM.

5. Randomly select and display an integer from 1 to 100 and then another integer from the remaining 99.

6. Create an array B of exactly 20 different integers from 1 to 100. Choose the integers randomly. Display the array, but only after it is completely determined.

7. Read 20 different English words into an array A$. Then create another array B$ containing exactly 10 different words randomly selected from those in array A$.

8. Starting with D(1) = 1, D(2) = 2, D(3) = 3, . . . , D(52) = 52, rearrange the entries of D as follows: select an integer K from 1 to 52 and swap D(K) with D(52), select K from 1 to 51 and swap D(K) with D(51), select K from 1 to 50 and swap D(K) with D(50), and so on. The last step in this process is to select K from 1 to 2 and swap D(K) with D(2). Then display the entries of D in four adjacent columns, each containing 13 numbers. Explain in what sense your program shuffles a standard bridge deck and deals one hand in bridge.

9. A retail store will soon carry a new product. A preliminary market analysis indicates that between 300 and 500 units will be sold each week. (The survey is no more specific than this.) Assuming that each unit costs the store $1.89, write a program to simulate sales for the next 16 weeks. Allow the store management to specify the selling price to obtain output showing the week, the estimated sales in number of units, the total revenue, the income (revenue − cost), and the cumulative income. Allow the user to try many different selling prices during a single program run.

10. Carry out the task specified in Problem 9, but this time assume that the market analysis says the number of units sold per week (300–500) will cluster about the midpoint (400), as described in Section 17.4.

11. Juanita Fernandes is offered the opportunity to transfer to another sales territory. She is informed that, for each month of the past year, sales in the territory were between $18,000 and $30,000, with sales of $25,000 or more being twice as likely as sales under $25,000. A 4% commission is paid on all sales up to $25,000 and 8% on all sales above that figure. Simulate the next 6 months' sales, and print the monthly sales and commission to give Juanita some information on which to base her decision to accept or reject the transfer.

12. The IDA Production Company will employ 185 people to work on the production of a new product. It is estimated that each person can complete between 85 and 95 units each working day. Experience shows that the absentee rate is between 0 and 15% on Mondays and Fridays and between 0 and 7% on the other days. Simulate the production for 1 week. Display the results of this simulation in four columns showing the day of the week, the number of workers present, the number of units produced, and the average number produced per worker.

13. Two knights begin at diagonally opposite corners of a chessboard and travel randomly about the board but always making legitimate knight moves. (The knight moves either one step forward or backward and then two steps to the right or left or else two steps forward or backward and one step to the right or left.) Calculate the number of moves before one knight captures the other. However you number the squares, each knight's move should be displayed as it is taken.

14. A single trip for a knight is defined as follows. The knight starts in one corner of the chessboard and randomly makes N knight moves to arrive at one of the 64 squares of the chessboard. (See Problem 13 for a description of an admissible knight move.) Write a program to simulate 1000 such trips for a knight to determine how many times each square was reached at the end of a trip. These counts should be presented as an 8 × 8 table displaying the counts for the 64 squares. Allow the user to obtain a frequency table for many values of N during a single program run.

15. SIM is a game in which two players take turns drawing lines between any two of the six dots numbered 1 through 6 in the following diagram:

```
          1     2
          •     •
    6 •             • 3
          •     •
          5     4
```

The first player's lines are colored red; the second player's are colored blue. The loser is the first player to complete a triangle with three of these six dots as vertices. For example, if the second player draws a line (blue) between dots 2 and 4, 6 and 4, and 2 and 6, this player has completed a blue triangle and hence loses. Write a program in which the computer is the second player. The computer is to record all moves and announce the end of each game with a message stating who won. [*Hint:* Use a 6 × 6 array H(I,J) to record the moves. If the first player types 3,5 to indicate that a red line is drawn between these two dots, set H(3,5) and H(5,3) to 1. If the computer picks 2,6 (to be done randomly), then set H(2,6) and H(6,2) to 2. Note that a triangle of one color has been completed when there are three different numbers I, J, K for which H(I,J) H(J,K), and H(K,I) are all 1 or all 2.]

16. Write a program for the game of SIM described in Problem 15, but this time the second player is a person, not the computer.

17. Write a subroutine to generate random numbers between 0 and 1 by averaging N random numbers rather than 5 as in Section 16.4. Include this subroutine in a program that allows the user to specify a positive integer N to obtain a frequency table showing counts of how many of 500 random numbers generated by the subroutine are in each of the 10 intervals 0–0.1, 0.1–0.2, . . . , 0.9–1. The user should be allowed to obtain tables for many positive integers N during a single program run. The program should halt when the user types zero. (Be sure to try the cases N = 1, 10, and 20.)

18. Display 20 sets of three integers D, L, and F with $0 \leq D < 360$, $5 \leq L \leq 15$, and $1 \leq F \leq 4$. (*Note:* If you interpret D as a direction and L as a length, you can create a design using these numbers. Starting at a point on a piece of paper, draw a line of length L in the direction given by D. At the end of this line segment draw one of four figures as specified by F— for example, different colored circles the sizes of a dime, nickel, quarter, and half dollar. Using the end of this first line segment as a new starting point, repeat the process by using the second of the 20 triples D, L, F. This process illustrates, in a very elementary way, what some people refer to as random art.)

■ 16.6 A Statistical Application

Programmers are often confronted with tasks that cannot be programmed to run within a specified time limit. When this happens, it is not always necessary to abandon the tasks. It may be that satisfactory results can be obtained by doing only part of the job. The following example, which illustrates one such situation, makes use of the statistical fact that the average of a large collection of numbers can be estimated by taking the average of only a fraction of the numbers, provided that the numbers picked are chosen randomly.

EXAMPLE 9

A researcher has compiled three lists of 500 measurements each. For each set of three measurements, one from each of the three lists, a series of calculations (which is known to take about one-hundredth of a second) must be carried out to determine a value V. The researcher needs to know the average of all such values V. We are to write a program to assist in this task. Because of heavy use of the computer, the program must take no longer than 30 minutes to execute.

PROBLEM ANALYSIS

On the surface this appears to be a simple programming task. We can read the three lists into arrays A, B, and C, determine V for each set of three numbers A(I), B(J), C(K), being sure to add each V to a sum accumulator SUM, and then divide SUM by the number of V's added. If the calculations that determine V are carried out in a subroutine that begins at line 800, we can use the following program segment to determine the required average:

```
300 LET SUM=0
310 FOR I=1 TO 500
320    FOR J=1 TO 500
330       FOR K=1 TO 500
340          GOSUB 800        'Calculate V.
350          LET SUM=SUM+V
360       NEXT K
370    NEXT J
380 NEXT I
390 PRINT "REQUIRED AVERAGE IS";SUM/500^3
```

If you use this program segment to find the average, you'll have a long wait. Let's estimate how long. Each list contains 500 measurements, so there are $500^3 = 125,000,000$ sets A(I), B(J), C(K) to process. Since each takes one-hundredth of a second, the total time needed to calculate all V values is $125,000,000 \times 0.01 = 1,250,000$ seconds, which is $1,250,000/60 = 20,833.33$ minutes, or 347.22 hours, or about 14.5 twenty-four-hour days.

About the only way out of this dilemma is to use only a fraction of the sets A(I), B(J), C(K). Since the time needed to calculate all of the V values is 20,833.33 minutes, using only 1 in 1000 will reduce the time to about 20.83 minutes. This is within the 30-minute limit specified in the problem statement. To ensure that the average we obtain is a reliable estimate of the average desired, the sets A(I), B(J), C(K) must be chosen randomly. In the following program segment we use the expression INT(500 * RND) + 1 to select subscripts from 1 to 500 randomly. The statement FOR N = 1 TO 125000 is appropriate since using 1 in 1000 of the sets A(I), B(J), C(K) means that a total of $125,000,000/1,000 = 125,000$ sets will be used.

```
300 LET SUM=0
310 FOR N=1 TO 125000
320    LET I=INT(500*RND)+1
330    LET J=INT(500*RND)+1
340    LET K=INT(500*RND)+1
350    GOSUB 800              'Calculate V
360    LET SUM=SUM+V
370 NEXT N
380 PRINT "ESTIMATE OF AVERAGE:";SUM/125000
```

■ REMARK 1   When this program segment is executed, the same subscripts I, J, K may be selected more than once. Since each set A(I), B(J), C(K) has an equal chance of being selected, however, the effect on the final average will be statistically insignificant.

■ REMARK 2   It is not necessary to use 125,000 of the sets A(I), B(J), C(K) to obtain a reliable estimate of the average desired. Indeed, random number generators used with BASIC will eventually repeat the sequence of random numbers being produced. If you use only 12,500 of the sets (1 in 10,000), you will probably get just as accurate an estimate of the average as you would with 125,000 sets.

■ 16.7 Monte Carlo

The speed of modern computing machines, together with their ability to generate good random sequences, allows us to approach many problems in ways not previously possible. The following example illustrates one such method, called the **Monte Carlo method.** When you complete the example, you should have little difficulty explaining why this name is applied to the technique involved.

EXAMPLE 10   **Consider the following figure of a circle inscribed in a square:**

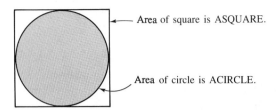

Area of square is ASQUARE.

Area of circle is ACIRCLE.

If darts are randomly tossed at this figure and tosses landing outside the square are ignored, we can expect the number of darts falling within the circle to be related to the number falling on the entire square as the area ACIRCLE of the circle is related to the area ASQUARE of the square. We will use this observation to approximate the area ACIRCLE of the unit circle (circle of radius 1).

**PROBLEM
ANALYSIS**

As noted in the problem statement, we can begin by writing this approximate equation:

$$\frac{\text{Area of circle}}{\text{Area of square}} \approx \frac{\text{Darts falling in circle}}{\text{Darts falling in square}}$$

With the variable names

ACIRCLE   =   Area of circle
ASQUARE   =   Area of square
DCIRCLE   =   Darts falling in circle
DSQUARE   =   Darts falling in square

the approximate equation becomes

$$\frac{\text{ACIRCLE}}{\text{ASQUARE}} \approx \frac{\text{DCIRCLE}}{\text{DSQUARE}}$$

Solving for ACIRCLE, we get

$$\text{ACIRCLE} \approx \text{ASQUARE} \times \frac{\text{DCIRCLE}}{\text{DSQUARE}}$$

The more darts thrown (randomly), the better we can expect this approximation to be. The problem, then, is to simulate this activity and keep an accurate count of DSQUARE and DCIRCLE. To simplify this task, let's place our figure on a coordinate system with its origin at the center of the circle:

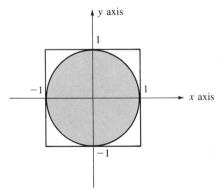

A point (x, y) will lie in the square if both x and y are between -1 and $+1$. Such a point will lie within the circle if

$$x^2 + y^2 < 1$$

To simulate tossing a single dart that falls in the square, we randomly generate two numbers, x and y, each between -1 and $+1$. The following algorithm describes this process for 10,000 points (x, y) generated in this way. Since each point (x, y) lies in the square, we can use a loop beginning

FOR DSQUARE = 1 TO 10000

On each pass through the loop, we generate x and y as described; if the point lies in the circle, we'll add 1 to DCIRCLE. Step (b3) of the algorithm displays the approximate area ACIRCLE after every 1,000 tosses.

THE ALGORITHM

a. Let DCIRCLE = 0   (Darts falling in circle)
b. For DSQUARE = 1 to 10,000
   b1. Generate x and y between -1 and $+1$.
   b2. If (x, y) is in circle, add 1 to DCIRCLE.
   b3. If DSQUARE is a multiple of 1000, display DSQUARE and the approximate area ACIRCLE = ASQUARE × DCIRCLE/DSQUARE.
c. Stop

Since $2 * \text{RND} - 1$ gives a random number between -1 and $+1$, and since the area ASQUARE of the square with side length 2 is 4, this algorithm translates easily into the following program:

THE PROGRAM

```
100 REM        A MONTE CARLO SIMULATION
110 REM
130 REM DISPLAY HEADINGS AND ASSIGN OUTPUT FORMAT F$.
140 REM
150 PRINT  " NUMBER OF      ESTIMATED AREA"
160 PRINT  "DARTS THROWN   OF UNIT CIRCLE"
170 PRINT  "------------   --------------"
180 LET F$="    #####            #.#####"
190 REM
200 REM ******************************************
210 REM        SIMULATE TOSSING 10000 DARTS.
220 REM
230 LET DCIRCLE=0                   'Darts falling in circle
240 LET ASQUARE=4                   'Area of square
250 FOR DSQUARE=1 TO 10000
260     LET X=2*RND-1
270     LET Y=2*RND-1
280     IF X^2+Y^2<1 THEN DCIRCLE=DCIRCLE+1
290     IF DSQUARE/1000<>INT(DSQUARE/1000) THEN 310
300     PRINT USING F$,DSQUARE,ASQUARE*DCIRCLE/DSQUARE
310 NEXT DSQUARE
320 END
RUN
```

NUMBER OF DARTS THROWN	ESTIMATED AREA OF UNIT CIRCLE
1000	3.23200
2000	3.15000
3000	3.12667
4000	3.14300
5000	3.13920
6000	3.14133
7000	3.13886
8000	3.13750
9000	3.14711
10000	3.14560

REMARK

Since we know that the area of a circle of radius 1 is π (approximately 3.1416), we see that the final estimate is accurate to two decimal places. To obtain greater accuracy, you might be tempted to use more than 10,000 points. Indeed, if RND were a true random number generator—that is, if it actually performed a random experiment such as tossing coins to generate numbers—you could expect to obtain any degree of accuracy desired by taking DSQUARE large enough. The fact that RND is not a true random number generator places a limit on the accuracy obtainable.

■ 16.8 Modular Arithmetic and Random Numbers

The realization that the use of random numbers in computer programs makes possible new and promising applications of the computer brought about an intensive search for ways to generate sequences of numbers possessing the attributes of random sequences. In this section, we describe a method for generating such sequences that has its basis in modular arithmetic. The method is one of the very first tried and is probably still the most widely used.

To illustrate the method, let us start with 33 as the first number in a sequence to be generated. To obtain the second number in the sequence, we multiply the first by 33 to obtain $33 * 33 = 1089$; however, we will keep only the last two digits, 89, of this product. To obtain the third number, multiply the second by 33 to obtain $89 * 33 = 2937$ and again keep only the 37. (To keep the last two digits of any product, divide the product by 100 to obtain a quotient and a remainder; the remainder will be the last two digits. Thus, if $89 * 33 = 2937$ is divided by 100 the quotient is 29 and the remainder is 37. When we divide the product by 100 and keep only the remainder, we say we are multiplying modulo 100; 100 is called the *modulus*.) Continuing to multiply each new number obtained by 33 modulo 100, we get

$33 * 33 = 89$ mod 100
$89 * 33 = 37$ mod 100
$37 * 33 = 21$ mod 100
.
.
.

The first 20 integers in the sequence so generated are

33, 89, 37, 21, 93, 69, 77, 41, 53, 49, 17, 61, 13, 29, 57, 81, 73, 9, 97, 1

Although these numbers were not randomly generated (we know exactly how they were produced), they are rather uniformly distributed between 0 and 100. For example, the interval 0 to 25 contains five integers as do the intervals 25 to 50, 50 to 75, and 75 to 100. If we want numbers between 0 and 1, we can divide each of these twenty numbers by 100, the modulus, to obtain

.33, .89, .37, .21, .93, .69, .77, .41, .53, .49, .17, .61, .13, .29, .57, .81, .73, .09, .97, .01

The process just described can be generalized by using numbers other than 33 and 100. In the following description of this procedure, S is used to denote the starting value and M to denote that multiplication is to be done modulo M. The product of two integers A and B modulo M is the remainder R obtained upon division of the product AB by M and is given by

```
R=A*B-M*INT(A*B/M)
```

Algorithm to Generate Sequences of Numbers Between 0 and 1

 a. Assign values to M and S.
 b. Let A = S.
 c. Replace A with A * S modulo M.
 d. A/M is the next number.
 e. Go to step (c) if another number is desired.

If M and S are chosen appropriately, the numbers generated will have many of the attributes of random numbers. The program that follows uses $M = 2^{27} = 134,217,728$ and $S = 5^9 = 1,953,125$. The first 100 numbers generated by the algorithm are displayed. We use a PRINT USING statement to avoid the exponential form that would otherwise be used for some of the numbers. Line 200 ensures that five numbers will be displayed on each line.

```
100 REM ASSIGN OUTPUT FORMAT.
110 LET F$=".######       "
120 REM INITIALIZE STARTING VALUE S AND MODULUS M.
130 LET M=2^27
140 LET S=5^9
150 REM GENERATE 100 RANDOM NUMBERS.
160 LET A=S
170 FOR N=1 TO 100
180    LET A=A*S-M*INT(A*S/M)
190    PRINT USING F$,A/M;
200    IF N/5=INT(N/5) THEN PRINT
210 NEXT N
220 END
RUN
```

.709430	.257827	.400745	.625170	.981427
.185363	.870218	.621112	.124809	.062784
.337099	.947539	.592915	.888228	.918056
.161427	.757541	.048992	.159934	.892505
.463627	.344976	.406942	.929196	.708945
.637107	.292836	.929551	.448788	.120792
.358115	.757185	.525653	.224344	.792201
.442220	.723934	.132426	.300629	.767218
.949606	.934484	.097237	.478121	.534915
.779967	.498923	.947894	.787949	.314953
.766037	.063589	.351397	.295223	.130359
.599345	.773146	.733931	.193797	.176778
.338585	.181512	.392690	.909332	.556717
.048375	.515124	.923405	.447031	.546351
.317964	.020357	.376684	.156732	.653963
.789149	.385196	.894504	.403706	.254774
.676639	.019278	.280298	.151697	.236821
.371235	.759049	.822296	.575478	.332057

Whether the numbers generated using these values for M and S emulate random numbers is of course a very relevant question. Problem 2 of Section 16.9 describes one of the many statistical tests that can be used in making this evaluation.

To assist you in making promising choices for M and S, we state the following guidelines that, experience has shown, increase the likelihood that "good" random sequences will be obtained.

1. M should be large. (For a variety of reasons, powers of 2 are popular.)
2. M and S should have no common factors. (We used 2^{27} and 5^9 for these values.)
3. S should not be too small in comparison to M.

The method described in this section is called the **power residual method:** "power" because successive powers of a single number S are used and "residual" because the numbers used are residues (remainders) upon division by a fixed number M. In all likelihood, the RND function provided with your BASIC system will generate random numbers using a method not unlike the power residual method.

■ 16.9 Problems

In Problems 1–3, write a program for each task specified.

1. A principle of statistics tells us that the mean (average) of a large collection of numbers can be approximated by taking the mean of only some of the numbers, provided that the numbers are chosen randomly. Generate a one-dimensional array L containing 500 numbers (any numbers will do), and display the mean M of these 500 numbers. To test the stated principle of statistics, randomly select approximately 30 numbers from L and display their mean. Use a loop to repeat this process 20 times. The 20 means obtained should cluster about M.

2. Let L be an array of N numbers between 0 and 1. Using array L, determine an array C as follows: C(1) is a count of how many entries of L are between 0 and 0.1, C(2) a count of those between 0.1 and 0.2, and so on. If L emulates a random sequence, we can expect each C(J) to be approximately E = N/10. In statistics, the value

$$X = \frac{(C(1) - E)^2}{E} + \frac{(C(2) - E)^2}{E} + \cdots + \frac{(C(10) - E)^2}{E}$$

is called the *chi-square statistic* for C. If it is small, it means that the C(J) do not differ drastically from the expected value E. For the present situation, statistics tells us that if X $\geq$ 16.92, we can be 95 percent confident that L does not emulate a random sequence. Thus, unless X < 16.92, we should reject L as a potential random sequence.

a. Assuming that N and the list C are known, write a subroutine to compute and display the chi-square statistic X.

b. Use the subroutine of part (a) in a program to test RND as a random number generator. For any positive integer N $\geq$ 200, the program is to determine the counts C(1), C(2), . . . , C(10) for N numbers generated by RND and then determine and display the chi-square statistic. The program should halt if a value of N less than 200 is typed.

[*Note:* If C gives a count of numbers in intervals other than (0, 0.1), (0.1, 0.2), and so on, a critical value other than 16.92 must be used. The test described here is called a *chi-square goodness-of-fit test* and is described in most introductory statistics books.]

3. Let a function y = f(x) have positive values for all x between A and B as in the following diagram:

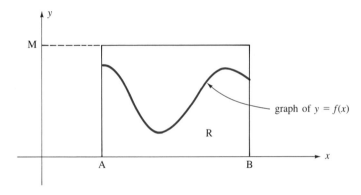

A point (x, y) with A < x < B will lie in the region R if 0 < y < f(x). If M is a number such that f(x) $\leq$ M for all such x, the area of the rectangle of height M shown in the diagram is M * (B − A). Use the Monte Carlo method to approximate the area R. Try your program for the following cases:

    a. $y = 1 - x^3$, A = 0, B = 1

    b. $y = \sin(x)$, A = 0, B = $\pi/2$

    c. $y = \sin(x)/x$, A = 0, B = 1

■ 16.10 Review True-or-False Quiz

1. The RND function generates sequences of numbers by using a well-defined algorithm.   **T F**

2. If 100 numbers are generated by the statement LET R = RND, then approximately half these numbers will be less than 50.   **T F**

3. With equal likelihood, the expression INT(2 * RND) will have the value 0 or 1.   **T F**

4. With equal likelihood, the expression INT(3 * RND) + INT(2 * RND) will have one of the values 1, 2, 3, 4, or 5.   **T F**

5. Let L$ be an array of 100 different names. If we wish to select exactly 20 of these names randomly, we can generate 100 random numbers between 0 and 1 and select the Ith name in array L$ if the Ith number generated is less than 0.2.   **T F**

6. A certain experiment has two possible outcomes: Outcome 1 and Outcome 2. To simulate this experiment on the computer, you can generate a number R = RND and specify that Outcome 1 occurs if R is less than 0.5 and Outcome 2 occurs otherwise.   **T F**

7. RND/RND = 1.   **T F**

8. The value of the expression INT(17 * RND) + 1 is an integer from 1 to 17.   **T F**

9. The value of the expression INT(5 * RND) + 5 is an integer from 5 to 10.   **T F**

10. The loop

```
500 LET S=0
510 FOR K=1 TO 100
520    LET S=S+RND
530 NEXT K
```

will generate random numbers S between 0 and 100. Moreover, the S values will cluster about the midpoint 50 of this interval.   **T F**

17

Sorting

Many programming tasks require sorting (arranging) arrays according to some specified order. When lists of numbers are involved, this usually means arranging them according to size—from smallest to largest or from largest to smallest. For example, you may be required to produce a salary schedule in which salaries are displayed from largest to smallest. When lists of names are involved, you may wish to arrange them in alphabetical order. The principal reason we sort data is to allow needed items to be found in a timely manner. This applies not only to printed data used by people but also to data that must be searched by computers.

For the reasons cited, much attention has been given to the problem of sorting and many different sorting algorithms have been developed. The *bubble sort* algorithm described in Section 14.5 is but one of these. Although this algorithm can be used for many of the applications encountered by beginning programmers, it is too slow for programming tasks that require sorting large quantities of data. In this chapter, we will describe some of the techniques used to write efficient sorting algorithms and present two very fast sorts: the Shellsort (Section 17.2) and the Heapsort (Section 17.3). The Insertion sort described in Section 17.1 is included not for its speed but because the sorting method is used in the Shellsort. In Section 17.4 we describe the Binary Search algorithm, a very fast search algorithm that is used with data that have previously been sorted. In Section 17.5 we describe a Merge-Sort algorithm that can be used to combine two or more previously sorted data files into a single sorted file. A comprehensive treatment of all topics covered in this chapter, and many more, can be found in *Sorting and Searching,* by Donald Knuth.*

■ 17.1 Insertion Sort

The sorting algorithm described in this section is called an *insertion sort* and is somewhat more efficient than the bubble sort (about twice as fast). Although it is not one of the fastest sorting algorithms, it is easy to understand and will help us describe an algorithm that is very fast.

Suppose the list A(1), A(2), . . . , A(N) is to be sorted in ascending order. We start with a list containing only the one entry A(1). Then we compare the next term A(2) with A(1) and these are swapped if necessary to give a list with the two entries

A(1), A(2)

The Art of Computer Programming, Vol. 3: Sorting and Searching, by Donald E. Knuth (Reading, MA: Addison-Wesley, 1973).

in the proper order. Next A(3) is compared with A(2) and, if necessary, with A(1) to determine where it should be inserted. We illustrate with the following list:

3 2 5 4 1

Start with a single entry list: 3
Insert the 2 before the 3:   2, 3
Place 5 after the 3:   2, 3, 5
Insert 4 between 3 and 5:   2, 3, 4, 5
Insert 1 before the 2:   1, 2, 3, 4, 5

Let us examine this process of insertion more carefully. Suppose the first I entries of array A

A(1), A(2), A(3), . . . , A(I)

are in order and A(I + 1) is to be inserted in its proper place. Temporarily assigning the value of A(I + 1) to the variable T, we proceed as follows.

If $T \geq A(I)$	no swap is necessary and no further comparisons are required.
If $T < A(I)$	let $A(I + 1) = A(I)$. (This moves A(I) one position to the right.) Note that T "remembers" the original value of A(I + 1).
If $T \geq A(I - 1)$	let $A(I) = T$ and the insertion is complete.
If $T < A(I - 1)$	let $A(I) = A(I - 1)$. (This moves A(I − 1) one position to the right.) T still remembers the original value of A(I + 1).

.
.
.

.
.
.

(Continue this process until T—that is, A(I + 1)—has been inserted in its proper place.)

This process describes a loop in which we make the comparisons

$T < A(J)$

for J = I, I − 1, I − 2, and so on until the proper position J + 1 for T, the original value of A(I + 1), is found. If T is less than each of the other entries A(J), we will eventually obtain J = 0, and even in this case J + 1 = 0 + 1 = 1 gives the proper position for T. The following algorithm shows a concise way to carry out the process described.

a. Let T = A(I + 1).   (Number to be inserted.)
b. Let J = I.   (Compare T with A(I) first.)
c. While J > 0 and T < A(J)
    c1. Let A(J + 1) = A(J)   (Move A(J) to the right.)
    c2. Let J = J − 1   (Next subscript for comparison.)
d. Let A(J + 1) = T.   (Insert T in proper position.)

To sort a list A(1), A(2), . . . , A(N), this procedure must be repeated for each value of I from 1 to N − 1. The flowchart in Figure 17.1 describes this process and the subroutine in Figure 17.2 that was coded directly from the flowchart can be used in any program to sort an array A of N numbers into ascending order.

■ **REMARK 1**

In the subroutine shown in Figure 17.2, we introduce the variable DONE to avoid the statement

```
WHILE J>0 AND T<A(J)
```

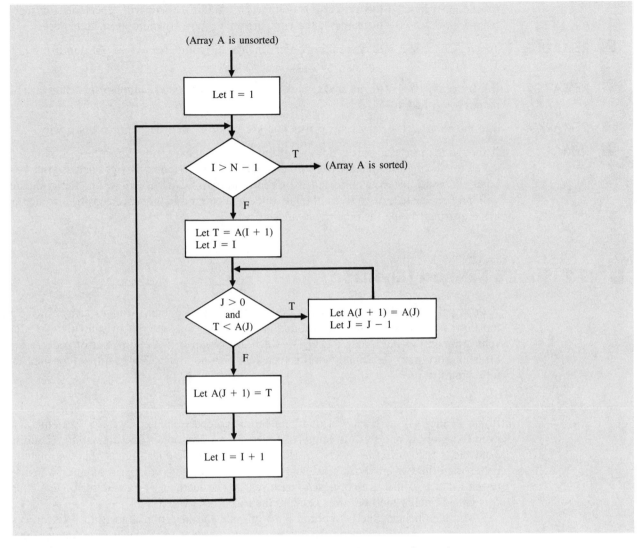

Figure 17.1 Insertion sort algorithm. Sort array A with N entries into ascending order

```
500 REM INSERTION SORT SUBROUTINE
510 REM
520 REM SORT ARRAY A OF SIZE N
530 REM INTO ASCENDING ORDER.
540 REM
550 FOR I=1 TO N-1
560    LET T=A(I+1)              'Value to be inserted
570    LET J=I                   'Compare T with A(I) first.
580    LET DONE=0                'Position for T not yet found.
590    WHILE J>0 AND DONE=0
600       IF T<A(J) THEN 630
610          LET DONE=1          'Position for T found.
620          GOTO 650
630       LET A(J+1)=A(J)        'Move A(J) up one position.
640       LET J=J-1              'Position for next comparison
650    NEXT   (or WEND)
660    LET A(J+1)=T              'Correct position for T=A(I+1)
670 NEXT I
680 RETURN
```

Figure 17.2 Insertion sort subroutine

for the inner loop. If the correct position for T is A(1), line 640 will repeatedly subtract 1 from J until J = 0. In that case, the comparison T < A(J) would be meaningless.

■ **REMARK 2** To sort the array A into descending order, change the comparison T < A(J) in line 600 to T > A(J).

■ **REMARK 3** If a list of N strings (for instance, names) is to be alphabetized, simply use string variable names for A and T.

■ **REMARK 4** The insertion sort is very fast for lists that are "almost" in order. Can you see why?

■ **REMARK 5** Although the insertion sort is not one of the most efficient sorting algorithms, it is ideally suited for sorting lists that are to be entered by using a slow input device such as your keyboard. If you input your unsorted list directly into A(1),A(2), and so on, the computer will have adequate time to insert the last value you entered in its proper position while you are preparing to type the next input value.

■ 17.2 Shell's Method (Shellsort)

A principal reason for the inefficiency of the bubble sort is that it moves array entries at most one position at a time. (Recall that in the bubble sort all comparisons involve adjacent array entries A(I) and A(I + 1), which are swapped if they are out of order.) The insertion sort improves slightly on this technique, but not much. For example, consider the following list.

    4 2 3 1 7 8 9

Either of the two methods will make numerous comparisons and swaps to sort this list, even though only one swap is actually needed. Certainly, no sorting algorithm should be expected to recognize this one swap. However, the example does suggest that we might do better than the two methods presented. The key is to allow comparisons and swaps between list entries that are not next to each other. The method we now describe does this. It is called **Shell's method** after Donald Shell who discovered it.*

The idea behind Shell's method is to precede the insertion algorithm by a process that moves "smaller" values to the left and "larger" values to the right more quickly than could be accomplished by making comparisons involving adjacent entries only. To illustrate the method, we'll sort the following list.

    7 1 6 3 4 2

First, think of the list as divided into two parts

    7 1 6   and   3 4 2

and compare the first, second, and third entries of these sublists, swapping the pairs of numbers that are not in order. We will indicate the comparisons to be made as follows:

    7 1 6 3 4 2

Thus, 7 and 3 will be swapped, 1 and 4 will not, and 6 and 2 will. This gives us a new list:

    3 1 2 7 4 6

Note that these three comparisons resulted in moving the "small" values 2 and 3 to the left and the "large" values 6 and 7 to the right, each by more than one position.

We now have a rearrangement of the given list in which entries three positions apart are in order. Similarly, we can rearrange the list so that entries two positions apart are in order. First, we make the comparisons

---

*"A High-Speed Sorting Procedure," by Donald L. Shell. *Communications of the ACM*, 2 (July 1959), pp. 30–32.

$$\underbrace{3\ 1\ 2}\ 7\ 4\ 6$$

to give

2 1 3 7 4 6

and then the comparisons

$$2\ 1\ \underbrace{3\ 7\ 4}\ 6$$

to give

2 1 3 6 4 7

Note that this step involves sorting two sublists. First

3 2 4   (1st, 3rd, and 5th entries)

and then

1 7 6   (2nd, 4th, and 6th entries)

With Shell's method, these sublists are sorted by using an insertion sort. If we now make the comparisons

$$2\ \underbrace{1\ 3\ 6\ 4\ 7}$$

from left to right—swapping pairs that are not in order—we will obtain the sorted list

1 2 3 4 6 7

With Shell's method, these comparisons are made by using an insertion sort. But since the list is "almost" in order—entries two positions apart and entries three positions apart are in order—this insertion sort will be very fast.

Let's summarize the process just used to sort a list of length 6:

A(1), A(2), A(3), A(4), A(5), A(6)

First, the list was rearranged so that entries *three* positions apart were in order—that is, each of the following two-element lists was sorted.

A(1), A(4)

A(2), A(5)

A(3), A(6)

Next, the list obtained was rearranged so that entries *two* positions apart were in order— that is, each of the following three-element lists was sorted.

A(1), A(3), A(5)

A(2), A(4), A(6)

Finally, the list was rearranged so that entries *one* position apart were in order, which resulted in a completely sorted list. While carrying out this process, each partial list was sorted by using the insertion method.

We now describe Shell's method for sorting an array A of length N.

a. Select an integer S from 1 to N/2.
b. Sort the array A so that entries S positions apart are in order.
c. If S = 1, stop. The array is sorted.
d. Pick a new and smaller S (S ≥ 1), and go to step (b).

For the list with six entries the values S = 3, S = 2, and S = 1 were chosen. The successive values S = 3, 2, 1 are not always to be used. The sequence of S values that yields the fastest sort is not known. The most common practice, and one that gives a fast algorithm, is to use the successive S values INT(N/2), INT(N/4), INT(N/8), and so on, until the value S = 0 is reached. The flowchart in Figure 17.3 displays the steps in the algorithm for this sequence of S values.

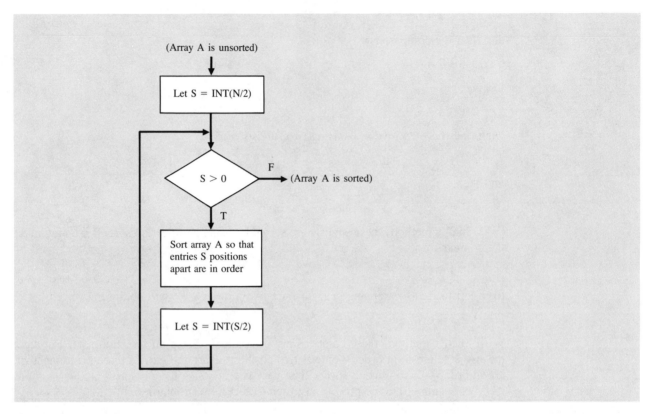

(Array A is unsorted)

Let S = INT(N/2)

S > 0   F → (Array A is sorted)

T

Sort array A so that entries S positions apart are in order

Let S = INT(S/2)

Figure 17.3   Flowchart to sort array A with N entries by Shell's method

The only part of this flowchart that may be difficult to code is the box corresponding to step (b) of the written algorithm. To accomplish this, each of the following lists must be sorted.

A(1), A(1 + S), A(1 + 2S), A(1 + 3S), . . .

A(2), A(2 + S), A(2 + 2S), A(2 + 3S), . . .

.

.

.

A(S), A(S + S), A(S + 2S), A(S + 3S), . . .

As indicated in the worked-out example, these partial lists will be sorted by using the insertion method. Note that each of these partial lists can be written

A(K), A(K + S), A(K + 2S), . . .

where K is an integer from 1 to S. The flowchart in Figure 17.4, which sorts lists of this form, is identical to the insertion-algorithm flowchart (Figure 17.1) except that it uses increments of S rather than increments of 1. In particular, a value T being inserted in its proper place is compared with A(J) for J = I, I−S, and I−2S, and so on, as long as J ≥ K and T < A(J). To sort all of the lists indicated above, we must carry out the process shown in Figure 17.4 for all values of K from 1 to S. The Shellsort subroutine shown in Figure 17.5 uses a FOR loop initiated by the statement FOR K = 1 TO S to accomplish this. This subroutine was coded directly from the flowcharts shown in Figures 17.3 and 17.4. It can be used to sort any list of numbers in ascending order. It is very fast.

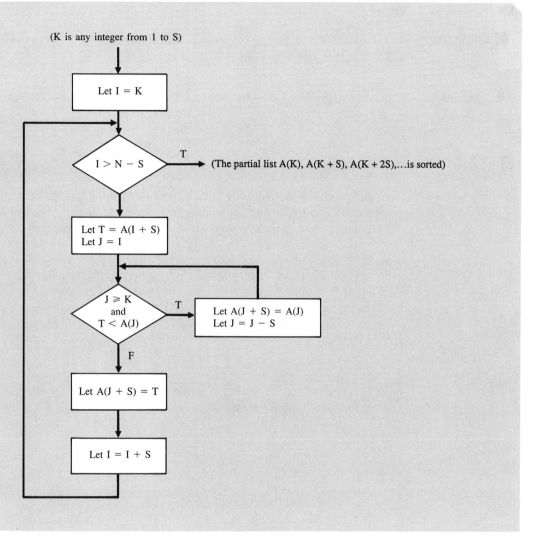

(K is any integer from 1 to S)

Let I = K

I > N − S →T→ (The partial list A(K), A(K + S), A(K + 2S),...is sorted)

Let T = A(I + S)
Let J = I

J ≥ K
and
T < A(J) →T→ Let A(J + S) = A(J)
Let J = J − S

F

Let A(J + S) = T

Let I = I + S

Figure 17.4   Flowchart to sort the list A(K), A(K + S), A(K + 2S), A(K + 3S), . . . , by the insertion method

Figure 17.5
Shellsort subroutine

```
500 REM SHELLSORT SUBROUTINE
510 REM
520 REM SORT ARRAY A OF SIZE N
530 REM INTO ASCENDING ORDER.
540 REM
550 LET S=INT(N/2)
560 WHILE S>0
570    REM SORT ARRAY A SO THAT ENTRIES
580    REM S POSITIONS APART ARE IN ORDER.
590    FOR K=1 TO S
600       FOR I=K TO N-S STEP S
610          LET T=A(I+S)              'Value to be inserted
620          LET J=I                   'Compare T with A(I) first.
630          LET DONE=0                'Position for T not yet found.
640          WHILE J>=K AND DONE=0
650             IF T<A(J) THEN 680
660             LET DONE=1             'Position for T found.
670             GOTO 700
680             LET A(J+S)=A(J)        'Move A(J) up S positions.
690             LET J=J-S              'Position for next comparison
700          NEXT  (or WEND)
710          LET A(J+S)=T              'Correct position for T=A(I+S).
720       NEXT I
730    NEXT K
740    LET S=INT (S/2)
750 NEXT  (or WEND)
760 RETURN
```

REMARK 1   If the array A must be sorted into descending order, simply change the comparison T < A(J) in line 650 to T > A(J).

REMARK 2   If a list of N strings is to be alphabetized, simply use string variable names for A and T.

■ 17.3 The Heapsort

As mentioned at the outset of this chapter, much attention has been given to the topic of sorting and many sorting techniques have beeen developed. The bubblesort algorithm is an example of an **exchange sort**—pairs of list entries are compared and if they are not in order they are *exchanged*. The insertion sort and the Shellsort are examples of **insertion sorts**—values are *inserted* into previously sorted lists or sublists. In this section we present the **heapsort,** a very fast sorting algorithm that requires a technique significantly different from the exchange and insertion methods. The heapsort is an example of a class of sorting algorithms called **tree sorts.** The reasons for the terms *heap-* and *tree sort* are suggested by the following brief discussion concerning the heapsort subroutine.

The idea behind the heapsort algorithm is to envision the array

A(1),A(2),A(3),A(4), . . . ,A(N)

as if its entries were organized as in the following diagram for the case N = 9. (The diagram is called a **binary tree.**)

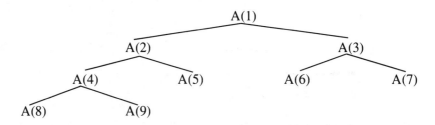

The heapsort first rearranges the entries in array A so that each entry in the tree is at least as large as the two entries immediately below it. You may check that this condition is expressed by writing

$A(K) \geq A(2K)$ and $A(K) \geq A(2K+1)$, for K = 1,2, . . .

Lines 540–690 of the subroutine (Figure 17.6) accomplish this. An array whose entries are arranged in this way is called a **heap.** If you trace lines 540–690 of the subroutine for the nine-entry array

71 67 48 98 64 13 37 58 14

you will obtain the heap

98 71 48 67 64 13 37 58 14

Envisioned as a tree, these entries would be organized as follows:

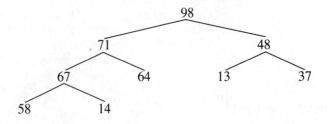

```
500 REM ********** HEAPSORT SUBROUTINE ***********
510 REM SORT ARRAY A OF SIZE N INTO ASCENDING ORDER.
520 REM
530 REM ---------- CREATE INITIAL HEAP -------------
540 FOR K=2 TO N
550    REM INSERT A(K) INTO THE HEAP
560    REM    A(1),A(2),...,A(K-1)
570    REM TO GIVE ANOTHER HEAP
580    REM    A(1),A(2),...,A(K)
590    LET I=K
600    LET T=A(K)
610    LET J=INT(I/2)
620    IF J=0 THEN 680
630       IF T<=A(J) THEN 680
640       LET A(I)=A(J)
650       LET I=J
660       LET J=INT(I/2)
670    GOTO 620
680    LET A(I)=T
690 NEXT K
700 REM ------ SORT ARRAY INTO ASCENDING ORDER -----
710 REM
720 FOR K=N TO 2 STEP -1
730    REM TEMPORARILY STORE A(K) IN T,
740    REM PLACE A(1) IN ITS PROPER POSITION A(K),
750    REM AND THEN ADJUST THE ENTRIES
760    REM    T,A(2),A(3),...,A(K-1)
770    REM TO GIVE A HEAP
780    REM    A(1),A(2),...,A(K-1)
790    LET T=A(K)
800    LET A(K)=A(1)
810    LET I=1
820    LET J=2
830    IF A(3)>A(2) AND K-1>=3 THEN J=3
840    IF J>K-1 THEN 920
850       IF A(J)<=T THEN 920
860       LET A(I)=A(J)
870       LET I=J
880       LET J=2*I
890       IF J+1>K-1 THEN 910
900       IF A(J+1)>A(J) THEN J=J+1
910    GOTO 840
920    LET A(I)=T
930 NEXT K
940 RETURN
```

Figure 17.6 Heapsort subroutine

The next step in the heapsort algorithm is to swap the largest entry A(1) with the last entry A(N) so that the largest entry is in its proper position. The entries in the shorter array

$$A(1),A(2),A(3), \ldots , A(N-1)$$

would then be rearranged into a heap and the process repeated with this shorter heap. For the given nine-entry array shown on page 326, we obtained the initial heap

98 71 48 67 64 13 37 58 14

If you take K = 9 and trace lines 790–920 of the subroutine for this array, you will obtain A(9) = 98, and the first eight entries will be rearranged into the heap

71 67 48 58 64 13 37 14

Envisioned as a tree, these eight entries would be organized as follows:

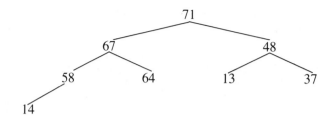

At this point, the largest entry A(1) = 71 would be swapped with the last entry A(8) = 14, the first seven entries would be rearranged into a heap, and the process would be repeated for this shorter seven-entry heap. Continuing in this way, the original list will be sorted very quickly into ascending order.

A complete discussion of the heapsort algorithm and why it is fast is beyond the scope of this introductory book. We present it simply as an alternative sorting subroutine that you may find useful. For long lists it is very fast, considerably faster than the bubble-sort, the insertion sort, and the Shellsort.

■ 17.4 Binary Search

Suppose an array A of length N has been sorted in ascending order. The first step in a "binary" search for a specified value V is to compare V with the "middle" term A(M). When this is done, one of three things will happen.

V = A(M), in which case V is found.
V < A(M), in which case V is in the left half of the list, if at all.
V > A(M), in which case V is in the right half of the list, if at all.

Thus, if V is not found by these comparisons, the search may be confined to a list half the length of the original list. The next step would be to compare V with the "middle" term of this smaller list. If this "middle" term is V, the search is complete. If not, the number of terms to be considered is again halved. Continuing in this manner, we could search the entire list very quickly. We illustrate by searching the following list of 13 numbers for the value V = 67.

    28 31 39 43 48 52 **60** 62 67 73 77 86 89

V = 67 is compared with the middle term, 60. Since it is larger, only the last six terms need be considered.

    62 67 **73** 77 86 89

This shorter list has two "middle" terms. When this happens, let's agree to use the left-most of these. Thus, V = 67 is compared with 73. Since it is smaller, the search is confined to the two values

    62 67

These final two values are both "middle" terms, so 62 is used. V = 67 is larger than 62, which leaves only the term 67. This final comparison results in a match, and V = 67 is found.

Note that V was compared with just four "middle" terms. In the same manner a search for any value V can be completed by comparing V with at most four such "middle" terms. If none of these four values is V, it must be concluded that V is not in the list. Using this method on any list with fewer than 2^N terms, we will either find V by comparing it with at most N "middle" terms or be sure that V is not in the list. Thus, a list with $1023 = 2^{10} - 1$ terms requires 10 or fewer steps to find V or to conclude that it is not present. In contrast, a sequential search of a list with 1023 terms requires 1023/2 comparisons, on the average, to do the same thing.

As simple as a binary search may appear, care must be taken to state the algorithm precisely so that it can be programmed (coded) without bugs. Perhaps the safest way to do this is to use two variables, say L and R (for left and right), to store the leftmost and rightmost positions yet to be searched. Thus, at the outset L = 1, R = N, and the middle term is M = INT((1 + N)/2). If V < A(M), only the terms in positions L through M − 1 need be considered, so R will be replaced by M − 1. Similarly, if V > A(M), L will be replaced by M + 1. The position of the next middle term is M = INT((L + R)/2). If L ≤ R, the comparison of V with A(M) must be repeated. However, if L > R, no more comparisons are required and we must conclude that V is not in the list. The flowchart shown in Figure 17.7 displays an algorithm for carrying out this process. The binary search subroutine on page 330 was coded directly from this algorithm.

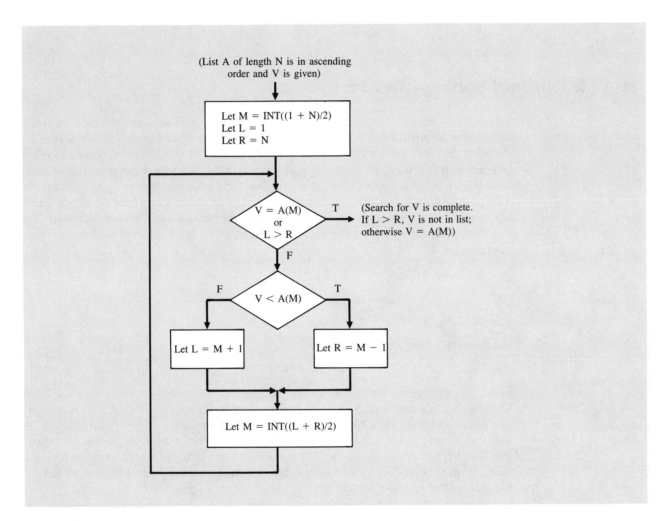

Figure 17.7 Binary-search algorithm

■ **REMARK 1**   If an alphabetized list of words, such as names, is to be searched for given name, simply use A$ and V$ rather than A and V.

■ **REMARK 2**   If the array A is in descending order, change the condition V < A(M) in line 780 to V > A(M).

■ **REMARK 3**   If you know that the entries in a list are in ascending order, but know nothing else about the list, then the binary-search algorithm is the fastest search algorithm available to you.

The Binary Search Subroutine

```
700 REM BINARY SEARCH SUBROUTINE
710 REM TO SEARCH ARRAY A FOR THE VALUE V
720 REM M=0 DENOTES THAT V IS NOT IN ARRAY A
730 REM OTHERWISE A(M)=V
740 LET M=INT((1+N)/2)
750 LET L=1
760 LET R=N
770 WHILE V<>A(M) AND L<=R
780    IF V<A(M) THEN R=M-1 ELSE L=M+1
790    LET M=INT((L+R)/2)
800 NEXT  (or WEND)
810 IF (L>R) THEN M=0
820 RETURN
```

■ 17.5 External Sorting—The Merge Sort

The bubble sort, insertion sort, Shellsort and heapsort algorithms are instances of **internal-sorting algorithms.** This term is used to indicate that all the data being sorted are stored in the computer's main memory at the same time. If the data to be sorted do not fit into memory, the usual practice is to sort them in parts, store these parts as files by using one or more secondary storage devices, and then merge these files into a single sorted file. This process is called **external sorting**—the data to be sorted are stored on external storage devices, and are never stored in their entirety in the computer's main memory.

In this section we describe one of the many methods used to merge sorted files into a single sorted file. We illustrate the method by showing how two lists of numbers

$$A_1 \leq A_2 \leq A_3 \leq \cdots \leq A_m$$

and

$$B_1 \leq B_2 \leq B_3 \leq \cdots \leq B_n$$

can be merged into a single list

$$C_1 \leq C_2 \leq C_3 \leq \cdots \leq C_{m+n}$$

First, we compare A_1 with B_1 and store the smaller as C_1. Suppose B_1 is smaller. Then $C_1 = B_1$ and we compare A_1 with B_2. If this time A_1 is smaller, then $C_2 = A_1$ and we compare A_2 with B_2. (If it happens that two values being compared are equal, we will assign the A entry to list C.) We continue in this manner until all terms in one of the two lists have been stored as C entries. The remaining terms in the other list are then placed in the C list as they appear. This process is called a **merge-sort** process since two sorted lists are *merged* into a single *sorted* list.

Applying this merge-sort method to the lists

$$A = 3 \quad 4 \quad 6 \quad 8 \quad 9 \quad 10$$
$$B = 5 \quad 8 \quad 8$$

we obtain

$$
\begin{aligned}
C_1 &= 3 \quad \text{since } 3 \leq 5 \\
C_2 &= 4 \quad \text{since } 4 \leq 5 \\
C_3 &= 5 \quad \text{since } 6 > 5 \\
C_4 &= 6 \quad \text{since } 6 \leq 8 \\
C_5 &= 8 \quad \text{since } 8 \leq 8 \\
C_6 &= 8 \quad \text{since } 9 > 8 \\
C_7 &= 8 \quad \text{since } 9 > 8
\end{aligned}
$$

$$C_8 = \left. \begin{matrix} 9 \\ 10 \end{matrix} \right\} \text{ since all of list B has been stored in C.}$$
$$C_9 = 10$$

If two lists, stored as File 1 and File 2, are to be merged into File 3, the same method can be used. The following algorithm shows one way to do this.

Merge Algorithm (To Merge File 1 and File 2 into File 3)

If the entries of Files 1 and 2 are in ascending order, the entries of File 3 will be in ascending order. If either file is empty, no merge takes place.

a. If either file is empty at the outset, go to step (j).
b. Read A from File 1 and B from File 2.
c. Write the smaller of A and B on File 3.
d. If either file is empty, go to step (h).
e. If A $\le$ B read a new A from File 1; otherwise, read a new B from File 2.
f. Write the smaller of A and B on File 3.
g. Go to step (d).
h. Write the larger of A and B on File 3.
i. If File 1 is empty, copy the rest of File 2 onto File 3; otherwise, copy the rest of File 1 onto File 3.
j. Stop

To help follow the action of this algorithm, we display the steps in the flowchart shown in Figure 17.8 on page 332. The merge-sort subroutine for two files shown below was coded directly from this flowchart.

Merge-Sort Subroutine for Two Files

```
600 REM SUBROUTINE ------ MERGE FILES 1 AND 2 INTO FILE 3 ------
610 REM
620 REM ALL FILES ARE ASSUMED TO HAVE BEEN OPENED AND FILE
630 REM POINTERS PROPERLY POSITIONED - USUALLY AT THE BEGINNING.
640 REM IF FILES 1 AND 2 ARE IN ASCENDING ORDER THEIR CONTENTS
650 REM WILL BE STORED IN ASCENDING ORDER IN FILE 3.
660 REM IF EITHER FILE 1 OR 2 IS EMPTY, NO MERGE TAKES PLACE.
670 REM     A DENOTES A VALUE READ FROM FILE 1
680 REM     B DENOTES A VALUE READ FROM FILE 2
685 REM
690 REM ----- ABORT IF EITHER FILE 1 OR 2 IS EMPTY -----
700 IF END#1 OR END#2 THEN RETURN
710 REM ---- BEGIN MERGE ----
720 INPUT#1,A
730 INPUT#2,B
740 IF A<=B THEN PRINT#3,A ELSE PRINT#3,B
750 WHILE NOT END#1 AND NOT END#2
760    IF A<=B THEN INPUT#1,A ELSE INPUT#2,B
770    IF A<=B THEN PRINT#3,A ELSE PRINT#3,B
780 NEXT  (or WEND)
790 REM HAVE REACHED END OF FILE 1 OR FILE 2.
800 IF A<=B THEN PRINT#3,B ELSE PRINT#3,A
810 REM ----- COPY REST OF FILE 1 OR FILE 2 ONTO FILE 3 ----
820 WHILE NOT END#1
830    INPUT#1,A
840    PRINT#3,A
850 NEXT  (or WEND)
860 WHILE NOT END#2
870    INPUT#2,B
880    PRINT#3,B
890 NEXT  (or WEND)
900 REM ---- MERGE IS COMPLETE ----
910 RETURN
```

■ **REMARK**   In the subroutine to merge two files, we use the end-of-file specifiers END#1 and END#2. If your system uses the end-of-file function EOF, change END#1 and END#2 to EOF(1) and EOF(2), respectively. If your version of BASIC allows neither END# or EOF, you must use the ON ERROR GOTO statement as described in Section 15.2.

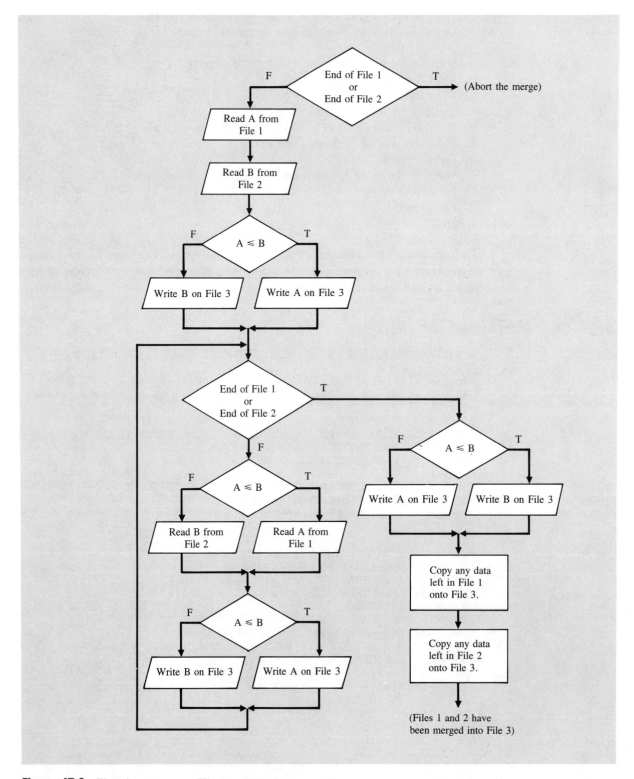

Figure 17.8   Flowchart to merge File 1 and File 2 into File 3

The method described for merging two files into a single file can be generalized to allow more than two files to be merged. The following algorithm and corresponding subroutine show one way to do this. Your version of BASIC may require changes to the subroutine as mentioned in the Remark on page 332.

Merge Algorithm (To Merge K Files, Numbered 1 through K, into a Single File, Numbered L)

One or more of the K files to be merged may be empty files. If the entries in each of files 1 through K are in ascending order, the entries in File L will be in ascending order.

a. Read the first entries of Files 1 through K into A(1), A(2), . . . , A(K). If file number I is empty, assign the "large" number 1E30 to A(I).
b. Find J such that A(J) is the smallest of A(1), A(2), . . . , A(K).
c. If A(J) = 1E30, stop; the merge is complete.
d. Write A(J) onto File L and read another value for A(J) from File J. But if the end of File J is encountered, assign 1E30 to A(J).
e. Go to Step (b).

The Merge-Sort Subroutine for K Files

```
100 REM ****** SUBROUTINE MERGE-SORT ******
110 REM THIS SUBROUTINE MERGES INPUT FILES 1
115 REM THROUGH K INTO FILE L (L>K)
120 REM
130 REM IF THE INPUT FILES ARE SORTED IN ASCENDING ORDER,
140 REM FILE L WILL ALSO BE SORTED IN ASCENDING ORDER.
150 REM
160 REM THE SUBROUTINE ASSUMES THAT ALL FILES
165 REM WERE OPENED IN THE MAIN PROGRAM AND THAT
170 REM THEY WILL BE CLOSED OR RESTORED THERE.
180 REM
190 REM FOR I=1 TO K, A(I) DENOTES A VALUE READ FROM FILE I.
200 REM ARRAY A MUST BE DIMENSIONED IN THE MAIN PROGRAM.
210 REM
220 REM READ FIRST ENTRIES OF INPUT FILES INTO
230 REM ARRAY A. SET A(I)=1E30 IF FILE I IS EMPTY.
240 FOR I=1 TO K
250    IF END#I THEN LET A(I)=1E30 ELSE INPUT#I,A(I)
260 NEXT I
270 REM ***** FIND J SUCH THAT A(J) IS LEAST *****
280    LET J=1
290    FOR I=2 TO K
300       IF A(I)<A(J) THEN LET J=I
310    NEXT I
320    REM ***** TEST FOR MERGE COMPLETION *****
330    IF A(J)=1E30 THEN 380
340    REM *** WRITE A(J) ON FILE L AND GET NEXT A(J) ***
350    PRINT#L,A(J)
360    IF END#J THEN LET A(J)=1E30 ELSE READ#J,A(J)
370 GOTO 280
380 REM ***** MERGE IS COMPLETE *****
390 RETURN
```

■ 17.6 Problems

Write a program to perform each task specified in Problems 1–15. The subroutines presented in this chapter may be used where appropriate.

1. Read an array L of integers from DATA lines, and then create two arrays A and B as follows. A is to contain the odd integers appearing in L, and B the even integers. A and B are to be sorted in ascending order before being displayed.

2. Read a list of positive integers into an array L and then create arrays L1 and L2 with L1 containing those values that exceed the average of all input values and with L2 containing the others. Sort L1 and L2 in descending order and display them as adjacent columns with the headings LIST1 and LIST2.

3. Read a list of positive integers into an array L and then create arrays L1 and L2 as follows. L1 is to contain those integers that exceed the *median* of the input list and L2 is to contain the others. L1 and L2 are to be displayed as adjacent columns and each column is to appear in ascending order. (The median of a list of numbers $a_1 \leq a_2 \leq a_3 \cdots \leq a_n$ is the middle term if n is odd and the average of the two "middle" terms if n is even.) (*Remark:* Only the array L needs to be sorted.)

4. Input an array L at the keyboard and display its contents. Then sort the array into ascending order and display the new ordering. Finally, modify L by deleting all values that appear more than once and display the modified array. For example, if $L(1) = 7$, $L(2) = L(3) = 8$, and $L(4) = L(5) = L(6) = 9$, then the new array is to have $L(1) = 7$, $L(2) = 8$, and $L(3) = 9$. Write your program so that many different lists of input values can be processed as described during a single program run.

5. Create an array A of N numbers by using the RND function and copy the array into a second array B. Sort array A by using a bubble sort and array B by using either the Shellsort or the Heapsort. Be sure to display a message at the start and end of each sort. The value N is to be input and in the range 1 to 1,000.

6. Create an array A of 1000 terms with

   $$A(I) = I^2 - I + 1$$

   Search this array for each of the following ten numbers (include them in DATA lines).

205663	676507	3131	225	62751
810901	202951	164212	678153	723351

   As each number is read, it is to be displayed along with the I value indicating its position in the array. If it is not in the array, an appropriate message should be displayed. Use a binary search. (A need not be sorted; it is in order.)

7. Create the array A as in Problem 6. Then search A for each of the 1000 values

   $$V = J^4 - J^2 + 1 - 1E6 * INT((J^4 - J^2 + 1)/1E6)$$

   where $J = 1, 2, \ldots, 1000$. For each V found in the array, display the J that gave it, the position M in the array A at which V is stored, the value V being sought, and the value of A(M). These last two values should be the same. Values of V not found should cause nothing to be displayed. (Use a binary search. A sequential search will take too long. Try it and see.)

8. Two input lists of positive integers, each appearing in ascending order, are to be read into arrays L1 and L2. The two arrays are then to be merged into a single array L whose entries are also in ascending order. L is to be displayed five numbers to the line.

9. Two input lists of positive integers, each appearing in ascending order, are to be read into arrays L1 and L2. The contents of these two arrays are then to be displayed as a single column, from smallest to largest. The arrays L1 and L2 are not to be merged into a single array.

10. Two lists of English words are presented in DATA lines. The word END terminates both lists. The two lists are to be alphabetized and displayed in two columns. Then the lists are to be merged into one alphabetized list, and this list is to be displayed using as little space as possible while still preserving the identity of the words. Two subroutines are to be used: one to sort a list and the other to merge two previously sorted lists into a single sorted list.

11. Two lists of numbers, each appearing in ascending order, are presented in DATA lines. Write a program to merge these two lists and store them in a file named NUMS so that the numbers in NUMS are also in ascending order. After NUMS has been created, display its contents, five numbers to a line. Use the following DATA lines and algorithm:

```
800 REM LIST1 COUNT AND VALUES
810 DATA 10
820 DATA 15,25,30,40,50,55,70,75,85,90
830 REM LIST2 COUNT AND VALUES
840 DATA 8
850 DATA 45,48,55,60,70,85,88,97
```

a. Read the lists into arrays L1 and L2.
b. Merge arrays L1 and L2 into file NUMS.
c. Display the contents of NUMS, five numbers to a line.

12. Two lists of English words are presented in DATA lines. The word END terminates each list. Write a program to read the two lists into arrays, to alphabetize each array, to merge the two arrays into a file named WORDS, and to display the contents of WORDS, three words to a line. Use the following DATA lines:

```
800 DATA PLIERS,HAMMERS,LEVELS,WRENCHES,SAWS
810 DATA SCREWDRIVERS,CHISELS,SQUARES,END
820 DATA NAILS,SCREWS,TACKS,TAPE,NUTS,BOLTS
830 DATA GLUE,PASTE,PAINT,STAIN,END
```

Problems 13–15 refer to the following files maintained by the AMCO Insurance Company. The file SALARY contains information about salaried employees, and the file HOURLY contains information about employees paid by the hour.

File SALARY

Employee name	Employee number
Adams John P.	351643
Dorr Mary L.	280455
Hart Thomas R.	386259
Poe Edgar T.	264359
Pratt Susan A.	242354
Zeoli Harold I.	283335

File HOURLY

Employee name	Employee number
Boyd Harry T.	539218
Dorr Martin P.	622055
Evans Janice T.	550044
Hart Thomas P.	622422
Nee Herbert T.	600245
Sands Susan Q.	502424
Toski John P.	522322

13. Write a program to help create the files SALARY and HOURLY. Note that the names for each file are in alphabetical order.
14. Write a program to merge files SALARY and HOURLY into a single file EMPLOY so that the names in EMPLOY are also in alphabetical order. End your program with a section that displays the contents of EMPLOY.
15. Write a program to display the contents of the file EMPLOY created in Problem 14, but with employee numbers appearing in ascending order.

■ 17.7 Review True-or-False Quiz

1. It is desirable to use sorting algorithms that compare and swap only adjacent entries, for such algorithms will not only be easier to understand but will generally be very efficient.   **T F**

2. If an array N$ of employee names and an array S containing the corresponding salaries of the employees are to be used to produce a two-column salary report with the names in alphabetical order, two loops will be needed, one to alphabetize the array N$ and another to make the corresponding changes to array S.   **T F**

3. Sorting algorithms are useful in producing printed reports in which lists of numbers appear in ascending or descending order or in which names appear in alphabetical order. Such tasks represent the principal and only major application of sorting.   **T F**

4. An array must be sorted in ascending or descending order before a sequential search can be made.   **T   F**

5. A binary search can be made only on lists that are sorted.   **T   F**

6. Each step in a binary search for a value V involves comparing V with an array entry A(M) to determine if V = A(M), V < A(M), or V > A(M). At most, 15 such steps are required to determine if a value V is included in an array of length 30,000.   **T   F**

7. The idea behind the insertion sort is to build a list by starting with one value and then placing each successive value in its proper position relative to all values included to that point.   **T   F**

8. The idea of the Shellsort is to use the insertion method on shorter and shorter partial lists.   **T   F**

9. One reason the Shellsort is efficient is that "small" values are moved to the left by more than one position at a time.   **T   F**

10. The Shellsort can be used to arrange a list of numbers in ascending or descending order but cannot be used to sort string data.   **T   F**

11. Algorithms used to sort data that are stored in a computer's main memory are called *internal-sorting algorithms*.   **T   F**

12. External-sorting algorithms can be used to sort data that will not fit in the computer's main memory.   **T   F**

13. External-sorting procedures often utilize internal-sorting algorithms.   **T   F**

18

Matrices

A two-dimensional array is usually thought of as a rectangular array having rows and columns. For example, a 2-by-3 array B with entries B(1,1) = 5, B(1,2) = 3, B(1,3) = 4, B(2,1) = 6, B(2,2) = 7, and B(2,3) = 9 would be visualized as the rectangular array of numbers

$$\begin{bmatrix} 5 & 3 & 4 \\ 6 & 7 & 9 \end{bmatrix}$$

having two rows and three columns. A one-dimensional array (list) A with entries A(1) = 4, A(2) = 8, A(3) = 2, and A(4) = 1 can also be thought of as a rectangular array

$$\begin{bmatrix} 4 \\ 8 \\ 2 \\ 1 \end{bmatrix}$$

that has four rows and one column.

We define a **matrix** to be any rectangular array of numbers. (The plural of *matrix* is *matrices*.) Thus, both one- and two-dimensional arrays are matrices. Because matrices have proved to be a useful aid in the solution of a variety of problems, the most common mathematical operations on matrices have been included in extended versions of BASIC. This chapter will describe and illustrate the BASIC statements used to perform matrix operations.

■ 18.1 Assigning Values to a Matrix: The MAT READ and MAT INPUT Statements

The MAT READ and MAT INPUT statements are used to assign values to matrices. The clarity and conciseness with which a program can be written by using these two statements are evident in the following examples.

EXAMPLE 1

Here is a program to read six numbers into a 2-by-3 matrix B and display the matrix B.

For purposes of comparison, the program is written in two ways: on the left with matrix statements and on the right with subscripted variables.

```
10 DIM B(2,3)        10 DIM B(2,3)
20 MAT READ B        20 FOR I=1 TO 2
30 MAT PRINT B;      30    FOR J=1 TO 3
40 DATA 5,3,4,6,7,9  40       READ B(I,J)
50 END               50       PRINT B(I,J);
RUN                  60    NEXT J
                     70    PRINT
  5   3   4          80 NEXT I
  6   7   9          90 DATA 5,3,4,6,7,9
                     99 END
                     RUN

                       5   3   4
                       6   7   9
```

The programming lines

```
10 DIM B(2,3)
20 MAT READ B
```

cause the computer to read six values from DATA lines. These values are assigned to the matrix B by rows; that is, B(1,1), B(1,2), B(1,3) will be read first, and then B(2,1), B(2,2), B(2,3) will be read. The MAT PRINT statement (line 30) is described in the next section.

■
□ **REMARK**

Matrices should be declared in DIM statements. If they are not, BASIC assumes that they are 10-by-10 arrays (11-by-11 where 0 subscripts are used).

EXAMPLE 2

Here is a program to assign values to a matrix during program execution.

```
10 DIM B(2,3)
20 PRINT "ENTER 6 VALUES-3 PER LINE."
30 MAT INPUT B
40 PRINT "THE 2-BY-3 MATRIX:"
50 MAT PRINT B;
60 END
RUN

ENTER 6 VALUES-3 PER LINE.
? 5,3,4
? 6,7,9
THE 2-BY-3 MATRIX:
  5   3   4
  6   7   9
```

In response to the question mark, the user must type the proper number of values to fill the first row of the matrix (matrices are always assigned by row) and then press the RETURN key. Another question mark will appear. The process should be repeated until the matrix, as defined, has been completely assigned. Only then will program execution continue.

□

More than one matrix may appear in a MAT READ or MAT INPUT statement.

EXAMPLE 3

```
10 DIM C(3,4),D(2,2)
20 MAT READ C,D
30 DATA 8,7,6,5,4,3,2,1
40 DATA 8,7,6,5,4,3,2,1
50 END
```

Two matrices C and D are declared in line 10. Line 20 instructs the computer to read the two matrices C and D. C is read completely before D is read, to give

$$C = \begin{bmatrix} 8 & 7 & 6 & 5 \\ 4 & 3 & 2 & 1 \\ 8 & 7 & 6 & 5 \end{bmatrix} \qquad D = \begin{bmatrix} 4 & 3 \\ 2 & 1 \end{bmatrix}$$

The general forms of the MAT READ and MAT INPUT statements are

ln MAT READ **a,b,c,...**
ln MAT INPUT **a,b,c,...**

where **a,b,c,...** denote matrices.

■ 18.2 The MAT PRINT Statement

The MAT PRINT statement is used to display matrices. The programming line

```
30 MAT PRINT B;
```

in Example 1 caused the matrix B to be displayed by rows; the semicolon after B indicates that B should be displayed using the packed format. If line 30 had been

```
30 MAT PRINT B,
```

the matrix would again be displayed by rows, but only one number would appear in each print zone, as shown in the next example.

EXAMPLE 4

```
10 DIM B(2,3)
20 MAT READ B
30 PRINT "USING THE PACKED FORMAT"
40 MAT PRINT B;
50 PRINT "USING THE PRINT ZONE FORMAT"
60 MAT PRINT B
70 DATA 5,3,4,6,7,9
80 END
RUN

USING THE PACKED FORMAT
 5  3  4
 6  7  9

USING THE PRINT ZONE FORMAT
 5              3              4
 6              7              9
```

If no punctuation follows the matrix in a MAT PRINT statement, the comma is assumed.

More than one matrix may appear in a MAT PRINT statement.

EXAMPLE 5

```
10 DIM C(3,4),D(2,2)
20 MAT READ C,D
25 MAT PRINT C,D;
30 DATA 8,7,6,5,4,3,2,1
40 DATA 8,7,6,5,4,3,2,1
50 END
RUN

 8              7              6              5
 4              3              2              1
 8              7              6              5
 4  3
 2  1
```

Matrix C is displayed first according to its format, followed by matrix D according to its format.

The general form of the MAT PRINT statement is

ln MAT PRINT **azbzcz...**

where **a,b,c,...** denote matrices and **z** is either a comma or a semicolon. The second matrix is displayed under the first, the third under the second, and so on.

■ 18.3 One-Dimensional Matrices

When we are using matrix operations, a one-dimensional array is regarded as a matrix with one column. Thus, the two dimension statements DIM A(5) and DIM A(5,1) are equivalent. If an array A with five elements is to be regarded as having one row with five entries, it must be declared with DIM A(1,5).

EXAMPLE 6   **Here are two programs that display a matrix with one row and a matrix with one column.**

```
10 DIM A(1,5)      10 DIM M(4)     [or DIM M(4,1)]
20 MAT READ A      20 MAT READ M
30 MAT PRINT A;    30 MAT PRINT M
40 DATA 3,1,6,5,4  40 DATA 4,3,2,1
50 END             50 END
RUN                RUN

   3  1  6  5  4      4
                      3
                      2
                      1
```

■ 18.4 Matrix Operations

BASIC allows the standard matrix operations of addition, subtraction, multiplication, and scalar multiplication. These operations are defined as follows.

Addition (subtraction). The sum (difference) of two matrices A and B of the same dimensions is formed by adding (taking the difference of) the corresponding entries in A and B.

Scalar multiplication. The product cA, where c denotes a scalar (number) and A a matrix, is formed by multiplying each entry in A by c.

Multiplication. The product C = A × B of the row and column matrices

$$A = [a \quad b \quad c] \qquad B = \begin{bmatrix} x \\ y \\ z \end{bmatrix}$$

is the 1-by-1 matrix

$$C = [ax + by + cz]$$

For example,

$$[1 \quad 2 \quad 4] \times \begin{bmatrix} 1 \\ 3 \\ 4 \end{bmatrix} = [1 \cdot 1 + 2 \cdot 3 + 4 \cdot 4] = [23]$$

$$[3 \quad 2] \times \begin{bmatrix} 1 \\ 5 \end{bmatrix} = [3 \cdot 1 + 2 \cdot 5] \qquad = [13]$$

Note that the number of columns of A must equal the number of rows of B. To find the product A × B of matrices other than row-and-column matrices, we consider the rows of A as row matrices and the columns of B as column matrices. Then, the entry in the Ith row and Jth column of A × B is found by taking the product of the Ith row of A and the Jth column of B as described above. The product matrix A × B will have the same number of rows as A and the same number of columns as B. For example,

$$\begin{bmatrix} 2 & 3 & 1 \\ 4 & 1 & 2 \end{bmatrix} \times \begin{bmatrix} 1 & 2 \\ 3 & 4 \\ 1 & 5 \end{bmatrix} = \begin{bmatrix} 2 \cdot 1 + 3 \cdot 3 + 1 \cdot 1 & 2 \cdot 2 + 3 \cdot 4 + 1 \cdot 5 \\ 4 \cdot 1 + 1 \cdot 3 + 2 \cdot 1 & 4 \cdot 2 + 1 \cdot 4 + 2 \cdot 5 \end{bmatrix}$$

$$= \begin{bmatrix} 12 & 21 \\ 9 & 22 \end{bmatrix}$$

The BASIC statements to perform these operations are as follows:

```
MAT S=A+B
MAT D=A-B
MAT S=(C)*A
MAT P=D*E
```

Matrices A and B must have the same dimensions so that A + B and A − B can be calculated. Also, so that the product P = D * E will be defined, the number of columns of D must equal the number of rows of E. The scalar C must be enclosed in parentheses as shown.

EXAMPLE 7   **Here is a program to compute and display A + B, 2B, and A ∗ B for the following matrices A and B:**

$$A = \begin{bmatrix} 2 & 3 & 4 \\ 6 & 7 & 7 \\ 4 & 4 & 3 \end{bmatrix} \qquad B = \begin{bmatrix} 1 & 2 & 1 \\ 1 & 2 & 1 \\ 1 & 0 & 0 \end{bmatrix}$$

```
100 DIM A(3,3),B(3,3),C(3,3)
110 MAT READ A,B
120 MAT C=A+B
130 PRINT "THE MATRIX A+B:"
140 MAT PRINT C;
150 MAT C=(2)*B
160 PRINT "THE MATRIX 2*B:"
170 MAT PRINT C;
180 MAT C=A*B
190 PRINT "THE MATRIX A*B:"
200 MAT PRINT C;
210 DATA 2,3,4,6,7,7,4,4,3
220 DATA 1,2,1,1,2,1,1,0,0
230 END
RUN

THE MATRIX A+B:
 3  5  5
 7  9  8
 5  4  3
THE MATRIX 2*B:
 2  4  2
 2  4  2
 2  0  0
THE MATRIX A*B:
 9 10  5
20 26 13
11 16  8
```

■ **REMARK 1**   The matrix C that is to be calculated must be dimensioned to the exact size in a DIM statement.

■ **REMARK 2**   Line 150 is typical of assignment statements that multiply a matrix by a scalar. Note that the scalar (2 in this case) is enclosed in parentheses. The statement is MAT C = (2) ∗ B, not MAT C = 2 ∗ B. The scalar may be any numerical expression, but it must be enclosed in parentheses.

■ **REMARK 3**   Matrix operations must be performed in assignment statements as shown in lines 120, 150, and 180. Statements such as MAT PRINT A + B are not allowed.

EXAMPLE 8   **A plumbing-supply company has developed the following data over one quarter:**

	April	May	June
Income	20,415	22,355	33,451
Expenses	19,041	20,851	26,152

Write a program to compute the monthly profit for these 3 months and the amount that should be put aside for tax purposes if the tax rate is 18% on all profits.

PROBLEM ANALYSIS

Let's read the income into a 1-by-3 matrix I and the expenses into another 1-by-3 matrix E. Then the profit for each month is given by the entries in the matrix P = I − E and the taxes are given in the matrix T = 0.18 × P.

THE PROGRAM

```
100 REM PROFIT AND TAX COMPUTATION FOR ONE QUARTER
110 DIM I(1,3),E(1,3),P(1,3),T(1,3)
120 MAT READ I,E
130 MAT P=I-E
140 MAT T=(.18)*P
150 READ A$,B$,C$
160 PRINT ,A$,B$,C$
170 PRINT
180 PRINT "PROFIT",
190 MAT PRINT P,
200 PRINT "TAXES",
210 MAT PRINT T,
500 DATA 20415,22355,33451
510 DATA 19041,20851,26152
520 DATA APRIL,MAY,JUNE
999 END
RUN
```

```
                APRIL         MAY           JUNE

PROFIT          1374          1504          7299
TAXES           247.32        270.72        1313.82
```

The matrix expressions that may be evaluated in matrix-assignment statements are very limited compared with the freedom allowed in forming BASIC expressions with LET statements. At most one operation may be performed in a single matrix-assignment statement. Statements such as

```
MAT X=MAT Y+Z-(3)*W
```

are not allowed. Furthermore, a matrix may not be used as an operand in a statement assigning values to the same matrix. Thus, statements such as

```
MAT A=A+B
MAT A=(2)*A
```

are not allowed.

■ 18.5 Matrix Functions

Certain matrix function are included in the BASIC language.

The CON Function

The statement

```
10 MAT D=CON(4,7)
```

will generate a 4-by-7 matrix D with each entry 1.

The ZER Function

The statement

```
20 MAT E=ZER(5,6)
```

will generate a 5-by-6 matrix E with each entry 0. The ZER function is useful when initializing all values of an array to 0.

The IDN Function

The statement

```
30 MAT F=IDN(3,3)
```

will generate the 3-by-3 identity matrix (1s in the upper-left to lower-right diagonal and 0s elsewhere). The product of the N-by-N identity matrix and any other N-by-N matrix A is A.

The arguments in these three functions need not be positive integer constants; they may be any BASIC numerical expressions. As illustrated in the following example, the functions CON, ZER, and IDN can be used to assign dimensions to matrices other than those given in DIM statements.

EXAMPLE 9   **Here is an illustration of the CON, ZER, and IDN functions.**

```
100 DIM C(20,20),Z(20,20),I(20,20)
110 PRINT "ENTER TWO DIMENSIONS FOR FIRST MATRIX."
120 INPUT A,B
130 MAT C=CON(A,B)
140 PRINT "THE";A;"BY";B;"MATRIX CONTAINING ALL ONES:"
150 MAT PRINT C;
160 MAT Z=ZER(B,A)
170 PRINT "THE";B;"BY";A;"MATRIX CONTAINING ALL ZEROS:"
180 MAT PRINT Z;
190 MAT I=IDN(A+B,A+B)
200 PRINT "THE";A+B;"BY";A+B;"IDENTITY MATRIX:"
210 MAT PRINT I;
220 END
RUN

ENTER TWO DIMENSIONS FOR FIRST MATRIX.
? 3,2
THE 3 BY 2 MATRIX CONTAINING ALL ONES:
 1  1
 1  1
 1  1
THE 2 BY 3 MATRIX CONTAINING ALL ZEROS:
 0  0  0
 0  0  0
```

```
THE 5 BY 5 IDENTITY MATRIX:
 1   0   0   0   0
 0   1   0   0   0
 0   0   1   0   0
 0   0   0   1   0
 0   0   0   0   1
```

■ **REMARK**

The matrices C, Z, and I are initially declared as 20-by-20 arrays in line 100. They are redimensioned in lines 130, 160, and 190 using the functions CON, ZER, IDN. If values other than 3 and 2 are input, this program will display matrices of different dimensions. The only restriction is that you cannot redimension a matrix so that it contains more entries (the product of its dimensions) than specified in the initial DIM statement ($20 \times 20 = 400$, in this example).

The TRN and INV Functions

BASIC contains the matrix functions **TRN** and **INV** to determine the **transpose** and **inverse**, respectively, of a matrix A. The transpose of a matrix A is the matrix whose rows are the columns of A, in the same order. Thus, the transpose of

$$\begin{bmatrix} 1 & 2 \\ 3 & 4 \\ 5 & 6 \end{bmatrix} \quad \text{is} \quad \begin{bmatrix} 1 & 3 & 5 \\ 2 & 4 & 6 \end{bmatrix}$$

The inverse of a matrix A is the matrix B for which $A \times B = B \times A = I$, the identity matrix. Only certain square matrices (same number of rows as columns) can have inverses. You may check that

$$\begin{bmatrix} 1 & 1 \\ 0 & 1 \end{bmatrix} \times \begin{bmatrix} 1 & -1 \\ 0 & 1 \end{bmatrix} = \begin{bmatrix} 1 & -1 \\ 0 & 1 \end{bmatrix} \times \begin{bmatrix} 1 & 1 \\ 0 & 1 \end{bmatrix} = \begin{bmatrix} 1 & 0 \\ 0 & 1 \end{bmatrix}$$

so that the inverse of

$$\begin{bmatrix} 1 & 1 \\ 0 & 1 \end{bmatrix} \quad \text{is} \quad \begin{bmatrix} 1 & -1 \\ 0 & 1 \end{bmatrix}$$

The functions TRN and INV are used in assignment statements as follows:

ln MAT **a** = TRN(**b**)
ln MAT **a** = INV(**b**)

where **a** and **b** denote different matrices.

The function TRN can sometimes be used to enhance the output of a program. For example, suppose a 3-by-6 matrix A is to be displayed. The statement

```
MAT PRINT A,
```

cannot be used unless your output device allows six zones per line. If the statement

```
MAT PRINT A;
```

is used, the six columns may not "line up" because of the packed format. However, if the two statements

```
MAT T=TRN(A)
MAT PRINT T,
```

are used, there are only three columns to be displayed, and the difficulty vanishes.

Neither the inverse nor the transpose of a matrix may be calculated in place. Hence, statements such as

```
100 MAT B=D*INV(C)
200 MAT M=TRN(A)+E
```

are not allowed.

EXAMPLE 10 **Here is a program to read and display a 3-by-3 matrix C and then to calculate and display both the inverse of C and the product of C and its inverse.**

```
100 DIM A(3,3),B(3,3),C(3,3)
110 MAT READ C
120 PRINT "MATRIX C:"
130 MAT PRINT C
140 PRINT
150 MAT B=INV(C)
160 PRINT "INVERSE OF C:"
170 MAT PRINT B
180 PRINT
190 MAT A=C*B
200 PRINT "MATRIX C TIMES INVERSE OF MATRIX C:"
220 MAT PRINT A
230 DATA 1,2,3,9,8,7,-2,5,-7
240 END
RUN

MATRIX C:
 1              2              3
 9              8              7
-2              5             -7

INVERSE OF C:
-.478947        .152632       -5.26316E-2
 .257895       -5.26316E-3     .105263
 .321053       -4.73684E-2    -5.26316E-2

MATRIX C TIMES INVERSE OF MATRIX C:
 1.             0             -1.24345E-14
 0              1.             3.55271E-15
-4.44089E-16   -3.55271E-15    1
```

The following example illustrates a common application of the matrix operations and functions.

EXAMPLE 11 **Let's write a program to solve the following linear system for x, y, z, and w.**

$$x + \ y + \ z + \ w = 2$$
$$x + 2y - \ z + \ w = 3$$
$$2x + 3y + \ z - 2w = 0$$
$$x + \ y + 2z - 2w = 1$$

PROBLEM ANALYSIS

Observing how matrix multiplication is performed, we can rewrite this system of equations in matrix form as follows:

$$\begin{bmatrix} 1 & 1 & 1 & 1 \\ 1 & 2 & -1 & 1 \\ 2 & 3 & 1 & -2 \\ 1 & 1 & 2 & -2 \end{bmatrix} \times \begin{bmatrix} x \\ y \\ z \\ w \end{bmatrix} = \begin{bmatrix} 2 \\ 3 \\ 0 \\ 1 \end{bmatrix}$$

Let A denote the indicated 4-by-4 matrix, and let C denote the 4-by-1 matrix on the right. With this notation, the matrix equation can be written as follows:

$$A \times \begin{bmatrix} x \\ y \\ z \\ w \end{bmatrix} = C$$

Now suppose A has the inverse B. (If it does not, this method doesn't work. However, if this system of equations has precisely one solution, which is the case in many applications, A will have an inverse.) Then, since B × A = I, the identity matrix, we can multiply both sides of the matrix equation by B to obtain the following:

$$\begin{bmatrix} x \\ y \\ z \\ w \end{bmatrix} = B \times C$$

The values for x, y, z, and w are thus the four entries obtained when the product B × C is performed. This analysis suggests the following simple algorithm:

THE ALGORITHM

a. Assign values to the 4-by-4 matrix A and the 4-by-1 matrix C from the given system of equations.
b. Calculate the inverse B of A and the product P = B × C.
c. Display the product P. This displays the values x, y, z, and w that satisfy the given equations.

The following program shows the power of the matrix operations. It would be a challenging task to write a program to solve such equations without using matrix operations.

THE PROGRAM

```
100 DIM A(4,4),B(4,4),C(4,1),P(4,1)
110 MAT READ A,C
120 MAT B=INV(A)
130 MAT P=B*C
140 PRINT "THE SOLUTIONS TO THE SYSTEM OF EQUATIONS:"
150 MAT PRINT P
500 DATA 1,1,1,1
510 DATA 1,2,-1,1
520 DATA 2,3,1,-2
530 DATA 1,1,2,-2
540 DATA 2,3,0,1
999 END
RUN

THE SOLUTIONS TO THE SYSTEM OF EQUATIONS:
-36
 23
 11
 4
```

■ 18.6 Problems

1. What is the output when each program is run?

a.
```
10 DIM A(4,1)
20 MAT READ A
30 MAT PRINT A;
40 DATA 2,4,6,8,1,3,5
50 END
```

b.
```
10 MAT D=CON(3,3)
20 FOR I=1 TO 3
30    LET D(I,2)=D(I,2)+4
40 NEXT I
50 MAT PRINT D;
60 END
```

c.
```
10 DIM H(4,4),I(8,8)
20 MAT I=IDN(4,4)
30 FOR J=1 TO 4
40    MAT H=(J)*I
50 NEXT J
60 MAT PRINT H;
70 END
```

d.
```
10 DIM A(4,3)
20 FOR I=1 TO 4
30    FOR J=1 TO 3
40       LET A(I,J)=I+J
50    NEXT J
60 NEXT I
70 MAT PRINT A;
80 END
```

e.
```
10 DIM A(5,5)
20 MAT A=ZER(5,5)
30 FOR K=1 TO 5
40    READ A(K,K)
50 NEXT K
60 MAT PRINT A;
70 DATA 7,9,1,3,5
80 END
```

f.
```
10 DIM M(8,8)
20 MAT M=ZER(5,5)
30 FOR I=1 TO 5
40    LET M(I,I)=M(I,I)+I
50 NEXT I
60 MAT PRINT M;
70 END
```

2. Each of the following programs contains at least one error. Correct them to ensure that each will run to completion.

a.
```
10 DIM A(8,1),B(8,1)
20 MAT READ A
30 MAT B=4*A
40 MAT PRINT B
50 DATA 4,3,2,1,3,5,7,9
60 END
```

b.
```
10 DIM M(2,2),D(2,2)
20 MAT M=CON(2,2)
30 MAT D=(M+M)+M
40 MAT PRINT D
50 END
```

c.
```
10 DIM A(2,3),B(3,2),C(2,2)
20 MAT READ A,B
30 LET C=A*B
40 MAT PRINT C
50 DATA 3,1,7,2,6,3
60 DATA 5,9,1,8,-3,0
70 END
```

d.
```
10 DIM A(2,3),B(2,3)
20 MAT READ A,B
30 MAT PRINT A+B
40 DATA 2,4,6,5,7,9
50 DATA 3,5,8,2,7,3
60 END
```

Write a program to perform each task specified in Problems 3–20.

3. Read a 2-by-3 matrix A from DATA lines and display both A and the transpose of A.

4. Read a 2-by-3 matrix A from DATA lines to determine its transpose B and the product A * B of A and its transpose. Display the three matrices A, B, and A * B.

5. Read two 3-by-2 matrices from DATA lines, and display the two matrices, the sum of the two matrices, and the transpose of this sum.

6. Input nine values for the 3-by-3 matrix A. Then display the matrices A and $A^2 = A * A$.

7. Display the cube $A^3 = A * A * A$ of any 3-by-3 matrix A whose entries are typed at the keyboard.

8. Read a 3-by-3 matrix A from DATA lines, and then display the matrices A, A^2, A^3, . . . , A^N where N is a positive integer. Have the user supply N. Try your program for the value N = 6 and the matrix

$$A = \begin{bmatrix} .2 & .4 & .4 \\ .01 & .02 & .97 \\ .8 & .05 & .15 \end{bmatrix}$$

9. Often when we are using the computer to manipulate matrices whose entries are integers, we generate matrices with entries that are not actually integers as desired but are very close to integers. For instance (see Example 10), the product of a matrix and its inverse, which should be the identity matrix, often has entries very close to 0 and 1 that should actually be 0 or 1. Write a subroutine to convert all such matrices to their correct integer form.

10. DATA line 500 contains the current salaries of the eight employees of a small business. Line 510 contains the individual merit increases to be given to each employee. In addition, each person is to receive a cost-of-living adjustment of 2.5% of the current salary. Calculate and display the new salaries using only the matrix statements.

```
500 DATA 14100,15350,15475,18324,22600,26582,31245,34335
510 DATA 750,630,780,1140,750,1330,1500,1450
```

11. Last year's budgets for the seven departments in a retail store appear in DATA lines. Because of inflation, it is decided to increase each budget by 3.4%. Using only matrix statements, display the new budgets and the total amount that must be budgeted for all seven departments.

12. A list of allowable medical-insurance claims for the preceding year is given in DATA lines. Because of a $50-deductible clause, each claim is to be reduced by $50. The amount actually paid on each claim is 80% of this reduced amount. Using only matrix statements, display the amount paid on each claim and the total amount paid.

13. An investment club owns shares in seven different companies. The first seven figures in the following DATA lines give the number of shares owned, and the second seven figures give the respective current values of these seven stocks.

```
300 DATA 100,275,350,65,840,975,355
310 DATA 37.50,12.125,42.75,87.375,125.25,8.75,34.375
```

Using only matrix statements, display the total paper value of this stock portfolio.

14. Write a program to display the transpose of the sum of two M-by-N matrices A and B.

15. Given two N-by-N matrices A and B, write a program to display the following.
    a. $(A + B)^2$ and $A^2 + 2AB + B^2$
    b. $A^2 - B^2$ and $(A + B)(A - B)$
    c. AB and BA

16. Write a program to display the two 4-by-3 matrices A and B side by side rather than one underneath the other. You may assume that both matrices contain integers of no more than four digits.

17. A square matrix A with positive entries is called a *regular stochastic matrix* if the sum of the entries in each row is 1. For example,

$$\begin{bmatrix} .1 & .9 \\ .6 & .4 \end{bmatrix} \quad \text{and} \quad \begin{bmatrix} .2 & .4 & .4 \\ .01 & .02 & .97 \\ .8 & .05 & .15 \end{bmatrix}$$

are regular stochastic matrices. For such a matrix A, it is known that the successive powers A, A^2, A^3, . . . approach a matrix T, all of whose rows are identical. Write a program to approximate T for any regular stochastic matrix A read from DATA lines. (A user should be allowed to input an error tolerance E. The matrix A^k to be used as an approximation for T is to be the first power A^k whose entries differ from the corresponding entries of A^{k-1} by less than E.)

18. Using the method of Example 11, write a program to solve linear systems of five equations in five unknowns.

19. Write a program to solve linear systems of N equations in N unknowns. You may assume that N will be 2, 3, 4, 5, or 6. Allow a user to type a value for N and then type the coefficients.

20. A matrix that has only one column is also called a *vector*. If the vector $\begin{bmatrix} x \\ y \end{bmatrix}$ is rotated through an angle of θ degrees, its image $\begin{bmatrix} x' \\ y' \end{bmatrix}$ is given by

$$x' = x \cos \theta - y \sin \theta$$

$$y' = x \sin \theta + y \cos \theta$$

or in matrix form

$$\begin{bmatrix} x' \\ y' \end{bmatrix} = \begin{bmatrix} \cos \theta & -\sin \theta \\ \sin \theta & \cos \theta \end{bmatrix} \begin{bmatrix} x \\ y \end{bmatrix}$$

Write a program to display the image of a vector when the vector and the angle are typed at the keyboard.

■ 18.7 Review True-or-False Quiz

1. Once a matrix B has been read from DATA lines, the entries of B may not be changed during program execution.   **T F**

2. In BASIC, *one-dimensional arrays* are considered to be *matrices* having one column.   **T F**

3. If a program contains the statement DIM A(10, 10), the matrix A can be given different dimensions by using the CON, ZER, or IDN functions. **T F**

4. If an 8-by-8 matrix B has been dimensioned in a DIM statement, it may be redimensioned during program execution only if both dimensions are kept less than or equal to 8. **T F**

5. In some programs it may be necessary to dimension a matrix more than once by using more than one DIM statement. **T F**

6. The statement MAT A = A+C is not allowed. **T F**

7. If A and B are both M-by-N matrices, their sum will be displayed by the statement MAT PRINT A+B. **T F**

8. Matrices must be assigned values by using matrix statements. **T F**

9. The statement MAT B = A*INV(C) is not allowed. **T F**

10. The two statements MAT A = (3)*B and MAT A = B+B+B are equivalent. **T F**

A Typical Session at a Time-Sharing Terminal

During a typical session at the computer terminal, you should be able to perform the following tasks:

1. Establish communication between the terminal and the time-sharing system (log-in).
2. Save your program for later use.
3. Retrieve and run a program that was previously saved.
4. Modify a saved program.
5. Break communication between the terminal and the time-sharing system (log-off).

In this appendix, the system commands that allow you to carry out these tasks are described.

■ A.1 The Log-In Procedure

The log-in procedure differs from system to system. Normally, you will need a **password** and a **user-number.** With these in hand, you should follow the log-in procedure described in the user's guide for your BASIC system.

Following is the display generated during a log-in to a typical time-sharing system.

The underlined characters are typed by the user.
(The time-sharing system identifies itself.)

```
USER NUMBER: ABC652      (The user number ABC652 is typed.)
PASSWORD:                (The password is typed but not displayed at the terminal.)
SYSTEM: BASIC            (The BASIC language is selected.)
NEW or OLD: NEW          (A new program will be typed.)
NEW FILE NAME: PROG2     (The name PROG2 is chosen.)
READY                    (The log-in procedure is complete.)
```

You may now type your program or any system command. For example, after READY is displayed, you may proceed as follows (underlined characters are typed by the user):

```
READY
100 LET S=13*2+9
110 PRINT S
120 END
RUN
 35
READY
```

```
LIST
100 LET S=13*2+9
110 PRINT S
120 END
READY
```

■ A.2 Saving Your Program

A file created under the NEW command is called a **local** or **temporary file.** It continues to exist only as long as you are logged into the system. To preserve such a file for later use, you may issue the SAVE command:

```
SAVE    (You type this.)
READY   (Displayed by the computer.)
```

The SAVE command creates a permanent copy of the current local file. This permanent copy is called a **permanent file** since it will continue to exist even after you log off the system.

The following display shows how you can type two programs and create a permanent copy of each of them (underlined characters are typed by the user):

```
NEW                         (Indicates that a new program will be typed.)
NEW FILE NAME: PROG1        (You name the program PROG1.)
READY                       (The local file PROG1 is empty.)
(Type your first program.)

                .
                .
                .

SAVE                        (Save PROG1 as a permanent file.)
READY                       (PROG1 also exists as the local file.)

NEW                         (Indicates that a new program will be typed.)
NEW FILE NAME: PROG2        (You name the program PROG2.)
READY                       (The local file PROG2 is empty.)
(Type your second program.)

                .
                .
                .

SAVE                        (Save PROG2 as a permanent file.)
READY                       (PROG2 also exists as the local file.)
```

If you now log off the system, the permanent files PROG1 and PROG2 will not be lost and can be used again at another time.

■ A.3 Retrieving a Permanent File

Let's assume you made the files PROG1 and PROG2 permanent by the SAVE command. If at a later session you wish to run these programs, you may proceed as follows (underlined characters are typed by the user).

```
                (log-in)

                .
                .
                .

NEW OR OLD: OLD             (A previously saved file is wanted.)
OLD FILE NAME: PROG1        (Request PROG1.)
READY                       (PROG1 is now the local file.)

RUN
(PROG1 will be executed.)
```

.
.
.

```
READY

LIST
```
(PROG1 will be listed.)

.
.
.

```
READY

OLD                          (Type OLD to request another permanent file.)
OLD FILE NAME: PROG2         (Request PROG2.)
READY                        (PROG2 is now the local file.)
```

At this point, the files PROG1 and PROG2 continue to exist as permanent files. They can be retrieved as local files by issuing the OLD command, and, as local files, they can be executed or listed by using the RUN and LIST commands. They can also be modified, as described in the next section.

■ A.4 Modifying a Permanent File

Often a program is saved before it is completely debugged. Let's assume a permanent file named POWER2 contains such a program. To modify POWER2, you must first use the OLD command to retrieve it as the local file. Having done this, you can modify the local file POWER2 just as you could when creating it under the NEW command. After making the necessary modifications, you can replace the permanent copy of POWER2 with the modified version by typing

```
REPLACE
```

The modified version is now the permanent file and can be retrieved at any subsequent session at the terminal.

The following display illustrates what has just been described (underlined characters are typed by the user).

```
LIST

100 LET A=5                  (Contents of POWER2.)
110 LET B=A^2
120 PRINT B
130 END
READY

100 LET A=7                  (Change line 100.)
LIST

100 LET A=7                  (Updated POWER2.)
110 LET B=A^2
120 PRINT B
130 END
READY

100 LET A=7                  (Change line 100.)

LIST
                             (Updated POWER2.)
100 LET A=7
110 LET B≠A^2
120 PRINT B
130 END
READY

REPLACE
READY                        (Updated version of POWER2 is now permanent.)

RUN                          (The local file POWER2 is executed.)
  49
READY
```

If in this example you type SAVE instead of REPLACE, the system will display a message such as

```
FILE EXISTS or POWER2 ALREADY PERMANENT
```

and will leave the permanent file POWER2 unchanged. If you really mean to replace the old version with the new one, you must type REPLACE. However, if you want to preserve the permanent file POWER2 and also save the modified version that now exists as the local file POWER2, you must first rename the local file. This can be accomplished by typing

```
RENAME, POWER3
```

where POWER3 is chosen as the new name for the local file. (You should consult the user's guide for your system to find the precise form of the RENAME command.)

Having renamed the local file POWER3 and assuming you had not previously saved a file under that name, you can type the command SAVE to create a permanent copy of POWER3.

■ A.5 Log-Off Procedure

Before you log off, be sure that all permanent files no longer needed are excised from permanent storage. Each BASIC system that allows you to SAVE programs also allows you to remove them from permanent storage. On some systems the command

```
UNSAVE PROG7
```

will remove PROG7 from permanent storage, whereas another system may require that you type

```
PURGE, PROG7
```

The precise form to be used will be described in the user's guide for your system. A listing of all your permanent files can usually be obtained with one of the system commands CATALOG or DIRECTORY.

To break the communication link between your terminal and the time-sharing system, type

```
BYE
```

If this command does not log you off your system, consult your user's guide.

Important: At this time turn your terminal off.

B. BASIC Language Cross-Reference Guides

B.1 BASIC–PLUS and VAX BASIC Cross-Reference Guide

	Keywords	Text reference	Differences
Assignment statement	LET	Section 3.5	The keyword LET is optional.
Data entry statements	INPUT	Section 5.1	The form INPUT *string; input variables* is allowed. The *string* is displayed and then a user must type values for the *input variables*.
	READ	Section 10.1	Same as in text.
	DATA	Section 10.1	Same as in text.
	RESTORE	Section 10.3	Same as in text.
Data output statements	PRINT	Sections 3.6, 7.1, and 7.2	Same as in text.
	PRINT TAB	Section 7.4	Same as in text.
	PRINT USING	Seciton 7.6	For *numerical* output values, same as in text. For *string* output values the following differences occur: ! specifies that only the first character of an output string is to be displayed. *n spaces*\ specifies that the first $n + 2$ characters of an output string are to be displayed.
Control statements	FOR/NEXT	Section 9.1	Same as in text.
	GOTO	Section 6.1	Same as in text.
	ON GOTO	Section 7.8	Same as in text.
	GOSUB	Section 11.1	Same as in text.
	ON GOSUB	Section 11.3	Same as in text.
	RETURN	Section 11.1	Same as in text.
	IF–THEN (to construct loops)	Section 6.1	Same as in text.
	IF–THEN (as a selection statement)	Section 8.1	The enhanced form IF *condition* THEN S1 ELSE S2 is allowed. S1 and S2 denote BASIC statements or sequences of BASIC statements separated by backslashes. In BASIC-PLUS, S1 must be single statement.

	ON ERROR GOTO	Section 15.2	Same as in text.
	END	Page 29	Same as in text.
	WHILE/NEXT	Section 6.2	Same as in text.
Other BASIC statements	DEF	Sections 12.3 and 13.8	Both numerical and string functions can be defined.
	DEF/FNEND	Section 12.4	Same as in text.
	DIM	Section 14.2	The smallest subscript is zero. **OPTION BASE n** with n equal to 0 or 1 specifies that the smallest subscript is n.
	REM	Section 3.7	An exclamation mark (!) can be used in place of REM. Also, a comment can be placed at the end of each line by preceding it with an exclamation mark.
	RANDOMIZE	Section 16.1	Same as in text.
File statements	*(See Miscellaneous notes concerning names of files.)*		
	OPEN	Section 15.1	Same as in Program A. File designator is preceded by a pound (#) symbol.
	CLOSE	Section 15.1	Same as in Program A. File designator is preceded by a pound (#) symbol.
	RESTORE#	Section 15.1	Not implemented.
	END#	Section 15.2	Not implemented. (Use ON ERROR GOTO.)
	FILE#	Section 15.1	Not implemented.
	INPUT#	Section 15.1	Same as in text.
	PRINT#	Section 15.1	Same as in text.
System commands	*(See Miscellaneous notes concerning names of files.)*		
	NEW	Page 351	Same as in text. Also, a program name can be specified just after the word NEW.
	LIST	Page 38	Same as in text. In addition: LIST n lists line number n LIST m–n lists lines m through n
	SAVE	Page 352	Same as in text. Also, a program name can be specified just after the word SAVE.
	OLD	Page 352	Same as in text. In VAX BASIC, the specified program with the highest version number is copied into memory.
	RENAME	Page 354	Same as in text except that no comma precedes the program name.
	RUN	Page 39	Same as in text.
	REPLACE	Page 353	Not implemented in VAX BASIC. In BASIC–PLUS, same as in text. Also, a program name can be specified just after the word REPLACE.
	UNSAVE	Page 354	Not implemented in VAX BASIC (See PURGE and DELETE, which follow.) In BASIC–PLUS, same as in text.
	PURGE	Page 354	To delete VAX BASIC files, type EXIT to return to the VMS operating system. The VMS command **PURGE** *fn.***BAS** deletes all files named *fn.*BAS except for the one with the highest version number. The command **DELETE** *fn.***BAS;***v* deletes the copy of *fn.*BAS with the version number *v*.
	BYE	Page 354	See Miscellaneous notes.
	CATALOG	Page 354	Not implemented in VAX BASIC. In BASIC–PLUS, type CAT to obtain a listing of file names in the disk's directory of files. (See Miscellaneous notes for listing of VAX BASIC files.)

BASIC functions	All numerical and string functions described in the text are implemented in both VAX BASIC and BASIC–PLUS. Differences are as follows.

Functions	Text reference	Differences
`LEFT$`,`MID$`, and `RIGHT$`	Section 13.1	Early versions of BASIC–PLUS use LEFT, RIGHT, and MID.
`ASC`	Section 13.7	Use ASCII instead of ASC.

Miscellaneous notes	

Variable names in BASIC–PLUS   After execution of the EXTEND statement, variable names can contain a letter followed by up to 29 digits, letters, and periods. If EXTEND has not been executed, names can contain at most one digit following the initial letter. The symbols $ and % designate string and integer variables as described in the text.

Variable names in VAX BASIC   Same as BASIC–PLUS in EXTEND mode except that the underscore character is also allowed.

Negation   A minus (−) symbol used to denote negation is carried out before any other numerical operations other than exponentiation (^).

Program termination   A running program can be halted by pressing the two-key combination Ctrl/C. This two-key combination also terminates a program listing.

Programming line   A programming line can contain many BASIC statements—simply separate successive statements with backslashes (\). Such a multiple-statement line can have only one line number.

Continuation lines   A single BASIC programming line can occupy many screen or printer lines. To continue a programming line to a new screen or printer line, type the ampersand character (&) and press the return key. Here is one way to write an IF–THEN–ELSE statement:

```
500 IF BAL<0                        &
       THEN PRINT "OVERDRAWN"       &
       ELSE BAL=BAL-DRAFT           &
          \PRINT "NEW BALANCE";BAL
```

Statement modifiers   The statement modifier IF, UNLESS, FOR, WHILE, and UNTIL allow the conditional or repeated execution of a BASIC statement. The following are illustrations:

```
100 PRINT BALANCE IF BALANCE>0
200 PRINT SUM UNLESS SUM=0
300 PRINT "*"; FOR N=1 TO 10
400 READ X WHILE X<=0
500 READ A,B UNTIL A=B
```

Immediate mode   Most BASIC statements can be typed without a line number. If this is done, the statement is executed immediately. This capability serves as a useful debugging tool. After a program halts, the values of any variables can be examined by using PRINT statements with no line numbers.

BASIC–PLUS file names   A file name can contain from one to six letters and digits followed by an optional extension consisting of a period followed by up to three letters and digits. If you do not include an extension when naming a BASIC program (this is the customary practice), the system assumes the default extension .BAS.

VAX BASIC file names   Same as in BASIC–PLUS, except that up to nine letters and digits can precede the extension. When the system copies a file to the system disk it includes a version number with the file name. The first time a file is copied it is given the version number 1; subsequent copies are given a number one greater than the previous version number.

Directory listing of files created in VAX BASIC   Type EXIT to leave VAX BASIC and return to the VMS operating system. Then type DIR to obtain a listing of the names of all files stored on the system disk.

Terminating a BASIC–PLUS session   When you enter the command BYE the system displays the prompt CONFIRM: and waits for a reply. To complete the log-out procedure, type Y (for YES). Other admissible responses to this prompt are explained in your System User's Guide.

Terminating a VAX BASIC session   First type EXIT to leave VAX BASIC and return to the VMS operating system. Then type LOGOUT.

■ B.2 Microsoft BASIC Cross-Reference Guide (for IBM and Other Personal Computers That Use Microsoft BASIC)

	Keywords	Text reference	Differences
Assignment statement	LET	Section 3.5	The keyword LET is optional.
Data entry statements	INPUT	Section 5.1	Microsoft BASIC allows the enhanced form INPUT *string; input variables* The *string* is displayed, and then a user must type values for the *input variables*.
	READ	Section 10.1	Same as in text.
	DATA	Section 10.1	Strings containing commas, colons, or significant leading or trailing blanks must be quoted.
	RESTORE	Section 10.3	Microsoft BASIC also allows the form RESTORE *ln* which causes the next READ statement to obtain data beginning with the first item in the DATA statement at line number *ln*.
Data output statements	PRINT	Sections 3.6, 7.1, and 7.2	PRINT directs output to the screen. To direct output to a printer, use LPRINT.
	PRINT TAB	Section 7.4	If TAB(*n*) is the last item in a PRINT statement, Microsoft assumes a terminating semicolon.

	PRINT USING	Section 7.6	The most significant differences in the output format string are as follows:
			  & specifies that an entire output string is to be displayed.
			  ! specifies that only the first character of an output string is to be displayed.
			  n spaces\ specifies that the first *n*+2 characters of an output string are to be displayed.

Control statements	FOR/NEXT	Section 9.1	Same as in text.
	GOTO	Section 6.1	Same as in text.
	ON GOTO	Section 7.8	Same as in text.
	GOSUB	Section 11.1	Same as in text.
	ON GOSUB	Section 11.3	Same as in text.
	RETURN	Section 11.1	Advanced Microsoft allows the form RETURN *ln* to return from a subroutine to line number *ln*.
	IF–THEN (to construct loops)	Section 6.1	Same as in text.
	IF–THEN (as a selection statement)	Section 8.1	Microsoft allows the enhanced form IF *condition* THEN *s* ELSE *t* where *s* and *t* denote BASIC statements or sequences of BASIC statements separated by colons.
	ON ERROR GOTO	Section 15.2	Same as in text.
	END	Page 29	Microsoft allows more than one END statement in a program. Each causes program execution to halt.
	WHILE/WEND	Section 6.2	Same as in text.
Other BASIC statements	DEF	Sections 12.3 and 13.8	Both numerical and string single-line functions can be defined.

	DEF/FNEND	Section 12.4	Multistatement functions not implemented.
	DIM	Section 14.2	The smallest subscript is 0. The statement

OPTION BASE *n*

with *n* equal to 0 or 1 specifies that the smallest subscript is *n*. Dynamic storage allocation is allowed (see page 246).

	REM	Section 3.7	A comment can be placed at the end of a line by preceding the comment with a single quotation mark. Everything that follows the single quote is the comment.
	RANDOMIZE	Section 16.1	The Microsoft form is

RANDOMIZE *n*

where *n* is an integer from −32767 to 32767. Different integers produce different sequences of random numbers when RND function is used.

File statements	OPEN	Section 15.1	Same as in text.
	CLOSE	Section 15.1	Same as in text.
	RESTORE#	Section 15.1	Not implemented.
	END#	Section 15.2	Not implemented. (Use EOF.)
	FILE#	Section 15.1	Not implemented.
	INPUT#	Section 15.1	Same as in text.
	PRINT#	Section 15.1	Same as in text.
System commands	NEW	Page 351	Clears that part of memory that contains the current program so that a new program can be typed at the keyboard.
	LIST	Page 38	LIST displays the current program. LIST *n* displays line number *n* of the current program. LISTR *m–n* displays line numbers *m* through *n* of the current program. Use LLIST to obtain printed lists.
	SAVE	Page 352	SAVE *"filename"* copies the current program onto a diskette (or cassette) and gives it the name *filename*. If another program is already stored on the diskette under the same name, it is replaced.
	OLD	Page 352	The Microsoft form is

LOAD *"filename"*

This command copies the program stored on the diskette (or cassette) under the name *filename* into memory. This program becomes the current program.

	REPLACE	Page 353	Not implemented. (The SAVE command does this.)
	RUN	Page 39	RUN causes the current program to be executed. The command

RUN *"filename"*

is equivalent to the two commands

LOAD *"filename"*
RUN

	RENAME	Page 354	The Microsoft form is

NAME *"oldname"* AS *"newname"*

This command changes the name of the diskette file *oldname* to *newname*. A file named *newname* must not already exist.

PURGE	Page 354	The Microsoft form is
		KILL *"filename"*
		This command deletes *filename* from the diskette directory of file names.
BYE	Page 354	Not implemented. Simply turn off the computer.

BASIC functions	All numerical and string functions described in the text are implemented in Microsoft BASIC. Differences are as follows.		
	Functions	**Text reference**	**Microsoft BASIC differences**
	RIGHT$	Page 215	RIGHT$(A$,N) denotes the string consisting of the last N characters of A$.
	RND	Section 16.1	The Microsoft form is RND(n).

If $n > 0$, the same sequence of random numbers is generated each time the program is run. The expression RND(0) always returns the most recent random number generated. To obtain different sequences of random numbers, use the RANDOMIZE statement as described in this cross-reference guide. [Another way to accomplish the same thing is to include a statement such as LET X = RND (any negative number) at the beginning of the program and then use RND(n) with $n > 0$ whenever a random number is needed. The sequence of numbers generated depends on the negative number used.]

Miscellaneous notes on Microsoft Basic	**Variable names** These names can contain any number of letters, digits, and periods. The first character must be a letter. The type of a variable is determined by the last character: $ for string variables, % for integer variables, ! for single precision real variables, and # for double precision real variables. If the last character is a letter, digit, or period, its type is single precision. Microsoft BASIC distinguishes between variable names by examining the first 40 characters in each name. Microsoft reserved words, which include all BASIC keywords, are not allowed as variable names.
	Negation A minus ($-$) symbol used to denote negation rather than subtraction is carried out before any other numerical operations other than exponentiation ($\wedge$).
	Program termination A running program can be halted by pressing the two-key combination Ctrl/Break. On many Microsoft systems, Ctrl/Break is used to terminate a program listing.
	Programming line A programming line can contain more than one BASIC statement—simply separate successive statements with colons. Such a multiple-statement line can have but one line number. A line is entered by pressing the ENTER key. Up to 255 keys may be pressed while typing a programming line.

■ B.3 APPLESOFT BASIC Cross-Reference Guide

	Keywords	**Text reference**	**APPLESOFT BASIC differences**
Assignment statement	LET	Section 3.5	The keyword LET is optional.
Data entry statements	INPUT	Section 5.1	APPLESOFT allows the enhanced form
			INPUT *string; input variables*
			The *string* is displayed, and then a user must type values for the *input* variables.
	READ	Section 10.1	Same as in text.
	DATA	Section 10.1	Same as in text.
	RESTORE	Section 10.3	Same as in text.
Data output statements	PRINT	Sections 3.6, 7.1, and 7.2	PRINT A;B causes the numerical values of A and B to be displayed with no intervening blanks.
	PRINT TAB	Section 7.4	Same as in text.
	PRINT USING	Section 7.6	Not implemented.

Control statements	FOR/NEXT	Section 9.1	At least one pass is made through every FOR/NEXT loop.
	GOTO	Section 6.1	Same as in text.
	ON GOTO	Section 7.8	Same as in text.
	GOSUB	Section 11.1	Same as in text.
	ON GOSUB	Section 11.3	Same as in text.
	RETURN	Section 11.1	Same as in text.
	IF–THEN (to construct loops)	Section 6.1	Same as in text.
	IF–THEN (as a selection statement)	Section 8.1	APPLESOFT allows the enhanced form IF *condition* THEN s_1:s_2:s_3: . . . where s_1,s_2,s_3 denote any BASIC statements. The statements that follow the keyword THEN are executed only if the *condition* is true.
	IF–THEN–ELSE	Section 8.1	Not implemented.
	ON ERROR GOTO	Section 15.2	Same as in text.
	END	Page 29	Many END statements can be used in one program. When encountered, the program run terminates with no message being displayed.
	WHILE	Section 6.2	Not implemented.
Other BASIC statements	DEF	Sections 12.3 and 13.8	Only functions with a single variable are allowed.
	DEF/FNEND	Section 12.4	Multiple-statement functions are not implemented.
	DIM	Section 14.2	Dynamic storage allocation is allowed. (See page 246.)
	REM	Section 3.7	Same as in text.
	RANDOMIZE	Section 16.1	Not implemented; however, the same effect is accomplished by the RND function (see below).

File statements	OPEN (for input)	Section 15.1	To open a file named DATA as an input file, APPLESOFT requires the two statements
			
			`PRINT CHR$(4);"OPEN DATA"`
			`PRINT CHR$(4);"READ DATA"`
			
			Subsequent INPUT statements will obtain input values starting from the beginning of file DATA.

	OPEN (for output)	Section 15.1	To open DATA as an output file, APPLESOFT requires the two statements
			
			`PRINT CHR$(4);"OPEN DATA"`
			`PRINT CHR$(4);"WRITE DATA"`
			
			Subsequent PRINT statements will direct the output to file DATA. Writing on the file starts at the beginning of the file.

	CLOSE	Section 15.1	The APPLESOFT statement to close file DATA is `PRINT CHR$(4);"CLOSE DATA"` All files that have been opened must be closed. If an input file is closed, subsequent input must come from the APPLE keyboard. If an output file is closed, subsequent output will be directed to the video display or printer.
	RESTORE#	Section 15.1	Not implemented. (The file pointer is automatically restored to the beginning of the file when the file is opened.)
	END#	Section 15.2	Not implemented. (Use ON ERROR GOTO.)
	FILE#	Section 15.1	Not implemented.
	INPUT#	Section 15.1	Not implemented.

	PRINT#	Section 15.1	Not implemented.
System commands	NEW	Page 351	Clears that part of memory that contains the current program so that a new program can be typed at the keyboard.
	LIST	Page 38	LIST displays the current program. LIST *n* displays line number *n* of the current program. LIST *m,n* line numbers *m* through *n* of the current program.
	SAVE	Page 352	SAVE *filename* copies the current program onto the diskette and gives it the name *filename*. If another program is already stored on the diskette under the same name, it is replaced.
	OLD	Page 352	APPLESOFT uses the form LOAD *filename*. This command copies the program stored on the diskette under the name *filename* into memory. This program becomes the current program.
	REPLACE	Page 353	Not implemented. (The SAVE command does this.)
	RUN	Page 39	RUN causes the current program to be executed. RUN *filename* is equivalent to the two commands. LOAD *filename* RUN
	RENAME	Page 354	RENAME *oldname, newname* changes the name of the diskette file *oldname* to *newname*.
	PURGE	Page 354	APPLESOFT uses the form DELETE *filename* to remove *filename* from the diskette.
	BYE	Page 354	Not implemented. Simply turn off your APPLE and any peripherals such as the video monitor.

BASIC functions

All the numerical and string functions described in the text, except the INSTR function, are implemented in APPLESOFT BASIC. There are two differences, as follows.

Functions	**Text reference**	**APPLESOFT BASIC differences**
RIGHT$	Page 215	RIGHT$(A$,N) denotes the string consisting of the last N characters of A$.
RND	Section 16.1	The APPLESOFT form is RND(*n*).

If $n > 0$, different random number sequences are generated each time the program is run. The expression RND(0) always returns the value of the most recent random number generated. To obtain the same random number sequence each time a program is run, you can include a statement such as LET X = RND *(any negative number)* at the beginning of the program and then use RND(*n*) with $n > 0$ to generate random numbers as they are needed.

Miscellaneous notes on APPLESOFT BASIC

Variable names These names can consist of up to 238 alphanumeric characters with the first a letter. However, only the first two characters are used to distinguish between any two variables. Variable names must not contain any of the APPLESOFT reserved words.

Spacing Although you are free to include blank spaces wherever you like while typing a program, some Apple systems will reformat your program according to their own special rules. In particular, if you indent a statement, it may not appear indented when you list it.

Negation A minus symbol ($-$), used to denote negation rather than subtraction, is carried out before any of the other numerical operations.

Program termination A running program can be halted by pressing the key combination Ctrl/C. Whenever a program halts, the current values of all variables are preserved and can be examined as described under immediate mode. The variable names and their values are cleared when you issue a RUN or LOAD command.

Programming line A programming line can contain more than one BASIC statement—simply separate successive statements with a colon. Such a multiple-statement line can have but one line number. A programming line can contain as many as 239 characters. When typing a line, end it with the RETURN key.

■ B.4 TRS-80 Model III BASIC Cross-Reference Guide

	Keywords	Text reference	TRS-80 MODEL III BASIC differences
Assignment statement	LET	Section 3.5	The keyword LET is optional.
Data entry statements	INPUT	Section 5.1	MODEL III BASIC allows the enhanced form INPUT *string; input variables* The *string* is displayed and then a user must type values for the *input variables*.
	READ	Section 10.1	Same as in text.
	DATA	Section 10.1	Strings containing commas, colons, or significant leading blanks must be quoted.
	RESTORE	Section 10.3	Same as in text.
Data output statements	PRINT	Sections 3.6, 7.1, and 7.2	PRINT directs output to the screen. To direct output to a printer, use LPRINT.
	PRINT TAB	Section 7.4	Same as in text.

	PRINT USING	Section 7.6	The most significant differences in the output format string are as follows:
			    ! specifies that only the first character of an output string is to be displayed.
			    %spaces% specifies that the first *spaces*+2 characters of an output string are to be displayed.

Control statements	FOR/NEXT	Section 9.1	At least one pass is made through every FOR/NEXT loop.
	GOTO	Section 6.1	Same as in text.
	ON GOTO	Section 7.8	Same as in text.
	GOSUB	Section 11.1	Same as in text.
	ON GOSUB	Section 11.3	Same as in text.
	RETURN	Section 11.1	Same as in text.
	IF-THEN	Section 6.1	Same as in text.
	IF-THEN-ELSE	Section 8.1	Same as in text.
	ON ERROR GOTO	Section 16.2	Same as in text.
	END	Page 29	Model III BASIC allows more than one END statement in a program. Each causes program execution to halt.
	WHILE	Section 6.2	Not implemented.
Other BASIC statements	DEF	Sections 12.3 and 13.8	Both numerical and string functions can be defined.
	DEF/FNEND	Section 12.4	Not implemented.
	DIM	Section 14.2	Dynamic storage allocation is allowed. (See page 246.)
	REM	Section 3.7	A comment can be placed at the end of a line by preceding the comment with a single quotation mark. Everything that follows the single quote is the comment.
	RANDOMIZE	Section 16.1	Not implemented.

File statements	OPEN	Section 15.1	To open a file named DATA, Model III BASIC uses the statement
			OPEN *mode, buffer,* "DATA"
			where *buffer* is a numerical expression (value 1–15) indicating which buffer is to be used, and *mode* is either the string constant "I" for an input file or "O" for an output file.
	CLOSE	Section 15.1	To close the file DATA Model III BASIC uses the statement
			CLOSE *buffer*
			where *buffer* is a numerical expression evaluating to the number of the buffer used by DATA.
	RESTORE #	Section 15.1	Not implemented. To restore the data pointer to the beginning of a file, close and reopen the file.
	END#	Section 15.2	Model III BASIC uses the statement
			EOF *buffer*
			where *buffer* is a numerical expression evaluating to the number of the buffer being used by the file.
	FILE#	Section 15.1	Not implemented.
	INPUT#	Section 15.1	Same as in text.
	PRINT#	Section 15.1	Same as in text.
System commands	NEW	Page 351	Clears that part of memory that contains the current program so that a new program can be typed at the keyboard.
	LIST	Page 38	LIST displays the current program. LIST *n* displays line number *n* of the current program. LIST *m–n* displays line numbers *m* through *n* of the current program. Use LLIST to obtain printed lists.
	SAVE	Page 352	SAVE *filename* copies the current program onto a diskette and gives it the name *filename*. If another program is already stored on the diskette under the same name, it is replaced.
	OLD	Page 352	The Model III BASIC form is
			LOAD *filename*
			This command copies the program stored on the diskette under the name *filename* into memory. This program becomes the current program.
	REPLACE	Page 353	Not implemented. (The SAVE command does this.)
	RUN	Page 39	RUN causes the current program to be executed. The command
			RUN *filename*
			is equivalent to the two commands
			LOAD *filename*
			RUN
	RENAME	Page 354	The Model III BASIC form is
			RENAME *oldname newname*
			This command changes the name of the diskette file *oldname* to *newname*. A file named *newname* must not already exist.

	PURGE	Page 354	The Model III BASIC form is
			KILL *filename*
			This command deletes *filename* from the diskette directory of filenames.
	BYE	Page 354	Not implemented. Simply turn off the computer.

BASIC functions	All numerical and string functions described in the text are implemented in Model III BASIC. Differences are as follows.

Functions	**Text reference**	**TRS-80 MODEL III BASIC differences**
RIGHT$	Page 215	RIGHT$(A$,N) denotes the string consisting of the last N characters of A$.
RND	Section 16.1	The Model III BASIC form is RND(n). If $n = 0$, RND(n) returns a random number between 0 and 1. If $1 \leq n < 32768$, RND(n) returns a random integer between 1 and INT(n).

Miscellaneous notes on Model III BASIC	**Variable names** These names can consist of any number of alphanumeric characters with the first a letter. However, only the first two characters are used to distinguish between any two variables. Variable names must not contain any of the Model III BASIC reserved words. **Negation** A minus ($-$) symbol used to denote negation rather than subtraction is carried out before any other numerical operations other than exponentiation ($\wedge$). **Program termination** A running program can be halted by pressing the BREAK key. **Programming line** A programming line can contain more than one BASIC statement—simply separate successive statements with colons. Such a multiple-statement line can have but one line number. A line is entered by pressing the ENTER key. Up to 255 keys may be pressed while typing a programming line.

C Answers to Selected Problems

■ Section 1.3

1. F **2.** F **3.** F **4.** F **5.** F **6.** T **7.** F **8.** T **9.** T **10.** F **11.** F **12.** F
13. F

■ Section 2.3

1. 5% discount
2. Decide whether the discount is applicable.
3. 693.50
4. 250.00
5. 80.00 and 0, 128.00 and 0, 176.00 and 48.00, 206.00 and 78.00
6. $4
7. $6 per hour
8. Step (c) is used to determine whether there is any overtime. G denotes gross pay. B denotes pay for overtime hours.
9. 21
10.
    1   1
    2   2
    3   6
    4   24
    5 120
    6 720
11. 55
12. 2, 4, 7, 8, 14, 28, 64
13. Process will *never* stop, since N is always less than 10.
14. Step (c) is ambiguous.
15. Variable names:

NAME   = name of an item
COST   = cost for the item NAME
PRICE   = sale price for the item NAME
QTY   = number of units of NAME sold
GROSS   = gross sales for the item NAME
INCOME = income from the item NAME

Algorithm

    a. Print column headings as specified.
    b. Read NAME and values for COST, PRICE, and QTY, for one item.
    c. Assign the value of the product QTY × PRICE to GROSS.
    d. Multiply QTY times (PRICE − COST) to obtain a value for INCOME.
    e. Enter NAME and the values GROSS and INCOME under the appropriate column headings.
    f. Return to Step (b) until the report is complete.

17. Variable names:

CORP	= corporation name
SHARES	= number of shares
PRICE	= current price for one share
EARN	= earnings for one share
EQTY	= equity represented by all shares of a corporation CORP
PE	= price/earnings ratio for one share

Algorithm

    a. Print column headings as specified.
    b. Read CORP and values for SHARES, PRICE, and EARN.
    c. Assign the value of the product SHARES × PRICE to EQTY.
    d. Divide PRICE by EARN to obtain a value for PE.
    e. Enter CORP and the values SHARES, PRICE, EARN, EQTY, and PE under the appropriate column headings.
    f. Return to Step (b) until the report is complete.

19. Algorithm

    a. Start with SUM = 0 and COUNT = 0
    b. Add the number on the top card to SUM, and add 1 to COUNT.
    c. Remove the top card and return to Step (b) until all cards have been processed.
    d. Divide SUM by COUNT to obtain the average AV, and proceed to Step (e) with the original stack of cards in hand.
    e. If the number on the top card exceeds AV, write the letter G on the card; otherwise write the letter L.
    f. Remove the top card and return to Step (e) until all cards have been examined.

20. Algorithm

    a. Press the CLEAR key.
    b. Insert your ID card into reader as shown.
    c. Enter your four-digit code and press ENTER.
    d. Enter amount of check and press ENTER.
    e. Place check in punch unit, blank side toward you.
    f. Remove check and ID card when these items are released by the machine.

■ Section 2.4

1. F **2.** T **3.** F **4.** F **5.** F **6.** T **7.** T **8.** T **9.** F **10.** T

■ Section 3.4

1. **a.** 17 **b.** 33 **c.** −2 **d.** −6 **e.** −15 **f.** system dependent: −9 or 9 **g.** 17 **h.** 9
   i. 0.25 **j.** −9 **k.** 64 **l.** 3
2. **a.** 3.5 **b.** 5 **c.** 0.75 **d.** 0.75 **e.** 10 **f.** 25 **g.** 4.5 **h.** 1.6667 **i.** 10 **j.** 3 **k.** −8
   l. −8
3. a, c, d, e, and j are not admissible.
4. **a.** 0.06*P **b.** 5*X + 5*Y **c.** A^2 + B^2 **d.** 6/(5*A) **e.** A/B + C/D
   f. (A + B)/(C + D)   **g.** A*X^2 + B*X + C   **h.** (B^2 − 4*A*C)^0.5
   i. (X^2 + 4*X*Y)/(X + 2*Y)
5. **a.** X + 1 + Y **b.** A^2 − B^2 **c.** A^3 + A^2*B + A **d.** A*B/C **e.** A/B/C
   f. X^4 + X^3*D + X^2*C + X*B + A **g.** P^Q^R **h.** 1/A/B/C/D

■ Section 3.8

1. **a.** 110 LET M=7
   b. 120 LET B=B+7
   c. 130 LET H=2*H
   d. 140 LET C2=(A-B)/2
   e. 150 LET A=(1+R)^10
   f. 160 LET X=X-2*Y
   g. 170 LET C$="COST"
   h. 180 LET A$="DOE,JANE"
   i. 190 LET Q$=P$
   j. 200 LET S$="*****"
2. **a.** 10 LET X=(A+B)*C
   b. correct
   c. correct
   d. 25 LET S=A+B
   e. correct
   f. 35 LET Y=4*10^0.5
   g. 40 LET A$="DISCOUNT"
   h. 45 LET D$="DIVIDEND"
   i. correct
   j. 55 LET M$="MONTHLY RENT"
   k. correct
   l. 65 PRINT "PRICE=";P
   m. correct
   n. correct
   o. 80 PRINT "ITEM #35"
   p. correct
3. **a.** RESULT 12
   b. AMOUNT= 108
   c. RESULT -2
   d. RESULT 5
   e. VOLUME 200
         VOLUME 125
   f. SOLUTION −1
   g. BOBBY LOVES
         MARY
   h. LIST PRICE 45
         DISCOUNT 4.5
         SELLING PRICE 40.5

4. a.

	A	B	C
100	1	–	–
110	1	2	–
120	1	2	1
130	1	2	3
140	4	2	3
150	4	5	3
160	4	5	2
170	4	20	2
180	2	20	2
190	2	20	11

b.

	N	Output
100	1	
110	1	1
120	2	
130	2	2
140	6	
150	6	6
160	42	
170	42	42

c.

	X	Y	Z	Output
100	0	–	–	
110	0	7	–	
120	0	7	7	
130	0	7	7	7
140	7	7	7	
150	7	343	7	
160	7	343	7	343

5. a.

	S	A	Output
100	0	–	
110	0	25	
120	25	25	
130	25	25	25
140	50	25	
150	50	25	50
160	25	25	
170	25	25	25

b.

	X	Y	Output
100	1.5	–	
110	1.5	0.6	
120	1.5	0.6	0.6
130	–1.5	0.6	
140	–1.5	0.6	–1.5
150	–1.5	0.6	0.6

c.

	N	C	S	G	P	Output
10	130	–	–	–	–	
20	130	3	–	–	–	
30	130	3	3.6	–	–	
40	130	3	3.6	468	–	
50	130	3	3.6	468		SALES 468
60	130	3	3.6	468	78	
70	130	3	3.6	468	78	PROFIT 78

d.

	A	P	Output
100	–	–	NTH POWERS OF 7
110	7	–	
120	7	7	
130	7	7	FOR N=1:7
140	7	49	
150	7	49	FOR N=2:49
160	7	343	
170	7	343	FOR N=3:343
180	7	2401	
190	7	2401	FOR N=4:2401
200	7	2401	

■ Section 3.9

1. F **2.** T **3.** F **4.** F **5.** F **6.** F **7.** T **8.** T **9.** F **10.** F **11.** T **12.** F **13.** F **14.** F

■ Section 4.9

1.
```
100 LET A=14
110 LET B=30
120 LET S=A+B
130 PRINT "SUM IS";S
140 END
```
Output: SUM IS 44

2.
```
100 LET X=5
120 LET Y=20
125 LET S=X+Y
130 PRINT "X+Y=";S
140 END
```
Output: X+Y= 25

3.
```
110 LET P=120
120 LET D=0.1*P
130 LET C=P-D
140 PRINT "DISCOUNT";D
150 PRINT "COST";C
160 END
```
Output: DISCOUNT 12
COST 108

4.
```
100 LET L$="AVERAGE"
110 LET A=9
120 LET B=7
130 LET M=(A+B)/2
140 PRINT L$;M
150 END
```
Output: AVERAGE 8

5. Syntax: `30 LET D=23000`
Programming: `40 LET R=.06`
Syntax: `50 LET A=R*D`
Output: `ANSWER IS 1380`

6. Programming: `50 LET A=(N1+N2)/2`
Syntax: `60 PRINT "AVERAGE IS";A`
Output: `AVERAGE IS 19.5`

7. Syntax and programming: `40 LET T=0.05`
Syntax: `70 PRINT "TOTAL COST=";S`
Output: `TOTAL COST= 126`

8. Syntax and programming: `60 LET X=-B/A`
Output: `SOLUTION IS -6.28571`

9. Programming: `165 LET T$=A$`
                 `180 LET B$=T$`
Output: `A$=STOCK`
                 `B$=BOND`
                 `A$=BOND`
                 `B$=STOCK`

10. Syntax: quotes missing in lines 170 and 190
Syntax: insert a semicolon before T in lines 170 and 190.
Programming: `185 LET T=V*R`
Output: `TAX ON FIRST CAR IS 297`
                 `TAX ON SECOND CAR IS 376.2`

■ Section 4.10

1. T **2.** F **3.** T **4.** F **5.** F **6.** T **7.** F **8.** T **9.** T **10.** F

■ Section 5.2

1. `120 LET A=100*(1.06)^X`
3. `120 LET A=X+0.045*X`
5. `120 LET A=X/19.2`
7. `120 LET A=X/(52*40)`
9. `120 LET A=2677.50+0.028*(X-17850)`
12. `120 LET A=X/133.84`
14. `120 LET A=X/1.8045`
16. `120 LET A=(1.8045/133.84)*X`
18. `120 LET A=(4*X/3.14159)^0.5`
20. `120 LET A=X/2.54`

■ Section 5.3

1. T **2.** F **3.** F **4.** F **5.** F **6.** T **7.** F **8.** F

■ Section 6.3

1. a.

1	1
2	3
4	7
8	15
16	31

b.

1	1
2	2
3	6
4	24
5	120
6	720
7	5040

    c. 1 2   **d.** 3 3 3
         4 5 6   2 2
                          1

2. a.

9		81	**b.** 1		1
7		49	2		5
5		25	3		14
3		9	4		30
			5		55
			6		91
			7		132

c. 1   **d.** 10   **e.** A   B   C
     1   2   B   A   C
     2   0   C   A   B
     3   A   C   B
     5   B   C   A
     8   C   B   A

3. a. Change line 30 to 30 WHILE N<25
    Change line 70 to 70 NEXT (or 70 WEND)

    b. Insert 25 WHILE P<1000
    Change line 60 to 60 NEXT (or 60 WEND)

    c. Insert 105 WHILE A<3
    Change line 130 to 130 NEXT (or 130 WEND)
    Insert 145 WHILE A<6
    Change line 170 to 170 NEXT (or 170 WEND)

    d. Insert 105 WHILE R>0
    Insert 115 WHILE S<=R
    Change line 140 to 140 NEXT (or 140 WEND)
    Change line 170 to 170 NEXT (or 170 WEND)

4. a. Change line 20 to 20 IF N<=1 THEN 60
    Change line 50 to 50 GOTO 20

    b. Change line 30 to 30 IF K>=8 THEN 80
    Change line 70 to 70 GOTO 30

    c. Change line 40 to 40 IF FIB>=10 THEN 99
    Change line 90 to 90 GOTO 40

    d. Change line 20 to 20 IF X<=0 THEN 90
    Change line 40 to 40 IF X<=4 THEN 70
    Change line 60 to 60 GOTO 40
    Change line 80 to 80 GOTO 20

    e. Change line 140 to 140 IF T$="A" THEN 240
    Change line 230 to 230 GOTO 140

5. a. T **b.** T **c.** F **d.** T **e.** F **f.** T

6. a. If $A < B$ control is transferred to line 10. Infinite loop.

    b. Line 21 will be executed next whether or not $X < X - B$.

    c. OK must be quoted. Syntax error.

    d. The condition $A^2 < 0$ is always false.

    e. Delete the comma. Syntax error.

    f. "DONE" is not a proper condition. Syntax error.

    g. OK must be quoted. Syntax error.

    h. "NOT DONE" is not a proper condition. Syntax error.

    i. Delete THEN 200. Syntax error.

7. a. Change line 60 to 60 IF N<=15 THEN 40

    b. Change line 140 to 140 IF A = B THEN 190
    Change line 150 to 150 LET D = B - A
    Change line 180 to 180 GOTO 140

    c. Change the line number of line 50 to 25
    Change line 40 to 40 LET T = .08*X

    d. Change line 50 to 50 LET R = N^(1/2)
    Change line 80 to 80 IF N<=10 THEN 50

8. **a.** Interchange the statements in lines 30 and 40.
   b. Change line 140 to 140 WHILE A<>B
   Insert line 165 INPUT A,B
   c. Change the line number of line 50 to 25.
   Interchange the statements in lines 60 and 70.

■ Section 6.4

1. F **2.** T **3.** F **4.** F **5.** T **6.** T **7.** T **8.** F **9.** F **10.** F **11.** F

■ Section 7.3

1. a. BASEBALL'S HALL OF FAME
   COOPERSTOWN, NY 13326
   b. PASCAGOULA RIVER
   BAYOU COUNTRY, U.S.A
   c. 5 TIMES 8 = 40
   d. HAPPY

         HAPPY

                  HOLIDAY

   e. 0   5   10   15   20
       25   30   35   FINI

   f. IF A= 5 A+2= 7

       IF A= 10 A+2= 12

       IF A= 15 A+2= 17

2. a.   10 PRINT X;"/";Y;"=";X/Y
   c.   30 PRINT "X -";Y;"= ";-X
   e.   50 PRINT "DEPT. NO.";Y+Y+X
3. a. Prints TEAFORTWO
   b.   30 PRINT "SLEEPING ";
       40 PRINT "BEAR ";
   c.   130 PRINT "7A";
   d.   155 PRINT
       170 PRINT X;
       180 LET X=X+1

■ Section 7.5

1. a.

SALES	COMMISSION
2000	200
2500	250
3000	300
3500	350
4000	400
4500	450
5000	500

b. BASIC BASIC BASIC

c. 1234567890
        0
         -1
          -2
           -3
            -4
     THAT'S ENOUGH

d. 7777777
        7
        7
        7
        7
        7

e. 1234567890
     * * * * *

f.

X	X^2
1	1
2	4
3	9
4	16

2. a. 10 PRINT TAB(6);"B";TAB(9);3
   b. 20 PRINT X;TAB(21);0.04*X;TAB(41);0.06*X;TAB(61);0.08*X
   c. 90 PRINT 0;TAB(16);0;TAB(31);0;TAB(46);0;TAB(61);0;TAB(76);0
   d. 25 PRINT TAB((80-N)/2); "...*name*..."where N = number of characters in *name*

■ Section 7.7

1. a. 123456789 **b.** 9.00 **c.** TIME 1 A= 0.00 **d.** 1/8=.125
    23.60   4.50   TIME 2 A= 0.01   3/8=.375
      23.6   2.25   TIME 3 A= 0.01   5/8=.625
                1.13   7/8=.875

2. a. POPEYE   **b.** RIVERBOAT   **c.** BOBBY LOVES JUDITH
                          BOATSWAIN   JUDI LOVES BOB

d. TAX–RATE 15   TAX–RATE 25   TAX–RATE 35

3. a. Same answers as Problem 2.

■ Section 7.11

1. F **2.** F **3.** T **4.** F **5.** T **6.** F **7.** T **8.** F **9.** T **10.** T **11.** F **12.** F

■ Section 8.3

1. a. T **b.** T **c.** F **d.** T **e.** F **f.** T **g.** F

2. a. Insert line 35: 35 IF N = 0 THEN 30
    Delete line 50.

b. Change line 40 to 40 IF (R = 7) OR (R = 11) THEN PRINT "OK".

c. Change line 40 to 40 IF (2 < Y) AND (Y < 8) THEN PRINT "BETWEEN".

d. Change line 40 to 40 IF X >=0 AND X <=100 AND X <>50 THEN PRINT "OK".

3. a. −1 **b.** 5 **c.** SMITH **d.** 5   **e.** 52
      −5   THAT'S ALL

■ Section 8.10

1. T **2.** T **3.** F **4.** F **5.** T **6.** F **7.** T **8.** T **9.** T **10.** T

■ Section 9.2

1. a. 4 **b.** 5 **c.** TIMES THROUGH LOOP= 2 **d.** +++/// **e.** LOOP **f.** No output
    5   1
    6   −3

g. 123456789   **h.** ITEM1 ITEM2 ITEM3 ITEM4
    V   V   1   2   3   4
     V   V
      V V
       V V
        V

2. a. Syntax error: 50 NEXT N

b. Programming error: 25 LET C=0
    Delete line 40.

c. Programming error:
    40 INPUT Y
    50 LET S=S+Y

d. Programming error: STEP S is admissible but the step value cannot be changed within the loop.

```
30 LET S=0
40 FOR N=1 TO 5
50 LET S=S+N
60 PRINT S
```

Section 9.4

1. a. 2 3 2 3 2 3   **b.** 13 16 11 14

   c. 2 3 4 5   **d.** 108   **e.**   7 7 7

       3 4 5   9 9 9

       4 5   111111

       5   131313

2. a. Syntax error: interchange lines 50 and 60.

   b. Programming error: include STEP $-$ 1 in lines 20 and 30.

   c. Programming error: `30 IF I<J THEN PRINT I;J`

   d. Programming error: `30 IF R<=C THEN PRINT "X";`

                                 `40 IF R>C THEN PRINT " ";`

Section 9.5

1. F **2.** F **3.** T **4.** F **5.** T **6.** F **7.** T **8.** F **9.** F **10.** T **11.** F

Section 10.2

1. a. 2 $-$3   **b.** CATWOMAN   **c.**   7   **d.** BAD VALUE: 22

     5 0   3   BAD VALUE: 84

     0 $-$5   18

                          $-$5

                           4

2. a. Change line 30 to `30 DATA 1,A`

   b. Replace ; in line 10 by ,

   c. Replace HELLO in line 20 by "HELLO"

   d. Change line 50 to `50 DATA "TOM DOOLEY, JR"`

3. a. Delete lines 130 and 170.

     Change line 50 to `50 PRINT A*A`

   b.
```
130 LET C=0
175 READ X
```
   c.
```
125 READ V
130 WHILE V<>999
140 LET C=C+1
150 READ V
```

Section 10.4

1. a. 9   **b.** 3   **c.** ROBINHEAD   **d.** 10 20 30

     3   5   10 20 30

     5   3

          5

■ Section 10.5

1. T **2.** F **3.** F **4.** F **5.** T **6.** F **7.** T **8.** T **9.** T

■ Section 11.2

1. a. 4 2 16   **b.** 2   **c.** 1 1   **d.** 8
     3 −7 −5   2   2 3
                   −2   3 6
                    5   4 10

■ Section 11.4

1. a. 5   **b.** A IS AN ARTICLE.
     5   AND IS A CONJUNCTION.
              BUT IS A CONJUNCTION.
              OR IS A CONJUNCTION.
              THE IS AN ARTICLE.

■ Section 11.5

1. T **2.** F **3.** F **4.** F **5.** T **6.** F **7.** F **8.** F

■ Section 12.2

1. a. 9 **b.** 6 **c.** 18 **d.** 26 **e.** −43 **f.** 2.4 **g.** 1200 **h.** 4 **i.** 3
2. a. 4 **b.** 5 **c.** 6 **d.** −4 **e.** 2865 **f.** 2860 **g.** 2900 **h.** 3000 **i.** 2864.714
3. a. 0 8 **b.** 1.1   1 **c.** XX   **d.** 3 **e.** *   **f.** 13.990 13.99
     1 8   1.21   1   XXXX   7   **   13.993 13.99
     2 6   1.331   1   XX   9   *****   13.996 14.00
     3 2   1.4641 1   21   13.999 14.00
     4 4
4. a. 10 IF ABS(A+B)=ABS(A)+ABS(B) THEN PRINT "EQUAL"
   c. 30 IF (INT(X)=X) AND (X>0) THEN PRINT "OK"
   e. 50 IF (INT(L/2)=L/2) AND (INT(L/25)=L/25) THEN PRINT
5. a. 20 LET X=INT(100*X+0.5)/100
   c. 30 LET X=INT(1000000*X+0.5)/1000000
   e. 40 LET X=1000*INT(X/1000+0.5)

■ Section 12.5

1. a. Programming error: 50 LET V=FNZ(X)
   b. Programming error: 20 DEF FNS(X)=X^2
   c. Syntax error: use FNC for FCN.
   d. Programming error: 30 DEF FNR(N)=X/N
2. a. 200   **b.** .5 2 .5 **c.** 0 3 **d.** 1 2 3 4 **e.** 10 **f.** 9 **g.** 1
     1400   1 4   .5 1 1.5 2   15   5
     0   2 5   20   13
                                 3 6   25

3. a. `125 DEF FNT(L)=L+0.05*L`
   b. `130 DEF FNI(R)=100*(R/100)*(1/4)`
   c. `135 DEF FNC(L,W)=(L*W/9)*12.95`
   d. `140 DEF FNT(E)=E*(27/1000)`
   e. `145 DEF FNF(C)=9/5*C+32`
   f. `150 DEF FNC(F)=5/9*(F-32)`
   g. `155 DEF FNM(F)=F/5280`
   h. `160 DEF FNM(K)=K/1.6093`
   i. `165 DEF FNK(M)=1.6093*M`
   j. `170 DEF FNR(X)=INT(1000*X+0.5)/1000`
   k. `175 DEF FNS(D,T)=D/T`
   l. `180 DEF FNS(X,Y)=X-(X*Y/100)`
   m. `185 DEF FNC(X,Y)=X/15*Y`
   n. `190 DEF FNA(R)=3.14159*R^2`
   o. `195 DEF FNV(R)=4/3*3.14159*R^3`
   p. `200 DEF FNS(A)=SIN(3.14159/180*A)`

■ Section 12.6

1. T **2.** T **3.** F **4.** F **5.** F **6.** F **7.** T **8.** T **9.** T **10.** F **11.** T **12.** T

■ Section 13.4

1. a. CYBER **b.** Z TO A **c.** CONSULTATION **d.** BIOPHYSICS
2. Same answers as Problem 1.
3. a. GREAT   **b.** ADD   **c.** 3 STEP
       SALT   LIST   2 LIST
       LAKE   STOP   4 STOP
       DESERT,   STEP   1 ADD
       UTAH
4. a. `10 PRINT LEFT$(A$,1)` or `10 PRINT A$(1:1)`
   b. `15 PRINT MID$(A$,2,1)` or `15 PRINT A$(2:2)`
   c. `20 PRINT MID$(A$,LEN(A$))` or `20 PRINT A$(LEN(A$):LEN(A$))`
   d. `25 PRINT LEFT$(A$,3)` or `25 PRINT A$(1:3)`
   e. `30 PRINT MID$(A$,LEN(A$)-2)` or
       `30 PRINT A$(LEN(A$)-2:LEN(A$))`
   f. `35 PRINT LEFT$(A$,1);MID$(A$,LEN(A$))` or
       `PRINT A$(1:1);A$(LEN(A$):LEN(A$))`
   g. `40 IF LEN(A$)=LEN(B$) THEN LET N=N+1`
   h. `45 IF LEFT$(A$,1)=MID$(A$,LEN(A$)) THEN PRINT LEFT$(A$,1)` or
       `IF A$(1:1)=A$(LEN(A$):LEN(A$)) THEN PRINT A$(1:1)`
   i. `50 IF LEFT$(A$,1)=MID$(A$,2,1) THEN LET X$="SAME"` or
       `IF A$(1:1)=A$(2:2) THEN LET X$="SAME"`
   j. `55 LET B$=LEFT$(A$,N)` or `LET B$=A$(1:N)`
   k. `60 LET B$=MID$(A$,2)+LEFT$(A$,1)` or
       `LET B$=A$(2:2)+A$(1:1)`
   l. `65 LET T$=MID(S$,2,1)+LEFT$(S$,1)+MID$(S$,3)` or
       `LET T$=S$(2:2)+S$(1:1)+S$(3:LEN(S$))`
   m. `70 LET F$=LEFT$(G$,3)+MID$(H$,LEN(H$)-2)` or
       `LET F$=G$(1:3)+H$(LEN(H$)-2:LEN(H$))`
   n. `75 IF LEFT$(A$,1)+MID$(B$,2,1)+MID$(C$,3,1)="YES" THEN PRINT "OK"`
       or `IF A$(1:1)+B$(2:2)+C$(3:3)="YES" THEN PRINT "OK"`
   o. `80 IF INSTR(1,A$,",")>0 THEN PRINT "COMMA"`
   p. `85 IF INSTR(1,A$," ")=0 THEN PRINT "NO SPACES"`

■ Section 13.6

1. a. M   **b.** CATDOG   **c.** HARRY
   A   1010   ALICE
           BEASTBEAST   LAST
                         LAST

■ Section 13.9

1. a. 31+31=62   **b.** E 5   **c.** 7 7   **d.** 0123456789:
   e. 42 WINS AND 21 LOSSES GIVES A PERCENTAGE OF .667
   f. CORRECT   **g.** 9876543210   **h.** COUNT: 47

■ Section 13.10

1. F   **2.** F   **3.** T   **4.** T   **5.** T   **6.** F   **7.** T   **8.** T   **9.** F   **10.** F   **11.** F   **12.** T
13. T   **14.** T   **15.** T   **16.** F

■ Section 14.4

1. a. 5   **b.** TO BE OR NOT TO BE.   **c.** 8   **d.** IRANGATE
        4
   b. PAYCHECK, JOHN   **f.** SAM
      DENVER, JOHN   JESS
      JOHN, ELTON   SANDI
      CASH, JOHN
2. a. DIM statement needed.
   b. Array A is redimensioned at line 30 after being implicitly dimensioned by line 10.
   c. Values of L$(6) through L$(10) are lost.
   d. 415 LET L=A(1)
      420 FOR J=2 TO 10
      430 IF L<A(J) THEN LET L=A(J)

■ Section 14.8

1. a. 1 4 9 16   **b.** 2 4 6   **c.** 2 3 5   **d.** YYYY
                                                NYYY
                                                NNYY
                                                NNNY
   e. DEVILS: HOOFERS: SAINTS:
      ED   ANN   DEB
      JANE   JIM   DOT
      JOHN   RON   RUSS
      SUE   RUTH   TIM
2. a. Interchange lines 220 and 230.
   b. Insert: 215 LET T=A(R1,C)
      Change line 230 to 230 LET A(R2,C)=T

■ Section 14.9

1. F   **2.** F   **3.** F   **4.** T   **5.** F   **6.** T   **7.** T   **8.** F   **9.** T   **10.** F

■ Section 15.3

1. a. SAM   **b.** JOAN PASS   **2. a.** J.D.SLOANE   **b.** J.D.SLOANE 565
      GREG   SAM   PASS   EXCESS: 3000   R.M.PETERS 265
      MARY   GREG FAIL   A.B.CARTER 505
                  MARY FAIL   A.B.CARTER   I.O.ULSTER 465
                  MARK PASS   EXCESS: 2400

                                    I.O.ULSTER
                                    EXCESS: 2000

■ Section 15.6

1. F   **2.** F   **3.** F   **4.** T   **5.** F   **6.** F   **7.** F   **8.** F   **9.** F   **10.** T

■ Section 16.2

1. a. 80   **b.** 0   **c.** 70   **d.** 100
2. a. T   **b.** T   **c.** either   **d.** either   **e.** T   **f.** T

■ Section 16.5

1. a. 10 PRINT 4*RND
  b. 20 PRINT 6*RND+5
  c. 30 PRINT 8*RND–5
  d. 40 PRINT INT(7*RND)+6
  e. 50 PRINT 2*INT(5*RND)
  f. 60 PRINT 2*INT(5*RND)+1
2. a. 1,2   (equally likely)
  b. 0
  c. –2,–1,0,1,2   (equally likely)
  d. 2,3,4   (3 about half the time; 2 and 4 each about one-fourth the time)
  e. 2,3,4,...,12   (not equally likely—simulates rolling a pair of dice)
  f. 1,2,3,4,6,9   (not equally likely)
3. ONE OF EACH, TWO HEADS, and TWO TAILS will be displayed about the same number of times. In practice, ONE OF EACH will occur about half the time.

■ Section 16.10

1. T   **2.** F   **3.** T   **4.** F   **5.** F   **6.** F   **7.** F   **8.** T   **9.** F   **10.** T

■ Section 17.7

1. F   **2.** F   **3.** F   **4.** F   **5.** T   **6.** T   **7.** T   **8.** T   **9.** T   **10.** F   **11.** T   **12.** T
13. T

■ Section 18.6

1. a. 2
4
6
8

b. 1 5 1
1 5 1
1 5 1

c. 4 0 0 0
0 4 0 0
0 0 4 0
0 0 0 4

d. 2 3 4
3 4 5
4 5 6
5 6 7

e. 7 0 0 0 0
0 9 0 0 0
0 0 1 0 0
0 0 0 3 0
0 0 0 0 5

f. 1 0 0 0 0
0 2 0 0 0
0 0 3 0 0
0 0 0 4 0
0 0 0 0 5

2. a. 30 MAT B=(4)*A   **b.** 30 MAT D=(3)*M   **c.** 30 MAT C=A*B   **d.** 15 DIM S(2,3)
30 MAT S=A+B
35 MAT PRINT S

■ Section 18.7

1. F **2.** T **3.** T **4.** F **5.** F **6.** T **7.** F **8.** F **9.** T **10.** F

Index

TO THE OWNER OF THIS BOOK:

We'd like to hear about your reactions to this textbook. Only through your comments and advice can we hope to improve the next edition of *BASIC: An Introduction to Computer Programming*. Under what circumstances did you use this book?

_____ As a student   _____ As an instructor

_____ As a computer hobbyist   _____ Other

1. What did you like most about BASIC? _____

_____

2. What did you like least about the book? _____

_____

3. Did you read all the chapters of the book? _____

(If not, which ones did you omit?) _____

4. Which special features were most interesting and informative? Why? _____

_____

_____

_____

_____

5. As you know, BASIC systems differ. Did you find the presentation of any of the BASIC statements to be especially troublesome to you? What changes do you feel will improve the book?

_____

_____

_____

_____

6. In the space below or in a separate letter, please let us know what other comments about the book you'd like to make. (For example, were any chapters or concepts particularly difficult?) We'd be delighted to hear from you.

_____

_____

_____

_____

_____

_____

_____

_____

_____

7. Optional:
   Name and address: _____

   _____

   _____

   _____

School: _____

Instructor's Name: _____

Date: _____

May Brooks/Cole quote you, either in promotion for *BASIC: An Introduction to Computer Programming* or in future publishing ventures?

Yes _____   No _____

Sincerely,
Robert J. Bent
George C. Sethares

- FOLD HERE -

- FOLD HERE -

198